America Is Elsewhere

America Is Elsewhere

THE NOIR TRADITION IN THE AGE OF CONSUMER CULTURE

Erik Dussere

OXFORD
UNIVERSITY PRESS

Oxford University Press is a department of the University of Oxford.
It furthers the University's objective of excellence in research,
scholarship, and education by publishing worldwide.

Oxford   New York

Auckland   Cape Town   Dar es Salaam   Hong Kong   Karachi
Kuala Lumpur   Madrid   Melbourne   Mexico City   Nairobi
New Delhi   Shanghai   Taipei   Toronto

With offices in

Argentina   Austria   Brazil   Chile   Czech Republic   France   Greece
Guatemala   Hungary   Italy   Japan   Poland   Portugal   Singapore
South Korea   Switzerland   Thailand   Turkey   Ukraine   Vietnam

Oxford is a registered trade mark of Oxford University Press
in the UK and certain other countries.

Published in the United States of America by
Oxford University Press
198 Madison Avenue, New York, NY 10016

Library of Congress Cataloging-in-Publication Data
Dussere, Erik, 1968–
America is elsewhere : the noir tradition in the age of consumer culture / Erik Dussere.
pages   cm
Includes bibliographical references and index.
ISBN 978-0-19-996991-3 (cloth : acid-free paper)—ISBN 978-0-19-996992-0 (pbk. : acid-free paper)
1. Detective and mystery stories, American—History and criticism. 2. Noir fiction, American—History and
criticism. 3. Film noir—United States—History and criticism. 4. National characteristics, American, in literature.
5. Masculinity in literature. I. Title.
PS374.D4D87   2013
813'.087209—dc23   2013008140

For Stephanie and Liv

{ CONTENTS }

{ ACKNOWLEDGMENTS }

Writing a book is a long, slow process that inspires a lot of whining, but it does have its rewards. I hope that the friends and colleagues who helped me in ways large and small, direct and incidental, will feel that they have some share in those rewards. It is impossible to do justice to all the contributions that others have made during the years when I was working on this book, but at least I can include some of their names here.

Thanks to those who read various sections of the manuscript while I was drafting them and who provided much useful advice, starting with my fantastic scholarship reading group: Despina Kakoudaki, Michael Wenthe, Jeff Middents, Fiona Brideoake, Jonathan Loesberg, and Deborah Payne. Other readers who made invaluable comments were David Pike, Marianne Noble, Richard Sha, and Graham Benton. My onetime student Phil Calderwood put his encyclopedic knowledge of film noir to work for me, and I have had useful conversations about the material with Joseph Chaves, Frédéric Mougenot, Elena Razlogova, Sondra Guttman, Jill Hartman, Dave Zirin, and Tony Lopez. Holly Hartman showed up at odd hours of the day to hear me read bits of the manuscript as papers at the American Literature Association conference. And really, all my colleagues in the Literature Department at American University deserve a shout-out for their support and encouragement and for being great people to work with, as do the students in my classes, who have helped me to think through many of the issues and texts that are discussed in the pages that follow.

Parts of the introduction and chapter 4 appeared in somewhat different form as essays in, respectively, *Film Quarterly* and *Contemporary Literature*, and I received useful suggestions from editors and outside readers in both cases. Thanks, too, to the anonymous readers for Oxford University Press, who provided generous and insightful commentary on the manuscript; to my excellent editor, Brendan O'Neill; and of course to Tanya Agathocleous, who is forever fabulous, and who suggested that I send the manuscript to Oxford in the first place.

A remarkable amount of infrastructural work had to be done just to make it possible for me to be in the position to write a book like this at all. Lisa Gitelman and Lisa Lynch brought me to Washington, D.C., and Abby Moser and Amy Holberg helped me feel welcome here. Chuck Larson hired me at American University, and then fought hard to hire me again. Chuck really seemed to believe in me as a teacher and a scholar when there was no particular reason for him to do so; without his efforts, this book might never have been written. The same goes for Roberta Rubenstein, whose advice and example throughout the years has been invaluable; Chris Warley, an unlikely motivational speaker who taught me how to interview for a job at the eleventh hour; and Jeff Middents, a good friend, neighbor, and colleague who has always been ready to lend a hand when things have looked dire.

My parents, Paul and Sally Dussere, are lucky enough to live only an hour's drive from one of the largest supermarkets in the United States (while my brother Michael lives close to the largest gas station I have ever seen). Anything that I accomplish owes a great deal to their love and support, and in addition growing up with them meant being in a community of unofficial film scholars, even if our analyses have sometimes lacked precision. ("Hey, it's that guy! You know; he was in that movie with that other guy."). I have been absurdly fortunate to have them to talk to and to watch movies with all these years.

No thanks could be enough for Stephanie Hartman, my partner in crime and everything else, but among other things her encouragement and interest have made the writing of this book possible, and she has patiently endured my many hijackings of our Netflix queue for research projects (like, say, frontloading the queue with fifteen obscure noirs, in hopes of glimpsing a gas station). Also, she has often freed up work time for me by entertaining our daughter for long summer afternoons—a labor of love, of course, but still. Which brings me to Liv, my favorite person in the world, ten years old now and probably unable to remember a time when I wasn't writing this book. So this one is for Liv and Stephanie, who make everything worthwhile.

America Is Elsewhere

Introduction

The American self can be taken to be a microcosm of American society,
which has notably lacked the solidity and intractability of English
society; it is little likely to be felt by its members as being palpably *there*.

—LIONEL TRILLING, *SINCERITY AND AUTHENTICITY*

My critique of America remains fundamentally incoherent. . . . All
I know is that although I live a freer life than many people, I want
to be freer still; I'm sometimes positively dazzled with longing
for a better way of being. What is it that I need?

—WILLIAM T. VOLLMANN, *RIDING TOWARD EVERYWHERE*

This book is an attempt to understand the relationship between consumer
culture and conceptions of national authenticity as it is expressed in American
fiction and film from the 1940s to the present. I will argue that the unprecedented rise of consumer culture that followed World War II reshaped American
national identity in important ways, and that as consumption and citizenship
were increasingly conflated, American cultural productions expressed a newly
urgent desire to discover or rediscover a version of the nation imagined as
authentic and opposed to consumerism. Over the decades that followed, this
cultural conflict between authenticity and consumption has evolved, and I
follow that evolution by tracing the tradition initiated in film noir and hard-
boiled fiction as it changes shape during American culture's movement into
the postmodern era.

The book is divided into three sections, which follow a loosely chronolog-
ical development. The first part sets out the key issues I discuss here by looking
at the late-modernist postwar period, during which hard-boiled fiction and
classic film noir became firmly established in American culture as exemplars
of the authentic. In part 2, I examine how this ideological structure of noir is
carried over into the conspiracy texts that define the emergence of postmodernism. Part 3 follows the noir tradition into the era of dominant postmodernism, examining novels and films that reformulate noir's assertion of
national authenticity, as well as those that ultimately undermine that assertion.
Throughout the book, my central focus is on the ways that the texts I examine

represent space, with particular attention to places of commerce—the sites of material culture where conflicts between authenticity and consumption are negotiated.

To make this argument requires a new way of reading noir, one that defines it as a response to the rise of consumer culture, as a *noir tradition* that continues and evolves long after the era of the forties and fifties in which it is generally located.[1] Studies of noir—which have generally focused either on film noir or on the "noir" hard-boiled fiction that is one of the key sources of the film cycle—nearly always pose the question, what is noir? In some cases the question is one of categorization: is it a genre, a style, a critical category, a free-floating principle? But my own analysis is concerned more directly with something like the question that Joan Copjec poses in her introduction to *Shades of Noir*, the question of "the genre's 'absent cause,' that is, of a principle that does not appear in the field of its effects" (xii). In arguing that the "principle" of noir is an ideological attempt to imagine a negation of American consumer culture, or a space outside of that consumerist national space, I am arguing for a continuity that links noir film and fiction of the forties and fifties, the "countercultural" conspiracy logic of the sixties and seventies, and the postmodern cultural productions of the last thirty years. While critical writings on film noir have often treated it as a response to the crisis and instability of the era of World War II and the decade that followed—a discontinuous reading in which noir arises from American transition and flux and then fades away[2]—I read noir as a response not to crisis but to affluence and national consolidation. This reading of noir as a response to consumer culture links it to the rise of the counterculture, with its critique of American affluence, and to the postmodern concern with exploring the contradictions of capitalism in the global consumer economy.

Reading noir as a response to, or an effect of, the pervasive presence of consumer culture in the postwar era makes it possible for me to build on previous noir scholarship—which has often looked at noir as a critique of American mainstream values—in order to offer a new conception of the term. The structural basis of the noir texts, in my reading, is contained and expressed in their staging of a conflict between consumerist America and an authentic American identity that takes the form of a negation of consumer culture. These texts are certainly not the only ones where these issues are present—indeed, these are issues that are absolutely central to postwar culture at all levels—but in the noir tradition the issues are framed in terms of a conflict that renders the issues and their relationship to questions of national authenticity visible, and that allows us to see how the problems raised by postwar consumer culture persist in the present. Noir is the site where this confrontation between two versions of America takes place most clearly, because noir texts are in their essence *about* authenticity; they are machines for the production of what I will be calling "authenticity effects."

When I use this terminology, I am drawing on a tradition—one that is expressed most clearly by Lionel Trilling, as I discuss below—that conceptualizes "authenticity" as a negative principle, one that is motivated by a desire to locate a space outside of social or economic systems perceived as artificial. The version of authenticity that concerns me—the one that is found in the texts of the noir tradition—is a discourse with a particular history, one that emerges as an oppositional response to traditions of commerce and the artifice that commerce seems to introduce into human relationships in general and American society in particular. In postwar America, this discourse takes the form of an assertion of and desire for an American authenticity imagined as the opposite of a mainstream American identity that has become indistinguishable from consumerism. In this sense, one could say that the capitalist dynamics of consumption and the commodity form *produce* authenticity as their inevitable opposite. Noir is a privileged site of investigation here because it consistently creates the effect of authenticity through its gritty-realist aesthetic, its claim to a cynical debunking, and its project of unmasking what it sees as the pretty lies and petty pieties of mainstream American discourse to discover the essential rot that they disguise. But in doing so, it makes the gap between authenticity and authenticity effect visible; its authenticity-based opposition to consumer culture emerges in the form of films and novels that are conscious of their status as commodities but that nonetheless attempt to take a critical posture toward the system of commodification.

The strategy by which noir texts represent this confrontation between consumer culture and authenticity is most clearly seen in their evocations of particular commercial spaces, which take both literal and symbolic forms. Space, in the terms set out by Henri Lefebvre and others, is produced in ways that correspond to the dominant ideological and economic order. In the postwar era, consumer capitalism's imbrication with American citizenship has been linked to its reorganization of American space. The familiar changes in the American landscape that we generally associate with the forties and fifties—suburban living, automobile culture, the new ways of buying represented by supermarkets, chain stores, and so on—all suggest the commodity as the dominant structure underlying our national space. Noir represents these new spaces in ways that claim a separation between two versions of America: the degraded, commercialized mainstream and the darker and more vital alternative offered by the noir aesthetic. The omnipresent national consumer culture produces anxiety, as citizens come to feel that the nation they inhabit is pervasively artificial and inauthentic. This feeling is particularly powerful when the spaces those citizens inhabit and negotiate every day are also organized by the logic of the commodity.[3] Noir responds to this experience of alienation by staging authenticity effects, which suggest the presence or possibility of an alternative America—one that is located outside of the commercial sphere.

This somewhat lengthy introduction is divided into two parts. The first part, "Authenticity Effects," is concerned with explaining and defining the central terms that I am using—*authenticity, noir, consumer culture, American (national) identity*—all of which are large and amorphous and therefore require me to explain exactly how I am using them. I will discuss the particular versions of these terms that I will be using, as well as the relationships between them, all of which is necessary in order to describe the shape of the argument I will be making. In the second part, "Out of the Past, into the Supermarket," I examine commercial spaces as representatives of postwar American consumer culture, taking the supermarket as an emblematic example. Then I bring all these threads together in a reading of three supermarket scenes in the noir tradition that recreates in miniature the evolution described throughout the course of this book.

1. Authenticity Effects

[In pulp fiction of the twenties and thirties we can] recognize the
authentic power of a kind of writing that, even at its most mannered
and artificial, made most of the fiction of the time taste like a cup
of luke-warm consommé at a spinsterish tearoom. I don't think this
power was entirely a matter of violence. . . . Possibly it was the smell
of fear which these stories managed to generate. Their characters lived
in a world gone wrong. . . . The law was something to be manipulated
for profit and power. The streets were dark with something more than
night. The mystery story grew hard and cynical about motive and
character, but it was not cynical about the effects it tried to produce nor
about its technique of producing them.

—RAYMOND CHANDLER, *TROUBLE IS MY BUSINESS*

Defining authenticity is a tricky thing. To begin with, the word "authentic" comes to us trailing a host of not-quite-synonyms—true, real, original, genuine—each of which requires explanation in itself, and all of which are used differently in different contexts. But the more onerous problem is that the term "authenticity" has no positive definition; it only has meaning when it is contrasted with some notion of the "inauthentic," so that any understanding of the word depends upon what a given writer or community imagines to be its opposite. In its various contexts, authenticity may be defined as the antithesis of society, artifice, imitation, modernity, conformity, or alienation—among other things. The authenticity I am talking about here refers to a historically defined cultural discourse with its own particular logic and rhetoric, one that emerges out of other discourses over time and is frequently given expression in American film and fiction during the twentieth century. It is imagined as the opposite of consumer culture, and because consumer culture had come to define the national identity by the 1940s, it is an authenticity conceived in national terms.

I have suggested that this specific sort of authenticity that emerges in noir texts is really an authenticity effect, a simulation of something that the texts desire and posit, and definitions of authenticity frequently return to that problem of simulation. Conceptions of the term seem, in other words, to contain their own debunking; authenticity is always an effect. This is certainly the case that emerges in Lionel Trilling's *Sincerity and Authenticity*, a series of lectures that he gave at Harvard University in 1970, which offer a powerful and subtle account of the discourse of authenticity. Trilling begins with the concept of "sincerity," which he describes in what are now fairly conventional terms as a component in the conception of the self that takes shape in the early modern era. The idea of sincerity—the desire to be faithful in outward expression to one's inner truth—becomes possible with the alteration of feudal class hierarchies and the breakdown of the assurance of immanent meaning provided by the premodern God. This change is aligned with the emergence, in more or less the terms in which we know it today, of the idea of society; the desire for sincerity is the desire for the self to be aligned truthfully with its expression in society.

Authenticity, Trilling argues, emerges out of the Romantic imagination and finds its fullest expression in modernism.[4] Within its logic, there is no longer any question of the self being aligned with society, because society is the opposite of authenticity and the authentic self is perpetually alienated from the social realm. This Romantic conception of authenticity is the one that informs existentialist philosophy. The individual, freed from the dogmas engendered by God-based belief systems, rushes headlong into the comfortable fetters provided by social norms and the commonplace; we act inauthentically when we model our particular existence on preexisting social frameworks, making an individual life an incarnation of the generality. Jean-Paul Sartre, in particular, devotes himself to depicting and delineating the modes of inauthentic behavior and "bad faith" at length, while authenticity itself is defined primarily in negative terms—as the opposite of the inauthentic norm—or in vague evocations of the importance of acting in accordance with one's individual freedom.[5]

This conception of the authentic has been taken up frequently in texts of the postwar era that are concerned with the problem of the individual's relationship to society and mass culture, and the prescription remains essentially the same. Authenticity is consistently conceived as a reaction; to act as an individual is to act in opposition to the surrounding culture. In the fifties and sixties a number of popular writers—David Riesman in *The Lonely Crowd* (1953), William Whyte in *The Organization Man* (1956), Herbert Marcuse in *Eros and Civilization* (1955) and *One-Dimensional Man* (1964)—made this argument, diagnosing the problem of these American decades as the problem of individuals who abandon their individuality by identifying themselves with the larger society. Marcuse's work made this point with particular passion. Adapting the Frankfurt School critique of mass culture so as to place the emphasis (literally: look at the italics in the following quote) on the abhorrent loss of individuality, he wrote in *One-Dimensional Man*, "Mass production and mass distribution claim the *entire* individual. . . . The result is not adjustment but *mimesis*: an immediate identification of the individual with *his* society and, through it, with the society as a whole. . . . In this process, the 'inner' dimension of the mind in which opposition to the status quo can take root is whittled down" (10). Like Trilling and the existentialists, these writers saw the problem of inauthenticity as a loss of selfhood, a false consciousness in which the individual subject "finds itself" in the society of which it is a part.[6] I will be arguing here that noir authenticity is a response not to the crisis of the existential self but rather to a crisis in the national imagination: the "problem" is not that individuals recognize themselves in society, but that they recognize themselves as Americans through their relationship to consumer culture. (That conflation of society and consumerism is itself visible in Marcuse's famous formulation: "People recognize themselves in their commodities; they find their soul in their automobile, hi-fi set, split level home, kitchen equipment. The very mechanism which ties the individual to his society has changed" [9].)

Leaving aside for a moment this crucial difference—my analysis of the way that authenticity becomes a cultural and ultimately national concern rather than (only) an existential one—I share with Trilling and the others a structural understanding of authenticity as the desire for something that is perceived to be lost and perhaps unrecoverable. For example, Trilling argues that the texts of modernism are crucial for understanding the problem of individuality in relation to mass culture because of the concerns about the loss of originality that emerge in the era of machines and mass production: "That the word [authenticity] has become part of the moral slang of our day points to the peculiar nature of our fallen condition, our anxiety over the credibility of existence and of individual existences. An eighteenth-century aesthetician states our concern succinctly—'Born Originals,' Edward Young said, 'how comes it to pass that we die Copies?'" (93). The assertion of authenticity, then, is a response to social anxieties about being inauthentic, the fear that one is not an original but rather a copy of the norm dictated by social forces. Alienation is the condition produced by the self so that it can prove to itself that it is not produced by society. From these comments we can extrapolate a first important point: Authenticity is not a thing or a state of being; it is, rather, a desire motivated by a sense that something has been lost, although it is not necessarily a nostalgic desire. As the nonexistent opposite of a reviled "inauthentic," it is the longing for a vaguely defined and perhaps unimaginable state of affairs, the longing for an *elsewhere*.

I will be arguing here that this desire for an elsewhere in noir texts is motivated by the presence—what is experienced in the American postwar era as the omnipresence—of consumer culture. Authenticity in this context is a reaction against the perception that the commercial principle has introduced artifice into every level of social interaction; it is the longing for an alternative to a national landscape rendered artificial by commerce. Trilling's more traditionally humanistic analysis, like the existential and psychoanalytic sources he draws on, imagines authenticity in terms of the alienated self, which is to say as the opposite of "society." In his brief discussion of Marxian alienation in *Sincerity and Authenticity*, he touches on the role of commerce in the development of modern authenticity. But Trilling reduces Marx's position to a bland humanism, wherein "money . . . is the principle of the inauthentic in human existence" (124), an idea so blithely generalized that Marx and Wordsworth can easily be contained in the same phrase, as in "the great enemy of being was having" (122). His naming of money as the inauthentic opens up the possibility of an inquiry into the role of the capitalist market in defining authenticity, but Trilling himself is ultimately interested in constructing a more general analysis in which commerce plays a supporting role.

But this generalization also suggests the extent to which Trilling sees authenticity as having a political dimension that goes beyond the concerns of the alienated individual. His addition of money to the discussion indicates that his definition of authenticity takes the form of a generalized negative political principle that opposes itself to large organizational systems such as "society" or "the market." As Amanda Anderson notes, Trilling's authenticity is "transgressive"; rejecting "the customary and conventional, authenticity is at heart an oppositional concept, built up out of negations" (*The Way We Argue Now*, 164). Here we can see the emergence of a second key point that builds on the first: as the desire for an elsewhere, authenticity takes the form of an attempt to locate a space or position outside of organizational systems associated with the mainstream or the dominant social or economic order.[7]

If authenticity is always an attempt to posit a space or position outside of some system, then the shape this dynamic takes in postwar America is the noir tradition's assertion of a national identity that is both alternative and central, an "other America" that is outside of and opposed to the capitalist formation that is manifested as a national consumer culture.[8] To understand the problem of authenticity in this postwar context as more than a problem of the human condition or of the decline of individualism, we need to pursue the concept of commodification as a central element in the organization of consumer culture. It is only when things and experiences are expressed in the monetary language of exchange value, and made available as items in a market, that an economy based on satisfying needs and wants through consumption becomes possible— and only then can authenticity be imagined as the hypothetical outside of that market system. This process is centuries old, and the sense that something crucial about human being and interaction is violated or rendered artificial by processes of exchange and monetization is at least as old as the beginnings of capitalism. But our current conceptions of commodification and the "consumer society" were shaped in the nineteenth century, and in the American context they are perceived as initiating a crisis in national identity in the middle of the twentieth.

This postwar crisis takes the form of a mutually dependent and evolving tension between authenticity and commodification—one that I will refer to as a dialectic, following Dean MacCannell's description of "the dialectics of authenticity." For an analysis of the simulation of authenticity in contemporary culture, I turn now from Trilling to the work MacCannell has done as a scholar of tourism.[9] The movement from tourism to noir is not as surprising as it might seem at first glance. The experience of watching film noir or reading hard-boiled fiction is itself a kind of tourism, a virtual slumming in which we inhabit an underworld of crime and passion, decadence and vitality, that is generally unavailable and inadvisable in our daily lives. Indeed, MacCannell has written about noir in these terms, describing it as a space that is appealing precisely because no viewer of noir would actually want to live there: "The best way to characterize *noir* sensibility is as 'false nostalgia' or 'constructed nostalgia.' What is produced is a sense of loss of something that was never possessed, something that never was" ("Democracy's Turn," 280). This sense that the thing that noir desires is something it has "constructed" is echoed in the concept of "staged authenticity" that MacCannell discusses in his classic study *The Tourist.*

Although MacCannell's subject is the way that rituals and events in other places are "staged" for tourists who come looking for the expression of a foreign culture, his analysis of this structure leads him to a more general theory. Staged authenticity, he argues, emerges from the condition of modernity, and what we look for when we travel to other countries is also what we look for at home: "The same process is operating on 'everyday life' in modern society, making a 'production' and a fetish of urban public street life, rural village life and traditional domestic relations. Modernity is quite literally turning industrial structure inside out as these workaday, 'real life,' 'authentic' details are woven into the fabric of our modern solidarity alongside the other attractions" (*The Tourist,* 91). In this way, the structure of tourist attractions allows us to reflect not only on our relationship to other cultures but also to our own. MacCannell concludes that the modern world is defined by a "dialectics of authenticity" in which people stage more and more elaborate, "spurious" structures in an effort to reproduce that which is perceived as genuine, and the more these spurious structures grow, the harder they quest for the authentic that seems forever to recede and to elude them.

This dialectics of authenticity is central to my reading of how noir operates, wherein the confrontation with consumer capitalism inspires noir to produce authenticity effects as a response. Given the importance of consumption to this understanding of noir, MacCannell's analysis is especially pertinent because he argues that commerce represents the principle of the inauthentic. The claim that America is or has become inauthentic underlies the assumptions that are persistently affirmed in the work of postwar cultural critics, who have often imagined the problem of modern alienation as a problem of the self versus society, in which society is inauthentic because it is conformist and thus hostile to the autonomy of the individual. This crisis of the individual is often understood as implying, by extension, a crisis of the nation. For instance, Daniel Boorstin, in his influential 1961 book *The Image: A Guide to Pseudo-Events in America*, suggests that mass culture and mass media have undermined American authenticity through a process of persistent fakery and simulation: "What ails us most is not what we have done with America, but what we have substituted for America. . . . We are haunted, not by reality, but by those images we have put in the place of reality" (6).[10] But the dialectical opposite of authenticity in MacCannell's analysis is not society, media, or the masses but rather commerce: "the dividing line between structure genuine and spurious is the *realm of the commercial*" (*The Tourist* 155; his italics). The definition of the authentic is that which cannot be bought, and so, within the dialectic, authenticity and commerce depend on each other for their existence and propagation: "The souvenir market, and by extension, the entire structure of everyday reality in the modern world, depends upon the perpetuation of authentic attractions which themselves are not for sale" (158). The world we inhabit is organized by the convolutions produced by two opposed and mutually dependent forces: the production of space and experience by consumer capitalism, on the one hand, and on the other the desire for authenticity that is created as an effect of that productive commodification.[11]

NATIONAL IDENTITY AND CONSUMER CULTURE

The dialectical relationship of authenticity and the capitalist marketplace is important to many elements of Western culture and selfhood generally, so for the purposes of this book it will be necessary to understand why that dialectic is particularly important in the American context, where authenticity is represented as a national anxiety.[12] America has consistently been self-conscious, ambivalent, and insecure about its national identity, and has looked for defining features in vague but assertive ideologies such as American exceptionalism and manifest destiny. The persistence of the effort to define America can perhaps be attributed to the fact that our national self-understanding is founded to such a large extent on constitutional principles and abstract ideas, rather than on claims of cultural or ethnic coherence. This is not to say, of course, that the United States as a nation has been less stable or less real than other nations. All forms of national identity are profoundly fictional—what is a nation if not a fiction with a history?—and despite its relative newness, America has had a considerably more coherent and consistent government than most European nations, at least since the early decades of the twentieth century. All nations have reasons to be self-conscious about their nationhood; in America that self-consciousness often takes the form of an anxiety (and a corresponding belligerence) about the absence of a historically constituted public culture.

This idea that America has historically been exceptional in its lack of a defining culture is also a way of understanding why it is the place where issues and developments in consumerism have been most visible. Many commentators have argued that market culture took hold in America more dramatically than in Europe in part because of the lack of "thereness" that Trilling identifies in my epigraph. Without the thick accretion of tradition or Arnoldian "culture" that characterized most European nations, this argument suggests, there was less America that needed eroding by the solvent of commerce. (Or, to employ a different metaphor, America offered more undeveloped space on which the productive energies of consumer capitalism could begin to build.) In *An All-Consuming Century*, Gary Cross argues that, as against the popular notion that America's hegemony in the late twentieth century is due to the triumph of liberal democracy as an idea, the ideology that has "won" and that characterizes the republic and its position in the world is consumerism. In making this case, Cross returns us to the idea that the market, itself placeless, has found a place in America specifically because the nation was already not "there"; consumerism has become the dominant culture here because of the thinness of the public sphere and the lack of a shared tradition, civic values, and cultural solidity:

> The predominance of markets over other social and cultural institutions in American history is particularly important. . . . The absence of an established national church, a weak central bureaucracy, the regional division of the elite, the lack of a distinctive national "high culture," the fragmentation of folk cultures due to slavery and diverse immigration, and finally the social and psychological impact of unprecedented mobility all meant that market values encountered relatively few checks. Americans have had a strong tendency to define themselves and their relationships with others through the exchange and use of goods. (4)

This materialist version of American uniqueness or exceptionalism offers an explanation for the way in which consumer culture has come to define mainstream America. The texts that I will be discussing in this book posit a split in which there are two Americas: the visible one, defined by consumer culture, and the vaguely imagined one that noir seeks to make visible—the alternative, authentic America.

The occasion for that split is not just the presence of consumer culture in America, but the process by which consumption has come to define American national identity. Although that definition became a cultural dominant in the postwar years that are the subject of this book, the process had deep historical roots. Since its beginnings in the early modern era, market culture has produced a characteristic tension between authenticity and artifice—with the emergent capitalist market signifying a dangerously artificial "placelessness" and mutability[13]—and one culture that was particularly invested in representing the market as artificial, and in representing itself as being opposed to that artifice, was that of the English Puritans with their Protestant reliance on "plain speech."[14] So the opposition between authenticity and commerce has shaped American identity in a tradition that, like the discourse of American exceptionalism, runs back to the Puritan settlers. As Jackson Lears observes in "Beyond Veblen: Rethinking Consumer Culture in America," American public culture emerged out of the "long tradition of Anglo-American Protestant culture: the Puritan's plain-speak assault on theatrical artifice and effete display" (75). This tradition informs American cultural anxieties about consumerism—conceived as a hedonistic display of artifice—that have intensified since the late nineteenth century. Warren Susman argues in *Culture as History* that "one of the fundamental conflicts of twentieth-century America is between two cultures—an older culture, often loosely labeled Puritan-republican, producer-capitalist culture, and a newly emerging culture of abundance" (xx)—a conflict that is important in the chapters that follow.

One legacy of the Puritan tradition in American culture, then, has been an ambivalence about the pleasures of that other American tradition: commerce and consumption. As Lears notes, a version of the Puritan strain is expressed in the work of Thorstein Veblen, whose *The Theory of the Leisure Class*, written at the turn of the twentieth century, has provided the most enduring American critique of commercial culture. Veblen's argument puts consumption at the center of discussions of economy and culture, arguing that the accumulation of commodities was a way of asserting status through a system of symbolic value that expressed itself in display and ornamentation. Veblen's scathing attack on what he identified as a ludicrous and wasteful display identified consumer culture as the very definition of inauthenticity, and in doing so set the stage for much of the cultural criticism that would emerge in the next century.[15]

In the last two decades, however, historians of consumption have stepped back from the moralizing positions that this idea of authenticity produces, and in the process have produced a new body of work that has resolved itself into a more or less consensual argument: that in the twentieth century, American national identity has developed in relation to consumer culture, and American citizenship has come to be defined by participation in that consumer culture.[16] This movement toward a national identity defined through consumption is the subject of Charles McGovern's comprehensive study *Sold American*, which shows how, during the period from 1890 to 1945, American citizenship became decisively associated with practices of consumption and "the quest for good became the pursuit of goods" (8). This shift occurred because of a number of social forces, including the advertising strategies of marketers and businesses, the work of academics and other professional critics, changes in government, and the emergence of various "consumer's rights" movements in the sphere of politics. All contributed to the national self-understanding in which "being an American meant being a consumer":

> Americans came to understand spending as a form of citizenship, an important ritual of national identity in daily life. Explicit political and civic language, images, and practices that equated voting with buying shaped common understandings of consumption. In entertainment and public discourse Americans saw their common heritage defined as much by goods and leisure as by political abstractions or historical figures. (3)

This conflation ultimately led to the emergence of the popular notion of the "American way of life," an idea that challenged the New Deal's focus on civic virtues and public life (even as it realized Franklin D. Roosevelt's vision of a culture of affluence) with the idea—and, swiftly, the ideological claim—that American identity found its best and truest expression in the realm of private accumulation and the pursuit of material wealth.

As citizenship and consumption were increasingly linked, so too advertising discourse in the first half of the century tended to define American national identity more generally in terms of the consumer marketplace. Advertisers drew on long-standing cultural traditions and beliefs in order to construct a vision of America that was reflected by and aligned with the practices of consumer capitalism. Mass production and massive availability of products signified democratic egalitarianism and the leveling of class distinctions; the abundance, novelty, and replacability of American consumer goods signified a forward-looking embrace of the new that rejected an outmoded European ownership model that valued tradition and durable quality; and consumer products became a way for immigrants to display their integration into American life. McGovern describes these developments as a new way of conceiving national belonging, a "material nationalism" in which commerce allows the restatement of a carefully chosen set of American common values in order to offer an illusory national identity reverse-engineered by way of the values of commerce itself: "Advertisers used their selective history and sociology to identify as 'decisively American' precisely those habits or traits most conducive to avid spending: an open mind, fierce individuality, a boundless appetite and curiosity for new things, a readiness to accept the modern, and a determination to find quality and satisfaction" (126). One of the most powerful versions of the American national "imagined community" that began to be imagined in the early decades of the twentieth century was one that located the nation's exceptional character, its common creed, and its definition of citizenship in values associated with consumption.[17]

This was the consensus that emerged in the postwar period—the consensus that produced the desire for authenticity as a response—and I have chosen to begin with texts from that period precisely because during the 1940s the culture of consumption becomes fully established and its association with citizenship is cemented.[18] This is the era of what Lizabeth Cohen calls the "consumers' republic." Cohen, like McGovern, suggests that not only our private lives but also our relationships to governmental and economic institutions are defined in crucial ways by practices of shopping and buying. Her analysis details the many formations this relationship between citizen and consumer has taken and the cultural and political effects it has created: "In the aftermath of World War II a fundamental shift in America's economy, politics, and culture took place, with major consequences for how Americans made a living, where they dwelled, how they interacted with others, what and how they consumed, what they expected of government" (*A Consumers' Republic*, 8). Within this tectonic shift, consumption becomes not just another cultural practice, but a way of understanding and organizing American national identity. It is during this period that noir film and fiction take their defining shape, one that responds to the conflation of consumption and national identity by employing the language of authenticity.

NOIR FICTION: THE CHANDLER EFFECT

The hard-boiled writing of the twenties—in particular the stories published by various writers in *Black Mask* magazine and the novels of Dashiell Hammett—is the starting point for the noir aesthetic. But Raymond Chandler's novels, stories, and screenplays from the thirties and forties have been the most influential body of work in shaping popular and critical understandings of noir.[19] This is largely due to the way that his work, much more explicitly than that of Hammett, depends upon the logic of authenticity. "Fiction in any form has always intended to be realistic," Chandler wrote in 1944 at the start of his famous essay, "The Simple Art of Murder." The essay is a manifesto for the streetwise "realism" of the hard-boiled detective novel, and its rhetoric and tone contain echoes of another manifesto for realism, Mark Twain's essay on "Fenimore Cooper's Literary Offenses," published fifty years earlier. Twain created an implicit critique of the adventure romance by drily pointing out factual errors, tonal absurdities, and the pervasive sense of unlikelihood in Cooper's "deerslayer" novels; the essay suggested that fiction was either realistic, on Twain's terms, or it was ridiculous and false. Chandler performs a similar dissection of works from the "Golden Age" of detective fiction—including those by Dorothy Sayers, Agatha Christie, and E. C. Bentley—singling out A. A. Milne's *The Red House Mystery* for particular scorn, and adopting Twain's method by piling up a lawyerly accumulation of damning evidence in order to produce a list of Milne's errors. But as the essay moves forward, it becomes clear that a strict realism based on accuracy and consistency is not really what Chandler is calling for. His essay posits and models a distinctly American style that defines itself against both the English detective tradition and a feminized consumer culture. The fiction he proposes is one that will assert an American identity that is genuine and at the same time opposed to the national mainstream, an identity whose avatar is a redemptive male detective figure. In reading "The Simple Art of Murder," then, it becomes clear that a distinction is necessary: Twain's essay is a manifesto for American realism, while Chandler's is a manifesto for American authenticity.

The essay calls for a fiction that is not only realistic, but also "honest," fiction that has "the authentic flavor of life as it is lived" ("Simple Art of Murder," 11). Chandler persistently satirizes what he sees as the feminine qualities of classical detective fiction of the English type, inventing prissy titles like *The Triple Petunia Murder Case* and *Death Wears Yellow Garters*, and making it clear that even a properly realistic mystery in this mold would still be unacceptably unmacho: "It would be fun to read [a successful plot of this sort], even if I did have to go back to page 47 and refresh my memory about exactly what time the second gardener potted the prize-winning tea-rose begonia" (10). The Britishness of these mysteries is exploited for comic effect here, but Chandler makes it clear that this form has its American version as well:

> This, the classic detective story . . . is the story you will find almost any week in the big shiny magazines, handsomely illustrated, and paying due deference to virginal love and the right kind of luxury goods. There are more frozen daiquiris and stingers and fewer glasses of crusty old port, more clothes by Vogue and décors by House Beautiful. . . . We spend more time in Miami hotels and Cape Cod summer colonies and go not so often down by the old gray sundial in the Elizabethan garden. (10)

The American incarnation of the classical detective story elicits the same attack on upper-class effeminacy that Chandler levels at the English books, but here the old money and old class structures have been replaced by the even more distasteful culture of American consumption, a mingling of the feminized and the inauthentic defined by slick magazines and apparently filled with the same products advertised in those magazines.

In opposition to the degraded commercial landscape that Chandler associates with the American adaptation of the classical detective story, he offers his version of the hard-boiled male detective-hero as a way of rescuing the nation from itself. Having begun the essay by asserting that fiction has always wanted to be realistic, he heads into the final movement by building a wave of rhetorical tension as he approaches his concluding sketch of the detective novel we need; Dashiell Hammett is the best we have had, but it turns out that he, and realism too, are "not quite enough" (17). At this juncture Chandler returns for a second sweeping claim—"in everything that can be called art there is a quality of redemption" (18)—that modifies the first. Realism is important for the detective novel, but the form is still incomplete if it is not "art"—if it lacks the capacity to redeem the fallen world it evokes. In the famous closing of the essay, he describes a detective figure who is a paragon of virtue, street smarts, and masculine attributes: "Down these mean streets a man must go who is not himself mean, who is neither tarnished nor afraid. The detective in this kind of story must be such a man. He is the hero; he is everything" (18). Chandler's novels present us with this man in the form of the detective-hero Philip Marlowe, picking his way distastefully among the debris and dreck of a mass-produced world. Marlowe's masculinity is presented as the vehicle of an authentic American identity that combines unblinking realism with a commitment to idealistic principles: this, Chandler suggests, is the real and defining spirit of America's better nature.

Like any theory of realism or mimesis, Chandler's contains an aesthetic imperative that suggests a set of moral or artistic goals. Chandler asserts that his hero "must" go down those mean streets, that a novel in which the protagonist does not spend his time seeking out mean streets and going down them without meanness can only aspire to represent the real, whereas a Chandler novel represents the real as the authentic. The hero's lack of "meanness," meanwhile, carries connotations of money, where to be mean is to be both cheap and concerned with base material or financial gain. Marlowe is not cheap; he is priceless—which is to say that he cannot be bought. The authenticity that Marlowe embodies, then, prescribes the enactment of an essentially romantic and sentimental vision that is opposed to commercial concerns as the necessary work of hard-boiled realism.

Chandler is absolutely correct in describing this quality as the thing that sets his work apart from that of Hammett, whose prose is less elegant than Chandler's but more experimental in its search for a style that is stripped of sentiment. For Hammett, realism is the vehicle for a series of self-conscious attempts to render the world in a radically objective way. Employing a cinematic outsider's view, accumulating detail without employing metaphor, and eschewing psychological insight, his novels aspire to render the world as a fragmented and depthless panorama in which nothing has an underlying meaning and nothing can represent anything else. Streets might be dark or dangerous, but not "mean," and men might be clever or quick but they are not heroes—there is no imperative for them to go looking for trouble, and they might even want to receive payment for doing so. Hammett's novels, particularly *Red Harvest*, *The Maltese Falcon*, and *The Glass Key*, employ this depthless style as a way of rendering an American landscape in which each person is a free agent among other agents who cannot be trusted, only manipulated. As such, his "realism" enables a leftist critique of a capitalist economy that dissolves bonds of love and fellowship and renders each person as a lone individual competing for survival.

This vision of the world surely has some foundation in Hammett's experiences as an operative for the Pinkertons, who were frequently employed as strike-breakers, and it is a vision that speaks to the American economy before the stock-market crash of 1929, one shaped by turn-of-the-century monopoly capitalism and marked by a lack of business regulation. Hammett's novels, written in the late twenties and early thirties, are responses to the economic conditions that created the Great Depression and to those that prevailed during the Depression itself. Chandler's novels, on the other hand, were published during World War II and the first decade of the postwar era. The Romantic concern with authenticity that runs through his fiction, and that remains mostly implicit in Hammett's flintier representation of America—we might say that Chandler romanticizes the solitariness that is for Hammett a critique of the individuating capitalist economy—is a response to the rise of consumer culture during this later period.[20]

The difference between the two writers is largely a matter of Chandler's desire to make hard-boiled realism an occasion for the performance of authenticity. It is that performance that defines much of noir fiction and film and that has captivated many of its fans and critics, as well as latter-day writers of crime fiction and makers of neo-noir films. Chandler's model, constructed around the desire for an anticommercial authenticity, is the one that we now most readily recognize as "hard-boiled" or "noir." "The Simple Art of Murder," like Chandler's novels, sets up a key opposition between authenticity and consumer culture. It juxtaposes the business of bestsellers and slick magazines against the gritty world of the detective-hero, and in doing so it employs a distinctive narrative style and voice. Terse, world-weary, and critical of a contemporary landscape that does not live up to Marlowe's stringent moral and aesthetic requirements, Chandler's discourse is a vehicle for the creation of authenticity effects.

In this version of the hard-boiled novel, authenticity is something constructed, imagined, and performed. The tough talk of its inhabitants, the brutal world of criminal doings and unjust social structures that it presents, the misogynist ethos of male camaraderie that it relies upon—all are performances not of the real or realistic, but of the authentic. Chandler's essay makes the case for this kind of writing, but it also enacts that case by way of tone—it dismisses the concerns and methods of literary criticism, presenting itself as a hard-boiled debunking of the critical essay form, performing authenticity in order to position its insights outside of the critical establishment:

> There is plenty of . . . social and emotional hypocrisy around today. Add to it a liberal dose of intellectual pretentiousness and you get the tone of the book page in your daily paper and the earnest and fatuous atmosphere breathed by discussion groups in little clubs. These are the people who make best sellers, which are promotional jobs based on a sort of

indirect snob appeal, carefully escorted by the trained seals of the critical fraternity, and lovingly tended and watered by certain much too powerful pressure groups whose business is selling books, although they would like you to think they are fostering culture. Just get a little behind in your payments and you will find out how idealistic they are. (1)

Here you have the hard-boiled attitude in a nutshell, as applied to the business of books. High culture is revealed to be just another racket, dependent on money, powerful groups, and an ideology founded on desires for class status. This critical position is enabled as much by the discourse—the effect of authenticity that the language creates—as by the observations Chandler makes.

Indeed, Chandler's discourse is organized around a rhetoric of debunking, an argument that conventional or mainstream ways of seeing and thinking fail to apprehend the truth of any situation. In the novels, this discourse is realized in the narration provided by Philip Marlowe as he explores and examines the Los Angeles through which he moves. His peripatetic habits are an important part of Marlowe's identity; as a figure for hard-boiled authenticity he is forever *moving through*, penetrating the American landscape and cityscape both through his physical movement and his jaded observations. Marlowe allows Chandler to render the world he describes as something to be seen through, an attractive illusion that Marlowe's language peels away to reveal corruption. In *The Long Goodbye* Marlowe finds himself watching a "girl in a white sharkskin suit and a luscious figure" with some fascination until, inevitably, "she opened a mouth like a firebucket and laughed. That terminated my interest in her. I couldn't hear the laugh but the hole in her face when she unzipped her teeth was all I needed" (87). The casually misogynistic description is itself an act of brutalization, employing metaphor in order to dehumanize; the woman becomes a grotesque agglomeration of inanimate things, her face an unzipped hole, as a way of registering Marlowe's disgust at her unrefined manner.

And if the world doesn't reveal its rot so easily, Marlowe will berate it until it does, as he does in the same novel with the honey-voiced Dr. Varley, who makes a good living keeping his old, sick patients well-sedated. Marlowe accuses Varley of running a profitable business while acting as if he is motivated by love:

"Somebody has to do it," he said. "Somebody has to care for these sad old people, Mr. Marlowe."

"Somebody has to clean out cesspools. Come to think of it that's a clean honest job. So long, Dr. Varley. When my job makes me feel dirty I'll think of you. It will cheer me up no end."

"You filthy louse," Dr. Varley said between his wide white teeth. . . .
He had a job to do, putting back the layers of honey. (136)

Marlowe persistently forces the world to reveal its underside, its ugly truth, and he does so through his linguistic formulations that act as summations, each one a pin that fixes the latest victim as a specimen for display, a new piece of evidence in the great debunking.

Acting as Chandler's tool for stripping away the false face of the world's hypocrisy, Marlowe asserts the belief that there is an underlying essence that must be revealed—a belief that is, at its core, sentimental. At the heart of *The Long Goodbye* is Marlowe's attachment and loyalty to a man named Terry Lennox, and at one point in the novel, when he is asked to take on a case, the prospective client says, "You can't judge people by what they do. If you judge them at all, it must be by what they are." Marlowe is struck: "I nodded vaguely. Because that was exactly the way I had thought about Terry Lennox" (95). The maxim is absolutely central to the worldview of Chandler's novels, in that it expresses a belief in getting past the untrustworthy surface of appearances and actions in order to uncover an authentic essence beneath. (This authenticity frequently takes the form of male comradeship—the idealized flipside of Chandlerian misogyny.)

Again, this is in many ways the opposite of Hammett's world, which is based on an aesthetic in which there are only appearances and actions, and to judge anyone by anything else would be a dangerous mistake. In the famous ending of *The Maltese Falcon*, Sam Spade denies Brigid O'Shaughnessy's appeal to essence, hers and his both; she claims that they are in love and that therefore he should not give her up to the police, while he refuses to admit that this appeal to something deeper could alter his response to her murderous and duplicitous actions, particularly her murder of his partner. In Spade's choice, both the similarities and the differences between Hammett and Chandler are on display. Both hard-boiled writers adhere to a worldview that affirms the value of bonds between men by devaluing and expunging the disruptive presence of women. But the value, the potential for authenticity, that they locate in relationships among men is not at all the same thing for the two authors. For Hammett this authenticity remains implicit and uncertain—Spade never liked his partner and is true to him only in a half-resentful observance of professional and patriarchal protocol—while for Chandler authentic bonds between men represent the value of an essence hidden beneath the world's ugly artifice.

Chandler's linguistic performance of authenticity is most clearly on display in his most famous stylistic technique—his flamboyant and defining use of simile. General Sternwood in *The Big Sleep* speaks slowly, "using his strength as carefully as an out-of-work show-girl uses her last good pair of stockings" (8). In *Farewell, My Lovely*, Moose Malloy wears an outfit so loud that "even on Central Avenue, not the quietest dressed street in the world, he looked about as inconspicuous as a tarantula on a slice of angel food" (3). As Christopher Raczkowski points out, Chandler's relentlessly metaphorical discourse creates a very different effect than the one created by Hammett, who carefully eliminates metaphor from his novels:[21] "While Hammett's narration metonymically slides along the surface, Chandler continually arrives at depth and interiority with these metaphors—intrinsic qualities, identity, essence" ("Metonymic Hats and Metaphoric Tumbleweeds," 112). The depth suggested by the metaphorical model is once again a strategy by which Chandler suggests that it is necessary to shatter the surface of things in order to see what they "really" are, employing language in order to strip away the false mask of American life and reveal its hypocritical artifice. That illusion is displaced and replaced by the effect of authenticity that is provided by Chandlerian discourse, an authenticity that is produced as a self-conscious performance, a deliberate effect.

The metaphors Chandler employs are so excessive in their construction and their frequency that they appear at times to be camping, self-consciously inviting the reader to see them as being "too much." Thus while the Chandlerian simile creates the effect of authenticity, it also renders visible the process of creating that effect, the "effect-ness" involved in the linguistic construction of authenticity. The tarantula on the slice of angel food is not appropriate or equivalent to the situation it describes (Moose Malloy being noticeably out of place); it is excessive to the situation, so that instead of clarifying the scene that is being described, it draws our attention to the performance of the metaphor. This performative excess also takes the form of a piling-on of metaphorical constructions. One chapter in *The Long Goodbye* begins with Marlowe telling us, "I drove back to Hollywood feeling like a short length of chewed string," which is followed up in the fourth paragraph with this triptych: "An hour crawled by like a sick cockroach. I was a grain of sand on the desert of oblivion. I was a two-gun cowpoke fresh out of bullets" (137). While the "short length of chewed string" does the job of evoking Marlowe's mental condition, the three consecutive images that follow add only their multiplying references—the atmospheric, the existential, the generic—in a performance that becomes increasingly outrageous. The Chandler style—the noir style—creates the effect of authenticity, but in a way that makes the construction of the effect visible.

FILM NOIR: DISCONTENT AND ITS CONTENTMENTS

Like Chandler's work, film noir represents itself as the opposite and the repudiation of consumer culture. It is organized around the performance of that repudiation, which is to say, once again, the performance of authenticity. Its critics and theorists, who are responsible for the creation and maintenance of "film noir" as a category, describe it as a dark and brooding refusal of American pieties and ideology, of sentimentalism and the commonplace, of Hollywood's facile optimism. The unsparing iconography of noir itself—the world-weary voiceover, the femme fatale, the trenchcoated detective, those brooding urban shadows—is familiar even to those who have never seen even one of the original films. And although these devices are now sometimes employed in the service of camp, the noir style still frequently appears as a marker of seriousness in film, television, comic books, and other popular media. This style continues to connote a kind of unflinching realism, and the effect derives in part from noir's self-conscious rejection of the commercial space it inhabits. That rejection serves to represent consumer culture as the polar opposite of noir, but the rejection is itself a symptom of noir's uneasy recognition that it exists within the network of consumption that circulates around all commercial film—the mainstream American consumerism that noir defines itself against.

The category of "film noir" itself has been the subject of much debate, in part because of the term's unusual origins and the category's uncertain status. People argue about the exact dates, but the American film noir cycle is often described as running from the early forties to the late fifties. ("Neo-noir" is a catchall term for any film made after that period that looks back in some way to the earlier films.) French critics invented this new category when they employed the phrase "film noir," already in use, to describe American crime films of the forties. Nino Frank published an article on the new *policiers* in 1946, and Jean-Pierre Chartier's essay "Les Américains aussi font des films 'noirs'" ("Americans Make 'Noir' Films, Too") appeared in the same year. The first book-length study of the subject is the now-classic *Panorama du film noir américain* (*A Panorama of American Film Noir*), published in 1955 by Raymond Borde and Étienne Chaumeton. Because it begins as an ex post facto critical category, because critics disagree about what films belong in that category, and because many of the films that *are* included cross generic lines— noir Westerns, noir gangster films, noir detective films, noir melodramas—it is problematic to describe film noir as a genre alongside staples like the Western or the musical. No Hollywood directors or producers ever knew themselves to be making a "film noir," and theorists of genre have often had a difficult time assimilating noir to their critical paradigms. Because of these difficulties in identifying film noir as a genre, scholars have tried using other terms. It has been variously described as a cycle (this was the choice of Borde and Chaumeton), a series, a style, a mood, a mode, or the expression of a zeitgeist. But since all of these terms are alike in their vagueness, they serve only as containers in which to gather a group of films, rather than defining or describing what noir is.

With that question still open, the critical work on noir has tended to focus at least as much on defining its topic as it has on interpreting the films, and that is a project with no definitive ending. Some critics have chosen to define noir by enumerating its stylistic or thematic elements, the most influential example being Paul Schrader's classic 1972 essay "Notes on *Film Noir*." But this approach can only ensure that the category remains amorphous and contested, as critics continue to debate the features, the boundaries, and the canon of film noir. James Naremore sums up the case this way: "Nothing links together all the things described as noir—not the theme of crime, not a cinematographic technique, not even a resistance to Aristotelian narratives or happy endings. Little wonder that no writer has been able to find the category's necessary and sufficient characteristics" (*More Than Night*, 10). Nonetheless, plenty of useful and interesting work on noir has been done in the last two decades, analyzing noir through such explanatory lenses as World War II's wartime culture; modernist urban space; European surrealism; European existentialism; American immigration and border crossings; anxieties about race, gender, and sexuality; psychoanalysis; and nationalism.[22] Each of these readings offers a useful key to understanding noir without, of course, providing a definitive explanation for it, and because the category of noir is so unstable, each new interpretation of noir tends to redefine the boundaries of the category itself.

So to attribute any coherent political stance to film noir—a grouping of films that has no movement or organization behind it, a critical category that is endlessly debated—is a difficult business. There is, nonetheless, a rough consensus among critics that noir tends to position itself oppositionally, providing a critical viewpoint on American politics of the forties and fifties, portraying the underside of the American Dream.[23] The films can frequently be read as a response to failures or contradictions in American institutions of government, society, and economy. James Naremore writes that for Borde and Chaumeton in *Panorama du film noir américain*, "noir is not merely a descriptive term, but a name for a critical tendency within the popular cinema—an antigenre that reveals the dark side of savage capitalism. . . . Noir produces a psychological and moral disorientation, an inversion of capitalist and puritan values, as if it were pushing the American system toward revolutionary destruction" (22). If so, then it is not surprising that Marxist critics like Mike Davis and Fredric Jameson have found in noir and the hard-boiled tradition the potential for a critical analysis of American capitalism.[24] Dean MacCannell writes that "there is a kind of innocent codependence of film noir sensibility and Marxist criticism, each providing the images and concepts that the other believes it needs" ("Democracy's Turn," 282). Although not all noir critics are Marxists, and not all critics see the films as politically progressive, it is clear that the noir tradition is concerned with the contradictions inherent in the American political economy, with the opposition between democratic ideals and capitalist structures.[25]

Both as a collection of films and as a critical category, film noir has a distinctive and conflicted relationship to the American consumer culture of which it is a part. The underworld that the films invoke is both an indictment and an artifact of capitalism, a populist intervention and a popular entertainment. These films tend implicitly to distance themselves from the artificiality of the movie-making system from which they emerge; thus the political critique of capitalism identified by noir's critics is performed in part through a formal critique of popular film. In this sense, there is an unexpectedly utopian impulse in noir: the suggestion that a filmic encounter with the "reality" of the urban and criminal underworld may also be an encounter with the presence and immediacy that people feel themselves to have lost when confronted with the apparent artificiality of consumer culture. Because noir offers this promise, it is important that these films present themselves as authentic. Through their streetwise attitude, moral ambiguity, and existential reflections on crime and death, they posit for themselves a film world that is less prettied-up than other popular films and ostensibly less commodified.

Noir drives this point home by providing a critique of consumption generally and of Hollywood's product in particular. In the first major study of film noir, Borde and Chaumeton argue that it is specifically dedicated to undermining Hollywood style:

> All the components of noir style lead to the same result: to disorient the spectators, who no longer encounter their customary frames of reference. The cinema public was habituated to certain conventions: a logic to the action, a clear distinction between good and evil, well-defined characters, clear motives, scenes more spectacular than genuinely brutal, an exquisitely feminine heroine, and an upright hero. (12)

As Borde and Chaumeton go on to explain, these conventions are systematically violated in the film noir cycle. But of course these crime films are themselves offered as entertainments with some sort of mass appeal. Although their serious subject matter and disillusioned tone suggests a gritty urban realism presumably absent in other Hollywood films, this tough-mindedness is really an authenticity effect created through a set of strictly mannered noir conventions: expressionistic lighting and scoring, hard-boiled dialogue that is formulaic almost to the point of parody, obsessively complex investigations of the past. Noir is gritty realism rendered through a stylized, filmic, and pleasurable mode of representation. Shimmering rain-soaked streets, white-hot gun flares in darkened rooms—these are confections offered to the moviegoer, visual treats whose tone of brutal cynicism has proved irresistible to generations of film critics and theorists.

The critical definition of noir itself emerges out of the postwar spread of American consumer culture. French critics used the phrase "film noir"—which had previously been applied to some French films of the thirties—to describe many of the American films that arrived en masse in Parisian cinemas after the years of the Nazi occupation, as part of a larger influx of American consumer products. Indeed, we might say that the category of noir is invented out of a political desire on the part of critics—first in France and later in other places, including the United States itself—to locate the inevitable destruction of American affluence and dominance in the heart of the American commodification machine itself. As I have said, noir is less a group of texts than a critical category constructed retrospectively. It is, in Naremore's terms, a discourse, and it is a discourse that is often deployed in the service of nostalgia. Its aura of darkness makes it highly marketable and available for commercial purposes, and "noir" is an extraordinarily successful brand. New! Improved! Noir! Lary May's romanticization of noir in *The Big Tomorrow* is an instructive example; he rightly sees the classic films as connected to the "rebel" screen stars of the fifties and the emergence of the counterculture in the sixties, all linked in their response to the "consumer paradise" (256) of the postwar period. But he seems unaware of the extent to which the rebel image has been, since the fifties, a consistently powerful tool for the marketing of films, clothes, vehicles, and pretty much everything else for sale in America.[26]

Noir, in other words, is cool. In our own present moment, in which noir is loved almost reflexively by audiences and critics alike, the idealized claim that film noir is "disturbing" or "disruptive"—what critic's heart is not warmed by perversity, cynicism, and brutality?—must be measured against the evidence that it is also pleasurable. When critics talk about noir as disturbing, it seems less that they are truly alarmed than that they are positing a hypothetical spectator of fantasized naïveté in order to claim the films as radical. (And criticism that deploys these kinds of descriptions shares a logic with the advertising blurbs that are used to sell movies. "Peerlessly disturbing!" "Radically disruptive!") I have suggested that these films stage a confrontation between democratic ideals and capitalist structures; they do so from a conflicted position, since these are Hollywood films that formally distance themselves from Hollywood conventions in order to construct their critique of consumer culture. Deciding whether this makes the films politically radical or radically co-opted is a critical cul-de-sac. But the consistency with which these films and their critics raise these issues suggests the extent to which noir expresses postwar American anxieties about consumer culture through its attempts to locate a space outside of that culture.

Caught between opposition to and complicity with Hollywood, classic noirs and later neo-noirs have struggled to differentiate themselves from other film entertainments, and from consumer culture as a whole, through the assertion that their visions represent an alternative, authentic America— one that has not been sold out. As Naremore's description of noir as an "anti-genre" suggests, the particulars of the alternative to consumerism offered by these films are hard to pin down; noir seems to exist purely as a force of opposition. But in its evocation of an underworld lurking just beneath the surface of the acknowledged social order, noir taps into a deep American sense that our real national identity resides somewhere outside of traditional institutions of government and economy, and outside of our inevitable, daily participation in the sphere of consumption. If the content of noir's definition of America remains vague—the hoped-for return of an undefinable national character—its critical strategy or tendency is clear: to disrupt the equivalence between American citizenship and consumer capitalism that has developed in the postwar era.

2. Out of the Past, into the Supermarket

Throughout this book, I will be arguing that the ongoing confrontation between authenticity and consumer culture that is staged by the noir tradition takes place most dramatically in the way that commercial spaces are represented in the texts I examine. In doing so, I am drawing on a critical tradition that argues that the development of capitalism has always been accompanied by developments in the organization and conception of space. Building on the work of the Marxist thinker Henri Lefebvre, scholars of geography have offered a body of analyses that imagine space not as something empty or neutral but as an entity that is produced in ways that reflect the structures of a given society and that reproduce the economic conditions that create it.[27] Capitalism, in Lefebvre's account, survives—avoids collapse and achieves its sustaining growth—by producing particular kinds of space. As Edward Soja puts it in *Postmodern Geographies*, "Socially produced space . . . is where the dominant relations of production are reproduced. They are reproduced in a [space] that has been progressively 'occupied' by an advancing capitalism, fragmented into parcels, homogenized into discrete commodities, organized into locations of control, and extended to the global scale" (91–92). That process is forever structuring and restructuring our spatial environments and experiences in order to produce the conditions that markets require. This suggests both that the analysis of spatial organizations is a way to understand social relations and that a refusal of those social relations must be imagined in spatial terms: "no social revolution can succeed without being at the same time a consciously spatial revolution" (92).

This urge toward a spatial revolution resonates with the noir response to commercial space, but the similarity is largely structural. Although noir responds to the problem that Marxist geography describes, it does so not in order to imagine a socialist space as an alternative but in order to reject the current organization of commercial space in the name of the incompletely imagined category of the national authentic. Moreover, as we shall see, the relationship to space that emerges in noir is often ambivalent, torn between the absolute rejection of commercial principles in favor of an authentic elsewhere and the possibility that commercial space may itself contain contradictory or imperfect versions of the dominant social relations.

The analysis of commercial space in noir is particularly relevant because the conflation of national identity and consumption that I have described was linked to changes in the spatial organization of American life in the postwar era. In the years after World War II, the nation's center of gravity altered as the "American Dream" came to be defined in terms of universal homeownership—and ownership of a modern and fully accessorized home—fuelling the well-charted movement from city centers to suburban sprawl. The interstate highway system and the American culture of the automobile developed in tandem, facilitating the move to the suburbs and enabling the emergence of commercial outlets designed specifically for people to reach by car—supermarkets, shopping centers, and ultimately indoor malls and superstores—as well as gas and service stations, commercial destinations that also contribute to the infrastructure of automobile culture. Lizabeth Cohen argues that these spatial changes constituted a new paradigm for the organization of American life: "An important shift from one kind of social order to another took place between 1950 and 1980, with major consequences for Americans. A free commercial market attached to a relatively free public sphere (for whites) underwent a transformation to a more regulated commercial marketplace . . . and a more circumscribed public sphere of limited rights" (286). The spatial changes that define postwar America, in other words, represent a new chapter in the relationship between the capitalist marketplace and the American nation, a new chapter in the production of the national landscape by commercial interests.

Consumer capitalism produces and reshapes a range of spaces within frameworks that enable its functioning and that serve to reproduce the conditions of consumer capitalism. One place where this process is especially visible is in those spaces where the business of consumption is organized and conducted. Commercial spaces, and stores in particular, are crucibles for our experience of consumer capitalism, locations where we take our place in the networks of relations among things that are the real point of the commodity structure. As geographer Robert David Sack makes clear in *Place, Modernity, and the Consumer's World*, the crucial tensions of twentieth-century life are encoded in these spaces of commerce, the "vast landscapes of consumption" that define our experience of space. That holistic experience of commodification is expressed in microcosm in the space of the store:

> Stores contain the commodities described in advertising. The store's environment must be attractive for these commodities to sell. This means that the store acts as an advertisement for the commodities, displaying them in a way that makes them as attractive as they were in the media ads. . . . This leads the stores themselves to possess the tensions that are contained in the commodities. (134–35)

Stores are not only places where commodities are displayed; they partake of the logic of the commodity in their location, organization, and operation. They are spatial expressions of the commodity form, sites where contradictions of consumption are present and conflicts around consumption are played out.

In order to locate and understand this process, I will be focusing my attention on the way that the texts under consideration here produce oppositional versions of national authenticity through their representations of a variety of commercial spaces, stores among them. In some cases the commercial aspect of the represented space is metaphorical or implicit and in others it is concrete and material; in fact, the material spaces of commerce that I discuss here always turn out to imply metaphorical spaces, and vice versa. Gas stations and supermarkets are significant as the nodes that define larger systems of economic and social circulation (the highways, the mobile goods, the money), while networks of global capital find their defining representation in the concrete space of the corporation (the office building, the magazine, the clock). In the chapters that follow, I will be arguing that the books and films I discuss employ particular commercial spaces in order to engage and sometimes contest the social and economic ideology of consumption that those spaces contain and embody, and thus to stage a tension between (national) authenticity and (consumerist) artifice. To begin this analysis, I will be focusing here on a paradigmatic American consumer space: the supermarket, which serves as film noir's *bête blanche*. I will examine how, in the context of post–World War II America, film noir encounters the supermarket—the store itself as well as the practices and meanings that derive from it.

SUPERMARKET EPIPHANIES

The evolution of commerce in postwar America runs parallel to the evolution of the supermarket, which can serve as a kind of microcosm for American consumer culture. In *Carried Away*, her history of "the invention of modern shopping," Rachel Bowlby cites the 1932 opening of the Big Bear store in Elizabeth, New Jersey, as the birth of the supermarket. (King Cullen, started in Queens in 1930, is another contender for "first supermarket.") Big Bear was really a discount warehouse, but its focus on self-service and on stocking household goods for low prices signaled a break with the previous model for large-scale shopping, the department store. Whereas the department store was international and cultivated an ambience of aristocratic luxury, the supermarket was an American invention designed to present an aura of pragmatism and democracy. It marked a movement away from urban centers toward a suburban, car-oriented lifestyle, as well as a movement from marketing aimed at bringing glamour to the middle class to marketing affordable food and sundries to the masses. This distinction is real, but it also has a powerful symbolic dimension. As Bowlby writes, "The department store is considered to be feminine, frivolous, French, and fashionable; in its Parisian form, it is one of the emblems of nineteenth-century modernity. . . . The supermarket, massive and materialistic, figures as an American invention" (9).

In fact, in the two decades after World War II the supermarket became the visual representation of America's emergence as a world power defined by abundance. In *Paradox of Plenty* Harvey Levenstein observes that in 1957, "when the U.S. government wanted to display 'the high standard of living achieved under the American economic system' at the Zagreb Trade Fair, it reproduced a supermarket stocked with American processed foods and produce" (114). The supermarket rose in tandem with the new national culture defined by the automobile, the highway, and life in the suburbs, representing the thoroughly modernized postwar America both externally—in its convenient placement by the roadside, surrounded by parking space—and internally, in its modern design, innovative layout, and self-service structure. This self-service model required a new model for marketing, too; companies redesigned packages in order to better catch the eye of the passing shopper, who was no longer guided by sales clerks. Warren Belasco writes in *Meals to Come* that the new supermarkets announced themselves as modern spaces through their futuristic design. These machines of efficient distribution "were also among the earliest and heaviest users of the 'streamline moderne' style—the up-to-date, slightly aerodynamic look of curved corners trimmed with stainless steel, black structural glass, enameled Art Deco letters, and neon signs" (175).

The postwar supermarket was a symbol of American modernity and innovation, and it also provided a representation of the "American way of life," in which American values were expressed in terms of national affluence. In *Shelf Life: Supermarkets and the Changing Cultures of Consumption*, Kim Humphery notes that the modern supermarket's "absurd, almost surreal field of 'choice'" is, like the consumer culture in general, "bound up with values of freedom and self-determination." Since these values are central to American self-definition, it is appropriate that, as Humphery notes, "the supermarket may have emerged as a cheap and efficient alternative to the traditional grocery store, but within two decades it . . . had become a symbol of all that was American" (6, 71–72). The distinctly American characteristics of the supermarket, then, are its emphasis on consumption made available to a mass market (signifying democracy and classless society) and its enormous range of choices (carrying the symbolic promise of freedom and independence). In this way the word "supermarket" itself has become shorthand for American consumer culture. By the 1940s, it was becoming the "dominant food-selling form in the United States" (*Carried Away*, 153). In the postwar period, when the United States emerged as the world's primary economic power, the supermarket model spread rapidly to European countries as well, along with the whole gamut of American products and popular culture (including the films that would eventually acquire the label "noir").

The supermarket's character as a symbol and emblem have made it a space that invites epiphany, a place where people and fictional characters confront America as something expansive, bland, bewildering, impressive, and terrible. Because the supermarket is so clearly a theater for the performance of American plenty and capitalist excess, it had particular resonance for Cold War politics, and there is a whole Cold War subgenre of the supermarket epiphany narrative. The Russian defector in the film *Moscow on the Hudson* (1984) collapses in the middle of a supermarket, overwhelmed by its disorienting vastness. There is even a story—often repeated as a fable of American affluence triumphing over Soviet ideology—that Boris Yeltsin relates about his visit to a supermarket in Houston in 1989: "When I saw those shelves crammed with hundreds, thousands of cans, cartons and goods of every possible sort, I felt quite frankly sick with despair for the Soviet people" (*Against the Grain*, 255). Whatever we may think of the story, the Cold War context makes an important point about supermarkets explicit: the supermarket epiphany is always, in one way or another, a moment in which America seems to reveal itself. The thing that is dimly seen, lurking vaguely around us all the time, snaps into focus just long enough for us to have the impression of apprehending it: American promise, or American monstrosity, glimpsed for a few flickering frames.

Most often, it is the monster that materializes. Kalle Lasn's epiphany about consumption in what he calls "America™" leads him to an ideological conclusion that is quite the opposite of Boris Yeltsin's. "Once you experience even a few of these 'moments of truth,' things can never be the same again," Lasn writes in *Culture Jam*. "When it happened to me I was in my neighborhood supermarket parking lot" (xiv). He goes on to describe his frustration with the system of putting quarter deposits into shopping carts in order to guarantee that the shopper will return them, which leads to a whole series of frustrations with the supermarket itself, which quickly becomes an emblem of the whole system to which "culture jamming"—Lasn's term for resistance to consumer culture—responds. The epiphany in the parking lot, Lasn claims, enables a whole new way of thinking about how to respond politically to the hegemonic America as defined by consumption: "I realized I had stumbled on one of the great secrets of modern urban existence. . . . Once you realize that consumer capitalism is by its very nature unethical, and therefore it's *not* unethical to jam it . . . once you start trusting yourself and relating to the world as an empowered human being instead of a hapless consumer drone, something remarkable happens" (xv). Specifically, taking this version of *The Matrix*'s red pill will allow you to see the truth that "a free, authentic life is no longer possible in America™" (xiii).

Lasn's revelatory moment is politically simplistic, but it suggests the extent to which supermarket epiphanies are often felt to reveal all that is wrong with the American way of life. Although *Moscow on the Hudson* plays its scene for laughs, the encounter with consumer culture is more often represented in film through the darkest kind of comedy—as in, for example, the several horror films that employ supermarkets and other commercial spaces as settings.[28] If the supermarket itself is imagined as horrific, it is because of the way that it cancels the liveliness of actual horror, with its visceral thrills and pumping blood; the real nightmare is in the way that the blank face of America swallows and covers over whatever monstrous crimes the filmmakers can invent. A fine epiphanic moment in this vein is presented near the end of the 2009 film *The Hurt Locker*. The "cowboy" bomb-defuser William James, who thrives on the adrenaline rush of his job, finally returns home to his wife and child only to discover that he cannot stand the tedium of everyday life in dull, civilized America and quickly signs up to go back to Iraq. His frustration is sketched quickly: all that is required is a shot of James pushing a shopping cart under the supermarket's fluorescent lights to convey the extent to which he is at odds with his surroundings. The idea is borrowed from the Western film tradition—the lone man who works to secure civilization and rule of law is himself unfit to live in a peaceful nation—and the film turns again to the supermarket as the spatial representation of a pervasively felt American emptiness by putting the cowboy in the cereal aisle.

In these scenes taken from the cinema and from life, the epiphany involves a portrayal of the supermarket as both a specific site of commerce and a synecdoche for larger systems of meaning, the placeless place in which American national identity and market principles are conjoined. One way of describing this twofold representation is offered by the authors of *Food and Cultural Studies*, who argue that the supermarket is a paradigm of what Anthony Giddens calls "disembedding," the process in which modern institutions "lift social relations out of local contexts and rearticulate them 'across indefinite tracts of time-space.' . . . This lifting-out is accompanied by the growth of *abstract systems* that mediate between people and institutions" (Ashley et al., *Food and Cultural Studies*, 113). This mediation occurs both at the level of social and material conditions—the way that this shopping model enables a more abstract relationship to food, money, and space—and at the level of cultural signification. A real social and commercial space that is also a metaphor for the omnipresence of the commercial in American daily life, the supermarket appears in all sorts of texts at moments of crisis or revelation because in this dual character it suggests the presence of the numinous, of the apparition of the American way of life itself in the real but estranged space of the Muzak and the misted produce.

This conception of the supermarket, and of consumer culture in general, as a numinous site of quasi-religious transcendence is a recurrent theme of postmodern fiction. (The work of Don DeLillo, in particular, frequently returns to this idea, and his *White Noise* is essentially a novel-length supermarket epiphany.) In a commercial encounter from Thomas Pynchon's *Vineland*, a character suddenly finds herself unable to cash her paycheck—the government program she works for has been cut off. Desperate, she rushes from store to store, finally arriving at a supermarket. While she waits for the inevitable rejection of her check, she has her own epiphanic moment:

> It was there, gazing down a long aisle of frozen food, out past the check-out stands, and into the terminal black glow of the front windows, that she found herself entering a moment of undeniable clairvoyance, rare in her life but recognized. She understood that. . . . it would all be done with keys on alphanumeric keyboards that stood for weightless, invisible chains of electronic presence or absence. If patterns of ones and zeroes were "like" patterns of human lives and deaths, if everything about an individual could be represented in a computer record by a long string of

ones and zeroes. . . . We are digits in God's computer, she not so much
thought as hummed to herself to a sort of standard gospel tune. (90–91)

The supermarket epiphany represents the disembedding that occurs in this
kind of commercial space in terms borrowed from the language of religious
revelation, but what is revealed each time is not the presence of God but of
systems in which consumer culture and national politics are conjoined. The
transformation of citizens into patterns of digital representation, bar codes, is
offered as a dystopian revelation of our inauthenticity; individual subjects are
constituted through the networks of commerce that define the nation, which
exists as the next level up of digital complexity. The supermarket is not only the
space within which we interact with these networks—within which the codes
are scanned in ways that are indecipherable to us—but also the symbol of
America as a thing made by structures of consumption.

   As these examples suggest, the supermarket takes this role in a whole range
of texts—fiction, film, personal history, cultural criticism—that meditate on the
meaning of America as a consumerist nation. As with the narrator of the Clash
song, the experience of inauthenticity often takes the form of being "lost in the
supermarket." So the dialectics of authenticity does not begin or end with noir—
far from it. But the noir tradition offers a paradigmatic statement of those issues
combined with a strategy that codifies the response to consumerism in terms of
authenticity. In order to trace the historical development of this strategy, I will
be looking now at three scenes from films that use the supermarket as a stand-in
for American consumer culture as a whole, drawn from three distinct moments
in the evolution of this dialectic: the classic noir *Double Indemnity*, the revisionist antinoir *The Long Goodbye*, and the postmodern neo-noir variant *The
Big Lebowski*. The discussion of these three films provides in miniature a version
of the argument I will be developing over the course of the book, in which
changing forms of American consumer culture—which tend to move toward
increasing abstraction and virtuality—elicit evolutions in noir's aesthetics of authenticity, with the confrontation between the two becoming visible in noir's
representations of commercial spaces. Each of the three movies reflects on the
relationship between noir and the supermarket as competing models for American self-definition. Taken together, they begin to suggest a paradigm for understanding film noir in terms of its ongoing engagement with the development of
American consumer culture from World War II to the present day.

THE MARKET AND THE UNDERWORLD

One of the films that arrived in France after the war and helped to shape early
critical definitions of noir was Billy Wilder's *Double Indemnity*, originally
released in 1944. Adapted from a novel by James M. Cain and with a script by
Wilder and Raymond Chandler, it provides an example of the classic film noir

and of how noir themes and styles represented a counterpoint to World War II–era consumer culture. This confrontation is most visible in the much-discussed "Jerry's Market" scenes, two extended sequences in which Walter Neff and Phyllis Dietrichson meet at a local supermarket, first to plan the murder of Phyllis's husband and later to deal with the fallout from the murder. In the latter scene, the film's plot has reached an especially tense moment, with Neff, who has grown wary of his partner in crime, arguing that they should stop trying to collect the insurance money and Phyllis angry that Neff has been spending time with her stepdaughter.

The scene begins with an establishing shot from above, showing the tidy geometry of the store and the people with carts winding among the aisles. During the next few minutes we slowly move closer to Neff and Phyllis and their surroundings dominate the screen less. But the supermarket continues to intrude on their conversation, in the form of passing shoppers and store employees—none of whom pays any attention to their frantic whispering. After several interruptions, as they stroll the aisles in a forced parody of shopping, the two end up divided by an aisle stacked so high with products that the camera has to give us a Neff's-eye view, looking slightly down at Phyllis. This separation by consumer goods is the point: Neff wants to turn back, to rejoin the citizen-consumers in the banal communal space of the supermarket, but Phyllis makes it clear that there is no turning back, and then Wilder makes it even clearer. The camera moves in for a stunned close-up on Neff and for the first time the supermarket recedes completely as his face fills the screen and his voice-over resumes, keying a fade to Neff sitting in the dark insurance office, recounting the story.

This scene sets out the opposition between supermarket and noir in the clearest possible terms. Its visual impact comes not only from its contrast with the scenes that precede and follow it—the bright interior space of the store as opposed to the dark insurance office after hours—but from the contrast between the store and the two characters who have made it the backdrop for their drama. Wilder uses the cheery mise-en-scene of the supermarket, with its bustle of polite shoppers and its orderly rows and pyramids of products, to throw his noir characters into relief.[29] In doing so, he makes use of the film medium's particular capabilities. Unlike radio or the written word, film is ideally suited to representing the space of the supermarket. As Anne Friedberg suggests in *Window Shopping: Cinema and the Postmodern*, shopping and film spectatorship each require a gaze that is simultaneously virtual and mobile, a gaze that originates in the nineteenth-century practice of *flânerie* and organizes a whole range of visual practices throughout the twentieth century (24). Both the film and the supermarket are inherently concerned with visual display and the organization of space, and both offer the aesthetic novelty of their design for the viewer's or shopper's perusal and delectation. Minus the two main characters, this scene from *Double Indemnity* could perhaps serve as a promotional film for the presentation of products in the modern supermarket, circa 1944.

FIGURE 1 Double Indemnity: *Film noir in the supermarket.*

Wilder uses the opposition between the aesthetics of noir and supermarket to create a more subtle opposition between noir and the rest of Hollywood film. In Jerry's Market, our two stock figures from hard-boiled noir, the femme fatale and the doomed sap who falls for her, are hopelessly out of place. Barbara Stanwyck in particular, with her platinum wig and dark glasses—look at me, I'm in disguise!—appears loaded to excess with signifiers of femme-fatality when placed among the shopping housewives and the neat aisles stocked with baby food and macaroni.[30] The noir woman is especially alien here because the supermarket shopper is usually imagined as a woman, but one who is a passive and receptive female consumer rather than the flinty, tough-talking Phyllis. For James Naremore, Phyllis is essentially continuous with the supermarket because her femininity is packaged and mass-produced: she is "visibly artificial," with a "cheaply manufactured, metallic look" (*More Than Night*, 89). But to the extent that she is visibly artificial, she is also visibly parodic; Phyllis's evident artificiality refers us mockingly to the unacknowledged artificiality of Hollywood femininity in general. In the same way, the bright, mass-produced emptiness of the store stands in for the bright, mass-produced emptiness that, the film implies, Hollywood typically produces.

This visual disjunction suggests that Walter Neff and Phyllis Dietrichson can no longer inhabit the same world as the "real" shoppers. Noir plotlines frequently evoke an underworld of crime, passion, and perversion that lurks beneath and alongside the world of respectable daily life. The plot typically begins with an apparently discrete event—a single death, a wrong turn, a flirtation—that leads the plot outward to reveal an expanding web of lawlessness and corruption. In *Double Indemnity*'s supermarket drama, the robust consumer society of the forties is haunted by two characters who inhabit that noir underworld. Neff and Phyllis have crossed the noir frontier and seem almost invisible to the respectable citizens who surround them, shoppers whose respectable citizenship is constituted here not through any official or institutional relationship but rather by their status as consumers.

In fact, the citizen-consumers are almost entirely oblivious to the two murderers in their midst, an implicit commentary on the supermarket as a new kind of social space organized around consumption and commodity fetishism. Kim Humphery cites a retail expert from the sixties, who suggested that in the new self-service stores "the package is an extremely important substitute for the personal relationship that people desire." Thus, as Humphery notes, "the notion of inanimate objects and physical spaces as the means by which to preserve, albeit in altered form, the communicative, social aspects of the shop was central to the development of the supermarket" (*Shelf Life*, 65). The space of Jerry's Market is superficially communal, but in fact the scene as filmed emphasizes the privatization and commercial purpose of the space, focusing our attention on barriers and awkward silences in order to suggest a "lonely crowd" of people lost in private reverie and communing only with their potential purchases. The noir underworld is presented as more vivid than the bland comforts offered by citizenship; the shoppers are docile shades, lacking the urgency and passion that motivate the conversation between Neff and Phyllis.

As the use of the supermarket in *Double Indemnity* shows, the noir conjunction of aesthetics and ideology is motivated, at least in part, by the rise of consumer culture in the postwar era and the increasing conflation of consumption and citizenship that this rise entailed. The juxtaposition between the underworld and the supermarket also figures noir's oppositional stance in relation to Hollywood film, its undermining of classical Hollywood narrative conventions. *Double Indemnity* thus presents itself as more unflinching and authentic, in its dark themes and cynical attitude, than other Hollywood movies of the time. It is in this sense that noir is countercultural (a link to the sixties that I discuss in depth in later chapters); it sets up a contrast between two versions of the nation, the mainstream consumer culture and the underworld of the deviant and dispossessed. Noir becomes the site of an American identity that is asserted as both alternative and original; it is the underground retreat of an ideal but undefined national character, a retreat that is itself outside the social and imaginative space of postwar citizenship because it rejects the equation of citizenship with consumption.

HOORAY FOR HOLLYWOOD

The era of classic film noir ended in the fifties, but in the New Hollywood of the late sixties and early seventies, filmmakers began to reevaluate American film genres and icons through the lens of a national culture changed by the new social movements associated with the sixties. Alongside the more visible political movements—including the civil rights movement, second-wave feminism, and gay liberation—the sixties produced a new wave of consumer advocacy that challenged practices in corporate marketing and production as manipulative and corrupt.[31] The consumer culture identified with the supermarket, and specifically its relationship to the woman as shopper, was often described as a form of conspiracy or brainwashing.[32] In Jennifer Cross's 1970 book *The Supermarket Trap*, she argued that American housewives were enmeshed in a plot constructed by marketers through the advertising and packaging of their products; the supermarket is a "bewildering, enticing, craftily packaged trap that awaits every housewife during her weekly shopping expeditions. . . . The contest is not an equal one, largely because most people are unaware that the trap exists, and of the competitive conditions within the food industry that sprung it, the marketing techniques that bait it so cunningly" (viii).

This vision of the supermarket as conspiracy is realized on film in the 1975 version of *The Stepford Wives*, in which a supermarket serves both as the communal center of the suburban Connecticut town of Stepford and also as the site where the film's anxieties about gender, conspiracy, and consumption are staged in their most disturbing form. The town's housewives are replaced one by one by compliant and physically enhanced robot versions of themselves, designed and constructed by an ex-Disneyland engineer; the tools of the marketing apparatus are being used to literally reshape women. In the film's final scene, the robot wives shop and greet each other vacantly. As they push their carts among the perfectly stacked aisles, the sixties' reading of the supermarket reaches its logical conclusion: a brightly lit space in which the colorful products are purchased by pretty automatons who are themselves the ultimate product of the consumer society. In this sense, perhaps the film's sneakiest suggestion is that men in positions of power fear feminism not only because it might ruin women as wives, but because it might ruin them as consumers. And although *The Stepford Wives* is itself an unlikely candidate for the neo-noir canon, it does contain at least one suggestion that the noir tradition offers an alternative to the artificial America of the suburbs: in this film about men conspiring to create more perfect shoppers, the only sympathetic male character is an ex-boyfriend named Raymond Chandler.

But films of the era that sought specifically to reckon with the legacy of noir did not generally give Chandler such gentle treatment. In the cultural context of the seventies, the hard-boiled noir narrative—with its retrograde gender politics and its masterful detectives—could only seem hopelessly old-fash-ioned. The only way to revisit noir was by making a kind of antinoir, such as Robert Altman's irreverent adaptation of *The Long Goodbye*, in which Ray-mond Chandler's private eye Philip Marlowe has been uncomfortably trans-planted to 1973. Since the classic era of film noir had ended some fifteen years earlier, the hard-boiled detective-hero had to be revived specifically in order to be reconsidered or parodied, allowing directors like Altman to create a com-mentary on an earlier mode of filmmaking.

Not only is Marlowe out of place in the Los Angeles of the seventies—represented by the spacey members of the women's commune next door, who spend their time baking pot brownies and doing yoga in the nude—but the style of the film is itself a rebuke to the classic films it parodies. Altman uses Chandler's novel as a source, and Leigh Brackett, who worked on the 1946 version of Chandler's *The Big Sleep*, wrote the screenplay; but the movie point-edly does not use a film noir style. Rather, it is made in the Altman style—with lovely, inventive cinematography by Vilmos Zsigmond. The camera pans and zooms and is kept wandering at all times (perhaps suggesting the shopper's mobile, distracted gaze), while the film image is "flashed" to minimize strong contrasts of light and dark. The narrative itself is loose and improvisational, and the casting and performance of Elliott Gould emphasize this looseness; he plays Marlowe as a lost, laconic hipster who mumbles to himself and whose tagline is, "It's OK with me."

In this context, the opposition between noir and supermarket is consider-ably less clearly defined than in *Double Indemnity*. Instead, Altman's attitude toward consumer culture is largely bound up with his attitude toward Holly-wood as a factory for the mass-production of images, including images from the noir tradition that he parodies. The film begins and ends with a tinny, old-fashioned version of the song "Hooray for Hollywood"; by letting us hear the scratches on the recording, as if we were listening to an old 78-rpm disc, it suggests that the Hollywood in which past incarnations of Marlowe lived is archaic and outdated. The first specific reference to noir itself comes in the form of a Hollywood security guard who specializes in impressions of movie stars—beginning with the Barbara Stanwyck of *Double Indemnity*. Film noir is accorded no special status here as a site of neglected or authentic American values; it is simply part of the larger movie-making industry, another artifact of the studio system.

This point is emphasized by Altman's undermining of noir conventions. In opposition to the complex and tightly patterned plots that characterized the forties noirs, we are given a shaggy dog story of a plot and a detective who seems to belong in the supermarket as much as he belongs anywhere. The film contains long, digressive scenes that do nothing to advance the narrative, and it ends abruptly on an act of sudden and absurd violence that violates any desire for consistency or closure. These choices seem indebted to a French

New Wave tradition that is interested not in straightforward social criticism but rather in an artistic interrogation and violation of genre conventions. This tone is set in the scene that plays out during the film's opening titles: Marlowe, in search of food for his cat—he gets the wrong brand—and brownie mix for his hippie neighbors, wanders the aisles of a local supermarket late at night in his forties suit, smoking his perpetual cigarette. Meeting this Marlowe—addled, anachronistic, running household errands for finicky pets—it is clear that he is precisely not the paragon of hard-boiled American manhood so lovingly created by Chandler. The dingy store and fluorescent lights themselves present a contrast with Wilder's bright stacks of commodities, and the film is casually cynical about consumer culture. When Marlowe asks for a particular brand of cat food, a store employee gestures at the rows of different brands and points out that "all this shit's the same anyway"—a phrase that neatly sums up Altman's feeling about Hollywood.

So the model set up by *Double Indemnity*, in which consumer culture and the noir underworld are placed in stark opposition, no longer holds up in *The Long Goodbye*. Nor is noir seen as a unique space in which Hollywood conventions are contested. Instead, Altman suggests that noir and supermarket are parts of the same system, and to put the detective in the macaroni aisle is only to show how the Hollywood production system is a part of the culture's pervasive "supermarket trap." As in *Double Indemnity*, the visual practices of filmmaking and film viewing are linked to visual practices of shopping and store display. But Altman's revisionist approach implies that in noir, too, these two kinds of visual pleasure are the same, that the Hollywood film viewer is always a shopping consumer. So here the potential for authenticity, for providing a critique of the culture supermarket, resides not in the noir style or narrative, but in the art-cinema style of New Hollywood directors like Altman—with nods to Godard and to the cultural politics of the sixties—whose demystification of classic Hollywood film is linked to his era's new and improved distrust of the consumer society.

FIGURE 2 The Long Goodbye: *From the mean streets to the cat food aisle.*

AMERICA ABIDING

Although seventies movies such as *The Long Goodbye* suggested that film noir was no longer relevant except in revisionist modes, noir styles and themes underwent a full-scale revival beginning in the eighties. Since then a whole new cycle of films loosely classified as "neo-noir" have appeared, ranging from the nostalgic revisiting of James M. Cain in *Body Heat* (1981) to the blue-screen visual pyrotechnics of *Sin City* (2005). In this period, few filmmakers have returned as consistently as the Coen brothers to themes and images borrowed from the noir tradition—but the Coens appropriate those themes and images in order to place them in a larger structure, a pastiche within which the meanings of noir are recontextualized and repurposed. *The Big Lebowski* (1998) uses Raymond Chandler's novels as a template, but although it too is an investigation of Los Angeles spaces, the Marlowe stand-in here is Jeffrey "the Dude" Lebowski, an addled, pot-smoking sixties survivor whose life is largely organized around his bowling schedule. Despite its unusual protagonist and its wholesale abandonment of noir iconography, *Lebowski* picks up the issues raised in my readings so far and holds them up for inspection, extending the confrontation between film noir and consumer culture into the contemporary imaginative space that goes by the name of "the postmodern."

The Dude himself brings together the two historical moments of noir represented by *Double Indemnity* and *The Long Goodbye*—the classic Chandlerian noir of the postwar era, the countercultural antinoir of the sixties era—and links them to the return to noir in the post-eighties era of dominant postmodernism. The narrator—an anachronistic Westerner called "the Stranger" in the credits—is insistent upon, but imprecise about, the relevance of the Dude to this last historical context, the nineties of the film's setting and release. He introduces the Dude in voiceover by saying,

> Now this story I'm about to unfold took place back in the early nineties— just about the time of our conflict with Saddam and the Iraqis. I only mention it 'cause sometimes there's a man—I won't say a hero, 'cause what's a hero?—but sometimes there's a man—and I'm talkin' about the Dude here—sometimes there's a man who, well, he's the man for his time and place, he fits right in there—and that's the Dude, in Los Angeles.

This introduction proceeds as the camera leads us toward and into Los Angeles, ultimately finding the Dude in a Ralphs supermarket. The camera tracks slowly up the aisle towards the Dude, shopping in his bathrobe—a movement that is echoed later in the film by the shots that track slowly down the lanes of the bowling alley. Both activities—bowling and shopping—define the Dude's way of life, one that is simultaneously inside and outside of the consumerist mainstream. They connect the Dude to the consumption of goods and leisure activities, but his way of participating in both suggests that, against all odds, leisure is trying to find a way to decouple itself from the alienating qualities of mainstream consumption.

Although he adheres to a vaguely understood version of New Left politics—and claims to have been one of the Seattle Seven and one of the authors of "the original Port Huron Statement, not the compromised second draft"—the Dude's real political potential resides in his way of being, his ethos. He does not work and has no desire to, and his dedicated laziness puts him at odds with the false work ethic and nationalist masculinity[33] that are championed by his namesake, the richer, older Jeffrey Lebowski for whom the Dude is mistaken. That other, "big" Lebowski is a vain phony who surrounds himself with the trappings of wealth, which he claims to have earned but actually is his first wife's inherited money, including a "young trophy wife," the keystone in his use of conspicuous consumption to construct an ideal image of himself. The Dude, by contrast, makes purchases only for pleasure (White Russian fixings, pot, bowling) and drives a car that becomes progressively more battered and squalid as the film progresses.

The Dude's position outside of the mainstream consumer economy is made visible upon his introduction in the initial supermarket scene. He is shown, in his bathrobe, at the register writing a check for 69 cents, with the telltale milk on his mustache indicating that he has already been sampling the wares. He is a kind of ghost in the machine, an unwitting trickster who partakes of the leisure that the consumer economy encourages without actually participating in that economy; instead he seems to be enjoying the ride to be had in slipping through its cracks. (Like Philip Marlowe, the Dude is an economically impossible character. Just as Marlowe never makes enough money from his cases to live on, the Dude has no visible source of income at all; both are fantasy figures representing the principle of a position or way of being that exists outside the consumer economy.) With his long hair and beard and bathrobe, he appears as a peculiar kind of Second Coming; he is the representative of a free-floating oppositional American identity that is found first in Chandler's noir detective, then evolves into the countercultural principle of the sixties, and emerges into the present as the Dude.

The film's appeal, in other words, is in its presentation of the Dude as the embodiment of an ethos, a mode of living that is opposed both to the film's self-proclaimed nihilists, who have no ethos (as bowling buddy Walter remarks, "Nihilists! Jesus. Say what you like about the tenets of National Socialism, Dude, at least it's an ethos"), and also opposed to the false ethos of the consumerist American way of life. It is this appeal to ethos that has inspired *Lebowski*'s unparalleled cult following, including the Lebowski Fests and the books and websites in which Dudeism is celebrated as a form of slacker theology.[34] Against nihilism and, more pointedly, against mainstream consumerist nationalism, the film appears to champion a generous, messy, and street-level American spirit, one that is both marginal and central, and one that looks

FIGURE 3 The Big Lebowski: *The Dude samples dairy products at Ralphs.*

back—in a mode that alternates between homage and critique—both to Chandlerian noir and to sixties counterculture.

The extent to which the Coens imagine this continuity is made clear in our hero's final words, "the Dude abides," which are given a visual emphasis: as he speaks he has already walked out of the camera's focus and into shadow, fading into the blurred backdrop of the bowling alley, into myth and symbol and ethos. This motto is taken up by the Stranger in his closing remarks: "The Dude abides. I don't know about you, but I take comfort in that. It's good knowing he's out there, *the Dude*, takin' 'er easy for all us sinners." Here, as with the Dude's Christlike appearance, the biblical reference has been repurposed. The Dude doesn't suffer for our sins; he is the principle of an oppositional stance that in his case takes the form of a Whitmanian loafing idleness.[35] The oppositional principle abides; it waits to be found in the American past of the noir texts (e.g., Chandler) and sixties texts (e.g., the Port Huron Statement) that it references, outside of the mainstream but nonetheless asserting its centrality to the spirit of the republic.

The Dude's relationship to the supermarket sets up the tension that the film explores between a mainstream, consumerist America represented by the big Lebowski and an alternative American identity that is both central and marginal. And this model for reading *The Big Lebowski* provides a way of answering the question that the Stranger does not answer at the film's beginning: why is the Dude "the man for his time and place"—particularly considering that the time is the moment of the first Gulf War? If he is considered as a principle that is opposed to or at least outside of the consumer economy, then the film is at pains to identify that consumer economy with the American conflict with Iraq. It is in the supermarket, while writing his check, that the Dude looks up and sees George Bush on a television announcing, in response to

Iraq's invasion of Kuwait, that "this will not stand, this aggression against Kuwait." By linking the Gulf War metonymically to the supermarket, the film suggests the extent to which the conflation of consumption with national identity extends to American foreign policy, wherein actions that protect the interests of oil companies and sustain the domestic market for oil consumption are framed and justified by the assertion that those actions represent national values, including America's strength, masculinity, and exceptionalist moral force.[36] The Dude is the man for his time and place because his way of being seems to provide a critique of and alternative to the republic of consumption, the supermarket within which the Gulf War makes sense.

But if *The Big Lebowski* provides a figure who is outside of the consumerist mainstream, it does not adhere to the clean opposition proposed by our other films from the noir tradition, in which consumerism is placed in opposition to some version of authenticity. *Lebowski* enacts a kind of critical play with the logics of consumer culture without actually positing an "authentic" alternative that is radically outside of commerce. So the relationship of the noir detective to the supermarket is different here than in classic noir like *Double Indemnity* (where the supermarket is opposed to noir) or antinoir like *The Long Goodbye* (where the detective's alignment with the supermarket undermines the noir genre). As with Elliott Gould's Marlowe in the latter film, the Dude appears at first to be a pathetically deteriorated version of the noir detective, but as I have suggested, the film ultimately celebrates his presence, and his successful detective work, in a way that is not undercut by his association with the supermarket. Instead, the film combines a critique of the large system of American consumer capitalism with a generous affection for commercial spaces that are associated with the messy local culture of Los Angeles, such as Ralphs and In-N-Out Burger.

These particular kinds of commercial space are used to evoke a marginal, down-at-heel Los Angeles of subcultural heterogeneity, as opposed to a national identity defined by consumer culture writ large. Indeed, the authoritarian police chief of Malibu, going through the Dude's wallet, is outraged to discover that his only form of I.D. is a Ralphs Shopper's Club card. Because the I.D. is from the local supermarket chain Ralphs, with deep roots in LA's culture—and the same store where the Dude wrote his 69-cent check—what might otherwise look like a damning equivalence of American identity with consumer culture appears here instead as an instance of the Dude slipping between the cracks of official ordering systems. Likewise, his preferred fast-food outlet is In-N-Out Burger: another local chain, and one of the few fast-food restaurants that Eric Schlosser has kind words for in *Fast Food Nation*. Schlosser's opposition between national and nation-defining mainstream organizations like McDonald's and the quirky local practices of In-N-Out mirrors the distinction that is implicit in *The Big Lebowski*. Commercial spaces—including supermarkets, fast-food restaurants, and of course bowling alleys—may have connections to local culture that separate them from the dominant, consumerist American way of life. (In the film's opening montage, there is a neat little glimpse of another site of local LA commerce, Benitos Taco Shop, as well.) The film leaves us not with a rejection of consumer culture as such, but with a profound ambivalence about the supermarket as symbolic space; it is uncertain whether to consider Ralphs as representative of national consumerism or of local street culture.[37] Although the film is faithful to its noir heritage in many ways, it approaches noir's anticonsumerist authenticity not as an axiom, but as a problem to be investigated and reconsidered. The Dude is ethos, but he is ethos without authenticity.

Each of the three films I have discussed here is engaged on some level with the aesthetics and ideology of noir, and each is searching for a position outside the mainstream of American consumer culture, for which the supermarket is an emblem. Each confronts the problem in a different and historically located way. In a classic film noir like *Double Indemnity*, the noir aesthetic is itself a site of resistance from which to provide a critique of consumer culture and popular film forms. For Altman's *The Long Goodbye*, made after the decline of the studio system, noir itself is hopelessly compromised as part of a mass-production system that can only be seen critically in retrospect. *The Big Lebowski* suggests that everything, itself included, is compromised, but not hopelessly; its political resistance to commerce as linked to nationalist traditions—putting the Gulf War in the supermarket—takes place through a generic play with noir in which consumption and authenticity are no longer imagined as purely opposed. Noir is the vehicle by which American film from the postwar period to the present stages the tension between two visions of national identity: on the one hand the pervasive everyday practices of consumer society, on the other the dream of an essential, undefinable America that exists somewhere on the margins, resistant to government and global capital alike. But in each of my three examples, the political engagement of the film is tied, one way or another, to its complicity in consumer culture, its status as an image that, however raw or disturbing it may be, has a lineage in the shop window and a kinship with the supermarket display.

THE SHAPE OF THE PROJECT

Throughout this study, I will be continuing the work that these first three readings have begun. I will be looking at representations of those commercial spaces in which the drama of authenticity is played out, in order to show how the authenticity effects in these texts are motivated by the desire to represent an alternative to the republic as we know it. When American citizenship is defined as a version of consumption, when the American Dream becomes the American way of life, when the American landscape is fully inhabited by the practices of commerce, where is the space in which one can locate authenticity?

That is the problem that these texts assert and take up in their various ways. Each text contains some conception of authenticity that is imagined as the opposite of the "consumers' republic," the "material nationalism," and in each case that opposite is posited as an alternative and vaguely defined other America— a better, truer America that has gone underground, an elsewhere. Here, again, authenticity is defined negatively, as the opposite of consumer capitalism. The tradition that begins with film noir and hard-boiled detective fiction consistently operates by creating authenticity effects, performances that suggest the lurking presence of this alternative America, an authentic presence that exists as the negation or critique of consumer culture.

There is, then, a second meaning to the term "authenticity effects." It describes not only the techniques and representational strategies by which noir-derived texts attempt to inhabit an oppositional position with regard to consumer culture but also the process by which authenticity is produced as an effect of consumption. The dominant consumer culture that emerged in the years after World War II, precisely because it came to define American citizenship and national identity so thoroughly, elicited a countercultural response— the sense of discontent and alienation that attended the emergence of the affluent society—that was expressed in noir film and fiction. Thereafter, developments in consumer capitalism produced new versions of the countercultural response, new developments in the language of authenticity; the two evolved in tandem. The discourse of authenticity that I identify here is essentially an effect of the America, with its distinctive spatial formations, that is produced in the era of consumer culture. But in describing the authenticity that is evoked in these texts as an effect, I am emphatically not arguing that we should dismiss it. Rather, this book begins from the premise that we must take seriously the desire for authenticity that is produced as an effect of consumption in order to recognize that any understanding of contemporary America must take into account the extent to which it is shaped by the dialectic of authenticity.

In writing about authenticity as a product and effect of commercial culture, I have sought to avoid making two of the common critiques of consumer culture, both of which are in any case widely available and often repeated. The first is the critique in which the rise of consumer culture is abhorred on the basis of an appeal to morality: it is destroying institutions, traditions, families, and so on. Consumer culture may in fact be undermining our humanity and our relationships to others, and if so there is no shortage of books and movies, articles and websites, that make the case—including, with differing degrees of explicitness, many of the texts under consideration in this study. But my goal here is, rather, to analyze the desire for authenticity that is the basis for these objections; to understand how authenticity emerges in the distinct discursive form it takes in postwar America; and to understand how it evolves during that era.

A second critique—in some ways the opposite of the first—argues that condemnations of consumption can have no political purchase when they are themselves participating in the marketplace. This paradox is clearly important to the work I am doing here. Films are made by Hollywood to be consumed and to make profits, and books are distributed and marketed by the publishing industry; they all are commodities and participate in the various logics and fetishizations that the commodity form puts in play. But this paradox should not lead us to devalue or dismiss the political potential of these texts. All critical positions on consumer culture begin within it or negotiate its networks at some juncture; this contradiction is a productive one, in ways that inform my investigation here. In the early chapters of the book, I am concerned with the way that the discourse of authenticity emerges in texts that are caught up in the system of exchange in one way or another, and in the later chapters I discuss texts that are engaged with the problem of how to envision a political resistance to consumer culture in a world-space that seems to have been constructed and inhabited at every level by global capitalism.

So in the chapters that follow I maintain a critical distance from, and a skepticism about, the various ways in which the noir tradition presents its vision of authenticity as an alternative that negates or rejects the consumerist American mainstream in absolute oppositional terms. This book, in other words, is not a brief in favor of noir authenticity. But neither is it an attack upon the logics of authenticity that I identify. Such attacks exist, particularly among liberal critics who view the authenticity-based politics of the sixties counterculture (which, as I argue here, is connected to the noir tradition), as an abandonment of real-world politics, a dead-end retreat in which cultural criticism substitutes for political intervention, enabling a disengaged and consumerist individualism; versions of this argument can be found in work by Thomas Frank, Sean McCann and Michael Szalay, and Joseph Heath and Andrew Potter.[38] These attacks on the politics of the counterculture—the politics of authenticity—have their merits, but their rejection of that politics rejects too much. Without championing the politics of authenticity, I have tried in this book to understand the discourse of authenticity as proceeding from real desires and discontents, as a crucial and persistent element in political and cultural traditions of American self-understanding.

In following the evolution of the discourse of authenticity, I am making the case for a tradition that comprises both film and fiction, originates in film noir and hard-boiled detective fiction, takes new forms thereafter, and continues to shadow the historical development of American consumption. Thus I describe the texts under consideration here as belonging to the "noir tradition" in order to emphasize continuities in the process by which classic noir evolves into conspiracy narrative in the sixties and then into cyberpunk and other neo-noir forms starting in the eighties. Following this general trajectory, the three sections of the book follow a rough chronology that runs from the 1940s to the early twenty-first century, and some of the novels and films I discuss in the latter stages of the book are aligned with the noir tradition in ways that are more attenuated than those I deal with in the early stages.

The first section comprises two chapters that examine consumption as a problem of noir masculinity in the immediate postwar era, through readings of film noir and detective fiction. Chapter 1 extends my analysis of commercial space by looking at the way that film noir represents the gas station, which inaugurates the spatial model within which the supermarket eventually emerges. A commodified space that is already being displaced by flashier commodities in the forties and fifties, the gas station is a crucial site for noir's staging of the confrontation between consumer culture and authenticity. Gas stations hold out the possibility of a last stand for authentic bonds between men to be affirmed, but in the films I discuss these bonds are always disrupted by the intrusion of female characters—incarnations of the famous femme fatale—who are dangerous not because of their sexuality but because they represent the irresistible corrosiveness of unrestrained capitalism.

The ambivalence with which noir represents the gas station is transformed into a stark opposition in the next chapter, which explores the postwar discourse around the executive figure, the hopelessly inauthentic "man in the gray flannel suit," and the corporation that defines him. Here the distinction between authentic men and inauthentic women is revealed as a distinction between two kinds of men, one that has more to do with class than with gender: the corporate executive as opposed to the streetwise detective. I focus on two novels, Kenneth Fearing's noir thriller *The Big Clock* and Raymond Chandler's detective epic *The Long Goodbye*, both of which negotiate the modernist problem of art's relationship to commerce through representations of corporate executives from the business of publishing. Both books suggest that the publishing executive is defined by his status as a member of the professional-managerial class, which represents the merging of American citizenship with consumerism; by contrast, the detective is rendered as a classless American, a fantasized and authentic alternative to the "organization man." In this sense, these books prefigure the countercultural logic that emerges fully in 1960s politics.

That historical shift is the subject of the book's second section, which is focused on the transformation of noir into conspiracy narrative during the sixties era, the moment of the emergence of postmodernism. Each of the chapters in this section describes a version of that transformation. The first, chapter 3, argues that in the sixties and seventies the political logic of noir authenticity is taken up in the new genre of the conspiracy narrative. While noir film and fiction seem to have exhausted themselves, their ideological resistance to consumer culture remains in the authenticity effects created by conspiracy texts. I argue that paranoid cinematic thrillers such as *The Parallax View* respond to the development of global capitalism by attempting to evoke the unrepresentable complexity and scope of multinational corporate networks. The America they describe is completely inhabited by forces that are too large to see, creating an imaginative impasse wherein authenticity takes the form of a recognition of the unknowability of conspiracy's functioning, so that we can only discover and perpetually rediscover the impossibility of political action.

The two chapters that follow employ conspiracy narrative in ways that attempt to reinstate political content through evocations of different kinds of authenticity. Chapter 4 returns to the questions raised by the sixties counterculture as seen in Thomas Pynchon's trilogy of California novels, *The Crying of Lot 49*, *Inherent Vice*, and *Vineland*. Pynchon's novels provide an especially consistent vision of the split between the two Americas, the mainstream one represented by the American way of life with its interlinking of political and commercial interests and the true, alternative republic whose promise is perpetually betrayed. Pynchon, I suggest, uses the logic of American exceptionalism in order to argue that America perpetually fails to achieve the ideal state it imagines itself to be, producing a left-leaning narrative of national self-betrayal. In these novels, the promise of authenticity resides with the outcasts, the left out and left over, who have no place in a mainstream America that is wholly inhabited by consumer culture and so retreat to hidden enclaves where the promise of the republic may be revived or reinvented.

The last chapter in this section turns to the African American counterconspiracy narrative, a genre that combines the African American literary tradition's conception of race as conspiracy with tropes from the exhausted form of the noir detective novel. While the alternative nationalism of Pynchon's novels looks to the American dispossessed as the true bearers of American identity, these novels of antiracist insurrection from the sixties and seventies argue for a form of black nationalism focused on the "authentic" space of the inner-city ghetto. The ghetto is produced during the postwar decades as the obverse of the new suburban mainstream and thus as a site where the effects of consumer capitalism's large systems can be witnessed as political effects. The three novels I focus on here—*The Spook Who Sat by the Door* by Sam Greenlee and Chester Himes's *Blind Man with a Pistol* and *Plan B*—envision the possibility of apocalyptic political action, but in doing so continue to rely on a historically distinct conception of black authenticity that imagines itself as the politically engaged alternative to a consumerist black middle-class.

The last section of the book takes two sets of paradigmatically postmodern texts as its subjects—one that relies on logics of authenticity, and one that does not. The project of representing the vast and abstract space of consumer capitalism that was so central in earlier conspiracy texts takes new forms in the cyberpunk genre—the focus of chapter 6. Beginning in the early eighties, films like Ridley Scott's *Blade Runner* and novels like William Gibson's *Neuromancer* employ the conventions of noir and hard-boiled detective fiction in a science-fiction context as a way of mapping the complexities and contradictions of the capitalist world system. I focus primarily on novels by Gibson in order to argue that the ethos of hybridity and bricolage that defines both cyberpunk and much of the critical discourse on postmodernism is, in the terms of my study, not a violation of authenticity but rather the postmodern form of authenticity. Although cyberpunk rejects essentialist identities in favor of a hybrid, "cyborg" aesthetic, that cyborg aesthetic is imagined as a new site of authentic resistance to the dominance of consumer capitalism.

In the final chapter I turn to the Coen brothers' *The Hudsucker Proxy*, not a neo-noir film in any obvious way, but one that employs noir as an element in its pastiche of Hollywood genre as a way of experimenting with the relationship between authenticity and consumer culture. The film looks back, from the perspective of the nineties, to the postwar era in order to introduce yet another mutation in the evolution of authenticity that began with classic noir. In its exploration of corporate spatial organization, it creates a symbolic space based on the principle of simultaneity, in which sixty years of Hollywood history are contained in the film's representation of the Hudsucker corporation building. This spatial model enables the film to think critically about film genre, particularly in its unlikely meshing of film noir with the screwball comedy. Ultimately the several genres and movie traditions that the film uses as its building blocks are themselves offered as consumer products, much like the Hula Hoop that Hudsucker manufactures and markets. In its refusal to condemn these consumer products, *Hudsucker* creates not the effect of authenticity, but a meditation on the dialectics of authenticity itself.

Each chapter raises its own set of issues that necessarily exceeds the capacity of the brief sketches offered here. Taken together, the chapters constitute an argument that the evolving confrontation between consumer culture and authenticity that is played out in the texts of the noir tradition is central to conceptions of American identity in the twentieth century and beyond. America itself is an elusive thing, more alive in idealized forms than in its government and institutions. People always seem to be taking to the highways in search of it, so it must be missing; people are always worrying about how to define it, so we must not know what it is. It is elsewhere, and wherever it is, it is better than the ersatz land we inhabit—this affluent nation full of citizens who are, we hear, alienated, empty, aching, lost, and dispossessed. My project is to follow the logic of the desire encoded in these assumptions, and the discourse of American authenticity that this desire produces, in order to discover the ways in which the noir tradition's novels and films employ that discourse in their ongoing attempts to reject or reimagine America.

PART I

Postwar Spaces, Postwar Men

Last Chance Texaco

GAS STATION NOIR

To understand the American roadside you must see it as a vital and inseparable part of the whole organism, the ultimate expression of the conspiracy that produced it. . . . You know this roadside as well as you know the formulas of talk at the gas station, the welcome taste of a Bar B-Q sandwich in mid-afternoon, the early start in the cold bright lonesome air, the dustless and dewy road and the stammering birds, and the day's first hitchhiker brushing the damp hay out of his shirt.
All such things you know. But it may never have sharply occurred to you that the Great American Roadside . . . is incomparably the most hugely extensive market the human race has ever set up to tease and tempt and take money from the human race.

—JAMES AGEE, *"THE GREAT AMERICAN ROADSIDE"*

I'm sorry, baby, I'm not buying.

—WALTER NEFF TO PHYLLIS DIETRICHSON, *DOUBLE INDEMNITY*

The gas station is a crucial location in film noir, a place where the conflicts at the heart of the noir cycle are displayed and played out. As an in-between space— one that is both indoor and outdoor, a place of stasis for people in motion—it contains contradictions and invites ambivalence. The editors of the collection *Moving Pictures/Stopping Places* observe that stopping places along the highway of cinema's great road trip "are marked by a vertiginous intensity . . . simultaneously disrupting and securing mobility; halting yet enabling movement; translating passage into the passage of time; heightening emotion as much as fostering motion; provoking transition as much as smoothing transit; registering identity whilst promoting anonymity" (3). Although these writers are primarily concerned with hotels and motels, the productive contradictions that they describe are relevant to the cinematic gas station as well. In the context of film noir, the gas station is particularly significant because it signifies the postwar commercialization of the American landscape while also bearing traces of the idealized masculinity that noir imagines as thriving in the now-lost world of the frontier and the open road.[1] The gas station is a commercial space, and therefore suspect, but it also potentially offers an image of gritty and masculine authenticity: America in grease-stained overalls.

The gas station is an easily overlooked feature of the American landscape—there are few commercial spaces we take for granted so completely, or try to get out of so quickly—and its appearances in noir could easily be overlooked as well. Gas stations are never at the center of the film noir narrative, but they hover persistently at the fringes, appear as the sites for important scenes and encounters, and play a key role in negotiating the oppositions that define the classic film noir cycle: country and city, crime and respectability, light and dark, male bonding and heterosexual desire, commerce and authenticity. All of these oppositions are put in play by the gas station's presence in film noir. The focus of this chapter is on the way that the latter two sets of oppositions—male bonding/heterosexual desire and commerce/authenticity—become versions of one another, so that issues of gender and commerce are intertwined.

One of the central features of film noir is its trademark gender politics, its special misogyny: the dichotomy between tough detectives and saps who fall for deadly women, the conception of femininity itself as a form of sinister artifice. In the films that I will be looking at here, noir's classic gender arrangements are much on display. I will argue that the gas station's role as a site of commerce enables a reinterpretation of noir's gender politics, in which it becomes clear that femmes fatales are figures for expressing anxieties about consumer culture and that male bonding is an attempt to imagine an authentic American identity outside of consumption. In the Introduction, I argued that noir imagines itself as the polar opposite of the consumer culture represented by the figure of the supermarket. The gas station adds a new twist to noir's representation of commercial space. As a distinctly masculine environment—one where, as Texaco's onetime motto suggested, "you can trust your car to the man who wears the star"[2]—the gas station is imagined as a place of male bonding, where relationships between men are forged, or tragically broken, or where unholy heterosexual compacts are made and signed in blood.

The Movie through the Windshield

Although one could assemble a long list of the kinds of interior spaces that bear meaning in film noir—diners, casinos, office buildings, banks, and hotels, for instance—few turn up as consistently as the gas station.[3] It appears in B-movie noirs as well as high-budget ones, in films central to the noir canon and in those whose status is more marginal, and it is often the site of important meetings, encounters, and turning points in the narrative. In Howard Hawks's *The Big Sleep* (1946), Bogart's Marlowe first meets the deadly Canino face-to-face in the service garage of a filling station; and Al picks up the conniving

Vera while filling up in Edgar G. Ulmer's *Detour* (1945). Fritz Lang included gas stations in his first two American films, the proto-noirs *Fury* (1936) and *You Only Live Once* (1937). The latter shows ex-con Eddie getting fired from his job and thus heading down the road to recidivism at a gas station (while in a later scene his wife Joan manages the nifty trick of hand-pumping her gas while holding the station attendants at gunpoint). A similar turning point occurs in Douglas Sirk's *Shockproof* (1949), when Jenny and Griff go on the lam after hearing on a gas station's radio that they are wanted. Gas station settings of various kinds are also important in *Decoy* (1946), *Crime Wave* (1954), *The Postman Always Rings Twice* (1946), *They Drive by Night* (1940), and *Thieves' Highway* (1949). Gas stations appear in many other noirs in less prominent roles, including *The Blue Gardenia* (1953), *Gun Crazy* (1950), *They Live by Night* (1948), *The Big Steal* (1949), *White Heat* (1949), and *Odds Against Tomorrow* (1959). Rounding out the list are some films I discuss in this chapter: *High Sierra* (1941), *Impact* (1949), *The Killers* (1946), *Out of the Past* (1947), *Kiss Me Deadly* (1955), and *Ace in the Hole* (1951).[4]

Although many of these sightings of gas stations in noir films are brief or seemingly incidental, their repeated appearance suggests their importance. They flicker past like something vaguely remembered, demanding to be understood. As Kelly Oliver and Benigno Trigo argue in *Noir Anxiety*, "Like the Freudian dream-work, the most significant and telling aspects of film noir often appear as insignificant details or marginal figures" (xv). While gas stations appear frequently, they rarely occupy center stage. Because they lurk persistently at the periphery of noir, it is necessary to ask what exactly they are doing there.

To begin with, their presence suggests the extent to which noir is organized around the tension between city and country. Although noir is often described as a specifically urban phenomenon—the hard-boiled detective pursuing an investigation through seedy back-alleys and rain-glazed city streets—the city can only bear meaning in these films insofar as it is opposed, implicitly or explicitly, to an image or idea of rural America. A particularly resonant example would be the character of Dix in *The Asphalt Jungle* (1950)—a title that suggests an intertwining of city and wilderness—who participates in the heist staged by the film in order to buy back his family farm in Kentucky, and dies as he reaches it. In fact, the noir canon is largely made up of characters in the city who dream of the country, characters exiled from the city who dream of going back or are dragged back against their will, and films that move back and forth between the two.[5]

In *Somewhere in the Night*, Nicholas Christopher emphasizes the role of the city in noir, while pointing out that the most important factor in the postwar development of the city is American car culture: "The automobile turns up significantly in film noir not only within the city, but often between cities, usually at night. The passengers are traveling between two sets of existential or emotional situations—or two sets of trouble—often symbolized by the cities at either end of the journey" (94). But although this is an accurate description of certain films—*Detour*, for instance—it misses the extent to which the journey itself is part of the equation, and the frequency with which the two poles of the journey are city and country, rather than city and city. The automobile links the urban and the rural, which may themselves turn out to be "two sets of trouble." A particularly dramatic example appears in Nicholas Ray's 1952 *On Dangerous Ground*. As the bitter and violent city cop Jim—sent to a rural region that he calls "Siberia" on a special assignment—drives out of town, we watch through his windshield as a series of fades show the changing landscape, as city streets and neon give way to bare trees and icy hills. On his trip back, we see the same transformation in reverse, and although it is never entirely clear which place represents the more "dangerous ground," Jim ultimately leaves the city behind to live in that rural Siberia with a blind and virtuous widow.

The gas station often plays a part in this negotiation between country and city. *High Sierra*'s (1941) gas station is where criminal protagonist Roy Earle befriends the countrified "Pa" and his family. Pa, who holds Roy in high regard, serves to connect Roy to his small-town roots; they forge a powerful bond, a bond between men that is disrupted by Roy's problematic wooing of Pa's crippled daughter, Velma. With the family as a vehicle through which Roy fantasizes a respectable life for himself, he pays for an operation to fix Velma's bad foot and then proposes marriage. But she is already in love with another man, and when Roy meets them he is horrified to discover that Velma is not the impossible embodiment of small-town innocence he had dreamed of. (Roy was hoping to marry a version of the blind widow from *On Dangerous Ground*; his mistake, apparently, was in removing Velma's disability.) Both urban crime— the legendary "big score"—and heartland respectability are revealed as false promises, dead ends, and there is nothing left for the film to do but to trace the path of Roy's dying: his suicidal return to crime and flight deeper into the countryside, where he is trapped and killed by the police on a mountainside.

A Mobil outpost in the oddball 1949 noir *Impact* offers a similar negotiation between city life and country life. Presumed dead after his beloved wife tries to have him killed on the highway, hard-driving San Francisco businessman Walter Williams drifts along in an aimless depression until he reaches Larkspur, Idaho ("pop. 4,501"—road signs are everywhere in the drifter's geography of noir). Here he happens upon a service station where the mechanic is an inept but beautiful widow. Walter takes over the mechanic's job, and begins to rediscover himself in this Norman Rockwell town where one chooses between apple or cherry pie, where one says grace at meals, and where someone's mother mends your socks. The dialogue of the characters is so filled with homegrown homilies that each line seems to have been embroidered and hung in a kitchen in middle America.[6] Walter's grease-monkey idyll can't last, but unlike Roy Earle he returns to the city rejuvenated by the country air. After beating a murder rap, he resumes his old life and job, though with the good woman from Idaho replacing the sinister city wife. *On Dangerous Ground, High Sierra*, and *Impact* are constructed around three very different stories, but in each film the negotiation between urban and rural space takes the form of a nostalgic longing for a lost purity that is represented by women who have not been tainted by city life. I will return to this gender dynamic—by considering the role of the pure woman's opposite number, the femme fatale—later in this chapter.

This opposition between city and country, both of which are either threatening or impossible, both of which inspire nostalgia for a past or imaginary ideal space, appears persistently in film noir.[7] Edward Dimendberg offers one useful way of thinking about this opposition in *Film Noir and the Spaces of Modernity*, arguing that noir's response to the problem of urban space in the postwar era takes two complementary forms. One is concerned with the concentrated space of the urban metropolis; the other, the tendency that I have been describing, is "centrifugal" noir, which concerns the tension between the city and the dispersed postwar space of suburbs, highways, and shopping centers that has grown up around it. The movement between the two is defined by the perceptual alterations of automobile culture, which creates a new kind of mobile and cinematic gaze. As an example of this new mode, Dimendberg cites the detective novels of Raymond Chandler and the film noir adaptation of Chandler's *Murder, My Sweet*: "It is as if each view of Los Angeles were seen from the window of a moving car, a discrete snapshot carried away from a scene with no thought as to its utility. . . . Marlowe perceives much of Los Angeles through the automobile windshield as he travels on surface streets and the outlying roads predating the highway system that emerged at the end of the 1930s" (168).

In these observations, Dimendberg begins to suggest a conjunction that is key to film noir: the experience of driving is analogous to the experience of cinema spectatorship. The two technologies emerged together at the end of the nineteenth century, and both offer consumer products that provide new kinds of visual mobility. In "Noir's Cars," Mark Osteen argues that cinematic automobility in noir is engaged with the postwar ideology of a privatized, consumption-driven social mobility: "newly purchased cars became signs of restored consumer power and renewed possibility—of a refurbished American dream" (184). The postwar driver inhabits a newly purchased space of identity, observing a film that unfolds a landscape of potential consumption and potential reinvention.

Noir brings these multiple and interlocking forms of mobility together; as in *On Dangerous Ground*, the American landscape is transformed into a movie that dramatizes the movement between city and country. In his study of how commerce in America moved from city centers to strips and sprawls, *Main Street to Miracle Mile*, Chester Liebs describes roadside buildings—gas stations, supermarkets, motels, drive-in theaters—as "the movie through the windshield." Starting around the time of World War I, "the most dramatic change in the windshield movie was the wholesale injection of 'commercials' into the roadside panorama. . . . Entrepreneurs began, almost spontaneously, to see ways to profit from the motorist's freedom to halt the windshield movie and step out into the picture" (5). If cars and movies are products that keep the consumer economy moving, they are also display windows. The movie through the windshield, if it is not itself a commercial, certainly provides a viewpoint from which one is compelled to watch the unfolding panorama of American commerce. That movie contains the paradox of consumer culture, which constructs a subject who must be constantly moving and constantly stopping, which dreams a subject whose mobile gaze is always a form of shopping.

This mobility is enabled by the gas station, which emerges now as a paradigmatic instance of the place in-between; the site that mediates among the urban, the rural, and the suburban; the commercial space where the shopper buys in order to keep shopping. In my introduction, I argued that the noir narrative provides a critique of consumer culture that takes place through the figure of the supermarket, and to understand the different confrontation that takes place between noir and the gas station, we might first consider how the gas station and the supermarket are linked historically. In his book *The Drive-In, the Supermarket, and the Transformation of Commercial Space in Los Angeles*, Richard Longstreth cites a 1938 *Saturday Evening Post* article about how an imaginary New Jersey family—named, appropriately enough, "the Muzaks"—encountered their first supermarket:

> The three Muzak children saw a glare of light down the street and simultaneously shouted, "Fire!" Poppa Muzak maneuvered the car out of traffic and parked. They elbowed through the sidewalk crowds, to stand finally with mouths agape. The glare came from red and white floodlights illuminating a square one-story building of modernistic design. Its seventy-five-foot plate-glass front was covered with banners announcing: "Supermarket Grand Opening." (77)

For Longstreth, the advent of the supermarket is the climactic chapter in a story that begins with the gas station, the story of how the primary mode of shopping in America became the experience of driving a car, pulling off the road into a parking area, and entering a brightly lit oasis to make a purchase.

This "supermarket" model, for which the gas station is the prototype, operates symbolically as a democratic leveling of class, organizing middle-class conspicuous consumption in a process that is homogeneous—both in appearance and in the interchangeability of products sold—and focused on economy and efficiency. From strip malls to Walmarts, from fast food to IKEA, this is the paradigm that structures the way that most Americans buy things (although in our time online shopping has begun to enable new developments in the mobile gaze of the consumer). It is a spatial model for our interaction with commodities of all kinds, the place where the automobile enables a meeting between corporation and consumer. Longstreth suggests that the innovation that led to this rearrangement of the American landscape was the gas station. His book traces the evolution in Los Angeles shopping facilities from the gas station to the "drive-in market" to the supermarket—a model "that would eventually revolutionize the planning of retail facilities" (4).

Although there were "super service stations" as early as 1914, it was during the twenties and thirties that the gas station, and the architecture of roadside commerce that it exemplified, reshaped the look of the republic.[8] In *The Gas Station in America*, John Jakle and Keith Sculle argue that what made the gas station novel was a marketing conjunction that they call "place-product-packaging," in which the spatial organization of the store becomes inseparable from the product the store is selling:

> Observe buildings, driveways, and pumps arranged in patterns and located across an array of sites or locations to reinforce each oil company's distinctive image. Integrate colors, shapes, and decorative details special to each firm. Add to the ensemble personnel in distinctive uniforms as well as labelled products specially packaged. Thus you have it: place-product-packaging—the networking of lookalike places defining trade territories, all supported through coordinated advertising. Consumers enter environments carefully calculated as corporate sign. (1–3)

The gas station, then, is not only part of a chain of standardized places for consumption; it is itself a sign, so that the organization of the outlet is itself both billboard and logo. Gas stations are branded spaces, and the spatial organization itself represents the brand; they sell commodities, and in order to do so, they sell "place" as a commodity.[9]

Gas stations in the twenties and thirties drew on these qualities to create images of their stations—in advertising and branded road maps—as oases of familiarity and reliability on the uncertain journey between here and there, brightly lit safe havens with friendly and competent men to attend to the customers. Chester Liebs observes that early gas stations were often designed to look like houses: "The sight of a little house selling gas along the roadside could . . . trigger a host of positive associations—friendliness, comfort, and security—in the minds of motorists whizzing by" (*Main Street to Miracle Mile*, 101). These commercial spaces, then, were often designed to package and market a standardized version of homey, rural Americana. The gas station's status as geographical logo suggested that travelers could easily, visually recognize the outlet, so that its corporate status became a source of trust: just as Americans in foreign countries now turn to McDonald's for a standardized taste of home, drivers could see the company logo as a stamp of reliability.

So the gas station seems at first, like the supermarket, to operate symbolically as the polar opposite of the film noir ethos, defined by a vampiric distrust of good cheer, safe havens, and mainstream American culture. But noir's relationship to the gas station is far more ambivalent. Unlike the supermarket, by the 1940s the gas station was no longer the dominant paradigm in American commerce. It had not yet been reclaimed—in the nostalgic mode of historic preservation or the postmodern mode of Robert Venturi et al.'s *Learning from Las Vegas*—as kitschy Americana, but it offered at least the possibility of being claimed by noir. Dimendberg argues that noir is defined by its "nonsynchronous" elements: "the nonsynchronous character of film noir is best apprehended as a tension between a residual American culture and urbanism of the 1920s and 1930s and its liquidation by the technological and social innovations accompanying World War II" (3). As with Dimendberg's decaying, transforming American cities, so too the gas station in the era of noir occupies a conflicted space. Displaced by grander, newer, more ambitious roadside stores, it retains a recent historical connection to the commercial vanguard while simultaneously, in its displacement, offering the possibility of a connection to the gritty, proletarian, self-consciously authentic ideology of noir.[10]

This ambiguous, nonsynchronous, half-authentic artifact is also one of the few commercial spaces that was designated and organized specifically as a masculine space. In the postwar forties and fifties, the growth of suburban and roadside shopping centers (of the sort that the gas station prefigured) led to a shopping culture and a form of commercial space designed around the woman-as-consumer. But the gas station had always presented itself as a haven presided over by male competence. Advertisements often featured smiling attendants in branded uniforms either standing in front of "their" gas stations ("Friendliness Lives Here!" reads a Tydol ad from the thirties) or giving directions or mechanical aid or even shelter to grateful travelers. These "little houses selling gas along the roadside" did not provide the domestic comfort of a maternal kitchen, but rather the complementary comfort of the suburban garage, with its promise of male comradeship and mechanical know-how. Jakle and Sculle suggest as much:

> For males, especially, the neighborhood gasoline station—with its ringing bell announcing customers, its smell of gasoline and grease signifying technology, and its brisk socializing indicating community—constituted a very important social setting indeed. Here could be found the exhilarating tension of mechanical and other problems faced and solved. In gasoline stations, both close to or far from home, young boys eagerly entered the exhilarating adult world. (3–5)

As the list of defining gas station features—customers, technology, community—indicates, this is a place of commerce that also offers a male identity organized around mechanical expertise and the company of other men. The gas station connotes male bonding and that connotation makes it possible for commerce to appear, symbolically, not as a contract between strangers in the marketplace, but as a compact among men of character. Film noir approaches this symbolic structure with ambivalence, desiring the utopian bonding of men, but compelled to disrupt and dispel it by introducing women into the film through the windshield.

Exile on Main Street

There are, arguably, two kinds of male protagonists in the world of film noir: the detective hero, whose heroism is defined by refusing the seductive wiles of the femme fatale character; and the sap, who allows himself to become the lover and protector of the femme fatale, and from that moment on is doomed. The plot that I will be examining in this section is about the doomed sap: as we learn in flashback, he has fallen in love with a beautiful woman—a woman who herself loves only money, the mistress of a powerful criminal. The sap runs off with the woman, but then she runs off with the money and ultimately goes back to the powerful criminal. The sap, left with nothing but now living under suspicion, heads for the sticks where he can live a quiet life at the fringes of respectability, working at a gas station. But then one day, by chance, a figure from the sap's past happens upon that gas station, setting in motion both the narrative and the machinery of events that will lead to our man's death.

This is actually the plot of *two* of the best-known noirs, both made right after the end of World War II: Robert Siodmak's *The Killers* (1946), and Jacques Tourneur's *Out of the Past* (1947). Both *The Killers* and *Out of the Past* begin with a movie through a windshield, both having credit sequences in which hired killers in black overcoats advance on small towns, while we watch the road's unfolding, looking forward from the car's backseat. *Out of the Past* begins with a series of picturesque landscape shots, which finally orient us with a roadside directional sign, after which we come to rest in a moving car with the mild-mannered thug Joe Stephanos, watching as the empty, mountainous terrain resolves itself into the Main Street commercial strip of Bridgeport, California. We turn in to a gas station, a sign on its roof giving the name of the film's protagonist, Jeff Bailey. Stephanos questions the young deaf-mute attendant about Bailey's whereabouts before crossing the street to a diner, where he proceeds to observe the ways of the locals and to offer contrast to them; this tough cynic is out of place in the gossipy small-town culture of the waitresses and customers.

The Killers opens with a considerably more ominous shot through the windshield (it is nighttime, the shot is claustrophobic, the music suspenseful) as the eponymous hit men drive into what a road sign announces as "Brentwood, New Jersey." The credits roll over a stark scene of darkness on Main Street pierced by shafts of light from a diner, with gas pumps in the foreground.

The killers walk slowly into the frame and then, once the credits are done, examine the closed Tri-State gas station, a place of peaceful order in which the white-eyed killers appear threatful and demonic. They walk across to the diner and proceed to terrorize the decent folk they find there, including young Nick Adams, until they discover that their target, the Swede, won't be coming in that night. Nick runs to warn the Swede, but Swede refuses to run. He waits unprotesting for his death to arrive, the very embodiment of existential resignation. (The scene, meanwhile, is composed of textbook noir visuals: the Swede's face hidden in shadow, the blazing guns of the killers that illuminate the room.) When Nick asks him why the men are coming to kill him, Swede sums up the story of many a noir protagonist: "I did something wrong, once."

At the Swede's autopsy, Nick tells the insurance investigator[11] about something that happened a week before, which we see in flashback. He and the Swede had worked together at the gas station, where one day a man pulled in. We don't know it yet, but this is Big Jim Colfax, the powerful criminal whose mistress, Kitty Collins, the Swede was in love with. Colfax sees the Swede, who has already recognized Colfax, and calls him over to check the car's oil and clean the windshield. The Swede, with the unmistakable film-noir resignation of a man who recognizes that he is already dead, complies while Colfax watches from the driver's seat, making sure of the Swede's identity and exercising his power as consumer in order to humiliate his erstwhile rival. The question of

FIGURE 4 *The killers case the gas station.* The Killers.

who is the audience and who is the actor in this movie as seen through the windshield becomes moot when, in a particularly tense moment, the Swede steps onto the other side of the screen, sitting next to Colfax in the car's passenger seat while he cleans the inside of the windshield. From this point on, the film will devote itself to investigating the mystery of why this apparently unremarkable scene was so upsetting to the Swede, and why the killers came to Brentwood to execute a gas station attendant.

Both films, then, are about failed attempts to leave the past behind—a past in the city, a past lived outside the law—by escaping into small-town life and legitimate work. As Joe Stephanos says to Jeff Bailey, looking around the gas station, "Funny racket to find you in . . . I guess because it's respectable." Jeff has in fact tried to start a new life in this little town, complete with a new fiancée, Ann, who is a version of the idealized rural woman in *High Sierra* and *Impact* and an ideal counterpoint to the dark-haired femme fatale Kathie. The two worlds of the film, those of urban crime and small-town life, are held apart as separate poles, each rejecting the other—Stephanos, who in his black overcoat is an incongruous presence in the sunny countryside, is killed by a well-placed cast of a fishing line and hook—but Jeff stands in the middle. It is appropriate that the gas station bears his name prominently on top, since both are stranded halfway between the two poles, neither of which is especially attractive. If the city is the site of crime, danger, and alienation, the town where Jeff has set up

FIGURE 5 *Big Jim Colfax watches the Swede through the windshield.*

shop is provincial, dull, and intolerant: Ann's parents in particular are unfairly hostile to Jeff and ready to believe the worst about him at all times. The gas station, then, suggests a kind of limbo located between city and country, inside and outside, past and present—but a limbo that is perhaps the only desirable, if not safe, location for the doomed male protagonist.

The extent to which the gas station is a site where film noir's ambivalent feelings toward mainstream American life are negotiated is made clear by the number of the films in which the gas station is connected to the possibility of a new beginning, often involving the (usually doomed) dream of settling down with a good-girl sweetheart. Moreover, for many noir men, the dream of a new beginning is linked—as with Jeff in *Out of the Past*—to their desire to own a gas station.[12] In Nicholas Ray's *They Live by Night* (1949), Bowie confides this dream to his lover Keechie, who has herself grown up in a service station. Steve Randall, of Anthony Mann's *Desperate* (1947), appears to be living the dream; he sends his wife and child off to the gas station—which, like Jeff's, will bear his name—in California while he stays behind to (successfully) face down the gangster who is pursuing him. In Fritz Lang's 1936 *Fury*—earlier I called it a "proto-noir"—Joe Wilson makes the mistake of leaving his gas station oasis. Early on in the film he is engaged to marry a charming woman and becomes the owner of his own station; he poses smiling by the pumps. But then he goes cross-country to visit the fiancée and the inevitable detour happens: he is stopped by police on the road, held in prison, and very nearly burned to death by a vigilante mob.

In these films, as in *Out of the Past*, the gas station is a vision of the desire for and impossibility of the postwar American dream. The "little house selling gas along the roadside" is a version of the dream of suburban home ownership, the house and family as extensions of the male self. It's a little place that a man can call his own, that in fact literally has his name on it, and that seems to come furnished with a lovely and good-hearted fiancée. But this dream is perpetually undermined, revealed to be a fantasy; the repressed urban past returns, the man is pulled back into it, and the promise of stability and marriage is shown to be false. The gas station, it turns out, cannot offer any lasting peace or heterosexual happiness. Instead it is a momentary refuge, a place not for married couples but for the brief assertion of authentic bonds between men before threatening women—representing the commerce that resides, temporarily disguised, at the heart of the suburban consumer's dream—arrive or return to claim the noir man.

In both *Out of the Past* and *The Killers*, the past from which the male character has taken refuge, the past that tracks him down, involves the dangerous woman with whom he has aligned himself. This figure, the femme fatale about whom one hears so much, is central to the functioning of film noir.[13] The femme fatale is of course a concentrated representation of patriarchal anxieties about sexuality and the feminine, but I want to suggest that she is also a figure representing pure and unrestrained commerce. As Molly Haskell remarks of Phyllis in *Double Indemnity*, the American femme fatale "is allied not with the dark forces of nature, but with the green forces of the capitalist economy" (*From Reverence to Rape*, 197). Frequently associated with high-end consumer goods—jewels, baubles, and costly accessories—the femme fatale is fetishized (by the film, by the male character) not only in the Freudian sense, but in the Marxian sense as well. We might say, in other words, that the unhealthy relationship at the heart of noir is really a relationship not of love or sex, but of economy, in which the femme fatale desires money and the male sap desires the deadly woman. He needs to pay for her, and the excessive quality of his desire for her (which is itself often linked to a desire for money) suggests the irrationality associated with commodity fetishism: for the noir man, acquiring the femme fatale is a kind of conspicuous consumption.

One place that we can see this phenomenon at work is in the scenes that introduce the femme fatale character. Over and over again—in *Double Indemnity*, *Gilda*, *The Postman Always Rings Twice*, and on and on—the woman's first appearance is surrounded with visual suspense, a lull out of which she emerges and stops the film dead for a stunned moment that captures the male character's drop-jawed fascination. This is, certainly, an instance of Laura Mulvey's scene of the woman-as-spectacle frozen in the male gaze, but it is also a scene of shopping. The man sees her through the store window of the cinematic look and *he has to have her*: how much is that murderess in the window?[14] It happens in *Out of the Past* when Jeff sees Kathie for the first time in Acapulco, emerging dramatically out of darkness and into light. And it also happens in a particularly complex way in *The Killers*. In that film, the scene of the Swede mesmerized by his first view of Kitty is heightened by a visual triangulation: Swede has brought his girlfriend Lilly to a party, and girl-next-door Lilly despairingly watches the ambitious Swede watching Kitty, the desired commodity that represents the possibility of a step up the class ladder.

Kitty, like Phyllis in *Double Indemnity*, is persistently associated with fetish objects that underline her (deceptive) status as an object to be purchased. Swede goes to jail for her when he claims to have stolen the jeweled brooch she is wearing, and long after he has lost her, he keeps a scarf of hers as a kind of stand-in; the scarf has a harp design on it, which Swede sees as a metonym for the Irish Kitty. A similar association is put into play late in the film when the insurance investigator Riordan makes an appointment with Kitty. She insists that they meet at a bar called "The Green Cat," whose name, with its echo of Kitty's name—her feline amorality—and her Irishness suggests that the bar in some sense *is* Kitty. She is, in other words, represented metonymically as a place of business, a commercial enterprise. (The bar's identification with Kitty is appropriate in another sense too; it is a trap for Riordan, as Kitty is for the Swede.) The fact that both Swede and Kitty are marked as immigrants by their ethnicity suggests the way that both strive for American wealth and status.

FIGURE 6 *Femme fatale as conspicuous consumption: Lilly watches the Swede watching Kitty.*

What Swede can never grasp, and what therefore dooms him, is that the status he desires in Kitty-as-commodity comes from her attachment to Big Jim Colfax, whose wealth Kitty will always return to, thus taking her place as an emblem of *his* conspicuous consumption. Swede, on the other hand, will always remain small-time; he will never rate a woman-as-ornament who would broadcast his status to the world.

In opposition to the deadly and amoral marketplace of desire which the woman represents, noir offers the possibility of bonds between men, and locates that possibility in the gas station. This homosocial bonding represents a form of noir authenticity because it is located outside of commercial interests; gestures of male solidarity are represented as rejecting the logic of the marketplace. These bonds are offered as an alternative to consumer culture, but it is an alternative that is never affirmed or stable. It is only a brief respite on the long, bleak highway of heterosexuality. Male friendships are always disrupted by the cold and self-serving logic at the heart of the male-female relationship, in which the femme fatale's artifice allows her to disguise rational economic self-interest as irrational sexual and romantic desire.

As we have seen, the gas station—associated with cars, mechanics, service garages—is traditionally thought of as a masculine space. Here manliness is performed and affirmed in the things that are required to service cars—technical expertise, physical labor, and the willingness to dirty one's hands—and conventionally feminine women are out of place. It is not surprising, then, that gas stations in film noir consistently appear as sites of male bonding. In *The Killers*, the Swede works with a younger man, Nick Adams, who clearly likes and admires him. After the scene in the diner, he runs desperately to the Swede's place to warn him that the killers are coming, and is baffled and disturbed by Swede's resignation in the face of his impending death. This model of male friendship is fleshed out in *Out of the Past*, in which Jeff's young deaf-mute employee is a silent, alert, and faithful presence throughout the film. He distrusts Joe Stephanos, warns and aids Jeff at key moments over the course of the film, and affirms male bonds over heterosexual romantic love in the film's resonant ending.

In the end, Jeff, like the Swede, commits a kind of suicide, calling the cops on Kathie rather than running away with her; when she realizes what he has done, she kills him and then is herself killed by the police. In a coda, we return to humble Bridgeport, where Jeff's girlfriend Ann is being wooed—at church, presumably on the way out of Jeff's funeral—by the hometown boy who has always been in love with her. Faced with the decision whether to commit herself to this man and by extension to the conventional small-town life he represents—he declares in this final sequence that what he likes about the town is that three people make a crowd, which could also be a veiled way of saying that he's glad Jeff is dead—Ann walks over to Jeff's station and asks the boy, "Was he going away with her? I have to know. Was he going away with her?" The boy nods assent, then watches as she walks back to her new boyfriend and, presumably, to marriage and a life of apple pie, the PTA, and a wholesome American dénouement. Having made this possible, the boy looks up at the gas station with its "Jeff Bailey" sign and gives it a smile and a "this one's for you" salute. The moment echoes the ending of Joseph Conrad's *Heart of Darkness*, in which Marlow cannot bring himself to tell Kurtz's fiancée (the "Intended") the dark truth of what he saw of the dying Kurtz in Africa. When pressed to recall Kurtz's last words—"the horror, the horror"—Marlow offers a lie, telling her that Kurtz's dying words were her name. The lie is an appropriate one, since "the horror" is not a bad description of Marlow's feeling about women in general and the Intended in particular, but it also conveys a sense that some things are "too dark," so dark that the polite and happy world constructed by civilization cannot be allowed to know about them.[15]

In *Out of the Past* the meaning is somewhat different. As in Conrad's novella, two men bond by keeping a woman in the dark—and out of the "darkness" in which authentic male modernism is steeped. But here the noble gesture involves painting Jeff as a villain so that his loved one can forget about him and go back to a life of rural values that the film pretends to affirm, while actually affirming the tough, stark gesture that links the boy to the doomed and heroic noir man. The gas station is not only the site of this resonant male bonding but also the symbolic vehicle through which it happens. The boy salutes the gas station *as* Jeff, having just offered a powerful lie on Jeff's behalf,

FIGURE 7 Out of the Past: *Posthumous male bonding at the gas station.*

in his name; it is as if, by the film's end, "Jeff Bailey" were less a person than a free-floating principle that comprises Jeff, the boy, and the gas station itself. That principle, affirmed in the final scene, is the assertion of a noir authenticity that is resolutely male. The gas station has now revealed itself to be a symbol of noir's ambivalence about the relationship between commerce and authenticity, an ambivalence that is worked out in part through the gas station's status as a site of male bonding and the breaking of those bonds by the femme fatale as a representation of unrestrained commerce.

All That Is Solid Blows Up

In the films that I will be looking at in this last section, the femme fatale's association with commerce in the form of a rapacious and amoral economic principle moves to the foreground. This shift in emphasis may owe something to more general shifts in the tone of film noir as it develops. In his classic essay "Notes on *Film Noir,*" Paul Schrader divided the noir cycle into three periods, with the third—fifties noir, basically—being the most demented and the most radical: "The later *noir* films finally got down to the root causes of the period: the loss of public honor, heroic conventions, personal integrity, and, finally, psychic stability. The third-phase films . . . seemed to know they stood at the end of a long tradition based on despair and disintegration and did not shy away from the fact" (59). The two movies I turn to now, Billy Wilder's *Ace in the Hole* (1951) and Robert Aldrich's *Kiss Me Deadly* (1955), are very much in this mold: cynical and hysterical texts that fix their unpleasant characters in a gaze without pity. Both films employ gas stations in ways that are inherited from earlier noirs such as *The Killers* and *Out of the Past*—in which the auto-mobile-made landscape becomes a site for understanding American identity— but the moral and sexual economy in these films is so altered that the meanings circulating around the gas station take new forms. We encounter new varia-tions on noir's juxtaposition of city and country, commerce and authenticity. Male bonding remains, but it is no longer a saving grace. The femme fatale persists, but she is no longer a sexual threat, since the male protagonist has no moral center that could be worth threatening or defending. With the mask of sex removed, the female characters in these films reveal what we have already begun to recognize; the femme fatale never was about sex, and now she can be seen for what she is: consumer capitalism in a tight dress.

· The action of *Ace in the Hole* is set primarily in and around a gas station in the desert. The big-city newspaper reporter Charles Tatum has, due to his re-lentless drinking, womanizing, and obnoxiousness, wound up stranded at the sleepy *Albuquerque Sun-Bulletin*, an outpost from which he is plotting his return to the big time. (His failure is linked to the failure of American automo-tive culture at the film's beginning, in which Tatum arrives at the *Sun-Bulletin* offices in his car, which is being pulled by a tow truck.) Sent out of town to cover a rattlesnake hunt, he and the young photographer Herbie pull in at Minosa's Trading Post, a gas station, store, and diner. But when Herbie goes inside to look for an attendant, it is as if he has stepped into a completely dif-ferent movie. The store is eerily deserted, full of local Indian handicrafts, and behind a door he finds an old Italian woman muttering prayers to a crucifix, seemingly deaf to his request to buy gas. The woman is the mother of Leo Minosa, who runs the station and who has been trapped by a cave-in while crawling into a nearby cavern to retrieve artifacts from Indian burial sites. Over the remainder of the film, Tatum exploits this tragedy, prolonging Leo's rescue by days in order to create a galvanizing story and media frenzy that he can use to leverage his way back to a high-profile New York newspaper job. In the process, the gas station becomes the center of a festival of consumption; people flock to the site with cars and campers, inspirational country songs about Leo Minosa are performed, a carnival sets up shop, happy American citizens and families who have been drawn by Tatum's sensational articles make the tragedy an occasion for festivity and commerce—and everyone is made to pay for the privilege by Leo's disaffected wife Lorraine.

In the process, the gas station becomes the site of an especially dark medita-tion on American consumer culture, one that indicts not just Tatum or the media, but the public as well. The gas station itself remains front and center visu-ally. In one of the film's central scenes, near the beginning, Tatum talks Lorraine into staying—so that she can play the role of the anguished wife that his human-interest "script" requires—by giving a speech about how "Mr. and Mrs. America" are going to flock to Minosa's and fill her pocketbook in the process. As he gives the speech, he and Lorraine are framed by the two (apparently back-projected) gas pumps, which serve as a visual reminder of how commercial space organizes the film's action. Lorraine continues to wait for her bus; when it arrives it fills the screen, and when it pulls away we see her walk between the pumps back into the station, where Tatum holds the door for her.[16] He and Lorraine, like Leo, are "buried" in rural New Mexico, he tells her, and although Lorraine shares his desire to get back to the city—they both want to go to New York—her desire, more relentless and pure than Tatum's, is to accumulate money.

Lorraine, in other words, is the film's new incarnation of the femme fatale. She is self-interested, greed-driven, antiromantic, contemptuous of men and morality; when Tatum tells her to go to church so she can better look like a distraught and devout wife, she says, deadpan, "I don't pray. Kneeling bags my nylons"—affirming her allegiance to bought objects rather than to people or principles. But, oddly, this femme fatale's relationship to Tatum is not at all about the question of sex. There is one implied sex scene, but there is no desire on screen, no seduction, and certainly no sense that sex could mean Tatum's downfall. He is already fallen, a Miltonic Satan who dominates the screen with cynical and compelling speeches, relentless energy, and sheer physical presence

FIGURE 8 *Unholy heterosexual compacts made under the sign of commerce.* Ace in the Hole.

throughout the movie. Whereas the classic femme fatale is defined, at least on the surface, by her sexuality and thus her ability to captivate the weak male hero and lead him astray, Lorraine seems to have shed even the pretense of sexual interest, along with the deception that is typically a defining quality of the dangerous noir woman. She is absolutely straightforward in asserting that all she wants is money, and as the film goes on she is revealed as an avatar of amoral and disinterested American capitalism. Other characters suffer and are punished—even Tatum is racked by guilt and finally dies of a wound inflicted by Lorraine—but when the circus is over, she takes her profits and quietly walks away.

If the femme fatale is no longer a threat to male integrity—if male integrity no longer exists—there is no longer the possibility of a compensating male bond. The gas station in *Ace in the Hole* remains a site of male bonding, but in a residual, parodic form that is already itself tainted by commerce. Tatum visits Leo in the cave regularly, and their interactions have the flavor of masculine kinship, with Tatum calling himself Leo's "buddy" and exhorting Leo to carry on, buck up, and sing songs from his army days. But although Leo clearly sees Tatum as his buddy, Tatum is motivated entirely by his desire to maintain exclusive access to Leo so that he can continue to control the flow of information and continue to scoop his competitors—a desire that ultimately causes Leo's death. Moreover, although Leo is the victim of Tatum's ambition and amorality, the film suggests that his own commercial ambitions have helped to doom him. He has gone into the cave to steal artifacts from the Indian graves in the hillside so that he can sell them at his gas station, and when Tatum first talks to him Leo speculates that his situation is punishment for this theft.

With the loss of male bonds as a site of authenticity that might act as counterpoint to the tide of consumer culture, that tide overruns the film. Pockets of authenticity, where some alternative to commerce might be imagined, exist only at the very margins of Wilder's world, in sources completely outside the mainstream of American life. Two such sources are the Indians and the inheritance of old-world European spirituality. As Leo points out, his store is a place for putting sacred Indian objects into the marketplace. The film reminds us persistently that the carnival of consumption surrounding Leo occurs in a place that was originally given a different kind of meaning, with a different kind of burial, by the displaced and original inhabitants of the land. Indians are often used this way in texts by the newer sort of American: not as people in themselves but as symbols of the white conscience, spiritual representatives of a pure and better America buried beneath the materialism of contemporary culture. (Tatum signals his hopelessly corrupted sensibility—not to mention his racism—at the film's beginning when he sees an Indian man and goes out of his way to offer a sardonic "How!" Later in the film, when the Indian man brings Tatum his lunch, he says, "Thanks, Geronimo.") Similarly, although Leo's mother is barely a character in the film, she operates symbolically as a representative of old-world immigrant spirituality, held separate from the festival of commerce around her: praying incessantly, she and Leo's father are essentially the only people in the film who take his predicament seriously or who seem genuinely to worry or grieve.

Indian tradition and old-world religion cannot offer a real alternative to commerce because they are so completely out of place, so tangential to the film's concerns and aesthetic, and this is also the case for the film's one other site of resistance to the flood of American commercialism: the *Sun-Bulletin* and its editor, Mr. Boot. (Indeed, the two sites of resistance are conflated in a scene that frames Mr. Boot next to Leo's mother's crucifix.) Waiting in the newspaper's office on his first visit, Tatum encounters a picture frame on the wall that contains an old-timey piece of needlepoint reading " TELL THE TRUTH," attributed to Mr. Boot. The editor is a decent man, committed to a vision of journalism in which ethics are more important than sensation. But as with the town of Bridgeport in *Out of the Past*, the film leaves us little room to embrace Mr. Boot's values as an authentic version of America. In a film that crackles with visual and verbal wit and incisive cynicism, the line "tell the truth" does not even have the minimal cleverness of a proverb or a cliché; it appears as a dull and outdated sentiment that is worthy of its embroidered form.

Although noir often pays lip service to the decency of the American heartland, it never manages to present that decency in a form that the audience can

FIGURE 9 *Tatum, unmoved by Mr. Boot's journalistic values or by old-world religion.*

genuinely embrace or see as more desirable than the criminality and corruption of the city. The attitude that Chandler's Marlowe expresses about mainstream American life in *The Long Goodbye* is representative: "An eight-room house, two cars in the garage, chicken every Sunday and the *Reader's Digest* on the living-room table, the wife with a cast-iron permanent and me with a brain like a sack of Portland cement. You take it, friend. I'll take the big sordid dirty crooked city" (249). In *Ace in the Hole*, although the greed, egotism, and misanthropy of Charles Tatum are horrific, there is nothing desirable on the other side of the equation either: Mr. Boot holding out pointlessly in his little office, and Mr. and Mrs. America amusing themselves mindlessly with whatever they are told to consume. The film is a closed box from which no light escapes, a vision of how anything remotely authentic in American life or American lives will be buried beneath a landslide of commercialism and empty spectacle.

Although Robert Aldrich's *Kiss Me Deadly* is a very different sort of film, it too contains an essentially nihilistic vision of America that emerges out of its meditation on the changing national landscape. Whereas the two poles that organize the action of *Ace in the Hole* are the city and the country, *Kiss Me Deadly* sets up an opposition between the city and its newly developing periphery.[17] As in a Chandler story, the hard-boiled detective Mike Hammer moves peripatetically through Los Angeles environments that range from the heart of the city to country roads and beaches, movement that is enabled by the car-friendly landscape of the fifties. Edward Dimendberg observes that in the film's survey of these various settings, the two that it returns to most consistently are the old, urban Bunker Hill district where much of the film's action takes place and the high-rise apartment where Hammer lives. These two principal settings provide a powerful contrast: each has a distinct spatial structure, and the contrast between the two suggests the tensions at work in postwar America, with the shift to a dominant consumer economy.

The most significant feature of the Bunker Hill settings in *Kiss Me Deadly* is the omnipresence of stairways. Indoors and outdoors, the endless stairways Hammer encounters in his investigation suggest an anachronistic form of urban planning, since they require a walking city subject; you can't drive on a stairway. At the same time, they organize space in a way that is chaotic, claustrophobic, and labyrinthine. The effect is emphasized by the canted angles, cluttered mise-en-scene, and jumpy editing Aldrich employs, so that the entire environment seems crazily skewed, disorienting, and ripe for violence—as when Hammer brutalizes a would-be attacker and then throws him down a really, really long flight of those outdoor stairs. Hammer's apartment, by contrast, exists in a space made up almost entirely of straight lines, vertical and horizontal. There are no stairs here—he takes an elevator—and the up-and-down of his building is set on a flat, straight highway. This is the automobile-made world, the familiar sprawling Los Angeles in which nobody walks anywhere, and the sound of car traffic is constantly audible inside

Hammer's apartment itself. Even the lines of the credit sequence run backward down the screen, designed to look as if they were written on the road for drivers to read. As in *Ace in the Hole*, Aldrich's film investigates these two sets of spaces, the claustrophobic city and the agoraphobic sprawl, not in order to value one over the other, but rather to reveal them to be two sides of the same dirty coin. And the detective who negotiates these spaces is perfectly at home in either of these corrupted landscapes.

Hammer is an unpleasant character, a greedy egotist who does sleazy divorce work, grins while he slaps and tortures people, and gets involved in the film's investigation only because he hopes to profit from it. This detective is no paragon of mean-street virtue, no knight in tarnished armor in the Chandler mold, and his difference from that type of classic, hard-boiled detective is indicated in large part through his consumer lifestyle and particularly his love of cars. His apartment is a kind of showroom for the latest in fifties lifestyle accessories—including an early answering machine for the PI who loves shopping for gadgets.

But before we have even seen the apartment, we could imagine it, given the character sketch offered in the opening sequence. When a woman calling herself "Christina," on the run from thugs who have trapped her at a mental hospital, forces Hammer to pull over, he snarls, "You almost wrecked my car." She responds a bit later by suggesting that Hammer's car—a flashy little convertible—tells her all she needs to know about him, that he is self-centered and that his vanity expresses itself through consumerism: "You're one of those

FIGURE 10 *The noir stairways of L.A.'s Bunker Hill neighborhood.* Kiss Me Deadly.

self-indulgent males who thinks about nothing but his clothes, his car, himself." In doing so, she describes him as a type: he is "one of those males," a new kind of man who defines himself through the things he owns. The gas station that they pull into during this opening sequence is a site of male-centered commerce. A neatly appointed little Chevron oasis with a friendly and deferential attendant, this is a place where Hammer is fully at home, a place for servicing his favorite commodity in a context that is distinctly masculine; Hammer has made a remark about taking "a trip off the road," which offers an occasion for the attendant to leer mildly at Christina. (The leer is abetted by the fact that Christina has escaped her tormentors wearing only a trenchcoat; the sadistic element in this misogynist male-bonding is brought out shortly afterward when we watch Christina's naked legs twitching as she is tortured to death by a group of fully clothed men.)

Our first stop at the gas station, then, suggests that in this film male bonding is no longer a site of authenticity, that a version of masculinity can itself be complicit with and produced through consumerism. But male friendship does begin to enter the picture as we learn about Hammer's relationship to the service garage near his place, which is run by an effusive Greek named Nick. (The screenwriter, A. I. Bezzerides, was himself of Greek and Armenian descent, and his noir screenplays consistently feature positive roles for immigrant characters.) Nick is a ridiculous character—maniacally shouting "Va-va-VOOM! Pretty POW!" whenever he wants to show appreciation for a car or a woman—but he is also a

FIGURE 11 Kiss Me Deadly: *The movie through the windshield.*

likeable character, and it is largely through him that Hammer is humanized for the audience. The two very different men share a bond that is rooted in their shared enjoyment of cars—which is to say, rooted in the culture of the mechanic's shop and the gas station, two kinds of businesses that are not identical but are closely linked in the meanings they contain. The connection that Nick and Hammer share makes automobile culture into more than just a site of conspicuous consumption; again, the in-between space of the garage allows the formation of male bonds that have more resonance than any other relationship we see onscreen. Nick's death—a killer releases a hydraulic jack, of a kind seen at the gas station at the film's beginning, and crushes him beneath the car he's working on—is the only event in the film that Hammer responds to with genuine feeling.

Indeed, the film has a schizoid attitude toward Hammer. Although he is clearly a contemptible sadist, in his interactions with characters who are marked by ethnicity or race—Nick, the old Italian moving man whom Hammer helps, the black employees at the nightclub he frequents—he is consistently friendly and likable. Hammer is like Charles Tatum of *Ace in the Hole* in that the film wants us to recognize him as (in his own words) a "real stinker," but it also wants us to find his shameless sleaziness compelling, and to witness his horror as he is forced to suffer the effects of his greed and cynicism. Like Tatum and unlike Jeff Bailey, he is already a fallen man or a kind of *homme fatale*, one who cannot be seduced by a femme fatale because the narrative cannot derive any force or feeling from his moral downfall.

So it is not surprising that in this film, too, the dangerous woman remains, but again in a manifestation that is disturbing in its purity: deception without seduction, sexuality without sex, and the accumulation of wealth above all. Gabrielle in *Kiss Me Deadly* resembles Lorraine Minosa, not only in her love of money but also in her disturbing, laconic affect. The line readings given by Gaby Rodgers and Jan Sterling in these respective roles make it appear that they are playing the same character, both using a flat drawl that makes them seem not so much lazy as irredeemable. "Never mind about the evil," Gabrielle says, when cautioned about the dangerous object at the film's center. "What's in the box?" They are not characters, but rather a misogynist vision of the female principle rendered as nonhuman, women for whom intelligence and scheming are not as effective as blunt, ruthless greed. (Carmen Sternwood in Chandler's novel *The Big Sleep* is the template for this animalistic femme fatale type, though minus the greed: a mindless, beautiful killer, she emits strange hissing noises and has no opposable thumbs.) Gabrielle does not symbolize the market's amoral logic as nakedly as Lorraine does, but her role is related insofar as it suggests the profit motive that, in *Kiss Me Deadly*, gives the fatal acceleration to the nation's fiery auto wreck.

At the center of the film's plot is the famous "great whatsit," the mysterious box that everyone is chasing and that both Hammer and Gabrielle assume to be something valuable—like perhaps the suitcase full of money that motivates so many thrillers. This box is literally hot, containing some sort of fissionable radioactive material, and when Gabrielle opens it she is engulfed in flames, while the material's terrible potential is represented in a hallucinatory fugue of demonic groans and hisses, followed by an atomic explosion on the California beachfront. This ending puts a whole range of meanings into play. As critics have noticed, Cold War anxiety about nuclear annihilation and patriarchal fears about female sexuality as something hidden, mysterious, and destructive are both present here.[18] While these themes are clearly important, the terms that I have set up here also suggest a continuity between this film and the other gas station noirs; when the temporary male bonding enabled by the gas station is, inevitably, disrupted by the intrusion of commerce, masculinity as a site of authenticity is revealed as impossible and the noir man is destroyed. The final explosion in *Kiss Me Deadly*, like the carnival of consumption in *Ace in the Hole*, suggests that this crisis of authenticity has national stakes, figuring the disappearance of authenticity metaphorically through the self-destructive potential of the American nuclear program.

Hammer's selfishness and greed are identified by the film as part of a larger social alteration in American postwar society, away from morality defined in terms of citizenship or community and toward a value system in which consumption defines the individual—a shift that is expressed most visibly here through automobility. The American culture of consumption, like the film's style, offers speed, novelty, and excitement—a zoomy car ride for the whole postwar generation as it hurtles toward annihilation. Once America's consumer society is set going, it is like the shiny new car—with bombs wired to the ignition and the speedometer—that Hammer receives as a gift; it moves toward an inevitable end in which the promise of an authentic America is vaporized. Va-va-VOOM! Pretty POW!

The climactic explosion in *Kiss Me Deadly* constitutes another instance of the ongoing attempt, and failure, in film noir to locate some sort of authentic space of resistance to the culture of consumption. The conjunction of automobility and apocalypse set up in that film appears in somewhat different forms in two other late-period noirs, *White Heat* (1949) and *Odds Against Tomorrow* (1959). Both contain gas station scenes, which are brief and would be easy to pass over if it were not for the fact that both films end with spectacular gasoline explosions. In each case, the explosion is weighted with the film's own set of symbolic concerns. *Odds Against Tomorrow* combines noir elements with the "social problem" genre of the fifties and sixties and concludes with a crude racial allegory. A racist white man and a racially conscious black man who have reluctantly agreed to pull a heist together are pursued by police into a gasoline refinery, shooting at each other as they go. The film concludes with the two men taking aim at each other and causing a huge gas explosion, in the wreckage of which their bodies are so charred that no one can tell them apart. *White Heat*, for its part, borrows elements from the gangster genre: James Cagney's Cody, like so many film gangsters, offers a dark version of the American success story, presented here with an Oedipal twist. Pulling a heist after the death of his criminal-mastermind mother, the increasingly psychotic Cody is pursued into the depths of a chemical plant, where he climbs to the top of a huge gasoline storage tank. There he commits a spectacular suicide, shooting into the tank and famously shouting, "Made it, Ma! Top of the world!" as the screen explodes into another American Armageddon.

In these films, the space of the gas station opens, through a metonymic chain, into dystopian and mazelike industrial spaces where noir men retreat hopelessly until there is nothing to do but to blow themselves up. These last stands are made, in other words, at sites of production: a final return to sites of a barren and forgotten industrial economy, to places that signify the outmoded and implicitly male process of labor that is being replaced by the cultural turn to consumption. It is a last-ditch grab at authenticity, one that offers no way forward and no way out. In the next chapter, I will pursue this analysis of the opposition between production and consumption as a crucial element in noir fiction's representation of the inauthentic postwar "organization man." As we have seen, a version of that opposition is also present in film noir, where the desire for an imagined authenticity clings hopelessly to the promise of male bonding in the gas station's signification of masculine labor and expertise. By the end of the noir cycle, that promise is thoroughly, and spectacularly, debunked.

Looking back from this perspective, by the light cast from these gasoline explosions, we can see that the gas stations in film noir have all offered this same desperate sense, that they are all Last Chance Texacos to which male characters retreat in mostly failed attempts to escape or to reinvent themselves. Forties films like *Out of the Past* and *The Killers* employ the classic noir gender dynamic in order to use bonds between men as a way of envisioning a space outside of commerce. Femmes fatales represent the commercial principle that disrupts those bonds, and the gas station serves as the in-between space where this drama can be played out. In later noirs, where the femmes fatales are revealed clearly as avatars of consumer capitalism or are simply absent, the promise of male bonding is revealed to be a false hope. These films posit and ultimately reject alternative sites of resistance to consumer culture—male friendship, rural values, the production economy—all nostalgic and all doomed and insufficient in the reshaping of national space that the consumer economy accomplishes. As ambivalent in-between spaces, the gas stations in these films are opportunities for noir to symbolize the conflict between the rise of the postwar consumer culture and the desire that that culture produces for an authentic America. The conclusion is predictably bleak, another dead end; the promise of male bonds is revealed as a fantasy; the men retreat toward death and irrelevance; and the women, those who are not caught in the traps that they have made, take the money and head down the road, thumbing a ride to the city.

The Publishing Class

DETECTIVES AND EXECUTIVES IN NOIR FICTION

In the credit sequence that begins each episode of the television series *Mad Men*, a show that follows the lives of men and women in the advertising business in the early sixties, a faceless man stands in a nicely appointed office in a tall building—presumably Madison Avenue in New York. The images are computer-generated and stylized in their simplicity: an assemblage of lines, within which the man is rendered as a suit—an executive type, rather than an individual—with head and hands minimally sketched in black silhouette. The office begins to dissolve, breaking up into its component lines. Now the man is in freefall, dropping through a landscape of skyscrapers on which advertising images are superimposed: blankly grinning and curvaceous women, offering products that guarantee happiness. He falls while the credits roll, a dream fall that seems to have no end. Then, in the final image of the sequence, a suit indistinguishable from the first is seated, lounging in a posture of relaxed control with a drink in his hand, one arm stretched casually over the back of the couch. We understand that he is the same man, the same type, that he is a master of the universe—male, white, and white-collar—and that he is nonetheless, at the same time, abandoned in a disastrous plummet. What are we to make of this contradictory figure?

In this chapter I will argue that the split character suggested by this credit sequence is a central figure in discussions of American identity in the postwar era. Cultural critics writing in the fifties and sixties persistently diagnosed this white male executive type as representative of a changing America and thus as a man divided against himself, caught between the Protestant work ethic and a leisure ethos, between inner-direction and outer-direction, between individualism and corporate bureaucracy, between production and consumption. This type represented a particular class position, that of the professional-managerial class, whose new centrality to the culture was enabled by the rise of consumer culture, its suburbanization of American space, and its readjustment of male identity away from production and labor and toward consumption and finding a place in the organization. As citizenship came to be equated with consumption, this class identity (which is also a gendered and racialized identity) became (for cultural critics who were themselves mostly white male professionals) the representative American identity.

In noir fiction, as in film noir, the rise of consumer culture and its identification with citizenship was represented as a crisis in which the consumerist "American way of life" smothered other national self-definitions. So in this chapter I will be looking at two novels in which the new class identity associated with the urban corporate executive is envisioned as the very definition of the inauthentic. This analysis requires a rereading of the way that the detective functions in noir fiction. These books set up a crucial opposition between the executive and the detective, which is to say, between two possible versions of male identity; if the executive is the embodiment of the American man as citizen-consumer, then the detective is the embodiment of noir fiction's attempt to imagine an alternative, idealized version of American identity—he exists as an oppositional principle and represents the negation of the citizen-consumer. In the terms I have been using here, the detective represents the principle of authenticity, bearing with him the sense that American national identity has been lost or betrayed and can perhaps be found or redeemed, even if its content cannot be articulated. Given this description, it is possible to say that the detective figure is a precursor to what in the sixties and seventies will be called the "counterculture."

As with the film noir texts that I discussed in the last chapter, then, the version of authenticity—of resistance to consumer culture—that these novels offer is bound up with a certain ideological attachment to masculinity. In the gas station noir, the male protagonists I have discussed were primarily unsavory antiheroes and doomed saps, and their stories were the acting-out of a crisis in which masculinity-as-authenticity was seen to recede, taking a brief and ambivalent refuge at the Last Chance Texaco before vanishing. The more or less heroic countercultural detectives I look at here provide the flipside of that narrative; the male detective is offered as a figure of resistance, poised against the tide of consumerism. In the process, what was implicit in the last chapter becomes explicit here. Gas station noir, I argued, makes it clear that the femme fatale is a function for expressing anxieties about consumer capitalism. In this chapter, the relevant opposition is revealed to be not the one between women and men but the one that occurs between two versions of masculinity, the authentic and the inauthentic. The conventional gender dichotomy between the male subject and some female threat—the femme fatale, consumption imagined as feminine—turns out to be a ruse. The real cultural anxiety is over what happens to male identity, as American identity, in the age of consumer culture.

This crisis is, again, played out in a symbolically charged space, but we turn now from the blue-collar gas station—an ambiguous in-between space where a version of masculine identity is still possible, however doomed it might be—to the white-collar milieu of the corporation, the antithesis of authentic male identity. In the process, we also turn from the concrete representations of gas stations to representations of corporate or organizational space that are considerably more virtual and symbolic. The corporation here is only the most visible manifestation of a postwar national space that organizes professional-managerial class identity through the mass distribution of print publications: books and magazines. Publication itself is central to the construction of America as a citizenry of consumers, with magazines—returning to their etymological roots—as the new stores, disseminating the same consumer options across the nation. Both of the books I will be looking at in this chapter, Kenneth Fearing's *The Big Clock* and Raymond Chandler's *The Long Goodbye*, invoke the new national space as a creation of magazine and newspaper publishing, and both use publishing executives and corporations as representatives of the "organizations" against which their detectives struggle. Most tellingly, this subject material leads both novels to meditate on their own status as publications that negotiate the anxieties surrounding artistic production and commercial production in the late stages of literary-historical modernism.

Mad Men

The year is 1953. Philip Marlowe is sitting in the bar of the Ritz-Beverly Hotel— "the third booth on the right-hand side as you go in from the dining-room annex," to be precise, as Marlowe always is when it comes to space in Los Angeles—drinking a Scotch and water. He is waiting for a publisher from New York, a man named Howard Spencer who has some detective work for Marlowe. The "high-powered publisher man" is now twenty minutes late, and Marlowe is disgruntled:

> Right now I didn't need the work badly enough to let some fathead from back east use me for a horse-holder, some executive character in a paneled office on the eighty-fifth floor, with a row of pushbuttons and an intercom and a secretary in a Hattie Carnegie Career Girl's Special and a pair of those big beautiful promising eyes. This was the kind of operator who would tell you to be there at nine sharp and if you weren't sitting quietly with a pleased smile on your pan when he floated in two hours later on a double Gibson, he would have a paroxysm of outraged

executive ability which would necessitate five weeks at Acapulco before
he got back the hop on his high hard one. (88–89)

Even for *The Long Goodbye*, a book in which Raymond Chandler has Marlowe
fix the modern world and its inhabitants with a contemptuous and literally
gimlet-eyed gaze, this seems a bit harsh. After all, Marlowe hasn't met Spencer
and knows almost nothing about him; yet he allows his irritation with the
tardy publisher to build, through the rhythm of the sentences, into an aria of
bile. In fact, the lack of information about Spencer turns out to be the key to
Marlowe's invective: his anger has nothing to do with Spencer himself, but is
directed instead at the executive *type* that Marlowe imagines him as personifying. (At later points in the book Spencer is described as thinking that he is
"very executive" [103] and speaking "in an executive sort of voice" [300].) The
anger and humor of the passage above are inseparable from the way that it
paints a remorselessly detailed picture of the representative of a particular
social class.

Designating and describing people as types is one of Chandler's characteristic strategies. His technique of detailed description—of people, clothing, furniture, space—allows him to evoke the whole social organization of life in Los
Angeles, and America, while also subjecting it to Marlowe's aggressive dismissal. Once a person has been identified as belonging to a type, Marlowe can
fix him or her in a verbal formulation that puts the detective in a superior position: the other person is now located in the proper stratum of the degraded
social world—wherein you are either part of the problem, or you are Philip
Marlowe. In the course of *The Long Goodbye*, Chandler gives this treatment to
cops, gangsters, millionaires, Mexicans, doctors, lawyers, and novelists, among
others. He spends two long paragraphs delineating the many different kinds of
blondes. Even his friend Terry Lennox, whose bromance with Marlowe is at
the emotional center of the book, is subject to typing: "Sure you're sorry. Guys
like you are always sorry, and always too late" (33).

But Marlowe's identification of this Howard Spencer, the publisher, as representing a certain kind of business executive—he works in New York, at the top of
a tall building, in a posh type of office with a posh type of secretary—is particularly resonant in the postwar context. In this chapter I will be looking at *The Long
Goodbye* alongside Kenneth Fearing's thriller *The Big Clock* in order to argue that
both books bring noir logic to bear on one of the central obsessions of American
culture during this era: the identity crisis of men in the professional-managerial
class. This crisis comes into particular focus when these men work in the "culture
industry" surrounding publication, either in the book market or in the world of
magazines. Inhabiting the commercial spaces that enable publication, they feel
themselves to be caught between high and low culture, between being productive craftsmen and being cogs in the machinery of mass-produced consumer
culture, between authenticity and commerce.

When one surveys American culture in the years between 1945 and 1965, it seems that everyone was looking for the same man, trying to diagnose his ills and sketch him for the authorities with a descriptive zeal that even Chandler couldn't match: William Whyte's "organization man," Herbert Marcuse's "one-dimensional man," the "other-directed man" David Riesman described in *The Lonely Crowd*, Sloan Wilson's "man in the gray flannel suit." All these famous terms were attempts to understand a particular kind of man, identified as white-collar, middle-class, living in the suburbs and commuting to the city, conformist, consumerist—and disaffected. By the late sixties this character would be under full assault as the culture began to shift decisively and the male executive became a pathetic figure subjected to vicious parody and full-on identity crisis in films like *Putney Swope* (1969), *Seconds* (1966), and *The Arrangement* (1969). But in the forties and fifties the organization man was at the center of discussions about the national character, busily representing the culture's central paradox: American affluence as the source of national malaise and anxiety. Riesman describes the "other-directed men" as "emerging in very recent years in the upper middle class of our larger cities," where they are "provided with the necessities of life by an ever more efficient machine industry and agriculture" and their lives are largely defined by "increased consumption of words and images from the new mass media of communications," which helps to create their outer-directedness, their desire to conform (34, 36).

Riesman's emphasis on the role of the consumption of mass media in constructing the outer-directed man is worth noting, because it offers a way to understand how these vague definitions of "organization men" are actually seeking to understand the constitution of a class identity. In Richard Ohmann's book *Selling Culture*, he argues that the rise of magazines around the turn of the century initiated "a national mass culture" in America, and that this rise occurred in tandem with the emergence of a new social entity, the professional-managerial class (PMC), which was constituted as a class and nationalized as *the* class through its consumption of these magazines.[1] He suggests that magazines offered a new kind of "social space," one that is appropriate, given the original meaning of "magazine": a warehouse or store. The magazine offers a whole range of miscellaneous items for the buyer's delectation; it is a commodity and also a collection of other commodities, a store in textual form. Alongside the commercial spaces I have discussed so far—the gas station, the supermarket—and complementing them, is the space of the magazine, a virtual space of consumption that also helped to constitute national identity.

This virtual and commercial space of the magazine made readers participants in a national culture that was centered on the metropolis and on New York in particular. By bringing New York to the reader, the reader was allowed to appropriate the social geography of the metropolis in order to better identify as part of a national "middle" class, one that eschewed class identity, as Ohmann observes: "as the mass magazines assembled their middle class audience . . . they projected a social space in which readers could understand themselves as autonomous, historically favored individuals" (255). America was held out as an "immaterial unity" within which members of the new professional-managerial class could imagine themselves as classless individuals, members of the amorphous "middle class" to which all Americans seem to believe that they belong. C. Wright Mills offered an extended analysis of this class position in his 1951 study *White Collar*, which argued that middle-class status was now equated with white-collar employment. More recently, in *The Twilight of the Middle Class*, Andrew Hoberek argues that the professional-managerial class evolved definitively into the "middle class" only after 1945, as the corporation became central to American business. This is the shift that so many postwar cultural critics presented as a crisis in American identity.

This sense of crisis is also a central element in postwar noir fiction—which is itself a mode of cultural criticism—and in order to understand its presence there, we need to consider both the texts and the historical moment they are responding to within the terms and development of the discourse of modernism. Modernism and mass consumption emerge together in the late nineteenth and early twentieth centuries, and the twinned emergence of these two phenomena is not an accident. Modernist writing—with its self-conscious difficulty, its avant-garde sensibility, and its dense thickets of allusion to literary tradition—imagined itself as a bastion against the commercial appeal of mass culture.[2] Its "writerly" quality, demanding an active and engaged reader to work through its experimental narrative and poetic techniques, has been seen as setting it apart from popular texts that offer themselves readily for the reader's "consumption."[3] Modernism, in other words, has been canonized as a way of describing the text that resists being consumed. Critics as politically diverse as T. S. Eliot and Theodor Adorno have valued modernist technique for precisely this reason, seeing it as an artistic bulwark against the commercial or the "culture industry" of Adorno's analysis.[4] Andreas Huyssen notes in his study of this "great divide" that "ever since their simultaneous emergence in the mid-19th century, modernism and mass culture have been engaged in a compulsive *pas de deux*. It indeed never occurred to Adorno to see modernism as anything other than a reaction formation to mass culture and commodification" (*After the Great Divide*, 24). Although the relationship of the modernist text to mass culture is a complex one—popular elements and texts are appropriated and deployed in modernist work in a whole variety of registers—mass culture does frequently appear to serve, as Huyssen has put it, as "modernism's Other."

If modernist art relies on mass culture as its defining Other, then in the realm of fiction the modernist text finds its consumable double most immediately in the print forms of mass culture: magazines, newspapers, and especially genre fiction. The modernist text, in this dichotomy, follows only the dictates of "art," while the genre book is written for money, for publication. William Faulkner, for example, supported his unprofitable modernist-novel-writing habit with more accessible stories that he published in the *Saturday Evening Post* and other magazines—putting his stories up for sale in the national store—and by working on film scripts such as the 1946 adaptation of Chandler's *The Big Sleep*. When he wrote a sensational book that seemed to fall into the genre of the crime thriller, *Sanctuary*, he gave the 1932 Modern Library edition an introduction that essentially disavowed the book, which was "a cheap idea, because it was deliberately conceived to make money. . . . I had just written my guts into *The Sound and the Fury* though I was not aware until the book was published that I had done so, because I had done it for pleasure. I believed then that I would never be published again. I had stopped thinking of myself in publishing terms" (337–38). The true modernist novel, the work of art, is written only for pleasure, not for publication; the genre novel, on the other hand, is written specifically to be published, to make money, and is therefore "a cheap idea"—not cheap in terms of cash realized, since *Sanctuary* was for many years Faulkner's best-selling book, but cheap because degraded precisely for being best-selling. A book tainted by commerce, by the business of publication, has no authentic value.

So it stands to reason that the modernist novel, on the one hand, and the detective novel or crime thriller, on the other, stand on opposite sides of this divide. However, the case of the American hard-boiled crime novel has always made the maintenance of the high/low cultural distinction difficult. Even during the thirties and forties, when most of Hammett's, Chandler's, and James M. Cain's novels were published, these writers had their champions among critics, and over the years they have acquired a quasi-literary status. The cultural arbiters at Library of America have published volumes of Hammett and Chandler, and Cain's *The Postman Always Rings Twice* appears in their 1997 volume *Crime Novels: American Noir of the 1930s and 40s* along with, among other books, *The Big Clock*. Indeed, contemporary critics have often pointed out that many of the concerns and techniques that define modernism are also central to the construction of noir fiction.

The hard-boiled detective fiction writers, however, were not comfortable imagining themselves as modernist writers, or as writers of any sort of literature. Rather, they saw themselves as occupying a curious middle space between modernist art and mass culture, a space from which they tended to reject the former as elitist and exhausted and to abhor the latter as commercial and degraded. As both Erin Smith and Sean McCann have shown, this rejection of high and low together proceeded from the hard-boiled writers' attempt to negotiate their position with regard to the literary marketplace, the problem of publication. In McCann's *Gumshoe America* he argues that American crime novels and the New Deal represent twinned, though not identical, attempts to imagine a space for public culture, that these novels became "entries in an ongoing meditation on the difficulty of imagining a democratic culture in a literary marketplace shaped by the institutions of mass communication and professional expertise" (4). The hard-boiled novel, having declared a plague on the houses of popular commercial publication and the modernist avant-garde, stakes out a position that is opposed to both—not middlebrow but antibrow— in the attempt to remain authentic. The alternative proposed by noir fiction, particularly in Chandler's novels, takes the form of a national imaginary, a utopianism without hope in which the "real America" is always receding; its ideal status is inseparable from its perpetual betrayal.

This sense of an ideal American culture that is continually crowded out of the actual public sphere emerges in part from the politics of the magazine marketplace in which hard-boiled crime fiction originated. The high/low hierarchy that distinguished modernist literature from genre fiction was reproduced within the marketplace by the distinction between the slicks—magazines like *Vanity Fair* or the *Saturday Evening Post* with high production values and a middlebrow audience—and the pulps, so named for the pulpy paper on which they were printed, which were more cheaply produced and had a largely working-class readership. The pulp magazine *Black Mask* was the main venue for the publication of crime fiction in the twenties and thirties, during which time it contained early stories by Hammett, Chandler, and a who's who of crime and detective writers.

The distinction between the slicks and the pulps was a profoundly gendered divide—the editors and writers of *Black Mask* imagined the battle between the pulps and the slicks as a struggle between masculine authenticity and feminine artifice. The profession of pulp writing was distinguished from literary writing as well as from the ostensibly feminized world of the slicks, reimagined as an artisanal and masculine craft; this was a way of rescuing male writers from Faulkner's dichotomy between artistic "pleasure" and "cheap" commercial hackwork. As Erin Smith's analysis of this gender politics in *Hard-Boiled: Working Class Readers and Pulp Magazines* makes clear, the problem of authenticity raised by hard-boiled fiction is inseparable from the problem of masculinity in the age of consumer culture, one faced both by the writers for, and the readers of, *Black Mask*: "What constituted manhood in a world where skilled artisanal work and the family wage that used to accompany it were eroding? If autonomous work and solidarity with shop-floor colleagues constituted a man's gender and class identities, where did a world defined increasingly by consumption and consumer choices leave him?" (64). As a response to this crisis of masculinity, the hard-boiled writers imagined their artisanal writing as a form of working-class production and therefore as the negation of the feminizing tide of consumption that threatened to erode masculine values and sources of identity.

The assertion of masculine identity was inseparable from an assertion of class identity—although it would be more accurate to say that, remaining true to the oppositional hard-boiled ethos, it is a *negation* of a different kind of class identity. If, as Smith argues, the male hard-boiled writers sought to imbue their profession with elements of blue-collar identity—with production rather than consumption—it could only be in the form of a residual, fantasized version of that identity. I will be arguing here that the male figure represented in noir fiction as an embodiment of the version of masculinity that these writers valued was himself precisely a fantasy figure. The hard-boiled detective is a male character invented in order to be the opposite not of women or the feminine but of the PMC corporate organization man, the executive and consumer. This opposition between two versions of masculinity that are defined by their class positioning (inside and outside of the PMC) is enacted within the space of publication, where the tension between commerce and authenticity is staged.

In other words, just as Ohmann suggests that the rise of magazines at the turn of the century was essential to the constitution of a new professional-managerial class, in the thirties and forties magazine and book publishing are the territories where that class identity is defined and contested in a context of corporate dominance. In the postwar era, the definition of the PMC becomes inseparable from that of the American middle class, the classless class whose male representative is the one-dimensional organization man in the gray flannel suit, and it is *this* abstracted American subject that the hard-boiled writers of the forties and fifties define their vision of authenticity against. It is this opposition—between the executive and the detective—that emerges in *The Big Clock* and *The Long Goodbye* and allows both books to negotiate the complex of issues surrounding modernism and mass culture through the social space of publishing.[5]

The March of Time

Kenneth Fearing's 1946 noir thriller *The Big Clock* renders the social space of the magazine as a literal space.[6] The corporation at the center of the story, Janoth Enterprises, occupies the upper floors of a tall office building in New York, with each floor devoted to a different magazine in Earl Janoth's publishing empire: the flagship is *Newsways*, but there are also *Commerce, Homeways, Crimeways,* the prototypical *People*-type magazine *Personalities* as well as magazines devoted to sports, food, romance, and something ominously titled *Plastic Tomorrow. Newsways* is a fictional version of *Time* magazine, where Fearing had worked for a few months in the early forties, and its publisher Earl Janoth appears as an unpleasant portrait of Time Inc.'s founder and chief, Henry Luce (although on the whole, Janoth and Luce are quite different). Luce was the successor to William Randolph Hearst as America's leading media magnate, and his publications defined mass media in the postwar era. These magazines eschewed the yellow journalism and robber-baron excess of Hearst, but Luce was no less devoted to using his empire to shape American opinion.

His famous essay "The American Century," published in *Life* in 1941, exhorted the nation not only to join the war in Europe, but in the process to take its rightful place as the world's dominant cultural and economic force.

The *Time* corporation that Luce built and shaped serves as an ideal example of the "organization"—and of the class of men who worked within it— that pervades so much of the cultural criticism of the forties and fifties. Although *Time* was founded in 1923, with *Fortune* following in 1930 and *Life* in 1936, it was not until the forties—an era during which American corporations generally expanded and centralized their operations—that it took on its defining role as a force for shaping and homogenizing national consciousness and opinion. As a corporation devoted to publishing, which is to say to the selling of culture and ideas, Time Inc. drew many young, ambitious intellectuals into its orbit. These men in gray flannel suits as often as not felt their intellectual ambitions to be in conflict with the organization—a top-down hierarchy devoted to the commercial distribution of a consistent product—of which they were a part.

Many of the public intellectuals of the postwar era did stints at Time Inc. publications, and they used that experience as a template for their portraits of disaffected men caught in the gears of the corporate machine; one could almost say that *Time* crystallized the defining conflicts of this class. Like Fearing, Sloan Wilson drew on his experiences at *Time* in his portrait of *The Man in the Gray Flannel Suit*. William Whyte wrote *The Organization Man* after working at *Fortune* magazine in the forties. (Irving Howe also worked for *Time*, and another major cultural critic of the fifties, Vance Packard, wrote for *American Magazine*—a *Time* competitor—before writing his trilogy of books dissecting the culture of consumption and its subjects, starting with *The Hidden Persuaders* in 1957.) Considering its status as a journal devoted to wealth and capitalism, *Fortune* attracted a surprising number of radicals; the leftist Dwight MacDonald served as its editor for a time, and James Agee and Walker Evans did the initial work for their searing study of rural poverty during the Depression, *Let Us Now Praise Famous Men*, while on assignment for the magazine.

Several former *Time* employees went on to write novels set at thinly disguised versions of the magazine, usually involving characters who find themselves conflicted about their work there and often featuring a Luce stand-in as the villain. A representative example is John Brooks's 1949 *The Big Wheel*, which borrows the title metaphor, describing the corporation as a vast revolving machine, from *The Big Clock*. The book concerns an editor at a magazine called *Present Day* (big clocks, present days—it's all *Time*, of course). He is an inheritor of robber-baron wealth who flirted with radical politics as a young man and now has aligned his ideals with those of the magazine. His crisis comes when he is forced to recognize that the corporation he works for *is* a machine designed to manufacture profit, and that its functioning has no relationship to his beliefs:

I see it all now; how too well I see it. We get out an intellectual magazine that has to make money. We sell ideas. The two, you see, are mortal enemies, selling and ideas. You cannot sell the truth for money.

And me? The trouble is . . . I was born half-salesman and half-thinker. The blending of two fine American strains. . . . But right now, I have a vision of the truth: I don't quite believe the ideas I sell, either. (212)

The crisis that *Time* magazine creates is the meeting of art, ideas, and culture on the one hand with the structure of commerce on the other; in other words, it is the crisis created by publication, which forces these divergent forces together, that divides the editor against himself. What is striking about the novels and essays that sought to diagnose Postwar Executive Man is that they identify not only a type of man but also the moment of his becoming conscious of his own predicament. He is defined by the conflict between art and commerce, he knows that he is so defined, and he perceives himself, unhappily, to be a cog in a corporate machine. To leave one's job at *Time* in order to write a novel is, after all, an iconic gesture of self-purification, an assertion of one's commitment to art over commerce. The novelists and sociologists are diagnosing themselves.

In *The Big Clock*, this internally divided and self-aware individual is manifested in the central character, George Stroud, who works at *Crimeways*. His job there frequently involves tracking down criminals and other people; we are told that he is very good at this, but his skills are augmented by the fact that he can draw on all the resources of every branch of the Janoth corporation in pursuing these investigations. Stroud lives in the suburbs with his wife and daughter, commutes to the city by rail, and feels himself to be trapped in the routines of his life. He breaks the routine one day by having more than a few drinks with Pauline Delos, whom he knows to be the mistress of his boss, Earl Janoth, and after a night of bar-hopping they spend the night together. Months later, he and Pauline go off for a dirty weekend in Albany, then spend an evening antique shopping in New York. After he drops Pauline off, Janoth appears at her apartment and she tells him about her affair, although without telling Stroud's name; they argue, and he kills her. Janoth runs to the apartment of his cold-blooded partner Steve Hagen, and together they concoct a plan: they will locate the mystery man who had been with Pauline and pin the murder on him. Stroud is chosen to head the investigation, and all of Janoth enterprises is put at his disposal to help him to hunt himself down.

Stroud is therefore both executive and detective, internally split not only by psychology but also by occupying two narrative functions and social types simultaneously. And although he is officially in charge of the investigation, in fact he can only truly be a horrified witness, watching from the center of the panopticon as the machinery of the corporation closes around him in an inexorably narrowing trap. As Stroud goes through the motions in this symbolic hunt for himself, it becomes clear that at the center of the book is a question: Who is George Stroud? *The Big Clock* is a parable of a man forced to confront himself, to watch as he is publicly revealed and dissected. But the novel's investigation of who Stroud is, and of what kind of man he might be, is not posed as a question about psychological or existential identity, but rather as a question about socio-economic identity. Early on, we are given a scene of Stroud in the classic scene all literature and film seems to fall back on to represent problems of the self: looking at himself in the mirror. In this scene, he confronts his job at Janoth as a crisis of masculinity, seeing himself as working in a "gilded cage full of gelded birds" (10). He tries to imagine a future for himself in which he has worked as a producer rather than as a cog in the engine that drives the consumer economy, one in which he has spent his life working for a railroad or an airline: his escape from the emasculating world of publishing involves a fantasized return to a more directly productive and masculine form of employment.

This initial desire to see himself as a different sort of man is given urgency by Fearing's insistence on showing Stroud what sort of man he actually is. One effect of the book's unusual narrative structure, which employs multiple narrators, is that we see Stroud from both the outside, in others' perceptions of him, and the inside, in the sections he himself narrates. Moreover, as the manhunt proceeds, a sketch of Stroud begins to emerge as the Janoth employees put together their sketch of the mystery man, and Stroud is thus confronted with this portrait of himself. Appropriately, the most vivid elements of this portrait are contributed by the painter Louise Patterson, who as we shall see is responsible for another sort of portrait of Stroud, too. Patterson, who has a bohemian's distrust of men in suits, offers this description, which is quoted to Stroud: "He was a smug, self-satisfied, smart-alecky bastard just like ten million other rubber-stamp sub-executives" (122). And later she asks herself, "This ordinary, bland, rather debonair and inconsequential person killed that Delos woman? It didn't seem possible. . . . What would he know about the terrible, intense moments of life?" (158–59). One of his coworkers, Emory Mafferson, remarks that "for all I knew, Stroud was merely another of the many keen, self-centered, ambitious people in the organization who moved from office to office . . . never with any real interest in life except to get more money next year than this, and always more than his colleagues did. Yet I had a feeling Stroud was not that simple" (139).

These summings-up of Stroud all portray him as a representative type, an organization man, but as that last remark of Mafferson's suggests, there is also a sense throughout that there is more to Stroud, hidden underneath his bluff and facile manner. Stroud himself believes this, even as he worries that the manner may actually be him after all. Faced with the trap he is being forced to set for himself, he ultimately takes a defiant attitude that he expresses as the assertion of an individual's revolt against a system that encourages robotic conformity:

Newsways, Commerce, Crimeways, Personalities, The Sexes, Fashions, Fu-tureways, the whole organization was full and overrunning with frus-trated ex-artists, scientists, farmers, writers, explorers, poets, lawyers, doctors, musicians, all of whom spent their lives conforming instead. And conforming to what? To a sort of overgrown, aimless, haphazard stenciling apparatus. . . . Why should I pay still more tribute to this fatal machine? It would be easier and simpler to get squashed stripping its gears than to be crushed helping it along. (114)

The language suggests the postwar obsession with individual authenticity of the sort that Lionel Trilling describes in *Sincerity and Authenticity* (as dis-cussed in my introduction), which takes the shape here of a self-serving coun-terculturalism. But in the process of asserting his individualism Stroud also touches on the book's central metaphor: the corporation as machine. The "big clock" is a figure not only for a single corporation but also for the system of capitalist economics of which the corporation is a synecdoche: "It would still be running as usual, because all other watches have to be set by the big one, which is even more powerful than the calendar, and to which one automati-cally adjusts his entire life" (5–6).

The extent to which people must adjust their lives to the movement of the big clock is perhaps the most pressing concern of the novel, and the source of its prevailing mood of nightmarish, conspiratorial entrapment. As a major organ of the postwar period's mass media, Janoth Enterprises is in the business of manufacturing not just a product but also a cultural consensus: "What we decided in this room, more than a million of our fellow-citizens would read three months from now, and what they read they would accept as final. . . . They would follow the reasoning we presented, remember the phrases, the tone of authority, and in the end their crystallized judgments would be ours" (27). The most frightening part of this arrangement, in Fearing's vision, is that there is really no one running the clock, no robber barons or bosses one can point to as villains, only the amoral steamroller of the market. Although Janoth and Hagen act maliciously and self-interestedly, they justify their actions by reference to the importance of the "organization": "There is more at stake than your private morals, personal philosophy, or individual life. The whole damned organization is at stake," Hagen tells Janoth (81). Hagen himself is utterly cold and uncompromising, a kind of human manifestation of the corporation itself—as Stroud remarks, "his mother was a bank vault, and his father an In-ternational Business Machine" (85–86).[7]

This kind of description is not limited to cold-hearted bastards like Hagen, either; throughout the book people are described, in George Stroud's flip, sar-castic narration, in terms that confuse the line between the individuals and their place in larger organizing systems. At a party early on, Stroud describes how "Georgette and I met and talked to the niece of a department store," and shortly afterward he says, "I met a small legal cog in a major political engine. And next Janoth's latest invention in the way of social commentators" (4–5). In these dismissive remarks, Stroud suggests that corporate organizations are like machines, and that the people he meets and works with are the gears that enable these engines of commerce to operate. His tone implies that he himself is set apart from these cogs—that he has access to an authentic self that the others do not—but as a split character he himself seems at other times to be part of the machine. While Stroud struggles to articulate an authentic identity for himself, he also feels himself to be a cog in the corporation, which is the most consistent portrayal of American life offered in the book. Fearing is faithful to this vision at the level of plot as well: At the book's anticlimactic climax, as the investigation closes in mercilessly on Stroud, he is saved by a profoundly undramatic corporate merger: a bland group of men in suits arrive, and control of the company passes from Janoth to another cog. Stroud escapes from the blind behemoth that was about to step on him, but ultimately his story is irrelevant to the behemoth's progress.

The book's most paranoid and satirical melding of the corporation and the man is presented as a story idea that the *Futureways* staff is researching. The story concerns a plan called Funded Individuals, "the capitalization of gifted people in their younger years for an amount sufficient to rear them under controlled conditions, educate them, and then provide for a substantial investment in some profitable enterprise through which the original investment would be repaid" (28–29). Although no one in the book bats an eye at this Philip K. Dickian plan, it clearly stands as a figure for the dystopian way in which identity throughout the book is structured by the functioning of capitalism, a final movement in the literal incorporation of the human subject into the business machine. If this is not a genuinely oracular conceit, it does at least presage the way that the vast and unlocatable networks of multinational capitalism will be represented in the postmodern conspiracy texts I discuss in later chapters.

In the future, then, it may be possible for the corporate ethos to become fully autonomous, inhabiting the psyche itself and existing, like the capitalist market, outside of any specific location; but in the novel's present the big clock is still represented physically, in the form of the Janoth Building. If Fearing's novel opens up for our viewing the social space of the organization, the space enabled by magazines and commerce, populated by admen and executives, this defining social space is represented as actual space, the corporation as building. Fearing spends three pages explaining the various branches and functionings of the Janoth magazines by explaining which floor each magazine occupies—the executive offices are of course on the top floor—even going so far as to give the office numbers of several *Crimeways* editors (a man's identity is his floor and his office). As the investigation comes closer to Stroud, the building becomes a literal trap, the exits are sealed, and the space within which

George Stroud can move around constricts as eyewitnesses move up through the floors, one by one, hoping to make an identification. When he enters the building just before all this, Stroud has been meditating on his recurring image of the Janoth organization as a blind, horribly efficient crushing machine, at which point he looks up at the building, which, "covering half a block, looked into space with five hundred sightless eyes as I . . . delivered myself once more to its stone intestines. The interior of this giant God was spick-and-span, restfully lighted. . . . A visitor would have thought it nice" (145).

The Janoth building—monolithic, clean, well-lighted, efficient—offers a symbol of the corporation as perfect trap, but Fearing also proposes an alternative and opposite kind of urban space in the book, one that contains the potential for resistance to the monolith. Stroud and Pauline Delos visit Gil's, a hangout of Stroud's that contains the bartender Gil's personal museum, described here as "an inexhaustible quantity of junk" (34). Gil runs a liquor-fueled game in which he claims that everything in the world is behind the bar, and challenges patrons to stump him; invariably, he produces something from his junkpile and concocts a story explaining its history and how it answers the patron's request. This milieu, where the detritus of consumer culture is collected and revalued, given new meaning by Gil's whiskeyed imagination, is the antithesis of the clean corporate world. Stroud has cultivated this dive as a retreat into messy vitality that serves as an antidote to his Janoth-organization identity; an especially pretentious coworker who is assigned to stake out Gil's in search of the mystery man finds the place horrifyingly lowbrow.

The same is true of the other haunt that he takes Pauline to, Antique Row. As with Gil's, the pleasure of this collection of shops is more in the exploration of interesting junk than in the finding of beautiful treasures: "Pauline and I dawdled over . . . spinning wheels converted to floor and table lamps, and the usual commodes disguised as playchairs, bookshelves, and tea carts. All . . . reflecting more credit to the ingenuity of the twentieth century than to the imagination of the original craftsmen" (46–47). It is, again, a festival of goofy bricolage, and in these private haunts Stroud seems to find the version of himself that his oddball employment history before Janoth suggests. We are told that he and Georgette ran a roadhouse, in addition to his stints as an all-night broadcaster and "a race-track detective." In this alternative space, Stroud-the-detective seems to replace Stroud-the-executive. Again, the book's vision of an authentic space that provides the possibility of resistance to the corporate machine is based on the principle of the quirky and irreducible individual, who is identified with low culture rather than middlebrow conformity.

But if the retreat from the middlebrow corporate ethos embraces a form of low culture, it also turns out to embrace high culture in the form of the modernist work of art. Stroud, it turns out, is interested in contemporary art and as a hobby he collects paintings by an artist named Louise Patterson. During his visit to the antique shops he finds a painting that he recognizes as hers and buys it (outbidding the incognito Patterson herself, which explains some of her initial dislike for him). Stroud's alternative identity, located in the city's authentically messy, lowbrow spaces, also aligns him with the avant-garde sensibility associated with modernist high art. Earlier in the story, Stroud enthuses over the sound-effects performer on a popular radio adventure serial because of his ability to create long sequences of sound drama: "I explained to Pauline . . . that some day this fellow would do a whole fifteen- or thirty-minute program of sound and nothing but sound, without voice or music of course, a drama with no words, and then radio would have grown up" (33). He finds in the mass medium of radio the possibility of an experimental art form whose modernist exploration of the possibilities of radio representation would make it suitable for "grown up" people of sensibility.

The Patterson painting suggests Stroud's mostly hidden affinity with the avant-garde, but the artwork, haggled over and sold to the highest bidder, also contains the contradictions involved in publication that we have seen—the selling of culture—displaced here onto the market for art. Not only are we privy to the buying of the piece, but the painting itself and the interpretations that surround it lead us back to the problem of the marketplace. The painting, we eventually learn, is titled *Study in Fundamentals*, and it portrays one hand giving a coin to another hand: "That was all," Stroud remarks. "It conveyed the whole feeling, meaning, and drama of money" (50). The *Study* is indeed connected to the fundamental themes of capitalism, corporations, and people for sale that are at the heart of *The Big Clock*. Together, Pauline and Stroud rename the painting *The Temptation of St. Judas*, and as a riff on this title Stroud offers a reevaluation of Judas as a kind of saint that is also potentially a description of Stroud himself. The picture is yet another "portrait" of Stroud: "Judas must have been a born conformist, a naturally common-sense, rubber-stamp sort of fellow who rose far above himself when he became involved with a group of people who were hardly in society, let alone in a profitable business. . . . A man like that, built to fall into line but finding himself always out of step, must have suffered twice the torment of the others" (53). This is really an inverted portrait of Stroud, who is, perhaps, built to fall out of line, but it conveys the novel's sense that there is something almost sanctified about the lowlifes, the castoffs, and the bohemians who offer an alternative to the Janoth building—including Louise Patterson, on whom Stroud has a bit of an unlikely crush at the book's end.

So although we first see the painting being put on the marketplace, what Fearing ultimately champions is the way that the painting transforms money into "art" by painting a portrait of money that conveys the feeling and drama of exchange. Paradoxically, Stroud has to remove this painting about money from the marketplace in order to preserve its importance—and this is all the more important because its value has shot up hugely as a result of the media attention it has garnered during the manhunt. In the novel's final scene, Stroud and Patterson meet for a friendly drink (or twelve) at Gil's bar, but when she asks for the painting back he refuses. He says that it is not for sale at any price, because "that particular picture gave me an education. It is continuing to give me an education. Maybe, sometime, it will put me through college" (174). Stroud seems to perceive his individualist nonconformity to be linked to the alienation from and resistance to mass culture that the modernist artwork represents.

Fearing, having painted his own picture of Judas, or of Stroud, offers his own formal nod to modernist technique in the multiple first-person narratives of the book. Although his style is not experimental in the mold of Faulkner or Woolf, it draws on their innovations in order to blend modernist form with pulp plotting—a common tendency among writers of noir fiction. Drawing on all the feeling, meaning, and drama of money as they shape identity, Fearing initiates the postwar moment in America with his own formally inventive diagnosis of the corporation and corporate man, using the figure of publication to explore the contradictions he faces. (Publishers here fare even more poorly than they do in Chandler; the novel ends abruptly with this headline, seen by Stroud from a cab window: "EARL JANOTH, OUSTED PUBLISHER, PLUNGES TO DEATH"—a fantasy, perhaps entertained by more than one former writer for *Time* magazine, of the demise of Henry Luce?)

The Big Clock presages the discourse of the "organization man" that emerges fully in the fifties, and offers its own version of the encounter between consumer culture and noir authenticity, staged in the conspiratorial space of the publishing corporation. The authentic version of male identity that Fearing imagines, the detective locked in a schizoid battle with the inauthentic executive on the battleground that is George Stroud, is grounded in an argument for individualism. Like Riesman, Whyte, and other cultural critics, Fearing conflates the critique of consumerism with the critique of conformity, and the result is a vague counterculturalism that champions the individual. This attempt to imagine a space that can serve as an alternative to the American mainstream in which consumption and citizenship are imbricated is picked up by Raymond Chandler—in his postwar novels especially—but in a way that suggests that the stakes are not those of the self but of the nation. In those books the redeeming male figure of the detective is no longer a reassertion of the value of the individual; instead, he becomes the fantasized bearer of a national authenticity.

Modernism and Money

The thematic heart of Chandler's 1953 novel *The Long Goodbye* is the tragic betrayal of idealized and nostalgically inflected male bonds. This theme will be familiar to any reader of Chandler; Philip Marlowe's actions throughout the novels rest on this foundational loyalty to masculine friendship. *The Long Good-bye* is the final, elegiac statement of this theme, a book organized around the unlikely friendship between Marlowe and the wealthy drunk and kept man Terry Lennox. One early morning, Terry comes to Marlowe's apartment and asks him for a ride across the border to Tijuana. Marlowe obliges, and then is thrown in jail when it is learned that Terry's wife, the heiress Sylvia Lennox, has been bludgeoned to death, and Marlowe refuses to cooperate with the police investigation. Throughout the book, Marlowe maintains his loyalty to his absent friend through many twists and turns of plot, even when he receives a five-thousand-dollar bill that he assumes is from Terry, even when he learns that Terry has died in a small village in Mexico and everybody considers the case closed. At the novel's end, Marlowe proves that Terry did not in fact kill his wife and deduces that he did not die in Mexico. Instead, two friends whose lives Terry had saved during the war intervened, staged Terry's death, and gave him a new identity, via plastic surgery, as the eccentric and effeminate Señor Cisco Maioranos.

The book is in fact largely concerned with Marlowe's sympathetic but troubled relationships with two men, each of whom suggests the extent to which *The Long Goodbye* is a meditation on literary modernism. The first, Terry Lennox, is a character drawn from the history of modernist writing, a "hollow man" alienated from the contemporary world and from himself. His physical scarring and moral emptiness are both products of his experiences as a soldier and war prisoner in World War II, a conjunction that recalls the iconic and damaged men returning from World War I in modernist texts like Hemingway's *The Sun Also Rises*, Woolf's *Mrs. Dalloway*, Faulkner's *Soldier's Pay* and *Flags in the Dust*. The darkness at the story's heart, he is identified throughout as an absence. When he tries to renew his friendship with Marlowe at the book's end, Marlowe rejects him as a "fifty-dollar whore" and refuses to call him anything but "señor" or "amigo," keeping the false Cisco Maioranos identity between them,[8] while Terry himself admits that he is an act without an actor: "'An act is all there is. There isn't anything else. In here'—he tapped his chest with the lighter—'there isn't anything'" (378). The second of these men is Roger Wade, a popular writer with ambitions to be a modernist author. The presence of these figures, and of the book's other references to modernist writers, brings modernism out of the realm of "literature" and back into the realm of publication. Although Marlowe likes both men, he ultimately rejects Terry, and watches Wade reject himself, and in both cases the problem—as I will argue here—is that both men allow themselves to be bought.

This is not to say that *The Long Goodbye* is itself a modernist novel. Chandler's book, like *The Big Clock*, borrows elements from the modernist toolkit while remaining skeptical about modernism's canonization as the definition of the "literary" aesthetic. Written in the moment of "late" or canonical modernism, the novel creates a commentary on modernist literature. As we have seen, hard-boiled fiction tends to define itself against both low and high, commercial and artistic. In Chandler, this project is a more radical version of Fearing's attempt to carve out an alternative space from which to critique the corporate ethos; he too rejects modernism not as an aesthetic strategy, but as a dominant mode of "literature."

Marlowe's superiority to his surroundings depends on a balancing act: he has to know the world of high culture well enough to puncture the pretentions of the rich and·mighty, but he has to maintain an attitudinal distance from that world in order to avoid becoming pretentious or literary himself. Marlowe cites the proto-modernist Flaubert in order to undermine an author who lectures him about the writing process, but adopts a mocking tone toward the iconic modernist T. S. Eliot in his exchanges with the black chauffeur Amos. He has offered—rather condescendingly—to buy Amos a copy of Eliot's poems, and when the two men meet again the chauffeur says, ""'I grow old . . . I grow old . . . I shall wear the bottoms of my trousers rolled." What does that mean, Mr. Marlowe?' / 'Not a bloody thing,'" Marlowe answers. "It just sounds good" (356). As represented by Eliot, modernism is branded as empty aestheticism, the beautiful work of art that has nothing to say about the social world, nothing to say to a black chauffeur or a streetwise private eye. It is also effete; Marlowe remarks of Eliot that "the guy didn't know very much about women"—in contrast, one can infer, to Chandler's text for the working-class man, which knows enough about women to describe nine distinct varieties of blondes (without liking any of them—Eliot would surely approve on that count) and which is offered not only as a book about the social world, but also as a political commentary on it.

But, true to hard-boiled fiction's refusal to embrace either literary culture or mass culture, the book has harsh words for both. Indeed, Chandler's skepticism about modernism is more than matched by his polemic against consumer culture. At his most efficient Marlowe can set himself apart from both low and high culture in the space of a few lines—"I went to a late movie after a while. It meant nothing. . . . It was just noise and big faces. . . . At three a.m. I was walking the floor and listening to Khachaturyan working in a tractor factory. He called it a violin concerto. I called it a loose fan belt and the hell with it" (86)—but his disgust emerges most vividly and consistently in his many diatribes against the former, the commercial culture.

Surveying the chintzy mass-produced world that Los Angeles is becoming with a sneer, Marlowe offers dismissals of television, radio, housing, trendy food, and the selling of Christmas, just to name a few. When he meets the dour media mogul Harlan Potter, he raises his eyebrows at the fact that Potter "hated everything," but one could easily say the same of Marlowe, and this lecture of Potter's could easily be his:

In our time we have seen a shocking decline in both public and private morals. You can't expect quality from people whose lives are a subjection to lack of quality. You can't have quality with mass production. You don't want it because it lasts too long. So you substitute styling, which is a commercial swindle intended to produce artificial obsolescence. Mass production couldn't sell its goods next year unless it made what it sold this year look unfashionable a year from now. We have the whitest kitchens and the most shining bathrooms in the world. But in the lovely white kitchen the average American housewife can't produce a meal fit to eat, and the lovely shining bathroom is mostly a receptacle for deodorants, laxatives, sleeping pills, and the products of that confidence racket called the cosmetic industry. We make the finest packages in the world, Mr. Marlowe. The stuff inside is mostly junk. (234–35)

Chandler's critique of consumer culture emerges as a response to the postwar context, to what I have been describing as the increasing conflation of consumption with American citizenship. The American way of life is contained in and represented by its white kitchens and shining bathrooms, all of which are part and parcel of the conspiracy of consumer capitalism.

The critique of commerce can be found throughout Chandler's six major novels, but it becomes a defining obsession in the two postwar books, *The Little Sister* and *The Long Goodbye*. (The final, dismal *Playback* is in a category by itself.) In *Gumshoe America* Sean McCann notes that the earlier novels tend to identify villainy with the vestiges of an older formation of capital, Gilded Age industrial plutocracy—as with, for example, the decadent oil money of the Sternwoods in *The Big Sleep*—whereas the postwar novels replace this clear-cut class warfare with a concern about the rising tide of commercial culture:[9]

> For Chandler . . . the surprising economic growth of the postwar years and the changes it wrought—the end of chronic mass unemployment, the apparently unstoppable expansion of a new suburban middle class, the now indisputable authority of mass entertainment and mass consumerism—all seemed marks of a dramatic alteration of American society. Nearly overnight, the United States had come to seem to Chandler less a society riven by hierarchical class antagonism than one built on a shallow, comfort-driven, and market-oriented consensus. (173)

In these late novels the result is that, like Harlan Potter, Marlowe stands alone against a world that is morally defunct. But while Potter retreats into an isolated bastion that preserves his lost "quality," Marlowe is out on the streets working to reinvent America's lost better self in himself, as himself. Chandler's response to the conflation of consumption and citizenship in the postwar fifties is to imagine Marlowe, the detective, as an embodiment of the authentic American self.

One of the consequences of the book's confrontation with consumer culture is that it also confronts its own image in the form of the conventions of hard-boiled detective fiction, now codified in the mass media. Just as *The Long*

Goodbye is aware of high-cultural modernism's conventions and status in the culture, it is also aware of the conventions and status of noir fiction. Marlowe frequently refers to his actions as a performance, or speaks as if reading wearily from a script—confronted by the police, he deadpans, "This is where I say, 'What's this all about?' and you say, 'We ask the questions'" (38)—or refers to himself ironically in the third person, commenting on "Marlowe's" behavior. The reader of *The Long Goodbye* is witness to the hard-boiled detective story becoming conscious of itself as genre; whereas in "The Simple Art of Murder" Chandler forcefully set the hard-boiled school apart from Sherlock Holmes and Miss Marple, he now must set it apart from its own multiplying copies:

> I turned to another channel and looked at a crime show. The action took place in a clothes closet and the faces were tired and over familiar and not beautiful. The dialogue was stuff even Monogram wouldn't have used. The dick had a colored houseboy for comic relief. He didn't need it, he was plenty comical all by himself. And the commercials would have sickened a goat raised on barbed wire and broken beer bottles. (99)

Although Chandler is clearly repulsed by the show itself, with its cheap production—Monogram was the studio known for its B-movie crime flicks—and persistent falseness, it is the commercials that he saves for the patented Marlovian verbal knockout. Commerce turns the unique cultural production of the hard-boiled writer into watered-down genre dreck.

This issue is explored in a more extensive way—and again self-consciously—through the character of Roger Wade (the popular novelist with modernist-literary ambitions) around whom many of the book's questions about publication circle. Earlier in this chapter we saw Marlowe sitting in a hotel bar waiting for the publisher Howard Spencer. When Spencer arrives he hires Marlowe to locate one of his writers—Wade, who is troubled and alcoholic and has gone missing—so that he can finish his latest book. Wade has written a series of best-selling "sex-and-swordplay" novels, and is clearly an important property for Spencer's publishing house. But his publishing success is persistently interpreted by the novel's characters as the reason why he is a troubled and self-hating alcoholic. He imagines himself to be capable of more important, more honest, less commercial work.

Given these terms, it is not surprising that this imagined work would take the form of modernist experimentation. At one point, Marlowe finds some pages that Wade has written while drunk, and Chandler emphasizes the importance of these pages by reproducing them at length, giving them almost an entire chapter to themselves. This passage is, as Sean McCann points out, a parody of the by-now clichéd modernist stream-of-consciousness writing, and it has some Hemingwayish repetitions (Sterling Hayden is got up in Hemingway drag to play Wade in the 1973 film). Even Police Lieutenant Bernie Ohls sees in Wade's writing the quasi-Freudian circling of an absent trauma that often characterizes modernist writing: "The guy had something on his mind. He wrote all around it but he never quite touched it" (278). Wade clearly wants to work in this modernist style, and becomes irritated when the writing becomes self-consciously pretty:

> Yes, I am sick, darling. But don't give it a thought, darling, because this sick is my sick and not your sick, and let you sleep still and lovely and never remember and no slime from me to you and nothing come near you that is grim and gray and ugly.
>   You're a louse, Wade. Three adjectives, you lousy writer. Can't you even stream-of-consciousness you louse without getting it in three adjectives for Chrissake? (205–6)

Wade's "modernist" writing expresses his (and the book's) anxiety about the commercial character of his professional writing as well; after one illogical turn of phrase he writes, "Does this sentence make sense? No. Okay. I'm not asking any money for it. A short pause here for a long commercial" (204). Writing that is done for the marketplace has to make sense; literary writing, because it is not for publication, is the vehicle for self-expression—parodied here as narcissistic whining.

Wade's dilemma is a version of the conflict between culture and commerce that we have seen in *The Big Clock*; his genre fiction has made him rich, but because he has ambitions to do more "serious" writing, he is conscious of his work as phony and hopelessly romanticized, and conscious that what he considers to be its phoniness is what makes it popular. As a result, Wade wallows in self-recrimination: "All writers are punks and I am one of the punkest. . . . I have a lovely wife who loves me and a lovely publisher who loves me and I love me the best of all. I'm an egotistical son of a bitch, a literary prostitute or pimp—choose your own word" (174). Prostitute and pimp serve here—as they do throughout the novel and any number of other books, films, and rap albums—as the ultimate terms with which to express contempt for someone who is, in one way or another, for sale; prostitution's metaphorical force comes from the way that it signifies the way that commerce is felt to introduce inauthenticity into human relationships at every level. *The Long Goodbye*, itself of course a work of genre fiction, uses a writer of a different kind of genre fiction to express the conflict all such work negotiates, and to express the anxiety (of Wade, of Chandler) that all genre fiction is hopelessly commodified. Wade's novel, after all, no longer exists as a work of inspiration; it exists as a product desired by a publisher so that it can be sold in the marketplace. Wade himself is just a function of authentification that needs to be propped up and kept sober long enough to finish writing its commodity.

This meditation on publishing is taken further through the character of Harlan Potter; as in *The Big Clock*, the most powerful and dangerous figure in this book is a publisher. Potter's character combines elements of both Henry

Luce, the most powerful publisher of the fifties, and William Randolph Hearst, whose ownership of newspapers across the country gave him enormous power and influence. His appearance in the book is an instance of one of the structural conventions of the noir detective story—we might call it the confrontation with Mr. Big—that both connects it to and separates it from the conspiracy story that it eventually evolves into. The hard-boiled detective novel generally begins with a crime; as the detective pursues the investigation he finds that this seemingly isolated crime expands outward, involving larger and larger spheres of social power, until ultimately the distinction between crime and the functioning of society disappears. The detective is left in an ambivalent position, and the story draws our attention to his limited sphere of enforcement. He can solve the local crime in a local way, but he cannot solve the problems of society and political economy that enable the crime at a further remove. He can only act as social critic, pointing to the powerful politicians and businessmen, the Mr. Bigs and Harlan Potters, who bear social responsibility.

The Long Goodbye's use of Harlan Potter as a Mr. Big suggests the extent to which Chandler's late fiction is beginning to move toward conspiracy narrative, toward an indictment of larger social and economic networks and forces, while still remaining in the tradition of detective fiction. The book frequently points out that business and crime are part of the same racket, with Marlowe concluding that "organized crime is just the dirty side of the sharp dollar"—and that there is no clean side (352).[10] Potter himself haunts the text from quite early on as a vast and ominous presence; he is the father of the murdered Sylvia Lennox, and everyone speculates about how the invisible hand of his influence is shaping the events that surround the case. His power is so large that it is hard to see, his wealth so immense that it defies comprehension and is necessarily (in Chandler's world) immoral: "A man doesn't make your kind of money in any way I can understand," Marlowe tells him, and when Marlowe is leaving, Potter says, "don't go away thinking that I buy politicians or law enforcement officers. I don't have to" (231, 236).

We are almost already within the logic of the conspiracy novel here, in this identification of a power so large and impersonal that it might be tempting to just call it capitalism, the sharp dollar itself. But by personifying this power in the character of Potter, and by allowing Marlowe to confront him, Chandler indulges in a bit of nostalgia for the world of his early novels, in which bad people at the top of the social and economic ladder could be identified and blamed. Both Hearst and Luce, Harlan Potter brings together representations of the wealthy capitalist fat cat and the new media machine of consumer culture, the villains of early and late Chandler combined in a single figure. *The Long Goodbye* hovers uncertainly between these two paradigms: the hard-boiled detective story, and the conspiracy narrative into which the social critique that the hard-boiled detective story enables will logically evolve.

The Organization, Man

The tension between commerce and authenticity that is at work in Marlowe's confrontations with these various characters—Terry Lennox, Roger Wade, Harlan Potter—is also central to the novel's representation of postwar Los Angeles spaces. This attention to spatial arrangements is one of the hallmarks of Chandler's fiction. Throughout the novels, Marlowe's attention to the changing landscape of his city is matched by his interior decorator's eye, and this investigation of space is the key to Chandler's investigation of American life in the forties and fifties. The social space within which classes and identities are constructed is, for Chandler, always represented in terms of actual space, even if the two are not always equivalent in any straightforward or allegorical way.[11] The catalogue of significant spaces rendered in *The Long Goodbye* goes on and on—Harlan Potter's house, the Wades' house, the Foucauldian poetry Marlowe employs to evoke the space of prison, the disorienting space of the Ritz-Beverly (where the bar is separated by glass from a swimming pool), Mexico and its American borders—but most of all, the novel is concerned with representing a postwar space that encroaches on the autonomy of the private detective and threatens to make him just another "organization man."

The majority of the novel takes place in the suburbs of Los Angeles, and one of the consistent themes of the book is the postwar movement from city center to suburbs, which Chandler renders in elegiac terms—another of the book's long goodbyes. The suburbs are described as either cheaply built monstrosities blighting the landscape or exclusive enclaves of the rich and contemptible. Even the seedy Dr. Verringer laments the new order: "'This peaceful little valley will become a real estate development. There will be sidewalks and lampposts and children with scooters and blasting radios. There will even'—he heaved a forlorn sigh—'be Television. . . . I hope they will spare the trees . . . but I'm afraid they won't. Along the ridges there will be television aerials instead'" (125). The movement to the suburbs, an invasion of the American natural landscape that is equated with the new consumer culture's overrunning of the American national consciousness, signals the end of an era for Chandler. What is perhaps most startling is that Marlowe himself has moved to the suburbs and is living outside of the city in a detached house rental. He maintains a distance between himself and the other suburbanites he meets, and from the conformist middle classes in general. But if *The Long Goodbye* is able to imagine a detective in the suburbs, why not a detective in a gray flannel suit?

This specter is raised when Marlowe begins his search for Roger Wade. Like George Stroud, he reflects that when conducting a manhunt it is useful to have an organization to call on, and so he pays a visit to a friend who works at the Carne Organization—presumably modeled on the Pinkertons, although Chandler has gone out of his way to give this detective agency a corporate sheen. Marlowe sums up the building with one of his trademark descriptions, which is marked by an even greater aversion than usual:

> They had the second floor of one of these candy-pink four-storied buildings where the elevator doors open all by themselves with an electric eye, where the corridors are cool and quiet, and the parking lot has a name on every stall, and the druggist in the front lobby has a sprained wrist from filling bottles of sleeping pills.
>
> The door was French gray outside with raised metal lettering, as clean and sharp as a new knife. THE CARNE ORGANIZATION, INC. GERALD R. CARNE, PRESIDENT. Below and smaller: *Entrance*. It might have been an investment trust.
>
> Inside was a small and ugly reception room, but the ugliness was deliberate and expensive. The furniture was scarlet and dark green, the walls were a flat Brunswick green, and the pictures hung on them were framed in a green about three shades darker than that. The pictures were guys in red coats on big horses that were just crazy to jump over high fences. There were two frameless mirrors tinted a slight but disgusting shade of rose pink. The magazines on the table of polished primavera were of the latest issue and each one was enclosed in a clear plastic cover. (111)

The corporate atmosphere of the building creates a sharp contrast with Marlowe's own office, which is shabby and makes no effort to present his business as a business. Meanwhile, despite the colorful lobby, Marlowe's friend's office at Carne is uniformly gray, a representation of the white-collar worker's office space as prison cell, with all the panoptic trappings. An "inspirational legend" framed on the wall reads "A CARNE OPERATIVE DRESSES, SPEAKS AND BEHAVES LIKE A GENTLEMAN AT ALL TIMES AND IN ALL PLACES. THERE ARE NO EXCEPTIONS TO THIS RULE," and the office contains a security camera by which the boss can monitor his employees.

The visit to the Carne Organization crystallizes Marlowe's role in Chandler's fiction as an oppositional figure, a fantasy of the authentic spirit of America stalking the streets of Los Angeles. It is tempting to try to read Marlowe according to his class position, as a classic American entrepreneur or small businessman, but in fact this is a category mistake, because Marlowe has no locatable class identity; he does not have a "realistic" existence in that way—this approach would be like trying to analyze Elmer Fudd as a representative hunter. As every reader of Chandler notices, Marlowe never makes enough money to support himself, because his ethical code prevents him from taking, or keeping, most of the money he is offered, except a little bit here and there for "expenses."[12] By my accounting, he makes a total of twenty dollars over the course of *The Long Goodbye*, during which time he persistently refuses money, gives money back, and gives money away—forgoing potential earnings in the thousands of dollars. If he is a businessman, he is the world's worst, and his "job" is really to be a kind of knight-errant, a comparison that is particularly explicit in *The Big Sleep*.[13]

The comparison to knights would presumably have suggested for Chandler and his contemporary readers an implied link between Marlowe and a vaguely imagined European aristocratic tradition that would serve to set him outside of the American class system entirely, while not implicating him in any direct way in the more rigid hierarchies of European class distinction. This suggestion that Marlowe is a sort of "natural aristocrat" operates in *The Long Goodbye* as well. As I have observed here, Marlowe is nauseated by the postwar consumer landscape, but he does have a kind of reverence for certain brands—Rolls-Royce, Rose's Lime Juice—that have an English provenance and that seem to suggest a lost world of aristocratic "quality" and "class" that is essentially alien to the American tradition. Inhabiting this position outside of American class enables Marlowe to pull off the necessary trick of rejecting consumerism without embracing the traditionally masculine position of production. A detective is not, after all, a producer in any traditional sense of the word. Rather than being aligned with working-class or puritan traditions of productivity, Marlowe is invented as the embodiment of a masculinity that is abstract and countercultural in its authenticity: the opposite of consumer culture.

In other words, Marlowe is all authenticity and no reality; he does not have a class identity because he exists as the fantasized *negation* of the identity and social position represented by the publisher Howard Spencer and the whole white-collar professional-managerial class, the executive middle-class of the postwar era. Unlike George Stroud, who is both detective and executive, Marlowe suffers no identity crisis—because he is pure detective, and thus diametrically opposed to the executive status of the Carne operative and the corporate organization in which he is a cog. Everyone is a type, everyone fits into a socioeconomic slot—except Marlowe. He exists as the impossible, delusional principle of a masculine subject position that transcends class entirely.

The anxiety that haunts Marlowe, then, is that he must be vigilant at all times in order to avoid the possibility of exchanging himself for money, of being "bought"—hence his bizarrely idealistic refusal to take money from anyone. The gangster Mendy Menendez mocks Marlowe for his knight-errant attitude, calling him "Tarzan on a big red scooter"; Menendez understands Marlowe's position, but considers it ridiculous to place one's values outside the marketplace, thus becoming a "cheapie." He himself offers a melding of consumer culture with amoral criminality, which is to say the American way:

> I got to make lots of dough to juice the guys I got to juice in order to make lots of dough to juice the guys I got to juice. I got a place in Bel-Air that cost ninety grand. . . . The best of everything, the best food, the best drinks, the best hotel suites. I got a place in Florida and a seagoing

yacht with a crew of five men. I got a Bentley, two Cadillacs, a Chrysler station wagon, and an MG for my boy. Couple of years my girl gets one too. What you got? (76)

I like that Chrysler station wagon especially, the way it brings all the nouveau-riche excess within the sphere of suburban conspicuous consumption, and so places the criminal Mendy on a continuum with the commuting executives.

Mendy and Marlowe understand each other perfectly in their perfect opposition: Mendy despises Marlowe for absenting himself from the economy, while Marlowe despises Mendy for participating in the capitalist economy (that cycle of "juicing the guys I got to juice") as a crime in itself. Marlowe even gets angry enough to punch Mendy in the gut because the gangster persists in calling him "cheapie." The force of the insult is not in the suggestion that Marlowe is small-time, but in the suggestion that he is for sale; in an echo of Faulkner's "cheap idea" for a moneymaking book, cheapness designates the compromises of the marketplace. As in his meeting with Harlan Potter, Marlowe expresses an abhorrence for the process of money-making itself; business is a crime and crime is a business. When Menendez asks, "How did I get so big?" Marlowe answers with an echo of his response to Potter: "*I wouldn't know*. You probably started out as a pimp in a Mexican whorehouse" (76, my italics). That repeated assertion that Marlowe "wouldn't know" how these men make their money operates both as an assertion of moral superiority—no decent person would know—and as a depiction of capitalist business-crime as conspiracy: the networks of economic power are too encompassing to be "known" by anyone. And once again, pimping and whoring provide the perfect analogue for the selling of oneself and others that the economy requires, a point Marlowe reiterates in his final dismissal of the gangster: "No wonder Terry didn't come to you for help. It would be like borrowing money from a whore" (79).

In this last insult Marlowe attempts, as he does throughout the book, to set Terry apart from the other men in the book, so that he might be worthy of Marlowe's friendship. But the effort is doomed. As a kept man, taking expensive presents from his rich wife, Terry is very much for sale. By the end, in the "fifty-dollar whore" guise of Señor Maioranos, Terry has become a creature of pure artifice, the apotheosis of a postwar culture in which identity is defined by one's relationship to the marketplace. In their final conversation Marlowe suggests that he himself can be bought in a different way: "You bought a lot of me, Terry"—finally using his real name—"For a smile and a nod and a wave of the hand and a few quiet drinks in a quiet bar here and there" (378). This of course only cements Marlowe's status as the man with no price tag: the only way you can "buy" him is with the authentic coin of male camaraderie, and Terry undermines this transaction when his currency turns out to be both dirty and counterfeit.

All these issues are contained in concentrated form in the five-thousand-dollar bill that Terry sends to Marlowe from Mexico earlier in the novel, along with a farewell note. Upon receiving it, Marlowe performs the little memorials to their friendship suggested in the note—a gimlet, a cup of coffee, and a smoke—but observes that "it didn't seem quite enough to do for five thousand dollars" (86). It is an ironic observation, of course, because the huge bill is both an absurd overpayment and also an inadequate substitute for the friendship it is meant to stand in for; the gift of money allows Marlowe to reject once again the system of value that money organizes, and to reassert an alternate value system. He solves the problem of the bill by transforming it into an artwork, a "portrait of Madison," and refers to it in this way not only to himself but to others, who are inevitably baffled. As with the "portrait of money" at the center of the narrative in *The Big Clock*, Marlowe applies a different value-system to this bill: by making money into artwork, he eliminates its exchange-value and instead makes it into a symbol of the "drama and feeling of money." The bill is, after all, a published, printed, mass-produced artifact, and Marlowe works to reenchant the banknote, giving presence and heft to something that is designed not to be owned or kept, that is supposed to serve as the almost abstract representation of capital.

In turning the bill into an artwork, however, Marlowe does not transform it into a purely aesthetic object, but rather one that resonates with Chandler's broader national concerns. It is not just a portrait, but a portrait of Madison, one of the "founding fathers." As advocate of the Constitution, author of the Bill of Rights, and one of the driving forces behind the *Federalist Papers*, Madison is well-suited to stand in for America's national origins. (If Chandler had wanted to choose the most impressive denomination available, he could have gone straight to the *ten*-thousand-dollar bill, but a portrait of Salmon P. Chase would have lacked the national symbolism that Madison makes available.) By looking back to the moment of the country's inception and to its founders, Chandler identifies the conflated meanings contained in the bill-as-object, which links the nation to the abstract sign of money. Moreover, he then separates the two: by taking the bill out of circulation and reimagining it as an art object with historical and political meaning, Chandler suggests that when the nation is purged of its economic value, it finds its better self as a repository of national ideals. "Madison" becomes a stand-in for a kind of American essence that is betrayed and lost when American identity is defined by consumer culture and the logic of the dollar.

This thread within the book contains Chandler's project in miniature. The purging of the "dirty side of the sharp dollar" is analogous to Marlowe's position within the novel; he too is working to purge the economic taint from America by reinventing an ideal American subject, the one represented by him, the idealized male detective-hero.[14] The culture of consumption has consistently been imagined as feminine, and this tradition is picked up in Chandler, but the central opposition he is concerned with is not between rugged individualist man and entrapping consumerist woman, but between authentic man (the hard-boiled detective) and inauthentic man (the consumerist execu-tive). In Chandler, the anxiety about sex that frequently surfaces is in fact a displaced anxiety about commerce.[15]

So the conflict in *The Long Goodbye*, as in *The Big Clock*, is not an opposi-tion between masculine and feminine principles, but rather an opposition between two male paradigms. The first, the executive or "organization man," is given a distinct class identity, while the second, the detective, is rendered through sleight of hand as an ideal and classless American subject. The first is the representative of the "type" of masculinity created by the merging of American citizenship and consumer culture; the second is the negation of the first. Marlowe's version of masculinity is presented as the vehicle of an authen-tic American identity, one that is simultaneously alternative and central. As such, Marlowe himself is a figure of fantasy. In *The Long Goodbye* his function is to serve as the opposite of a postwar America in which citizenship and con-sumption have become conflated; he is the imagined opposite of this America and the representative of a vague and hoped-for alternative America. The prin-ciple of opposition that is imagined into being as a response to and redemption of an unlocatable national ideal, Marlowe is what I have been calling an au-thenticity effect.

Defined by his negations, Marlowe stands alone, surveying the degradation and detritus of the commercial thing America has become, forever saying goodbye. In its pure and all-encompassing opposition, his dour idealism has a structural similarity to the countercultural critiques that will emerge in the 1960s. *The Big Clock* and *The Long Goodbye*, for all their differences, both have a place in the prehistory of that counterculture; both respond to the rise of consumer culture and its identification with citizenship by moving toward a social critique of the corporation that represents American capitalism in terms of conspiracy.[16] In the sixties and seventies, this noir model of social critique evolves fully into the conspiracy mode, and that transformation is the subject of my next section.

PART II

Maps of Conspiracy

The Gumshoe Vanishes

CONSPIRACY FILM IN THE SIXTIES ERA

It is more strange than I can say. Nothing of it appears above the surface; but there is an immense underworld, peopled with a thousand forms of revolutionary passion and devotion. . . . And on top of it all, society lives! People go and come, and buy and sell, and drink and dance, and make money and make love, and seem to know nothing and suspect nothing and think of nothing . . . and day follows day, and everything is for the best in the best of all possible worlds. All that is one-half of it; the other half is that everything is doomed! In silence, in darkness, but under the feet of each one of us, the revolution lives and works. It is a wonderful, immeasurable trap, on the lid of which society performs its antics.

—HENRY JAMES, *THE PRINCESS CASAMASSIMA*

You mean, if you didn't see it, it's not there.

—*THE PARALLAX VIEW*

Jorge Luis Borges's 1945 detective story "Death and the Compass" begins with the mysterious murder of a Talmudic scholar. The police assume it is a case of robbery, but the private detective Erik Lönnrot finds this approach to be too pedestrian: "Here lies a dead rabbi," he says. "I should prefer a purely rabbinical explanation" (2). He takes the dead man's collection of books and dedicates himself to studying them, taking particular interest in the scholarship on the Tetragrammaton, the four-letter name of God. Soon two more murders, apparently connected, have been committed at different locations in Borges's unnamed city, the three killings together mapping out the points of an equilateral triangle. Since the third murder is announced as the last, the police assume the killing spree is at an end. But Lönnrot, inspired by the idea of the Tetragrammaton— and backed up by Borges himself, who loads the story with references to diamonds, rhombs, rectangles, and other four-sided shapes—posits the necessity for a fourth murder at a location that makes a perfect square on the map. He goes alone to this location, where he is ambushed by his criminal nemesis, Red Scharlach. Scharlach explains that the three murders—one of which was faked, the other two unrelated—were pieced together by him into a trap for Lönnrot. Knowing the detective's scholarly bent and passion for abstract deduction, Scharlach created a mystery that only Lönnrot would solve. Having explained it, he kills the detective.

Borges's story offers a satirical take on Edgar Allan Poe's stories featuring the abstract reasoning of Auguste Dupin—in fact, Lönnrot explicitly compares himself to Dupin—generally considered to be early entrants in the genre of the classical detective story. But if "Death and the Compass" is a parody, it is also a parable, illustrating the hairsbreadth that separates the detective story from the conspiracy narrative. The clues that the detective follows as he closes in on the criminal can, with a slight change of perspective, become a net in which he himself is caught; a solution can be a trap; and a plot is also, of course, a plot. Borges's detective story, like those of Poe, is essentially abstract; it is interested in detection and conspiracy as purely formal and intellectual exercises. His parable illuminates a key structural element of the conspiracy plot. Each of these narratives turns on a paradox or aporia in which our knowledge as readers has form but no content; the revelation is that we cannot know what we seek to know, that there are forces beyond our ability to know. Like a roll-er-coaster ride, it is a vertiginous and pleasurably disorienting experience, the epistemological thrill that is produced endlessly in texts ranging from films such as *The Matrix* to Foucault's *Discipline and Punish*: everything you know is wrong; nothing is what it seems; the truth is stranger than you *can* think.

The Borges story, like many of his writings, manages to prefigure the tendencies and techniques that will come to define postmodern cultural production. In this section of the book I will be suggesting that the decade of the sixties, the moment of the emergence of postmodernism in the American context, is also the moment at which the noir detective plot evolves into the conspiracy narrative.[1] In this transformation, many of the conventions of the noir detective story disappear, but what I have been describing as the core principle of noir—the attempt to locate an "authentic" alternative to the America in which national identity and consumer culture have become conflated—remains. Throughout I have been arguing that this attempt is staged in noir's representations of commercial spaces, and the final correspondence between "Death and the Compass" and postmodern conspiracy narrative is the way that both unfold in spatial terms; Scharlach's geometrical trap is an augur of paranoid geographies to come.

In the early chapters of this book, I was concerned with the way that spaces of commerce—the supermarket, the gas station, publication—give concrete expression to the newly dominant consumer culture of the postwar era and thus provide opportunities for texts of noir film and fiction to stage their opposition to American consumption through the creation of authenticity effects. I have been arguing that during the forties and fifties, noir film and fiction persistently defined themselves against the consumerist American mainstream, offering cynical debunkings and stripped-down aesthetics as an alternative vision of America. This alternative took the form of an assertion of authenticity, of a vaguely imagined opposite of the nation as it appeared in the postwar years—the "inauthentic" nation defined by consumption and suburbia, by shopping spaces and men in gray flannel suits. But in doing so, these films and books also had to confront their own conflicted status as commodities circulating within the consumer economy. They created effects of authenticity that were haunted by their own artificiality and by the repressed knowledge that their authenticity was always an effect of the consumer culture that it defined itself against.

This logic is both preserved and transformed in the texts of the noir tradition that come after the "classic" texts. Starting with this chapter, my analysis will move beyond those films and novels of the classic period in order to pursue the dialectic of consumption and authenticity that is initiated in postwar noir and to analyze the forms that dialectic takes as it evolves. As a result, some of the texts that I examine from this point on—over the course of the next five chapters—may appear to be tangentially connected to classic noir. But I will be making the case that they are crucial to the noir tradition that I am defining here. These texts engage the central problem that classic noir articulates, thus revealing the central role played by that problem in debates about and representations of American identity over the last half-century. Just as defining "noir" in the first place requires locating the principle that underlies its construction—the discourse of authenticity—so, too, following the logic and the development of that principle requires us to look beyond the more obvious boundaries of the "noir canon."

To begin this investigation, in these next three chapters I argue that in the sixties and seventies, as the icons of noir and the detective genre with which it is associated are revised and undermined, the conspiracy narrative becomes the vehicle for the production of a new kind of authenticity effect that responds to the globalization of corporate entities and the rise of multinational capital. Space, in this context, becomes more virtual and less specifically locatable than in the earlier chapters—we have already seen the beginning of this process in the evocation of the corporate "space" of publication—but nonetheless spatial representations continue to be the crucial category through which these texts represent the landscape of the national consumer culture. The global perspective does not dilute but rather intensifies the attempt of these conspiracy texts to imagine a specifically American authenticity, one that is invoked even more insistently, though more desperately, in an increasingly postnational world where nostalgia for a lost ideal seems more and more to be the only mode in which it is possible to represent America.

In the last section I argued that noir texts set up versions of an opposition between the authentic and the consumer culture, but conspiracy texts suggest that authenticity resides in the recognition that there can be no access to the

desired alternative to consumer culture. America is represented as being entirely effaced, and conspiracy texts of the sixties and seventies suggest that they
have caught a snapshot of the nation in the moment of its being rendered
obsolete as a category by the forces of multinational consumer capitalism.
Whereas in the last chapter we saw that Raymond Chandler could still posit
Philip Marlowe as a redemptive male detective figure, struggling heroically
against conspiratorial forces, in the conspiracy texts I will be looking at here
that redemptive figure has been emptied of his masculinity and of his ability to
point to the powerful forces that create the conditions for crime. Like the nation, the detective-hero no longer has any real existence, and authenticity consists in representing the shadowy shape of these twinned absences.

In the chapters that comprise part 2 of this book, "Maps of Conspiracy," I
present three ways of describing and understanding the movement from noir
detective story to conspiracy narrative, and each one offers a distinct approach
to the political issues raised by that movement. I begin, in this chapter, with an
articulation of the political problem itself. I get at this by examining how Hollywood's conspiracy films of the sixties and seventies—with particular attention to Alan J. Pakula's *The Parallax View* (1974)—represent American spaces
that have been radically emptied of detective-style agency and national
meaning. This emptying-out indicates the political problem at hand: although
the films build a powerful critique of the nation as a construct of multinational
corporate forces, they cannot represent the possibility of resistance to this vast
trap. The crisis of noir at the moment of the emergence of postmodernism is
that authenticity can only take the form of authenticity's absence.

The Descent of Noir

Conspiracies—or more accurately, cultural anxieties about conspiracy—arise at
particular times and for particular reasons; the type of conspiracy narrative that
I am interested in here emerges in the context of 1960s America. As Peter
Knight argues in his study *Conspiracy Culture*, "the 1960s . . . witnessed a broad
shift from conspiracy theories leveled against already victimized people on the
charge of counter-subversion of the status quo [for instance, the McCarthyism
of the fifties], to conspiracy theories proposed by the people about abuses of
power by those in authority" (58). Whereas previously the fear of conspiracy
was a fear of subversive organizations that were seeking to destroy the American nation and undermine its way of life, in the sixties and seventies this fear
was increasingly focused on the extent to which the American government, in
conjunction with industry and commercial interests, was operating in ways and
according to policies that undermined the principles of the nation and the autonomy of its subjects. This shift away from the right-wing "paranoid style" that
Richard Hofstadter famously diagnosed in 1963, toward a left-leaning political

critique of the American way of life, is part of the same set of cultural changes that enabled the New Left and the social movements of the sixties.[2] The antiwar movement, second-wave feminism, and black power, among other movements, all express in some form the belief that American politics, laws, culture, and commercial institutions in some combination are aligned against the interests of a wide variety of American individuals and communities.

Furthermore, during the sixties—and the seventies, when the cultural changes of the sixties began to find full expression in American cultural production—paranoia came to seem like a rational approach to living in an America that appeared to be in crisis; as Joan Didion wrote of her nervous breakdown in *The White Album*, a book that simmers with dread and intimations of apocalypse, "an attack of vertigo and nausea does not now seem to me an inappropriate response to the summer of 1968" (15). The assassinations of the Kennedys, Martin Luther King Jr., and Malcolm X, as well as the Manson family killings, the racial tensions and violence still alive in the wake of the civil rights conflicts and the Watts riots, and the escalating battles between antiwar protesters and police—all these contributed to the sense that the nation was a dangerous, divided place, ripe for conflagration. Much of this danger appeared to come from the authorities—the government, the police, the FBI and CIA—who often operated in clandestine ways that violated any notion of transparent democratic process. By the time Watergate and the Pentagon Papers came along in the early seventies, they just seemed to confirm what everyone had already agreed to suspect about the unseen functioning of governmental power.

This emerging notion of a split between a secret or subterranean government[3] and the public face of government that provides its alibi is structurally similar to the representation of economic institutions that noir film and fiction offers, in which business provides the respectable mask behind which an amoral and destructive capitalism operates to undermine American ideals. But the difference between these two situations is worth delineating, because they represent two distinct representational modes that are uneasily conflated both in the conspiracy narrative and in the politics of the counterculture. The anxieties Knight describes about secret government suggest that sixties-era conspiracy theory is essentially a left-libertarian model, in which individual liberties are under threat from a hostile government and the technocratic ethos it has embraced: a conspiracy of the state against its citizens. The "noir" anxiety, on the other hand, is that the nation is no longer functionally important because its principles and interests are now inseparable from commercial interests: a conspiracy of the puppet state against the authentic republic. The former set of concerns is the one that critics most often identify with sixties politics. I will be arguing that in the films I consider here, the latter anxiety is foremost, and that to the extent that the films are concerned with the loss of individual subjectivity, it is because they are concerned with the loss of the national ideals embodied in the male detective-hero.

The noir model of conspiracy narrative begins with a version of the conflation of crime and capitalism that is central to the films and novels of the postwar era. We have already seen in Fearing's *The Big Clock* and Chandler's *The
Long Goodbye* that the noir worldview suggests that crime is essentially just a
subset of corporate activity; that all crimes, investigated thoroughly, eventually
lead to the homes and offices of the rich and powerful; and that American
capitalism inevitably produces crime and is fundamentally criminal itself. In
postwar noir, however, there is still the possibility of identifying and confronting the powers that shape the society and the economy. Sometimes they even
appear as individuals, such as the seemingly omnipotent media magnate Harlan Potter in *The Long Goodbye*, whose branching networks of power and influence are so vast that Philip Marlowe can only infer them. Nonetheless, even
if Marlowe cannot convict Potter, he can still (metaphorically) indict him; and
if he cannot alter the workings of economic power, he can still point to them.
Conspiracy narrative employs a style of investigation borrowed from noir, but
it suggests the next logical step: there is no longer an identifiable culprit at the
investigation's top level, only further systems in a structure so large that it
cannot be described.

This transformation of noir detective narrative into conspiracy narrative in
the sixties provides a way of explaining and reformulating the apparent split
between the two kinds of conspiracy—a split that seems to take place at the
moment of the sixties. As we have seen in Peter Knight's formulation, the history of conspiracy culture is *discontinuous*: a "paranoid style" of right-wing
anxiety about subversive anti-American forces is replaced in the sixties by a
left-libertarian conception of American government and corporate capitalism
as elements in a conspiracy against the American people. Taking this as a starting point, I am proposing a *continuity* in which that second type of conspiracy
emerges out of what I have been calling the "noir tradition." In the sixties, the
iconography and narrative conventions of both film noir and hard-boiled detective fiction were revived in order to be violated or rejected in antinoir and
antidetective texts.[4] With these generic elements stripped away, the ideological
logic of noir—the oppositional attitude toward consumer capitalism defined
through the assertion of a lost, authentic America—is taken up by conspiracy
film and fiction. The iconography and narrative conventions of noir do continue to be widely disseminated, particularly after 1980 or so, in neo-noir and
in new variations on hard-boiled crime fiction. But for the most part these
texts do the opposite of what conspiracy texts do—they preserve a version
of noir that reinvents and extends its generic grammar without evoking its
political logic.[5]

Although conspiracy narrative retains a version of the political logic of noir,
its undermining of the detective figure and its focus on large systems of power
and commerce also call the possibility of political agency and efficacy into question. The post-sixties conspiracy model suggests that the political and economic

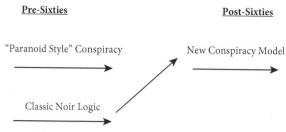

FIGURE 12 *From noir to conspiracy.*

systems with which the individual is faced in the era of multinational capitalism are ungraspably huge, so that those systems can only be confronted at the conspiratorial level—which is to say that the individual cannot confront them at all. In *The Geopolitical Aesthetic*, Fredric Jameson suggests that conspiracy film, whatever its failings or failures, works toward that confrontation with the ungraspable. In what is clearly an invocation of his claim from *Postmodernism* that political action in the postmodern world has to begin with some form of "cognitive mapping," Jameson goes on to suggest that conspiracy texts "constitute an unconscious, collective effort at trying to figure out where we are and what landscapes and forces confront us in a late twentieth century whose abominations are heightened by their concealment and their bureaucratic impersonality. Conspiracy film takes a wild stab at the heart of all that" (3). Building on this description, I will be arguing here that the epistemological paradox of conspiracy—I know there is something to know, but I don't and can't know what it is—is also a political paradox. Because they cannot know, individuals cannot act; politics, in Jameson's formulation, can only take shape through the "unconscious, collective" representations offered in conspiracy narratives. These narratives take this set of issues as their subject: the powerlessness of individual agents in the face of the global economy, combined with an attempt to represent the unknowability of that economy.

This attempt takes place within the context of an especially dramatic and ambitious moment in American cinema. During the "New Hollywood" period running from 1967 until the late seventies, the cultural changes of the sixties era and their challenge to the self-conception of the American nation were expressed in a new kind of filmmaking, particularly through a powerful wave of generic transformation. Genres that had evolved gradually within a stable framework of conventions during the studio era now appeared in radically altered forms, all of them slouching toward conspiracy. The musical, the war film, and (crucially) the Western were taken apart and rebuilt as cynical and self-aware films in which a critique of American culture and heritage took place in part through a critique of Hollywood's history of representing America.

Perhaps the most dramatic example of this transformation is the hard-boiled detective film associated with film noir. Noir was already a special case, a cycle of films that, as we have seen, was often regarded by its critics as "anti-genre" and that already contained a critical evaluation of American life and Hollywood film. But in hard-boiled detective films, this critical tendency still took place within the conventions of a genre in which it was the job of the detective to trace a crime as far into the underworld, as far into the halls of political or capitalist power, as the case demanded. In the paranoid post-sixties era, this plot structure could not sustain itself. Along with the other genres, it was taken to the chop-shop, and what emerged was a kind of antinoir.[6] As I argued in the introduction, seventies films such as Robert Altman's *The Long Goodbye* (1973)—as well as *Chinatown* (1974) and *Night Moves* (1975), among others—interrogated and undermined the noir detective genre, self-consciously incorporating references to classic hard-boiled films while constructing stories in which detectives are unable to solve the case or become unwitting pawns in a larger plot.

These films suggested that the noir detective story had become culturally irrelevant in the seventies, but the noir politics of authenticity was preserved in the characteristic genre of the New Hollywood era, the conspiracy thriller. This cycle of films evoked a wide range of conspiracies, some drawn from the headlines, some expressing countercultural politics, some with science-fictional premises, some satirizing the conspiracy plot itself, but all suggesting the lurking presence of large and intangible forces organizing American lives. In addition to the trilogy of films by Alan J. Pakula that I will be discussing here, the cycle included titles such as *Point Blank* (1967), *The President's Analyst* (1967), *Vanishing Point* (1971), *Executive Action* (1973), *Serpico* (1973), *The Conversation* (1974), *Three Days of the Condor* (1975), *The Stepford Wives* (1975), *Twilight's Last Gleaming* (1977), *Capricorn One* (1978), *Invasion of the Body Snatchers* (1978), *Coma* (1978), *The China Syndrome* (1979), and *Winter Kills* (1979).[7] With the rise of the conspiracy film—cynical in its outlook, eschewing narrative closure and happy endings—the moviegoing experience in the New Hollywood era became an excursion into radical paranoia and political criticism. Whether explicitly or metaphorically, these films asked us to suspend our belief in the government, the police, the rich and powerful, the patriarchy, and big business. But the specific villains in these films were less important than the generalized atmosphere of unease that they created, a paranoia in which spatial representations borrowed from noir were adopted and altered in order to evoke the claustrophobically large system of multinational capitalism.

Space, in other words, had to be represented differently in these films, as their investigation moved from particular sites in the American landscape to the global systems of commerce that seemed to be undermining any form of national identity. Edward Dimendberg has argued that in its representation of the city, classic noir expresses the "distinctive spatiality" of late modernism, marked by "nostalgia and longing for older urban forms combined with a fear of new alienating urban realities" (7). My discussion of the gas station similarly suggested the extent to which noir's late-modernist vision is an attempt to represent the contradictions contained in the geography of the postwar moment, as the city center gives way to spaces of consumption produced by the new geography of the suburbs and automobility. The meanings of noir are inseparable from these historically located representations of space.

If noir is organized by a late-modernist topography in which incipient signs of an emergent, dispersive media culture coexist with nostalgia for the centralized city, then conspiracy film's representation of space is characteristic of the early postmodernism of the sixties era.[8] In these films, a residual desire for modernist wholeness remains within a new vision of totality as absolute dispersion. Conspiracy cinema renders the American spatial arrangements of the sixties and seventies in order to represent the individual's confrontation with an expanded commercial sphere that can only be seen in the form of its effects and symptoms. The corporation, still operative here as an architectural entity, now extends outward until its boundaries are no longer visible and "America" appears to be merely a shelter for some of the corporation's local operations. To see what becomes of noir's vision of authenticity in this context, I will be looking here at Alan J. Pakula's "paranoid trilogy" of seventies films—in particular its middle entry, *The Parallax View*—in which the geographical contours of conspiracy are on full display.

The Space of Conspiracy

Pakula's trilogy is made up of three films released between 1971 and 1976: *Klute, The Parallax View,* and *All the President's Men.* Although they were not conceived in advance as a trilogy, the three films share a sensibility and, more importantly, a visual design that expresses that sensibility, due in large part to the cinematographer who worked on all three films, Gordon Willis. Legendary in Hollywood as "the prince of darkness," Willis was an influential figure in creating the new look of seventies films, a visual style that ignored studio-era lighting protocols and often left the stars' faces in shadow, as in his work on *The Godfather* films. Together, Pakula and Willis employed a post-noir style that used underexposure to keep audiences uncertain about the action, framed characters within looming environments to emphasize their helplessness, and manipulated offscreen space to suggest the presence of unseen threats. The result was a conjoining of theme and image into a logic of conspiracy that suggested the loss of agency in a world organized by powers beyond the individual's grasp.

The first film of the trilogy, *Klute,* is a fairly conventional thriller: Jane Fonda plays Bree, a Manhattan call girl menaced by an obsessive ex-client and protected by Donald Sutherland as a private detective named "Klute." This isn't a conspiracy scenario, strictly speaking, but the film creates an atmosphere of paranoia through its visual choices and spatial dichotomies. Bree is often shot from an exterior perspective, seen through a window or skylight or fence, giving us a stalker's-eye view of her, and the stalker, who is a corporate executive, is always shown high up in a suburban office building. From this impersonal, antiseptic aerie he seems to look down, like Sauron's eye in a business suit, on the street-level bustle and urban messiness of Bree's life. The contrast suggests that a kind of freedom is available in the street life of the city, in the space defined by the illegal commercial transactions of prostitution or drug-dealing, although that freedom is endangered when it becomes visible to the powers that be. The political logic of conspiracy emerges as a new development of the noir ethos, locating threat and harm not in the urban jungle of thieves and gangs but in the bland and fluorescent offices where power resides.

The creepiest scene from *Klute* also initiates Pakula's most powerful visual tool: the manipulation of offscreen space to create the effect of paranoia. The scene is a fairly long single shot, which initially frames Bree's upper body in bed, reading a book, until the phone rings. She picks up, no one is there, she hangs up the phone and sits up, spooked. Then, as the phone begins to ring again, the camera pulls back slowly to reveal her large dark room, bit by bit, until Bree is a distant figure in a tiny pool of light. There is nothing threatening in that particular space; rather, the scariness of the shot comes from its use of the apartment space as a metaphor for the threat that lurks beyond and unseen and that now seems to have become pervasive. The camera pulls back just far enough to reframe Bree as small and solitary, hemmed in by forces she cannot locate, suggesting that this is the limit to which the individual consciousness can extend. Even in the apartment there can be no safe space: the domestic has been violated, and the use of the telephone for that violation indicates the intrusion of outside forces into the home in a way that resonates with the film's theme of surveillance. Her phone has already been tapped by Klute, and we have seen repeated scenes of the stalker in his office listening to a recording of Bree talking on the telephone. As in Francis Ford Coppola's *The Conversation*, made three years later, *Klute* employs a camera gaze that suggests that the characters are under constant observation by unseen forces; there is no longer any dependable private space, and the empty apartment is scarily inhabited by intersecting networks of power.

All the President's Men, the story of Woodward and Bernstein's experience with real-life conspiracy in the Watergate investigation, also employs images of emptiness to express paranoia. Woodward has his meetings with the mysterious Deep Throat in a parking garage, as if the revelation of the conspiracy required a visual corollary, a dimly lit, anonymous architecture that is vast and undifferentiable—a labyrinth in which you might never know your coordinates. At the second meeting, their conversation is interrupted by a screech of

FIGURE 13   Klute: *The limits of what we can see, the limits of what we can know.*

tires, and Woodward turns to look. When he turns back, Deep Throat is gone. Pakula creates the impression of emptiness in this case not through tracking, but through a series of quick shots: first the long series of close-ups on Woodward and Deep Throat as they talk; then Woodward turning, the car racing away, Woodward turning back; and then a shot with the camera still focused on the place where Deep Throat was, as if it were trying to locate a ghost. Following this are long shots of Woodward alone in the cavernous, concrete emptiness of the garage. (The effects of this scene are emphasized in the following scene: walking home, Woodward feels that he is being followed, turns, and confronts an empty street.) Here, as in *Klute*, Pakula uses the revelation of a space that had been offscreen to express the experience of the individual confronting conspiracy; something that had previously been hidden or ignored is now brought into view, but there is nothing there to see. Our awareness of the unknown something is simultaneously an awareness of our inability to know it.

But *All the President's Men* is about a plot that is ultimately exposed. It is, after all, the story of an actual conspiracy: the cover-up surrounding the criminal abuse of executive power that led to Nixon's resignation. And since it is the story of that conspiracy being exposed by two low-ranking *Washington Post* reporters, it also makes a satisfyingly traditional Hollywood narrative about ordinary individuals bringing down the powerful and corrupt. The film is set, of course, in Washington, D.C., and it uses that setting to emphasize the extent to which this is a specifically American story, one that puts into play issues of democracy, individuality, and free speech. Consider the striking scene in the Library of Congress, where Woodward and Bernstein have gone to hunt for clues. As they sift painstakingly through endless piles of paper, the camera again, as in *Klute*, moves back to reveal a larger space, this time moving up and up until the reporters are unlocatable: tiny figures in the vast geometry of the reading room, seen from above.[9] The government, for which the library stands in metonymically, is presented in this shot as a conspiracy, vast and complex, but it is one that can be negotiated by our diligent reporters. They may be dwarfed, but we know that their efforts will ultimately (with some crucial help from Deep Throat) locate the corruption and trace it to the highest offices of power. The connection between their plucky labor and the monumental space of the library that the shot enables can be seen as validating an abstract version of the system of American values itself: free individuals affirm the nation's core meaning by thwarting the corrupt forces within it. In this film Pakula offers an idealized vision of an America whose citizens are capable of purging the abuses of its political system. But in *The Parallax View*, which turns from the question of governmental corruption to the effacement of the nation itself by capitalist forces, no such optimism is available; Pakula inverts the logic of *All the President's Men*, systematically undermining the American ideal and the individual who seeks to locate it within the web of conspiracy.

The Parallax View begins with a shot of a Northwestern Indian totem pole against a clear sky. After a few seconds, the camera moves to the side, revealing that behind the totem pole is Seattle's Space Needle. It is the Fourth of July, Independence Day, and in a few minutes the famous landmark is going to be the site of a senator's assassination. This opening shot is the film's first instance of "parallax," a term that describes how an object looks different when viewed from different perspectives. The film itself is organized by this technique of shifting visual perspective; it is almost an essay on cinema's capacity for exploring the tension between the seen and the unseen. Even Godard never managed to shake our faith that seeing is believing, that the visual is the privileged method for providing truth, and *The Parallax View* uses that faith, phrasing its questions about what is true and what is knowable in a vocabulary of onscreen and offscreen space. As the opening image of the totem pole and the Space Needle tells us, the knowledge these questions will be concerned with is specifically American: one version of America hides another, or gives way to another. But here the search for a "real" America, unlike the one we have seen in noir film and fiction, will yield only a shifting series of hollow husks, a shell game in which any one you point to will turn up empty. After the assassination, a Warren Commission–style panel declares that the killer acted out of "a misguided sense of patriotism," but the film itself will suggest that the patriotisms available to us are all misguided.

Released two years before *All the President's Men*, *The Parallax View* features its own maverick investigative reporter, Joe Frady (played by Warren Beatty). He becomes convinced that the witnesses to the Space Needle assassination are themselves being killed one by one, and ultimately traces the murders to the Parallax Corporation, which recruits and trains assassins. Frady poses as a sociopath—it's not much of a stretch—and infiltrates the organization; but Parallax learns his identity and lures him to the site of another assassination, where he discovers that he has been set up to take the blame for the killing. In its dark visual design, its lone-wolf investigator, and its murder that

FIGURE 14 *Two versions of America: the totem pole and the Space Needle.* The Parallax View.

leads to a hidden underworld where power, wealth, and corruption mingle, the film's roots in the noir detective genre are clear. (And in a related vein, Frady's name itself is clearly a parodic version of the TV series *Dragnet*'s LAPD Sergeant Joe Friday—Friday is now a Frady?)

The noir detective story is the primary referent, but *Parallax* also stretches out to encompass a large swath of Hollywood film history in its effort to revise mythologies of the American past. Critics have pointed out that Frady's path leads peripatetically from crisis to crisis in an echo of Hitchcock's *North by Northwest*, itself a kind of conspiracy film.[10] As with Hitchcock's memorable crop-dusting or auction sequences, *Parallax* is structured as a series of entertaining set-pieces that take us through a representative assortment of American landscapes, and the dramatic opening atop the Space Needle recalls Hitchcock's love of staging climactic scenes on national monuments. In its tour through American spaces and the genres they are associated with, the film isn't shy about working with shopworn movie clichés. There is even a Western-style scene in which Frady walks into a redneck bar, orders a glass of milk, and gets into a smash-the-bottles-and-chairs brawl as a result, as well as a more or less gratuitous car chase with comic bits of Appalachian fiddle mixed into the musical score—echoes of Beatty's turn in *Bonnie and Clyde*—and Frady wearing a cowboy-style Sheriff's hat. (The chase ends with Frady crashing the car—where else?—in the middle of a supermarket.) Noir provides the visual and narrative structure, but the film seems to be intent on bringing the whole Hollywood past—and, more specifically, its tradition of the embattled male hero—within the scope of its revision.

Indeed, while these elements indicate how much American film history *Parallax* takes in, Frady himself is a classic Hollywood hero only in the broadest outlines. *Chinatown*'s Jake Gittes is flawed and sleazy, but he is a fully realized character, whereas Frady is nearly empty; he is identified as a loner and maverick in the mold of the American male genre-film hero, but he is essentially a blank, the perfect subject for a film in which individual subjects are no longer effectual because Pakula's concern has shifted to systems, nations, corporations. This theme is realized in the film's use of sequences or shots that frame tiny human figures against vast artificial landscapes. These are especially noticeable as the film approaches its bleak conclusion; whereas the early sequences of the film take place primarily in outdoor settings or relatively organic indoor spaces—apartments, restaurants—in the latter part much of the action follows Frady as he negotiates large, confusing networks of concrete, steel, and glass. The Parallax Building itself has ridges that curve seamlessly at its bottom into the concrete that surrounds it, so that the people walking around it appear to be at the feet of a stony giant.

The framing of shots throughout the film creates this sense of human figures, human agents, who are dwarfed by the corporate architecture of their environments. Frady, following a Parallax agent, stands in front of the window-sheeted corporate building behind him in a medium shot, which is quickly replaced by a much longer shot, with Frady antlike and the building still filling the screen. That shot is followed by a long take of a lone, distant man riding an escalator, surrounded by geometries of impersonal metal and glass. In passages like this, it is as if the dwarfed figures in nineteenth-century American landscape painting had been transplanted to a dystopian man-made world in order to signify the absolute ascendance of the sublime corporation.

These sequences operate in a different way than the shots that open outward into paranoid space in *Klute* and *All the President's Men*; they are not sequences in which screen space opens up, but in which that space remains flat and looming. *Parallax* is more claustrophobic than the other films, because without introducing a specific threat it maintains a generalized sense of Frady's helplessness and turns every space into a potential menace. This is a part of Pakula's stylistic strategy, in which information is persistently hidden from or exposed to the film's frame in ways that are disorienting to the viewer. Close-ups, as Fredric

FIGURE 15 *Frady, standing in front of the Parallax Building . . .*

FIGURE 16 . . . *is dwarfed by the sublime corporation.*

Jameson observes, are used several times in the film to deprive the viewer of information about the characters' spatial surroundings, but this is only one example of a much larger strategy of concealment and revelation. A scene in a morgue is shot through a doorway, and it is not until after the scene has played out that Frady steps into view, altering our sense of who has what information. When Frady tracks down the elusive Austin Tucker, who was present at the assassination and has gone into hiding, Tucker steps warily into the camera's view from behind a boat. Once they have set off on the water, Frady sits at one end of the boat while Tucker and his bodyguard confer (and seem to conspire) at the other end, their words inaudible. The play of seen and unseen organizes the film's effects at every level: an airplane taxis by and then explodes seconds later offscreen; trains enter dark tunnels; characters are framed so that we only see their feet or their eyes; the film maintains the stillness of a surveillance camera rather than following the action; some scenes are so dark or shot so obliquely that the action is impossible to follow.

Nearly every shot in the film enacts this drama of the hidden and the revealed, but a paradigmatic scene occurs early in *Parallax*. Frady has an angry confrontation with the police, who have arrested him at the scene of a drug bust, and throughout the scene the cops remain offscreen while the camera holds on Frady, creating a sense of a menacing and unseen presence. This is a screen representation of the experience of conspiracy, and a microcosm of the film as a whole: power takes forms that are hidden or obscured, and without a visible opponent, the individual's response appears as a hostile and irrational flailing. This may also be a way for the film to signal the extent to which state authority is an imaginary presence in this vision of America, a proxy authority that does not even know that it has been superseded—it is both threatening and insubstantial. At the film's beginning and end, the Warren Commission stand-in makes its appearance as a panel looming in empty darkness, anonymous in the distortion of a fisheye lens. The investigators

FIGURE 17 *The beset individual: Frady contends with offscreen antagonists.*

speak with dry authority, concluding that each assassin—Frady ostensibly being the second—acted alone, and providing the film's final words: "There will be no questions."

This Is Not America

The aesthetic climax of *Parallax* is a film within the film that is shown to Frady at the corporate headquarters to test his responses. The film, which resonates with our knowledge of the related discourses of advertising, propaganda, and brainwashing, consists of a series of still images, including single words such as "love," "mother," "country," "god," "enemy," and so on. Multiple images follow each word, in ways that initially leave little room for subtlety: a movie cowboy beside a tyke for "father"; a farm and apple pie for "home"; George Washington and the Statue of Liberty for "country"; Hitler, Mao, and Castro for "enemy"; the blond comic-book version of Thor signifying "me." As the film proceeds, the images speed up and repeat in different combinations, while the sentimental music that lends emotion and force to the visual archetypes begins to warp into something like psychedelic rock. (The score of *Parallax* itself plays a similar trick: the main theme is vaguely patriotic and uplifting, but the introduction of minor notes gives it a sinister and suspenseful edge.) The pace and mood become chaotic and confused—at the climax there is a brief image of George Washington that also includes a swastika—before coming to a peaceful conclusion centered on the word "happiness." Even this scene makes unusual use of screen space. We see Frady sitting down in his one-seat movie theater, and we see him get up at the end, but we are never given a reaction shot, even at the test's conclusion. By keeping him completely out of the picture—unlike in, say, the analogous scene in *A Clockwork Orange* in which Alex is forced to watch violent images—Pakula deprives us of some important cues that might tell us how to read this scene.

FIGURE 18 *Frady prepares to watch the Parallax test film.*

The "film" itself is unusual in that it is not actually a film but a succession of still images, and it signals a persistent tension between *Parallax*'s film text and the unmoving pictures that recur within it. In addition to the test images, there are several scenes of Frady studying photographs, and at one point the camera freeze-frames on a Parallax agent we have seen before as if someone was building a dossier on him. (It is a familiar technique from crime films in which the police run down a list of criminals who they are seeking, but here the absence of an agent who might be taking the "photo" makes it another scene in which a generalized and unlocatable surveillance seems to be taking place.) The heavy-handed symbolism and emotional manipulation contained in the test's montage of still images are the aesthetic opposite of the film around it, which is as detached and analytical, as devoid of identificatory strategies, as Hollywood films ever get. Although we watch the test film along with Frady, it is presented in a mode that incorporates irony and a kind of anthropological fascination; the context asks us to consider intellectually the kind of images that are used by Hollywood or Washington to manipulate the emotions of other people and, of course, ourselves. The juxtaposition between the film and the still images it contains offers us explicitly what *Parallax* as a whole offers us implicitly: the sense that we are being allowed to occupy a position of critical distance from which we can recognize that an authentic America is no longer available. *Parallax* conceals the emotional force of this revelation behind the screen of its analytical detachment; it is designed to activate in its audience a form of nostalgia for the national authentic that has, the film suggests, been sold in complicated ways and without our knowledge or consent in the global marketplace.

The images contained in the test film, which look less like straightforward propaganda than like a harsh shuffling of the deck of American symbols, suggest the way that this pessimistic and nostalgic attitude toward the nation plays out in *The Parallax View*. In its conspiratorial worldview the corporation—and the system of global capitalism for which it is a synecdoche—has completely undermined and inhabited the functioning of the nation and its democratic institutions. This film expresses at the level of form the argument put forward by the president of TV network UBS in another dark seventies film, *Network* (1976):

> There are no nations, there are no peoples, there are no Russians, there are no Arabs, there are no Third Worlds; there is no West. There is only one holistic system of systems. One vast and interwoven, interacting, multi-variant, multi-national dominion of dollars. Petro-dollars, electro-dollars, multi-dollars, reichsmarks, rubles, pounds and shekels. . . . There is no America, there is no democracy. There is only IBM and ITT and AT&T. And Dupont, Dow, Union Carbide, and Exxon.

The viewer of *Parallax* may eventually realize that the senatorial candidate who is killed at the film's end is in fact the opponent of the candidate whose life Frady saves from a Parallax bomb in an earlier scene. Parallax has no investment in any political party; like any company, it is at the disposal of the unknown clients it serves, putting American politics in the all-too-invisible hands of market forces.

What remains of the nation, then, is only a collection of the most generic national signifiers. The heavy-handed American symbolism in the test film is basically indistinguishable from the patriotic boilerplate presented in the rehearsal for the final candidate's speech, the rehearsal at which he is killed and Frady is framed. This event includes a marching band playing "Yankee Doodle Dandy" in a room festooned with red, white, and blue while a crowd displays flip-card mosaics of Washington, Jefferson, Lincoln, and Teddy Roosevelt, and the candidate's speech runs through the standard pieties of American political discourse ("the promised land of liberty our forefathers created," etc.). Filming the rehearsal of the speech allows Pakula to draw our attention to the emptiness of the words and the event; while a recording of the speech plays, the candidate stands idly at the microphone and smokes, suggesting a cynical distance between the candidate and the empty patriotic rhetoric. What Frady discovers is that these empty images, this simulacrum America, is all that remains, a façade behind which capitalism does its business. This is a far more comprehensive conspiracy than the one in *All the President's Men*, because there is no question of corruption here; the government need not be in on the plot at all. (As Frady observes, "there is a bureaucratic tendency to cover up mistakes, but I got no reason to think any governmental agency was in on it. Or if they were, that they knew it.") Instead we get what is more disturbing: a nation that exists only as an empty accumulation of images, a government that is essentially a sham even if those who constitute it are unaware of the fact, while behind the scenes impersonal corporate entities pull the strings that move the politicians and the American people.[11] John McClure writes that the conventional conspiracy story is "reassuring" because it "proclaims . . . that conspiracies exist, that they threaten to destroy our democratic capitalist way of life, and that this very way (heroically individualistic, brilliantly analytic, technologically sophisticated, and deeply principled) is always throwing up heroes capable of defending it against its conspiratorial others" ("Forget Conspiracy," 254). That is the model exemplified by *All the President's Men*. *The Parallax View*, by contrast, is a perfect trap from which no such reassurance emerges, a trap that implicates heroic individualism, democracy, and capitalism in the conspiracy logic that its narrative and aesthetic techniques create. In the film's concluding image of claustrophobic space, Frady runs and runs through darkness toward his one chance of escape, a brightly lit door suggesting sunlight, outdoors, open space, the impossible outside. But as in Borges, or Kafka, Frady's understanding comes only at the final moment and the door on which he pins his hopes opens onto his death, in the form of a Parallax agent— or perhaps a duped lawman—who guns him down. After a whole movie's worth of unexpected figures emerging ominously out of the unseen, we must have expected this one.

The one purpose the simulacrum America still serves is to motivate people, whether they are voters or prospective assassins seeking positions with the Parallax corporation: the film argues not only that American democracy is a hollow shell, but that American individualism is, too. As I have suggested, Joe Frady is a version of the classic American male film hero, but one that has been emptied of content. He has all the right attributes—he is an investigator, an anti-authoritarian, a man who feels that he must work on his own to expose a conspiracy that others have failed to see—and it is precisely that set of attributes that makes him not only a (partly) successful sham Parallax operative but also a mirror image of the "real" Parallax operative suggested by the test film. (In order to get an interview with Parallax, Frady has to take a written personality test. He visits a clinic that studies violence, where they let the in-house sociopath, Ernie, take the test for him; the camera shift from Frady to Ernie suggests a mirroring—this is not just Frady's proxy, but his double.) The test images projected for Frady suggest that the ideal assassin is a model of beset individualism, a "me" who is menaced by forces on all sides, who longs to defend the values represented by "home," "god," and "country," and who feels that the state and its leaders are arrayed against him. In other words, he is not only potentially an assassin, but potentially the male protagonist of any Hollywood thriller or action movie—which is to say that he is in some ways the very model of the individual as constructed in the American imagination. The images of Frady contending with offscreen oppressors are similar to the images of the "me" who can be convinced that he must strike out violently at those in power.

Although there are New Hollywood conspiracy films, such as *Three Days of the Condor*, that provide the kind of individual hero that McClure describes, taken as a group these films suggest an emptying-out of the individual agent, with *Parallax* providing only the most radical version of this tendency. Coppola's *The Conversation*, for example, is a character study of surveillance expert Harry Caul, who has done everything possible to erase himself as a personality, to submerge himself in a professional identity that leaves no private self that could be revealed by the surveillance of others. When he does act, even in a limited way, it is only to discover afterward that he has misinterpreted a surveillance tape he made and that the tape itself is the instrument of a plot that has lured Harry's client to his death. In the film's final sequence, Harry is told that his apartment is bugged and responds by searching the apartment so thoroughly that at last he completely dismantles it, tearing apart the protective shell that constitutes his identity in a failed attempt to locate the flaw in the shell.

As in *The Conversation* and *The Parallax View*, John Boorman's antinoir *Point Blank* makes a manipulation by corporate interests into the occasion for the draining away of its protagonist's identity. Lee Marvin plays Walker, a hard-boiled antihero who escapes from Alcatraz in order to claim restitution from the partner in crime who has double-crossed him and left him for dead. Working on information from a mysterious figure named Yost, he moves relentlessly through the noir stomping ground of Los Angeles, and ultimately discovers that his money from the heist has been paid to a crime syndicate, the Organization. In a classic instance of the noir conflation of crime and business, the Organization is located on the top floor of an office building, in a space that is indistinguishable from any corporate headquarters. Walker demolishes the Organization, but in the process learns that the shadowy Yost has used him as a tool by which Yost can seize sole control of the Organization. In the dreamlike final scene, Yost calls for the hidden Walker to come out, while Walker fades into the shadows and disappears. Was it all a fantasy, playing across Walker's mind at the moment of his death at the film's beginning? As with the question of where exactly that bug in Harry Caul's apartment is located, it doesn't matter. What does matter is the way that New Hollywood protagonists are absorbed into the engulfing dreamworld of large commercial entities— ones that are either actually or metaphorically corporate—that they cannot fight their way out of. Ghosts of a heroic Hollywood tradition who don't realize they are obsolete, these characters act against conspiracy only to have their assertion of agency revealed as yet another manipulation at a deeper level.

In this radical emptying-out of the individual subject, the politics of authenticity reach a limit-point that is also a kind of impasse. The argument contained in the spatial logic of *Parallax* and in the conspiracy cycle generally suggests that these films can point to the historical shift to multinational corporations and name it as the site for the production of a national inauthenticity, the disappearance of the nation as a meaningful category in the world system of the global economy. But that is all. The films represent a crisis; the structure of noir authenticity has been both disassembled and extended in order to respond to the large systems of global capitalism, but the result is that the idea of an authentic America no longer has any political purchase and can exist only in the form of a nostalgia for the displaced category of the nation. To the extent that the argument of conspiracy and the social critique it implies is successful, it is also a kind of endpoint; it looks not for an exit, but for the signs that confirm our suspicion that all the doors have been locked from the outside.

In *The Parallax View* there is no obvious alternative to the world the film shows us. The space of the screen becomes a cage from which there is no way out, and the undermining of the individualist male hero eliminates the subject through which American films traditionally imagine political agency proceeding.[12] Texts like *Parallax* do not and perhaps cannot envision collective action, which might offer one path to a politics of resistance. Their annihilation of the individual male hero suggests the need for an authentic alternative, but that alternative remains unimaginable within the films themselves. Conspiracy films are representations of the multinational corporate production of space that describe the desire for an alternative to that space. As such, they create an effect of authenticity that emerges in response to increasingly abstract and virtual formations of consumer capitalism. As in the case of noir, it is an effect that takes the form of oppositional critique, but the alternative America it desires can no longer be envisioned or represented, and conspiracy takes the noir logic one step further by eliminating the detective, the male individualist who stood in opposition to consumer culture. The effect of authenticity is now located at an even farther remove, as the evocation of and nostalgia for authenticity's absence. Conspiracy narrative attempts to signal the presence of a consumer culture that is now global, that is too large and complex in its production of space and subjectivity to be represented. Its representational strategy is to indicate its own failure, a position whose implications for political action are left uncertain and, at least temporarily, impossible to articulate.

The political problem that is staged in *The Parallax View* shapes many of the texts of the noir tradition as that tradition evolves during the era of postmodernism's emergence. (Indeed, it is a political problem that is central to postmodern cultural production generally.) In the next two chapters I will be looking at two more groups of conspiracy texts from and about the sixties era, both of which attempt to articulate versions of authenticity that are not nostalgic but are instead engaged in the politics of their present moment and of the American pasts that they invoke. In doing so they make it clear just how powerful the logic of authenticity and the noir tradition are in constructing oppositional political positions in the postwar era, and how important it is in American political discourse to have recourse to an idea of America as the foundation of any articulation of an alternative or countercultural politics.

Flirters, Deserters, Wimps and Pimps

PYNCHON'S TWO AMERICAS

So the bad Ninjamobile swept along the great Ventura, among Olympic
visitors from everywhere who teemed all over the freeway system in
midday densities till far into the night, shined-up, screaming black
motorcades that could have carried any of several office seekers, cruisers
heading for treed and more gently roaring boulevards, huge double and
triple trailer rigs that loved to find Volkswagens laboring up grades and
go sashaying around them gracefully and at gnat's-ass tolerances, plus
flirters, deserters, wimps and pimps, speeding like bullets, grinning like
chimps, above the heads of TV watchers, lovers under the overpasses,
movies at malls letting out, bright gas-station oases in pure fluorescent
spill, canopied beneath the palm trees, soon wrapped, down the
corridors of the surface streets, in nocturnal smog, the adobe air, the
smell of distant fireworks, the spilled, the broken world.

—THOMAS PYNCHON, *VINELAND*

Could [the rejection of the Puritan idea of the "elect"] have been the
fork in the road America never took, the singular point she jumped the
wrong way from? . . . It seems to Tyrone Slothrop that there might be
a route back—maybe that anarchist he met in Zürich was right, maybe
for a little while all the fences are down, one road as good as another,
the whole space of the Zone cleared, depolarized, and somewhere
inside the waste of it a single set of coordinates from which to proceed,
without elect, without preterite, without even nationality to fuck it up.

—THOMAS PYNCHON, *GRAVITY'S RAINBOW*

The epigraph to Thomas Pynchon's novel *Inherent Vice* is taken from a graffiti
slogan of the countercultural protests that took place in Paris in May 1968—
"Under the paving-stones, the beach!"—a quotation that contains in miniature
the interlocking cluster of themes that I will be identifying in Pynchon's work.
This utopian rallying-cry of the soixante-huitards describes a scenario in which
two opposed principles occupy the same space: one, associated with play,

leisure, and nature, buried beneath another that suggests social order and the built world of property ownership. I will argue here that Pynchon's trilogy of novels about the 1960s and the counterculture dramatizes the movement from traditions of detective and noir narrative to conspiracy plot. In doing so, these novels articulate what I will refer to as the "Two Americas" model: two versions of the nation occupy the same geographical space, with the visible and consumerist republic twinned by the alternative, dispossessed America beneath. *The Crying of Lot 49*, published in 1966, makes the birth of the sixties era the occasion for the transformation of the detective novel into the conspiracy novel, and in the process formulates a series of questions about the possibility of political action in the postmodern context. The neo-noir *Inherent Vice* (2009) and the conspiracy novel *Vineland* (1990), in reflecting on the end and the legacy of the sixties, both attempt to answer those questions by connecting the sixties to other historical moments of possibility for the American Left.[1]

In the last chapter, I argued that the film *The Parallax View* represents one version of the process by which the noir detective story evolves into the conspiracy narrative. In that version, noir authenticity in its original form is no longer viable; if the nation (and the Chandlerian male hero who might redeem some sort of national identity) has been effaced as a category by systems of global capital, the only authentic position remaining is to point to the absence of national authenticity in a gesture that is both radical and nostalgic. This approach appears to disable any possibility of political intervention. The discovery that the world system has inhabited the nation in ways that cannot be fully known suggests that no critique can be realized, no action can be taken. Pynchon's books represent a different version of this evolution, one that acknowledges this problem and also argues the necessity for expressing some form of oppositional politics. In these books, the search for authenticity leads to the self-consciously rhetorical Two Americas model, with its new articulation of the claim that there is a better, truer America lurking somewhere outside the nation, outside of that mainstream America defined by an omnipresent consumer culture. This opposition between two distinct versions of America—the mainstream nation that is defined through consumer culture as the "American way of life" and the alternative, underground nation of the Left and the left-over—is central to all of Pynchon's novels, and is particularly apparent in his books that deal with the politics of the sixties.

Pynchon's books are concerned not with the disappearance of the nation as a category but with the betrayal of the nation's boundless promise—what Greil Marcus has described in a different context as "the inevitable betrayals that stem from the infinite idealism of American democracy" (*Invisible Republic* 89). The books are drawn persistently to those who have been dispossessed by national narratives and definitions, to the flirters, deserters, wimps, and pimps who live beneath—or hidden within—the official economy. I will be arguing that Pynchon's attention to these historical dispossessions is expressed as a version of American exceptionalism—the belief that there is a unique and re-demptive American destiny—and that this exceptionalism is the form that au-thenticity takes in his novels. Pynchon's work signals a recognition that, in order to intervene in a meaningful way in American politics, it is necessary to claim one's own position as an "American" one. Thus the books deploy authen-ticity strategically in order to place a homegrown Left tradition at the heart of American promise. An exceptionalist authenticity provides the rhetoric that Pynchon uses to construct this Left tradition; he employs it self-consciously as an effect in order to associate that Left tradition with the better, truer America he evokes.

In articulating this position, Pynchon continues the engagement with spa-tial systems that we have seen at work throughout the noir tradition in both its classic postwar and its conspiratorial sixties formations. The commercial space that Pynchon investigates is America itself. The land and landscape are envisioned as a commercial entity—as property—and *real estate* is Pynchon's recurrent figure for describing the transformation of America into a republic of consumption. Real estate, as a way of imagining the national landscape as an array of items offered up for purchase, provides the language through which these books begin to imagine the "American way of life" as a spatial conspiracy, realized in the ongoing spread of the postwar suburbs and the consumerist lifestyle that they represent. For Pynchon, this commercializa-tion of American space both constructs a new geographical model and enables a leisure economy that finds its paradigmatic expression in screen-based en-tertainment. Confronting the consumerist mainstream as a form of con-spiracy, his novels assert the presence of an alternative America of dispossessed weirdos, a hidden challenge to the real estate nation, which is made, once again, in the language of an authenticity that is imagined as the opposite of consumer culture.

Ballad of a Thin Woman

Published in 1966, *The Crying of Lot 49* is both a book about and a book of the emergent culture that is associated with "the sixties." The central character and detective, Oedipa Maas, begins the story as a square, a straight, a suburban housewife and former Young Republican who is plunged down the rabbit-hole of the sixties counterculture. There she discovers that the world around her is not what it seems, that she has been floating down the mainstream in a bubble, cut off from the cultural changes happening all around her. Like Bob Dylan's archetypal Mr. Jones, she finds that once she leaves that bubble, she herself becomes an alien, an outsider who doesn't get it.[2] Wandering through the "jumping" Berkeley campus, Oedipa finds herself on "a plaza teeming with corduroy, denim, bare legs, blonde hair, hornrims, bicycle spokes in the sun, bookbags, swaying card tables, long paper petitions dangling to earth, posters for undecipherable FSM's, YAF's, VDC's, suds in the fountain, students in nose-to-nose dialogue" (103). In order to begin deciphering this new or newly revealed world, Oedipa must become a "sensitive": the process of becoming a detective, an Oedipus capable of reading and interpreting the signs and codes she encounters, is at the same time the process of becoming clued or tuned in, so that she is no longer Ms. Jones, but rather someone who *does* get it.

The shape of this process is structurally similar to the investigation that makes up the bulk of any noir detective novel: an episodic narrative involving a series of encounters with eccentric people, each one leading on to the next and all threaded together by the protagonist's pursuit of a central mystery. The mystery here involves the Tristero, a conspiracy that may or may not exist, a version of the "underworld" that is so powerfully evoked in hard-boiled crime fiction. But the mastery that the traditional detective displays has here been replaced by Oedipa's tentative investigation, which not only leads to a conspiracy too large to be understood or uncovered but also grows to implicate or enfold Oedipa herself. There is no satisfying solution to the mystery—the book in fact ends deliberately at an indeterminate moment, suspended between knowledge and unknowability—and by the end there is no longer even an autonomous subject who can solve the mystery, since Oedipa's identity and future have become bound up with the uncertainty of the Tristero.

In this way, *The Crying of Lot 49* exemplifies the postmodern turn from detective story to conspiracy plot that I described in the last chapter.[3] The conspiracy narrative virtually defines the emergence of the postmodern novel in the post-sixties era. In his book on paranoia in postmodern fiction, Samuel Chase Coale refers to conspiracy as "the postmodern sublime," in which the longing for and the impossibility of transcendence or pure presence are experienced simultaneously (*Paradigms of Paranoia*, 6); tackling the same subject, Patrick O'Donnell suggests that "paranoia can be viewed as the reaction-formation par excellence to the schizophrenias of postmodern identity, economy, and aesthetics" (*Latent Destinies*, 11). For these critics and others, postmodern cultural production employs conspiracy as a way of representing the epistemological crisis brought on by the difficulty of comprehending the vastness of the late-capitalist global economy. In the sixties, hard-boiled detective fiction gives up its role as the popular foil and secret heart of modernism and is reborn as conspiracy literature. It is not accidental that this new kind of conspiracy novel takes the form of "literary" postmodernism; with its self-conscious enjoyment of popular culture forms and its attention to the failure of traditional systems of knowing, postmodern fiction has thrived on revisiting and revising the detective genre.

But Pynchon's use of conspiracy is not designed solely to offer a glimpse of dizzying postmodern aporia; here the experience of the sublime potentially offers access to the impossible and longed-for thing, the national authentic.

Conspiracy is the primary trope through which Pynchon organizes his Two Americas model, and his formulation of that model is inseparable from the history of the 1960s and the politics of the counterculture. In *Utopia Limited*, Marianne DeKoven argues that by looking at key texts produced during the sixties it is possible to witness the emergence of postmodernism; at this "pivot" moment, "certain aspects of sixties radical politics and countercultures, visible in representative texts, embodied simultaneously the full, final flowering of the modern and the emergence of the postmodern" (3). This formulation is useful for describing the emergence of the new form of postmodern conspiracy narrative, which takes the noir detective form and transforms the kernel of conspiracy plot that it contains into the dominant trope of the new form.

In *The Crying of Lot 49*, as in DeKoven's argument, the turn to the postmodern is linked to the emergence of countercultural politics. The novel provides a catalogue of secret societies, each with its own conspiratorial agenda: Inamorati Anonymous, the anarchist CIA, the radically right-wing Peter Pinguid Society, AC-DC, DEATH, WASTE, not to mention the shadowy but nonfictional Mafia. But the book's strategy is to imagine that all of its disparate secret societies, and any number of unaligned individuals, are united in a larger conspiracy: "a calculated withdrawal, from the life of the Republic, from its machinery" (124). This withdrawal is manifested in their use of the alternative mail service that Oedipa identifies with the Tristero. The withdrawal itself is more interesting than the bizarre details of the secret societies because it signals the desire for an alternative, the sense of lack, that motivates the creation of a counterculture. Like the detective figure in noir fiction, the Tristero is representative of an oppositional position that has no clearly defined content; it is the assertion of an alternative America that has no definite politics.

At this point, the book's formal postmodern question—how is it possible to know or verify the truth of the world?—is revealed to contain a *political* postmodern question: How is it possible for an alternative community to resist the dominant national identity if the only thing that makes it a community is its alternative positioning? How can a politics be founded on absence? And if it could be, would that really be a politics at all? The Tristero offers the possibility of resistance to the American mainstream and the consumer culture that defines it, but in doing so it is defined by and as a principle of opposition. *Lot 49*'s counterconspiracy only exists in the negative, as an effect of the mainstream it resists, its content apparently unrepresentable: it is the longing for an authentic way of being without a definition of the authentic—another American elsewhere.

The book is organized not as a solution but as the articulation of this political problem. Nonetheless, putting the problem in this form suggests, first of all, that there is a coherent and definable American mainstream, and that opposition to that mainstream is a worthwhile goal. To this end, Pynchon structures *Lot 49* as a historical allegory in which Oedipa represents some version of the American Everyperson as she moves from the post–World War II era to the crisis and challenge of the sixties. What little we know about Oedipa outside of the Tristero plot is sketched quickly at the beginning, and Pynchon loads the book's early sentences with signifiers of suburban consumerism and lifestyle. As Mark Conroy remarks, we learn almost nothing about Oedipa's psychology, history, or social background, but "what we get, to the extent that we get anything, is her profile as a consumer" ("The American Way and Its Double in *The Crying of Lot 49*," 50). She has just returned home from "a Tupperware party where the hostess had put perhaps too much kirsch in the fondue" to her TV and living room, after which she goes shopping at the local supermarket and comes home to read *Scientific American*, prepare dinner (lasagna, garlic bread, romaine lettuce), and mix the evening's cocktails before watching Huntley and Brinkley (9–11).

In the midst of this sequence, one that seems to have been cribbed from the pages of *Good Housekeeping* circa 1960, Pynchon hits a note that will recur throughout the book—the emptiness of this typically American life with its "fat deckful of days which seemed (wouldn't she be the first to admit it?) more or less identical" (11). The book's early pages establish a brief but decisive connection between the consumerist fifties and the sense of emptiness that Oedipa is forced to confront in more direct ways as she is pulled into the underworld that Pierce's will opens to her. Whether or not there is a Tristero, an alternative to mainstream America, what Pynchon insists upon is the *desire* for that alternative, the haunting sense that something is missing.

In evoking that sense of loss and that desire for an alternative, *The Crying of Lot 49* returns us to the problem of the postwar dominance of consumer culture and the new ways of thinking about citizenship that that dominance creates—a problem that Pynchon connects to the emergent cultural politics of the sixties. In the 1995 introduction to his 1969 book *The Making of a Counter Culture*—the book that coined the term—Theodore Roszak explicitly frames the politics of the sixties as a response to something that began much earlier, arguing that "the period of upheaval we conventionally call 'the sixties' is more appropriately seen within a broader setting that stretches from 1942 to 1972" (xi). For Roszak, the politics of the sixties can only be understood in the context of the "age of affluence" that accompanied the rise of consumer culture: "What I have called 'the counter culture' took shape between these two points in time as a protest that was grounded paradoxically not in the failure, but in the success of a high industrial economy. It arose not out of misery but out of plenty; its role was to explore a new range of issues raised by an unprecedented increase in the standard of living" (xii). Like the noir detective figure (although in somewhat different clothes), the counterculture was imagined as an alternative or antidote to consumer culture.

The sixties counterculture, in other words, represents the next development in the paradoxical combination of affluence and discontent that postwar cultural critics associated with the inauthentic "organization man." The affluent society was defined by the rise of the suburb; by the conspicuous consumption of automobiles and appliances; and by a conformist tendency that pushed all Americans to aspire to, and to define themselves as part of, the middle class. But consistently, throughout the postwar era, the comforts of American prosperity—the Pax Americana, the Cold War consensus—have produced traditions of discontent and resistance. The central paradox of the rise of consumer culture is that although it accompanied one of the highest standards of living known in history, it also produced a broad cultural sense of emptiness, alienation, and loss.

Pynchon's book, with its depiction of Oedipa as the discontented American subject and its exploration of sixties counterculture, is alert to the paradoxes of the affluent society. In his essay on *The Crying of Lot 49*, Conroy argues that the book "presents itself as an anatomy of postwar American consumer society" (45). He suggests that Pynchon represents consumption as the "secular" side of the larger system known as "the American way of life." The "sacred" side is "a kind of civil religion of American destiny, whose *arche* and *telos* authorize and guarantee the transactions of the commercial arena" (59). We might say that for Pynchon the American way is a loose-limbed conspiracy in which political and commercial entities have colluded to create the hegemonic postwar America from which his characters are alienated.

Oedipa, our everywoman, is representative in this regard as well: she finds herself not only alienated, but confused by her alienation. After all, what good is an unhappy American? So as she puts together the shadowy and unverifiable history—or counterhistory—of the Tristero, she discovers both the longing for an alternative to the life she knows and an explanation for that longing. The Tristero, in this version of events, originates in Europe in the sixteenth century out of a struggle for control of a postal monopoly. The loser of the struggle melodramatically renames himself "El Desheredado, The Disinherited" and begins a guerrilla campaign against the mail system involving both violence to postal carriers and an underground delivery service. This campaign threads its way through the events of European history, attenuated eventually from its original purpose so that the Tristero comes to exist only as a negative force, an abstract embodiment of the principle of disinheritance, an absolute Other. In the nineteenth century, having diffused in Europe, it sets up shop in the United States to compete with the Pony Express, the early messengers disguised as Indians, "their entire emphasis now toward silence, impersonation, opposition masquerading as allegiance" (174). The Tristero is a metaphor for conveying a sense of dispossession that haunts the promise of America, and so there is a neat logic to the Indian disguises, since the Indians are both the most completely dispossessed and also the most authentic and original Americans.[4]

Pynchon fuses the Tristero story to another, more concrete set of observations about America. Just two years before *The Crying of Lot 49* was published,

Michael Harrington titled his call-to-arms study of poverty in the United
States *The Other America*. It is this "other America" that Pynchon evokes in the
midst of the novel's long climactic meditation, as Oedipa considers the question of disinheritance:

> What was left to inherit? That America coded in Inverarity's testament,
> whose was that? She thought of other, immobilized freight cars, where
> the kids sat on the floor planking and sang back, happy as fat, whatever
> came over the mother's pocket radio; of other squatters who stretched
> canvas for lean-tos behind smiling billboards all along the highways, or
> slept in junkyards in the stripped shells of wrecked Plymouths, or even,
> daring, spent the night up some pole in a lineman's tent like caterpillars,
> swung among a web of telephone wires, living in the very copper rigging
> and secular miracle of communication. . . . She remembered drifters she
> had listened to, Americans speaking their language carefully, scholarly,
> as if they were in exile from somewhere else invisible yet congruent with
> the cheered land she lived in. (180)

In this passage we encounter the most heightened prose in the book, Pynchon dipping, as he does at key moments, into the tradition of the American
long sentence—inherited in part from Walt Whitman's catalogues and over-
full poetic lines—with its resonant tone of prophesy and summation, its
urge to create a language capable of responding to American vastness
and diversity. The tone here is resolutely serious, combining a sense of Oedipa's exhaustion with a straight-faced evocation of an almost mythological
America of squatters and hobos, as if Pynchon were seeking to transport us
to thirties America, to the outrage and eloquence of Walker Evans and James
Agee.[5] There is, too, a nostalgic note in the description of the other, con-
gruent nation these outsiders inhabit—a barely hidden world that, significantly, can be found "behind" billboard advertisements or in the junkyards
that are the inevitable obverse of consumption—as if that "invisible" nation
were the real one.

   In other words, Oedipa learns that the promise of America—"how had it
ever happened here, with the chances so good for diversity?" (181)—is fatally
undercut by the existence of those who are dispossessed, but at the same time
discovers that the true and vital version of America is the one represented by
the dispossessed. Again, Pynchon distinguishes between two Americas: the
debased and bland consumers' republic, on the one hand, and on the other, the
displaced, dispossessed "spirit" of America, both alternative and authentic.
The two Americas inhabit the same space; to use a digital metaphor of the sort
that Pynchon is fond of, they are different states of the same thing. The American land is both a one and a zero—and Pynchon is looking for a way to flip the
switch between them. This distinction suggests, then, that the true national
spirit has been betrayed, which is the reason that the Tristero takes root in

America. For Pynchon, the central drama that constitutes American history is the movement from boundless promise to endless betrayal.

Exceptionalist Authenticity

At this point we come back to the political question that lingers throughout *The Crying of Lot 49*, the one Pynchon presents but does not resolve: what exactly is the content of this authentic and alternative America in the present? If the Tristero functions only as an oppositional counterforce, then can it have any real effect or politics? After all, the Tristero exists as a way of linking up all the various groups who have chosen to withdraw from the life of the republic, groups with myriad goals and conflicting politics. If a nation is a fiction with a history, what uniting fiction might motivate and organize Pynchon's nation of outsiders, rebels, and loners, of "flirters, deserters, wimps and pimps," Oedipa among them? *The Crying of Lot 49* deliberately resists closure and in the process leaves us, again, not with an answer but with an articulation of the problem. In the final image of Oedipa waiting for the crying, we are offered a metaphor for the longing of the American citizen. Is there a Tristero or, as Oedipa fears, is there "just America," just the collection of things contained within the nation's borders?

This question suggests the extent to which Pynchon's fiction is engaged with issues that are raised in similar ways in the discourse of "American exceptionalism," which contends that there is, there must be, something to America beyond the collection of things that it contains. American exceptionalism describes a national tradition, stretching back to early Puritan settlers, within which spiritual and secular elements are blended in order to represent America as having a unique and sacred destiny in which the redemption promised in the New Testament will be enacted in and as America.[6] As Deborah Madsen puts it:

> Exceptionalism describes the perception of Massachusetts Bay colonists that as Puritans they were charged with a special spiritual and political destiny: to create in the New World a church and a society that would provide the model for all the nations of Europe as they struggled to reform themselves (a redeemer nation). In this view, the New World is the last and best chance offered by God to a fallen humanity that has only to look to His exceptional new church for redemption. Thus, America and Americans must sustain a high level of spiritual, political, and moral commitment to this exceptional destiny. (1–2)

The logic of exceptionalism has had a privileged place in putting the question "what is America?" at the center of discussions of national policy. American leaders have frequently answered that question in moral terms that have served as an alibi for the exercise of whatever kinds of power they have seen fit to use against those both inside and outside of the national borders. Indeed, the myth of American exceptionalism has frequently been derided by progressive and leftist scholars as a dangerous and reactionary ideology that has been used to justify imperialism, genocidal expansionism, regime change in Iraq—in fact, to justify any of our nation's criminal atrocities through the invocation of a higher destiny, a special status.

Given this history, and given Pynchon's sympathy with the American dispossessed, it is not surprising that scholars have generally seen in his work an attack on the myth of exceptionalism. Madsen, for example, argues that "Pynchon focuses upon the exploitation of [exceptionalist] cultural mythology to perpetuate internal class divisions and to further America's imperialist ambitions" (152). (The grammar is unforgivably ambiguous, but in context it's clear that she is saying that Pynchon is *against* perpetuating these things.) Indeed, Pynchon himself is quite aware of the tradition he is working against. In a famous passage from *Gravity's Rainbow*—part of which is cited here as an epigraph—Tyrone Slothrop reflects on the actions of his first American ancestor, William Slothrop, who in the 1630s becomes disillusioned with the mission of the Massachusetts Bay Colony. He ultimately writes a heretical tract called *On Preterition* in which he argues for the holiness of the Preterite, those who are not saved, when the few, the Elect, are. This sympathetic championing of dispossessed and outsider communities is so common in Pynchon that his critics regularly use "elect" and "preterite" as shorthand for the perpetual struggle of the privileged and powerful against the losers and the outsiders of history that is acted out in his books.

But I want to suggest here that this countercultural impulse one finds in Pynchon is itself a manifestation of the exceptionalist logic. In *The New American Exceptionalism*, Donald Pease argues that during the Cold War exceptionalism provided a "state fantasy" that supported the dominant political order precisely because it had no stable definition. If America is defined not by a set of values but by its difference from other nations, then its alleged exceptionalism becomes a kind of alibi that renders the nation ideologically unassailable:

> The United States differed from other nations in that its national fantasy was in fact a state fantasy. . . . American exceptionalism defined America as having already achieved the condition of the ideal nation that normally incited national desire. After it defined America as the fulfillment of the world's dream of an ideal nation, the fantasy of American exceptionalism eradicated the difference between the national ideal U.S. citizens wanted and the faulty nation they had, by representing America as having already achieved all that a nation could be. (21–22)

For Pease, exceptionalism enables Americans to erase the difference between fantasy and reality, suggesting that the nation in its present state is already the ideal nation.

But even if this ideological complacency may describe a dominant consensus position during the postwar era, this consensus was contested as inauthentic from within the noir and countercultural texts that I have been working with in this book. Noir authenticity depends upon the logic of American exceptionalism, making precisely the argument that Pease sees exceptionalism as having rendered impossible. It argues that the America that exists is not the ideal nation, and it is defined by the desire for a truly ideal nation that it posits without defining, a nation that resembles the one envisioned by American exceptionalism both in its ambition and its vagueness.

For Pynchon, this exceptionalist authenticity, insisting upon the centrality to American life of the alternative and the dispossessed, becomes the vehicle for an antinationalist nationalism, an antiexceptionalist exceptionalism.[7] It stands as the sign of democratic, inclusive, and egalitarian American values that have been lost, misrepresented, or betrayed for so long and in so many ways that they have become subversive. As Jeffrey Baker writes, "Pynchon reveals the sixties' counterculture's expectation that America ought to be able to do better" ("A Democratic Pynchon," 100). The place where Pynchon and the counterculture meet is precisely in this belief that the critique of contemporary America must take place in the name of the "real" American values. That belief is documented, for example, in Dotson Rader's memoir of the New Left; "America isn't really America," one friend is quoted as saying. "And it won't be until . . . the whole damn place is pure again, as clean as it was before Americans ruined it" (*I Ain't Marchin' Anymore*, 2). The redemptive promise of America is not something to be created in the future, but something original that has always existed only as a promise, as something to be recovered and realized.

Indeed, one of the surprising things about Pynchon's work is that despite the fact that he writes fiction that is mazelike and erudite, radically indeterminate, and archetypally postmodern in its emotional distance and refusal to yield definitive accounts or dependable knowledge, his novels consistently offer an almost touchingly naïve and heartfelt belief in the promise of America, coupled with outrage at the betrayal of that promise. This belief animates the ending of *The Crying of Lot 49*, giving it the resonant emotion that is the only reason to accept the nutty version of the Tristero's history that we are offered. It is the belief that moves Dixon to despair in *Mason & Dixon* when confronting the most profound instance of the betrayal of American promise, slavery: "Where does it end? No matter where in it we go, shall we find all the World Tyrants and Slaves? America was the one place we should *not* have found them" (693). Likewise *Vineland* describes the homeland in 1984—the year when George Orwell's vision met that of Ronald Reagan—as "the State law-enforcement apparatus, which was calling itself 'America,' although somebody must have known better" (354).

As these examples suggest, Pynchon's antiexceptionalist exceptionalism informs the whole broad sweep of American history that his fiction takes in, from the nation's colonial origins and colonialist expansion to its present moment. Likewise, this approach places Pynchon in the tradition that, in Sacvan Bercovitch's argument from *The American Jeremiad*, defines American literature itself: "American writers have tended to see themselves as outcasts and isolates, prophets crying in the wilderness. So they have been, as a rule: American Jeremiahs, simultaneously lamenting a declension and celebrating a national dream" (180).[8] Both Pynchon's American subjects and his approach to those subjects, in other words, stretch backward and find antecedents throughout the whole of the nation's history; they do not begin with the rise of consumer culture in the twentieth century. The argument I am making here is that the sixties are privileged in Pynchon's fiction because they represent the moment when the history of American consumer culture and the history of America's efforts to define itself meet at a crisis point, the moment when envisioning a more "authentic" America is at the heart of the national culture. In his trilogy of sixties books, the crisis of the sixties (that is, the belated crisis of postwar affluence) is always at the same time a crisis of American history generally—and is therefore an opportunity to reassert a homegrown tradition of the American Left. This dual project is expressed most clearly in the figure of real estate, where the long history of American land development is expressed by way of postwar consumer culture's impact on the national landscape.

Unreal Estates

The concern with real estate is already there in *The Crying of Lot 49*, which initiates a synecdochal model that is picked up in both *Inherent Vice* and *Vineland*; the creation of America as a republic of consumption is rendered through the representative phenomenon of California land development. Pierce Inverarity, we are told on the first page, made his fortune as a "California real estate mogul," and Oedipa's first intimation of conspiracy appears upon her arrival in San Narciso, the place where Pierce began his land speculation. It is a representative Californian space—"less an identifiable city than a grouping of concepts—census tracts, special purpose bond-issue districts, shopping nuclei"—and as she drives in, Oedipa's first view is of "a vast sprawl of houses which had grown up all together, like a well-tended crop, from the dull brown earth" (24). The agricultural image, ambiguous in its suggestion both of preindustrial land use and of property ownership, gives way to a metaphor that places San Narciso firmly in the realm of the man-made; the development reminds Oedipa of a circuit board, both containing a "hieroglyphic" meaning to be decoded: "so in her first minute of San Narciso, a revelation also trembled just past the threshold of her understanding" (24). The suburban landscape appears immediately as a conspiracy, a mystery in which two ways of understanding the space of San Narciso are simultaneously present. To understand

America as real estate is to evoke the hovering and numinous presence of the Tristero's other America, so that conspiracy and counterconspiracy become visible in the same moment.

Around this kernel the book's plot begins to accumulate. As Oedipa and the lawyer Metzger watch TV, Metzger identifies every product that is advertised as being connected in some way to Pierce's estate. Television and suburban real estate work in tandem—a conjunction I will be returning to in discussing *Inherent Vice* and *Vineland*—to suggest a pervasive ordering of San Narciso; it is a place defined not just by Pierce but by the principle of commerce that he represents. As the book progresses, these discoveries continue and multiply until it seems that there is no place in America that Oedipa can go without discovering both the trace of Pierce's money and the suggestion of the Tristero that inevitably follows, the commercialization of space evoking its opposite and dispossessed double: the two Americas.

Pierce's role in real estate, then, signals the extent to which he is a figure for capitalism writ large, a way for Pynchon to represent the branching largeness of an economic system that is "past the threshold" of any individual's understanding. He is a shadowy presence in the book, dead at the start, evoked vaguely in flashbacks as a shape-shifting presence, less comprehensible as an individual than as an idea or principle. The anarchist Jesús Arrabal, meeting Oedipa and Pierce, is disconcerted to recognize the extent to which Pierce is an "anarchist miracle," an apparition of capitalism in the flesh: "He is too exactly and without flaw the thing we fight" (120). When Pierce describes himself, in his role as real estate developer, as a "founding father," Pynchon invokes the term, loaded as it is in the American context, both with irony and gravity; if America is now entirely inhabited by consumer capitalism, then Pierce is in fact an appropriate founding father.[9]

In *The Crying of Lot 49*, then, Pynchon's investigation of consumer capitalism as a far-reaching conspiracy is expressed as a concern with real estate; the commercialization of American space is represented in the postwar spatial rearrangements of suburban land development. The long transformation of American land into property and the more recent evolution in that process, in which that land expresses the new dominance of the consumer ethos, produce—at least in part—the countercultural response of the sixties. This complex of issues is taken further in *Inherent Vice*—published in 2009 but set at the end of the sixties—a book in which California real estate is at the heart of another detective's investigations.

If *Lot 49* dramatizes the movement from detective story to conspiracy narrative, *Inherent Vice* is the book in which Pynchon portrays that movement as a demonstration of the continuity between noir politics and conspiracy politics. Like the Coen brothers' *The Big Lebowski*, it makes the link between noir and the counterculture explicit by creating a protagonist who is both a pot-smoking hippie and a Chandler-style private investigator. Doc Sportello is the sole agent of LSD Investigations ("Location, Surveillance, Detection"), whose emblem, "a giant bloodshot eyeball in the psychedelic favorites green and magenta" (14), is a parody of the Pinkertons' unblinking-eye logo. The book's plot is itself a catalogue of elements from noir film and fiction: the Los Angeles setting, the visit from a femme fatale figure with which the book begins, the apparently local investigation that swiftly becomes baroque in its complexity and reveals that criminal acts are linked to powerful businessmen and conspiracies of power, the scene in which the detective is knocked out (here by a spiked joint rather than a Mickeyed drink), the scene in which the detective confronts Mr. Big. Even the title *Inherent Vice*, with its origins in insurance practice, recalls the title *Double Indemnity*. The book is self-conscious about its noir references, as are Doc and the other characters. Doc (who isn't always clear on the distinction between real and fictional people) sees the hard-boiled dick, like the sixties freak, as an oppositional figure whose time is coming to an end: "Once there was all these great old PIs—Philip Marlowe, Sam Spade, the shamus of shamuses Johnny Staccato, always smarter and more professional than the cops, always end up solvin the crime while the cops are following wrong leads and gettin in the way" (97).[10]

Both Doc and Pynchon are committed to keeping that noir attitude alive, and the Left content that informs the oppositional stance is made clear by the book's use of the actor John Garfield. Garfield provides the most consistent link to noir in *Inherent Vice*; he is a role model for Doc, who frequently refers to his films, owns a suit that Garfield wore in the 1946 noir *The Postman Always Rings Twice* (pairing it with an outrageous tie that once belonged to Liberace), and uses the name of Garfield's character from that film, Frank Chambers, as an alias. Garfield is known for his Left-leaning politics and his status as a martyr of the Hollywood blacklist, qualities that seem to be reflected in his film roles playing rebels and outsiders, often in movies that displayed a distinct leftist sensibility. For Pynchon these roles connect Garfield to the countercultural ethos; at one point in *Inherent Vice*, Doc finds himself watching a 1951 noir, *He Ran All the Way*, on late-night TV—"John Garfield's last picture before the anti-subversives finally did him in, and it had the smell of the blacklist all over it"—and is mesmerized with horror by the ending: "It was somehow like seeing John Garfield die for real, with the whole respectable middle class standing there in the street smugly watching him do it" (254).

Inherent Vice draws on noir as a Left tradition that finds its continuation in the sixties counterculture, one that rejects the America of the respectable middle class in favor of a truer and more original America. The politics of the sixties are seen to contain the hope for this better America—a hope that is both a return and a revision. Doc is given some help with his case one night by a large plastic reproduction of a nickel that hangs on the wall of a stoner hangout; in fact, the nickel has a history of this sort of behavior: "Now and then, late at night . . . Thomas Jefferson turned from left profile to full face, unfastened the ribbon that held his hair back, shook everything out into a full-color red-headed freak halo, and spoke to selected dopers, usually quoting from the Declaration of Independence or the Bill of Rights" (294). As with the "portrait of Madison" in *The Long Goodbye*, the apparition of Jefferson as a hippie freak is a way for Pynchon to revalue the nation's currency, to separate the two Americas by separating the symbol of money from the symbol of America. The latter symbol is then aligned with the politics of the sixties and the larger Left tradition—Pynchon is careful to note that Jefferson is in "left profile"—so that that tradition becomes associated with the original promise of America. The sixties appear to be doomed as "the faithless money-driven world" (130) begins to reassert itself, but if *Inherent Vice* is to be an elegy for the sixties, it is also determined to be a critique of the thing that supersedes the sixties. The authentically freaky and Jeffersonian America is opposed to the commercial spatial arrangements of the "Supermarket Amerika" (119) that is represented by sprawling suburban real estate.

As in a Chandler novel, the geography of Los Angeles is central to the organization of *Inherent Vice*.[11] The book is largely structured around an opposition between the disorderly charm of Doc Sportello's Gordita Beach (apparently a fictional stand-in for Manhattan Beach)[12] and the threatened imposition of housing developments—the paving stones that will cover up the beach. Gordita Beach itself is one of those enclaves of outsiders that Pynchon treasures, home to a sympathetic assortment of surfers, stoners, New Agers, paranoids, and oddballs: another version of the various groups in *Lot 49* who have chosen to withdraw from the life of the republic. The new housing development that threatens this enclave is called "Channel View Estates," a name that is unsubtle in its linking of the construction of suburbs to the larger consumer economy by way of television and other screen-based leisure entertainment—a link that we have already seen at work in the synergetic operation of TV commercials and real estate in Pierce Inverarity's empire.[13]

As Doc's investigations circle around the construction of Channel View Estates, it becomes clear that this development, like Pierce's property in San Narciso, is a representative manifestation of the larger history of American land ownership and the dispossessions that that ownership has produced.[14] The new houses are replacing a black neighborhood that had been a Japanese neighborhood before the internment camps of World War II, leading Doc to ruminate on the "long, sad history of L.A. land use. . . . Mexican families bounced out of Chavez Ravine to build Dodger Stadium, American Indians swept out of Bunker Hill for the Music Center," and now "black pedestrians . . . looking for the old neighborhood, for rooms lived in day after day, solid as the axes of space, now taken away into commotion and ruin" (17, 19). When Doc finally has his meeting with Mr. Big, it plays out in much the same way as Philip Marlowe's meeting with Harlan Potter in *The Long Goodbye*. The wealthy Crocker Fenway is able to resolve the details of the case that Doc is working on, while he and Doc express contempt for each other across the divide between Fenway's quasi-aristocratic landowning class and Doc's alignment with the renters, the transients, and the underclass. Fenway, echoing Harlan Potter's contempt for mass culture, despises the suburban blight of Channel View Estates for his own reasons; from his class viewpoint the whole of contemporary consumer culture is a degraded mess from which the wealthy should both profit and wall themselves off. In fact, the Estates are a problem whose source is not Fenway, but something more diffuse and harder to locate; it takes the form of an entity that Fenway has dealings with, and even serves as the agent of, called "the Golden Fang."

The question of what exactly the Golden Fang is remains up for debate in the novel. It might be a large and efficient drug cartel, but it also appears at different moments during the book as a ship, as a cloaked and vampiric apparition with gold fangs, and as a corporate entity set up by a group of dentists that is located in a building shaped like, yes, a giant golden fang. As all of this shape-shifting and coy play between the literal and the figurative suggests, the Golden Fang is one of Pynchon's conspiratorial entities, a way of representing the large multinational systems that shape the lives of Americans. Both Thomas Jones and Bill Millard, in early essays on *Inherent Vice*, have noted that the Golden Fang seems to represent the global functioning of capitalism itself. Indeed, the Golden Fang Enterprises building that Doc visits looks like a hipper, sleeker version of the corporate headquarters in which the Organization Man goes about his business.

The Golden Fang, then, is a version of the conspiracy of the American way of life that is evoked in *The Crying of Lot 49*; it is both capitalism as world-system and also the local, national interface of capitalism, which takes the form of middle-class consumer culture. After Doc has come to terms with Crocker Fenway, a handoff is arranged between Doc and the Fang, and the agents appear not as fiendish spies, but as avatars of the American way:

> The Golden Fang operatives were cleverly disguised tonight as a wholesome blond California family in a '53 Buick Estate Wagon, the last woodie that ever rolled out of Detroit, a nostalgic advertisement for the sort of suburban consensus that Crocker and his associates prayed for day and night to settle over the Southland, with all non-homeowning infidels sent off to some crowded exile far away, where they could be safely forgotten. (349)

The Fang, with its many parts pervading the book and constructing the plot that Doc must try to negotiate—but that he cannot foil—takes the form of the bland and smiling mainstream, one that even here is associated with the transformation of land into commercial property via real estate and the automobility of the sprawl: the "*Estate* Wagon" that is an "advertisement" for a suburban ideology conceived in conspiratorial terms. This passage returns to

Pynchon's characteristic dichotomy between the visible America and the America of all those who are alienated from the nation as it is, the dispossessed who cling to some idea of America as it ought to be.

I have already suggested that this latter vision is given content in *Inherent Vice* through the deployment of noir as a repository of Left politics that is linked to an original or authentic vision of America. Intimations of another reality, another set of possibilities for the nation, are proposed throughout the book. As we have seen, founding father Thomas Jefferson gets a hippie make-over, and as in *The Crying of Lot 49*, Indians are put into symbolic play as well. Gordita Beach sits on the graveyard of a hallucinogen-smoking tribe "not un-like the hippie freaks of our present day" (355), associating the counterculture with another kind of original America. But the most explicit representation of an authentic and exceptionalist national identity that is offered in the book is its persistent evocation of the unreal estate of Lemuria, the mythical drowned land beneath the Pacific. Lemuria is invoked as a full-blown alternative nation, the lost continent of which California itself is an offshoot, an "ark"—as Doc's lawyer Sauncho remarks dryly, "Oh, nice refuge. Nice, stable, reliable piece of real estate" (352).

Lemuria represents the fantasy of a different kind of America, one that is both exceptionalist and leftist—a combination that the book desires but is un-able to manage coherently. In one of Pynchon's oddball historical readings, Doc has an acid trip in which he envisions war in Indochina in terms of a Manichaean battle between right-wing Atlantis (of which Nixon is an agent) and left-wing Lemuria (Ho Chi Minh). It would be hard to say, however, what exactly the leftist political values of the lost continent are. With no clear set of principles, the fantasized Lemuria offers instead the image of a free-floating opposition to the actual real-estate America that Sauncho describes: "The land almost allowed to claim its better destiny, only to have the claim jumped by evildoers known all too well, and taken instead and held hostage to the future we must live in now forever. May we trust that this blessed ship is bound for some better shore, some undrowned Lemuria, risen and redeemed, where the American fate, mercifully, failed to transpire" (341). As imagined here, Lem-uria offers the promise of redemption, the vision of an America that is as it ought to be, that defines Pynchon's antiexceptionalist exceptionalism. By placing that better national identity in a mythical elsewhere, Pynchon follows the trend that we have seen at work throughout the texts of the noir tradition; the conflation of national identity with consumer culture is countered by an authentic version of America that is defined by what it is not. Lemuria, like the book as a whole, is a statement of intent that is never followed to completion, a call for the return to a betrayed American leftism that it cannot quite describe.[15]

These themes return in the final pages of *Inherent Vice*, suggesting the extent to which this desire for the American elsewhere is at the core of the book. Doc finds himself driving through an epic and impenetrable fog—a motif that is employed both here and in *Vineland* as a Californian expression of the tension between the seen and unseen worlds, a metaphor for the experience of conspiracy, containing the possibility of a hidden nightmare or an ultimate redemption. Driving, listening to tunes on the radio, Doc isn't panicking: he has gas in the tank, "a container of coffee from Zucky's and almost a full pack of smokes" (368). He reflects that maybe

> it would stay this way for days, maybe he'd just have to keep driving, down past Long Beach, down through Orange County, and San Diego, and across a border where nobody could tell anymore in the fog who was Mexican, who was Anglo, who was anybody. Then again, he might run out of gas before that happened, and have to leave the caravan, and pull over to the shoulder, and wait. For whatever would happen. . . . For the fog to burn away, and for something else this time, somehow, to be there instead. (369)

A dream of crossing a border to a place where no one is dispossessed, of the fog lifting to reveal not the commercial real-estate America but a better, not quite imaginable something. Here is the Pynchonian exceptionalism in a nutshell, with its powerful expression of the desire for a set of values identified as authentically American but betrayed and absent from the visible republic, and its inability to describe what exactly those values are.

The critique of consumer culture that is offered by *Inherent Vice* is both representative of Pynchon's Two Americas model and also the most politically simplified version of that model. Narrating the last days of the sixties, the book associates the counterculture with noir authenticity without investigating either of those terms in depth—or perhaps it would be more accurate to say that the book retroactively attributes some of the sixties counterculture's incoherences to the past history of the American Left. The result is a critique of consumer culture that is essentially a condemnation. The contrast between the commercial space represented by real estate, on the one hand, and the unreal estate of the alternative America, on the other, is rendered in stark moral terms that lead to a ringing endorsement of exceptionalist authenticity. The book does, however, extend the investigation of the alternative America that is begun in *The Crying of Lot 49*, employing noir elements intertextually in order to suggest that the content of the authentic republic must be found in traditions of American leftism, and establishing a link between the politics of noir and the politics of the counterculture—one that we had already begun to see in postwar noir fiction. *Inherent Vice* wants to construct that vision of a homegrown American Left as the true American identity, but its effort to do so is hampered by the book's black-and-white opposition between consumerist real estate and countercultural authenticity as well as by the vagueness of the leftist histories to which it refers.

These ideas are taken further in *Vineland*, which, although it was written earlier, constructs a more sophisticated model for describing the Left content of the alternative America and the relationship of that alternative to the consumer culture that it confronts. In fact, a version of this model sneaks into the margins of *Inherent Vice* as well. Remember that coffee from Zucky's, the one that Doc is depending on to get him through the long miles of fog? The coffee, with its provenance from an actual deli in Santa Monica, reminds us that it isn't necessarily commerce as such that Pynchon wants to reject. As with *The Big Lebowski*, with its homages to Ralphs grocery, In-N-Out Burger, and Benitos Tacos, *Inherent Vice* teems with references to actual, local Los Angeles businesses that bear positive connotations by virtue of being part of the messy local culture: Tommy's Hamburgers, Pink's Hot Dogs, Zody's—not to mention the ones invented by Pynchon. These spaces, unlike the redemptive elsewhere of Lemuria, suggest that the enemy in Pynchon is not always consumer culture as such, but rather the large and homogenizing forces of capitalism that work in conjunction with normalizing definitions of national identity—the conspiracy of the American way of life, with its ideological fusing of capitalism and democracy.

If *Inherent Vice* often seems to envision a withdrawal into an impossible elsewhere as the only solution, it also holds out the possibility that a messy and vital culture may still flourish on the streets and in the stores of the republic. The balance between these two sites of possible resistance—the pure alternative (Lemuria) or the impure alternative (Zucky's)—leans toward the former in *Inherent Vice*, but both are present in all three of the books I discuss here; the tension between them is central to Pynchon's vision. *Vineland* takes the latter model much further, and it does so by moving from the actual space of real estate to the screen space which Pynchon sees as the other, virtual space that defines suburban life.

Visible Republic

The one explicit reference to film noir in *Vineland* is continuous with the essentially naïve critique of consumer culture that *Inherent Vice* performs. Late in the book, the teenaged Prairie meets a friend at a Hollywood shopping mall called Noir Center, which takes its theme from what Prairie thinks of as the "weird-necktie movies" of the forties and fifties. As the novel describes it, "Noir Center . . . had an upscale mineral-water boutique called Bubble Indemnity, plus The Lounge Good Buy patio furniture outlet, The Mall Tease Flacon, which sold perfume and cosmetics, and a New York–style deli, The Lady 'n' the Lox. Security police wore brown shiny uniform suits with pointed lapels and snap-brim fedoras" (326). Pynchon makes a familiar point here about the way that an omnivorous consumer culture can and will appropriate anything in order to create the illusion of novelty in both products and shopping spaces. The satire suggests that to appropriate the dark themes and images of film noir is the ultimate absurdity; the final frontier of American authenticity has now been paved over and sold to the highest bidder. But I will be arguing that this straightforward satire is at odds with the larger project of the book. *Vineland* leaves the conventions of detective form and noir behind, and perhaps this is because noir—as in *Inherent Vice*—is linked so closely to a complete rejection or negation of consumer culture, a rejection that becomes more complex and negotiated in *Vineland*. If noir itself is barely present here, nonetheless the book's conspiracy structure, in which commerce is once again seen to have fully inhabited the American landscape, extends the meditation on the relationship between consumer culture and authenticity that we have seen at work in *The Crying of Lot 49* and *Inherent Vice*, and in the noir tradition generally.

Like the other two novels, *Vineland* imagines an other America that exists simultaneously within and outside the visible republic, but this time it is not a magical land like Lemuria. Although there are intimations of supernatural forces at work—alien visitations, Godzilla sightings—*Vineland* provides a specific geographical location where the true, alternative America might be found, one that is concrete and metaphorical at the same time: Vineland County, in northern California. The name is a resonant one, first of all because it evokes a place lushly overgrown, a haven of the natural world, a land untouched by real estate. And indeed, the book is full of descriptions of Vineland as a place of natural beauty, of redwoods threatened by logging, of marijuana plants threatened by the DEA, while at the book's center is the story of an accidental revolutionary named Weed and the moment of sixties utopianism that dies when he does. The name itself contains an echo of "Vinland," the name Leif Erikson gave to the newly discovered continent of North America a thousand years ago. Thus Vineland is offered as a version of the original America, although at the same time it recalls the first moment of European contact with and claiming of the American land—a paradise already lost at the moment of origin.

It is appropriate, then, that the book also refers us to the Indians native to the region, the Yuroks. Drawing on Yurok lore, Pynchon tells a story about the woge, spirits of the natural world who "withdrew" (Pynchon uses the word twice in this brief tale) when humans arrived, some disappearing into the landscape, others going away "nestled all together in giant redwood boats, singing unison chants of dispossession and exile" (186). *The Crying of Lot 49* echoes loudly in this fable of ecology mingled with the history of European colonization: it is there in the language of "withdrawal" from the life of the nation, in the notion of a group exile performed in "unison," and in the symbolic use of Indians to refer to an original and betrayed America. If *Lot 49*, *Inherent Vice*, and *Vineland* mark the emergence, end, and legacy of the sixties, respectively, then Pynchon's ambivalent consideration of that legacy becomes a way of simultaneously modifying and concretizing his vision of the Two Americas, filling in the blanks, as it were, left by *The Crying of Lot 49*.

While *The Crying of Lot 49* posits the Tristero as a mysterious counterforce, an organization defined by the principle of opposition, *Vineland*, like *Inherent Vice*, gives a particular kind of content to that opposition. Instead of shadow histories and shadowy operatives, here we are offered a ragtag bunch drawn from the various branches of the American Left: aging hippies, certainly, and also Wobblies, communists, anarchists, and punks, as well as less political outsiders such as the Thanatoids, who represent that most dramatically dispossessed group of all, the dead. Although these groups often don't like or respect each other (as is the case, for example, with leftover hippie Zoyd Wheeler and his old leftie mother-in-law Sasha), they are increasingly thrown together in the enclaves available to alternative America, driven into smaller and smaller spaces as Ronald Reagan's America expands its reach in a kind of ideological clearcutting. As in *Inherent Vice*, there is an effort here to create continuities between the sixties counterculture and other leftist traditions, but in this case it is both more far-ranging and more concrete. Unlike the isolated, abstractly symbolic characters of *Lot 49* and the generic figures of *Inherent Vice*, those in *Vineland* are tied to families and histories, and through those networks to two great moments of possibility for the American Left in the twentieth century: the thirties and the sixties.

The relationship between the legacies of the New Deal and the New Left has been as troubled as that between Sasha and Zoyd, but as Pynchon suggests by putting these two in the same extended family, the relation between the two traditions is a necessary and productive one. In his essay "Between the 30s and the 60s," the social ecologist Murray Bookchin insists that the two historical moments must be understood together, that "the 60s are particularly significant because they tried to deal with problems that 30s' radicalism left completely unresolved" (248). For Bookchin, the trouble with the thirties is that its leftism was tied to the European political traditions from which it emerged; the value of the sixties, then, is in the attempt to create a specifically American radicalism, grounded in native utopian traditions. Thus the "agenda" of the sixties counterculture "stressed the *utopian* aspects of the 'American Dream' as distinguished from its *economic* aspects: the eschatological ideal of a 'New World,' of frontier mutualism, of decentralized power and 'participatory democracy,' of republican virtue and moral idealism" (249).

In this passage, Bookchin articulates a way of understanding the Two Americas problem as a conflict between two perhaps incommensurable versions of the American Dream that has organized national identity in the twentieth century and beyond. On the economic side, there is the ever-growing consumer economy; on the utopian side resides the American "better self," the ideal of an alternative and disinherited America. Bookchin describes sixties politics, in other words, as a version of the antiexceptionalist exceptionalism contained in Pynchon's work: an attempt to separate utopian democratic American values from materialist American values, and to assert the former as representative of the authentic nation. In *Vineland*, it is precisely this set of problems that Pynchon again takes up, except that he finds at least the possibility of an organically American (and not necessarily utopian) radicalism in the inheritance of both the sixties and the thirties.

These political traditions, and the conflicts between them, are at the heart of the family around which *Vineland* is organized: the former hippie and surfer Zoyd, who now gets by on mental disability checks from the government; his teenaged daughter Prairie, who lives with Zoyd in Vineland County; and her mother Frenesi Gates, whom Prairie has never met. Frenesi, like Caddy in *The Sound and the Fury*, is the now-absent object of everyone's desire, and she is crucial to the novel's structuring themes because of the fundamental conflicts she embodies: born immediately after World War II and named for a pop song, an artifact of the newly dominant consumer culture, her family history connects her to the radical labor politics of the thirties. A red-diaper baby, Frenesi's maternal grandparents, Jess Traverse and Eula Becker, were Wobblies. Jess was a labor organizer who worked to unionize loggers in Vineland until the timber company's bosses arranged to have his legs crushed under a redwood.[16] Frenesi's parents worked in Hollywood in the fifties, "always under dreamlike turns of blacklist, graylist, secrets kept and betrayed" (74), and despite her other compromises, at a crucial point in the book, Frenesi cannot bring herself to cross a picket line even to flee to safety with her family.

Caught within the contradictions that she has inherited, Frenesi perpetually and helplessly betrays her political values. We learn that in the sixties she was part of a radical filmmaking collective called 24fps, which among other things set out to document a campus takeover led by the mathematician and unlikely revolutionary Weed Atman. Frenesi became involved with Weed, but also with the federal agent, Brock Vond, who brought down the student uprising. By the novel's present, she, like Zoyd, is being paid by the state, working intermittently as an undercover operative, sexual betrayal now having become a tool of her trade. Frenesi, like her mother Sasha, tends to desire the sort of authoritarian, right-wing agents of the state who are completely abhorrent to her (and Pynchon's) political outlook. She is, in a sense, America, or the American citizen; against all her better judgment and best values, she is drawn to figures of authority who represent the opposite of those values.

The extent to which Pynchon turns to the tradition of the New Deal as a repository of America's best values is clear from the way that tradition haunts the book's landscape, another ghost nation threatened by real-estate America. The thirties remain imprinted on the California land, in "old WPA murals about Justice and Progress" (200), "the concrete art deco bridges built all over the Northwest by the WPA during the Great Depression" (316), the "New Deal earnestness" of Vineland architecture (317). The antique, ruined quality of these objects signals their status in the contemporary moment of the eighties, defined by what one character calls "the whole Reagan program . . . dismantle the New Deal, reverse the effects of World War II, restore fascism at home and around the world" (265). Like the Indians who are so invisible as contemporary people to mainstream America yet whose words haunt the landscape everywhere in the names of rivers, towns, and streets, the legacy of the thirties seems to survive only in its crumbling monuments—the New Deal left as another original and dispossessed America.

Pynchon clearly wants to reclaim this legacy for the present. Although the novel charts the failures and betrayals of the sixties and ultimately documents a quasi-military invasion of northern California by federal agents, in the final section we are given Pynchon's approximation of a utopian vision. It comes in the queer and charming form of the annual Traverse-Becker reunion, a gathering of old Wobblies and lefties and their children and grandchildren for a good old-fashioned family cookout in the edenic space of Vineland. This section is a celebration of messy Americana—with its RVs and cooking grills and potato salad—that would do John Mellencamp[17] proud:

> The eating . . . was the heart of this gathering meant to honor the bond between Eula Becker and Jess Traverse, that lay beneath, defined, and made sense of them all, distributed from Marin to Seattle, Coos Bay to downtown Butte, choker setters and choppers, dynamiters of fish, shingle weavers and street-corner spellbinders . . . waiting for Jess's annual reading of a passage from Emerson he'd found and memorized years ago. . . . "'Secret retributions are always restoring the level, when disturbed, of the divine justice. It is impossible to tilt the beam. All the tyrants and proprietors and monopolists of the world in vain set their shoulders to heave the bar. Settles forever more the ponderous equator to its line, and man and mote, and star and sun, must range to it, or be pulverized by the recoil.'" (369)

Vineland is skeptical and ironic about much that happened in the sixties, much that is spiritual, much that is American, but it is hard to find anything but a fond indulgence in its attitude toward the Becker-Traverse gathering. And this passage, where Pynchon again employs a Whitmanesque catalogue to evoke a whole range of outsider types and then ends on a resoundingly affirmative note from Emerson that is at odds with the apocalyptic undertones that run through the novel, puts the American literary past in the service of thirties leftism in order to assert a radical politics that is homegrown, optimistic, and commonsensical. The rhetoric of the passage places that leftism at the very heart of American life as it is lived and practiced.

But against this ending with its sense of possibility, much of Pynchon's book is devoted to a dystopian evocation of the mainstream, the "American way of life" which is defined by consumer culture. This culture of consumption, in fact, seems to be the real threat in the book, less cartoonish and more pervasive than the incursions of the militarized and fascistic federal government, which are themselves modeled on the actions of TV and movie law-enforcers. Throughout the book, Pynchon extends the analysis of the American-way-as-conspiracy that we have seen in *The Crying of Lot 49* and *Inherent Vice*, showing commerce and government to have a set of aligned goals that result in a nightmare vision of the national real-estate culture, one that is defined as artificial and juxtaposed against nature and landscape.

The natural haven of America, as represented by Vineland, is in danger of becoming real estate. As the logging proceeds and the pot plants are destroyed, the land itself is in danger of being incorporated into the national mainstream: "Developers in and out of state had also discovered the shoreline in the way of the wind, with its concealed tranquilities and false passages. . . . All born to be suburbs, in their opinion, and the sooner the better" (319). But in *Vineland* the anxiety about real estate shifts decisively into the metaphorical register. The conjunction suggested by *Inherent Vice*'s "Channel View Estates," and the similar linking of television to suburban real estate in *The Crying of Lot 49*, becomes fully realized in *Vineland*'s evocation of a nation defined by television and other screen-based leisure technology. Real estate's spatial transformations signal the advent of a consumer economy in which the most important claims to be staked are on the territory of the screen, the commodified and virtual space now inhabiting the space of the republic.

Tube Space

Signs of the consumer society are everywhere in *Vineland*. The question of how to interpret these signs is central to understanding the novel, and that question has often been at the heart of the argument that has taken place over the literary "value" of *Vineland*. Because of the seventeen-year waiting period after *Gravity's Rainbow*, and the reputation and following that Pynchon had acquired in the meantime, the expectations for the "new Pynchon" were both high and specific. As a result, when *Vineland* appeared and was found not to have the density or scope of *V.* or *Gravity's Rainbow*, it was largely reviled by Pynchon critics and readers who seemed to feel that they had been betrayed. The book has any number of defenders, including, notably, Salman Rushdie and Edward Mendelson, both of whom wrote early reviews in which they found value in the book's differences from Pynchon's earlier fiction: its more complex emotional resonances, its glimpses of possibility breaking through the paranoia, its evocation of community.[18] But Pynchon scholars have, by and large, treated *Vineland* like a red-headed stepchild, and the negative judgments have often pointed for evidence to the book's relationship to popular culture.

Many of Pynchon's most dedicated and insightful critics have reacted to the novel with something like revulsion on this account. David Cowart's essay "Attenuated Postmodernism: Pynchon's *Vineland*" is a useful example:

> The density of reference to the ephemera of popular culture is almost numbing. Pynchon refers often to movies, as in *Gravity's Rainbow*, but here he neglects historic films and art cinema in favor of *Gidget*, *Dumbo*, *20,000 Years in Sing Sing*. . . . Even more insistently jejune are the allusions to the titles, characters, stars, and music of such television programs as *Star Trek*, *The Brady Bunch*, *Gilligan's Island* . . . *Smurfs*, *ChiPs*, *Superman*, and *The Bionic Woman*. This depressing litany—the intellectual horizon of the American mass mind—subsumes less obvious manifestations of popular taste as well: mall culture, "roasts," video and computer games . . . even "sensitivity" greeting cards. (8)

I have actually shortened all the lists in the quotation above; Cowart in his horror seems to have been compelled to catalogue every instance of popular culture in the book. The only way that he can find any value in Pynchon's use of pop culture is if Pynchon can be effectively distanced from the references themselves, if his attitude can be seen as an "implicit judgment of this shallowness" (8). Joseph Tabbi hits the same note, arguing that *Vineland*'s "studied superficiality and restricted reference to the ideas and artifacts of mass culture make it the most self-consciously 'popular' of Pynchon's books, and this popularity is . . . an imaginative shortcut on Pynchon's part, an acceptance of a ready-made audience that frees him from the responsibility of creating the sensibility by which he will be understood" ("Pynchon's Groundward Art," 90). Both Cowart and Tabbi seem to feel that the pervasive references to consumer culture have made *Vineland* itself into a product for mass consumption, as indicated presumably by the relative straightforwardness of the style and narrative as compared with *V.* or *Gravity's Rainbow*. By this logic, the book is therefore inauthentic and unworthy of Pynchon's oeuvre.

Despite their overwhelming tone of disdain and disappointment, these critics are absolutely on target in pointing to the omnipresence of popular culture references in the book and in observing that the central aesthetic and political question of *Vineland* involves accounting for these references. But the question isn't whether the novel has too little ironic distance from these intertexts, but whether it has too much. It is immediately clear, in other words, that Pynchon opposes the natural and original America he locates in Vineland County to the all-devouring consumer culture he satirizes throughout the book. But often his satire appears to be easy and conventional, as in the description of the "Noir Center" mall, which seems to draw a clear line between the authenticity of film noir and the inauthenticity of consumer culture. Many of the book's satirical details, like those in *Inherent Vice*, express this simplistic critique of consumption, as if Pynchon had gone from postmodernist guru to vulgar Marxist.

But I want to argue that this content is at odds with the formal strategies the book employs. Ultimately, *Vineland* suggests that only through a formal incorporation of consumer culture is it possible for fiction to articulate a homegrown American radicalism for the post-sixties era. As Prairie's postpunk boyfriend Isaiah Two Four says to Zoyd, "Whole problem 'th you folks's generation . . . is you believed in your Revolution, put your lives right out there for it—but you sure didn't understand much about the Tube. Minute the Tube got hold of you folks that was it, that whole alternative America, el deado meato, just like th' Indians, sold it all to your real enemies, and even in 1970 dollars—it was way too cheap" (373). (The characters in *Vineland* are more compelling and emotionally complex than those in *The Crying of Lot 49* or *Inherent Vice*, but they still don't talk even remotely like anyone you've ever met.) Here Isaiah returns us to a familiar theme—the sixties as desire for an alternative and original America ("just like th' Indians")—in order to suggest that any Left politics that wants to look to the future as well as the past has got to understand the Tube.[19]

Television and other screen-based technologies of leisure are the primary forms of consumer culture that appear in *Vineland*. In his essay on the book's "entropy of leisure," David Thoreen observes that in this novel tracing the period 1945 to 1984, "video technology provides Pynchon with the perfect analogue to the consumption economy" ("The Economy of Consumption," 53). The references to television, movies, and video games are ubiquitous and multilayered, operating at several levels in order to better confuse the distinction between real life and screen space. The characters refer to shows and movies, but so does the narration, and the date of each film mentioned is given in parentheses, so that novelistic discourse becomes tangled up with that of film scholarship, or *TV Guide*.

But the interpenetration of the book and its intertexts goes further than this. Pynchon uses television and film references not only to saturate the content of the text but also to provide its aesthetic and narrative organization, its metaphors and plot developments. As these techniques emerge over the course of the book, it becomes clear that *Vineland*'s most powerful intervention into post-sixties politics is its attempt to construct a language that imbricates narrative and character construction with consumer culture. Early in the book, Zoyd describes his life as "like being on 'Wheel of Fortune,' only here there were no genial vibes from any Pat Sajak to find comfort in, no tanned and beautiful Vanna White at the corner of his vision to cheer on the Wheel, to wish him well, to flip over one by one letters of a message he knew he didn't want to read anyway" (13). Likewise, pot-smoking Zoyd and the DEA agent Hector Zuñiga (a "tubefreak" who can't keep TV and reality straight) have "a romance over the years at least as persistent as Sylvester and Tweety's" (22), while Zoyd describes his "inner feelings" to Frenesi by saying, "Feel like Mildred Pierce's husband, Bert" (57). For Prairie, performing a dramatic rescue, "it felt like being bionically speeded up, like Jaime Sommers, barreling through a field of slo-mo opposition" (328). These characters define themselves, both on the surface and at the deep level of identity and emotion, through television and movies; other characters read and understand them in this way, and the text itself tells their story using terms, coordinates, and trajectories borrowed from screen technology. Brock Vond even tries to make the ending of *Vineland* the ending of *The Empire Strikes Back*, announcing Vader-like that he is Prairie's real father.

The extent to which Tube space serves as a way of organizing the book becomes especially clear in Pynchon's references to video games, which are employed at significant junctures to describe the characters' actions. Takeshi's approach to the Kunoichi Retreat is "an all-day hard-edged video game, one level of difficulty to the next" (161), while an argument between Frenesi and her current husband is "a kind of alien-invasion game in which Flash launched complaints of different sizes at different speeds and Frenesi tried to deflect or neutralize them before her own defenses gave way" (87). One of the book's most resonant passages describes how, for Frenesi:

> [Brock Vond's] erect penis had become the joystick with which, hurtling into the future, she would keep trying to steer among hazards and obstacles, the swooping monsters and alien projectiles of each game she would come, year by year, to stand before, once again out long after curfew, calls home forgotten, supply of coins dwindling, leaning over the bright display among the back aisles of a forbidden arcade, rows of other players silent, unnoticed, closing time never announced, playing for nothing but the score itself, the row of numbers, a chance of entering her initials among those of other strangers for a brief time, no longer the time the world observed but game time, underground time, time that could take her nowhere outside its own tight and falsely deathless perimeter. (292–93)

In this passage, Pynchon goes into his most eloquent and distinctive register, building clause upon clause like a beatnik Henry James, putting one of his most powerful long sentences in the service of an extended video-game metaphor that is no longer satire but rather a sad, tender evocation of the lost promise of the sixties and the pathos of a generation that has not learned how to grow up. The passage of time and the movement of history, like the psychological developments and conflicts of the characters, is rendered through the figure of the virtual spatial arrangements and interactions made available on the screen.

In the description of Frenesi's video-arcade years, as in the "Wheel of Fortune" passage, Pynchon keeps a straight face while working through his pop-culture analogies, creating a tension between the language and the subject that allows these Tube intertexts to bear the weight of real emotion and concrete history. Pynchon holds this tension throughout *Vineland*, and it is in its essence a tension between two distinct versions of the Two Americas problem. One version, similar to the logic of *The Crying of Lot 49* and *Inherent Vice*, insists that a line can be drawn between the authentic America and the pervasive consumer culture; but the new version suggested by *Vineland* acknowledges that to formulate a workable politics in the post-sixties era will mean blurring that line. While the content of the book tends to keep the line firmly in place through its easy satire, the blurring occurs primarily at the level of form. In *Lot 49*, Pynchon evoked the lurking presence of an "other America," a diverse, polyglot, dispossessed nation lurking behind the smiling billboards. In *Vineland*, Pynchon adds a new twist by suggesting that the billboards, too, are a part of the America that must be evoked. The language itself insists that there can no longer be an uncontaminated space of resistance to the American way of life. Instead, what is required, and what is proposed in the form of the text itself, is an aesthetic that can ground Pynchon's oppositional politics in a world thoroughly suffused by consumer culture.

Making its poetry out of the odds and ends of the commercial world, *Vineland* cautiously begins to bridge the divide between consumer culture and alternative America. This ostensibly minor entry in the Pynchon canon is actually an evolution in his ongoing attempt to represent the problem of conspiracy and of the Two Americas that is so central to his fiction. Pynchon returns in *Vineland* to the issues raised in *The Crying of Lot 49*, and he does so in order to reformulate them, to give concrete political content to the logic of national dispossession and withdrawal offered by the earlier book. In the process, he invokes the legacy of the sixties and the counterculture as the historical moment that must be both recuperated and questioned. *Lot 49* evokes the sense of national loss and the desire for authenticity occasioned by the rise of consumer culture—the problem that gave rise to the counterculture; *Inherent Vice* links the countercultural withdrawal from the republic to a noir-derived authenticity that is distinctly, if vaguely, leftist. *Vineland* suggests that our present moment requires a politics that is not dependent on rejecting consumer culture in favor of some ideal of purity, utopia, or absolute withdrawal. Incorporating elements of consumer culture into its aesthetic and narrative structures, the book does not abandon the exceptionalist logic of the Two Americas but instead gives us an alternative America that can make meaning out of its relationship to the texts of consumer culture. In order to find a place in the confrontation between capitalism and democracy, between real estate and authenticity, it is necessary to have a home in Vineland, but also in the spilled and broken world. This is an alternative based not on withdrawal but on engagement, one that puts the sixties counterculture in a larger context of American Left politics stretching backward to the thirties and forward to the present in order to assert that political tradition as the heart of the authentic and original republic.

In making this rhetorical assertion that equates the Left tradition with the true national values, Pynchon seems to acknowledge that in American public discourse it is necessary to invoke the symbol of America, that any workable political position depends on some version of the logic of exceptionalism, the logic of noir authenticity. The novels work to purify that logic, to appropriate it in order to separate its promise of national redemption from the nationalist atrocities and materialist ambitions that the exceptionalist vision has embraced and abetted. In these novels, America is not the world's redemption; it can only redeem itself, by embracing the better version of itself that is to be found in traditions of homegrown leftism, of a (perhaps utopian) politics based on inclusion, equality, diversity, and participatory democracy. This reassertion of a version of authenticity gives Pynchon's later conspiracy narratives a political project that had seemed impossible in the more radical undermining of authenticity that takes place in texts like *The Parallax View* (and, in its own way, *The Crying of Lot 49*). With this in mind, I turn now to a third set of conspiracy texts, in which the generalized problem of American dispossession that Pynchon raises, the problem of the tension between conspiracy and counterconspiracy, is given another kind of specific content by sixties-era novels about African American revolution.

{ 5 }

Black Ops

GHETTO SPACE AND COUNTERCONSPIRACY

My books are set in the Negro ghetto. They are as authentic as
The Autobiography of Malcolm X.

—CHESTER HIMES, *INTERVIEW IN LIFE MAGAZINE*

In this chapter I identify a third version of the transition from the noir detective story to the conspiracy narrative that takes place in the sixties and seventies. We have seen that the novels of Thomas Pynchon confront the political problem raised by conspiracy texts such as *The Parallax View* by using what I have been calling the "Two Americas model." In this model, the nation as defined by its relationship to consumer capitalism is envisioned as a conspiracy called "the American way of life," which produces a counterconspiracy as its double: the authentic America that is represented by the nation's dispossessed and recruited by Pynchon as the contemporary expression of a leftist American tradition. The issue of dispossession is taken up in another way in the sixties-era genre that I discuss in this chapter: the African American counterconspiracy narrative. This genre, too, is part of the evolution of the noir tradition, following the path we have seen in the last two chapters by suggesting the exhaustion of noir and hard-boiled detective genre conventions while preserving the critical potential and the politics of authenticity contained in that tradition. The conspiratorial vision of these texts incorporates African American literary and cultural traditions in order to confront the crises of sixties America by imagining the possibility of collective revolutionary action. While the alternative nationalism of Pynchon's novels looks to the American dispossessed as the true bearers of American identity, these novels of antiracist insurrection from the sixties and seventies argue for a form of black nationalism focused on a space that is figured as authentic and that is also a product of consumer capitalism's history: the inner-city ghetto.

I will be arguing that in the sixties era, the historically distinct discourse around "black authenticity" finds common ground with the discourse of "noir authenticity" that is at the center of this book. The African American literary tradition and the noir tradition meet in counterconspiracy narrative, which claims a division between a consumerist black bourgeoisie and an urban black underclass that is defined spatially in terms of its exclusion from the suburban life of the consumers' republic. Thus the ghetto is represented as the site of an authentic and revolutionary black identity, a place where large political and economic forces are seen to have destructive effects on particular American communities, and where it becomes possible to envision collective (though not necessarily successful) forms of responsive political action.

The major figure in the story of noir's relevance to black counterconspiracy is Chester Himes, and I begin by showing how Himes's late book *Blind Man with a Pistol* dramatizes the disappearance of the hard-boiled detective novel and the emergence of the conspiracy plot. Through examination of this book, along with a brief look at the films of the "blaxploitation" cycle, it is possible to see the emergence of a new way of representing the ghetto as a site of potentially authentic resistance to American consumer culture. This potential is explored further in Himes's last, unfinished novel *Plan B* and Sam Greenlee's *The Spook Who Sat by the Door*. Both books imagine revolutionary and apocalyptic racial conflict that begins in the American ghetto; in the process, they extend the Pynchonian attempt to envision an oppositional politics of conspiracy, articulating a racially specific version of the Two Americas model.

Conspiracies of Cash

As with the New Hollywood antinoir films I discussed in chapter 3, Chester Himes's 1969 novel *Blind Man with a Pistol* works self-consciously within the noir tradition in order to show how the politics of the sixties—with emphasis on the politics of race—render that tradition obsolete, while the book simultaneously lays the groundwork for the postmodern conspiracy novel.[1] The last finished work in his series of Harlem Detective novels, *Blind Man* is a mystery with no solution, an investigation that leads only to more questions and crimes, that cannot be resolved because of hidden forces and agendas, and that ends in chaos and confusion. Claiming the upheavals of the sixties as his inspiration, Himes created a hard-boiled detective story that enacts its own obsolescence. By evoking a web of colluding forces that prevents his detectives from solving the novel's mystery, Himes begins the work that we have seen to be central to the various incarnations of sixties-era conspiracy narrative; he forces our attention to larger issues of institutional racism and other betrayals of the social contract that serve the interests of those with wealth and power. In doing so, *Blind Man* acknowledges and announces the death of the noir detective story.

Having already published five novels in the United States, in the fifties Himes relocated to Europe, where the publisher Marcel Duhamel convinced him to write a detective novel for Gallimard's *Série noire*. He wound up completing nine crime novels, all set in Harlem and all featuring the black police detectives

Coffin Ed Johnson and Grave Digger Jones. Himes's work in this series was violent, satirical, and bluntly written from the start, but the later books became increasingly cynical, strange, and gory, culminating in explosions of narrative and racial chaos—and *Blind Man with a Pistol* takes this trajectory to a kind of endpoint. It undermines the basis of the detective story—the promise it holds forth that the conspiracy of forces can be known and described or, at least in the noir tradition, pointed to—by multiplying its storylines indiscriminately instead of bringing them together, until they fly off crazily in all directions, unresolved and unconnected. Three corpses are discovered in the basement of the house of a hundred-year old black Mormon with eleven wives whose children go naked and eat from a trough. A gay hustler wearing a "black power" fez kills a white john—maybe—and steals his pants. A suspect in the case is murdered by a knife-wielding lesbian dancing in a downtown club. A massive riot breaks out on "Nat Turner Day" when three protest marches converge in Harlem, and the rioting escalates throughout the novel.

Chaos and violence are nothing new for Himes, but what is new is the complete inability of Coffin Ed and Grave Digger to solve any of the crimes and mysteries that face them. Throughout the Harlem novels, Himes's heroes wrap up each individual case like the good hard-boiled detectives they are, but in *Blind Man* they fail—not because of their own shortcomings, but because of conspiratorial forces. Some combination of institutional racism, ambition on the part of the detectives' superiors, a shadowy organization called "the Syndicate," and a mysterious "mister Big" has come together to block them from solving the case. These, of course, are exactly the sort of barriers that the detective in a novel is *supposed* to overcome—the whole point of being a male detective-hero is to discern and confront the hidden forces that are trying to stop him from solving the mystery, at least at the local level. But by the end of *Blind Man*, Grave Digger and Coffin Ed have made no progress and are reduced to shooting rats for amusement as the final, apocalyptic riot erupts. A requiem for the noir detective novel, *Blind Man* undermines the conventions of the genre in order to evoke a tangled web of deliberate and historical conspiracies, its sticky threads combining race, politics, and commerce.

Throughout his writing career, Himes was concerned with how the absurdity of race deforms the lives and daily interactions of his characters; so in this sense, the narrative chaos and conspiracies of skin in *Blind Man with a Pistol* are simply the next logical development in a career-long engagement with the illogic of race. But it is a development that is motivated by the politics of the contemporary moment, which is to say, the sixties. Up to this point in the Harlem novels, Himes had carried out his explorations of race in America through variations on a recognizable generic framework, and the occasion for his demolition of that genre is perceived by Himes to be a historical shift in the politics of race. In the preface to *Blind Man*, Himes explicitly suggests that the novel is meant as a response to the social conditions and political context of the sixties:

A friend of mine, Phil Lomax, told me this story about a blind man with a pistol shooting at a man who had slapped him on a subway train and killing an innocent bystander . . . and I thought, damn right, sounds just like today's news, riots in the ghettos, war in Vietnam, masochistic doings in the Middle East. And then I thought of some of our loudmouthed leaders urging our vulnerable soul brothers on to getting themselves killed, and thought further that all unorganized violence is like a blind man with a pistol. (5)

The content of the book deliberately reflects the racial politics of its present: the riots, which recall the Watts riots of 1965, among others; the presence of a bespectacled black Muslim minister and leader named "Michael X"; the variety of antigovernmental causes and protests, including references to the Black Panthers and Martin Luther King. Likewise, Himes's all-encompassing distrust of "loudmouthed leaders" resonates with the antiestablishment critiques propagated by the antiwar movement, the countercultural New Left, and Black Power in its militant, post–civil rights form.

But his distrust of organizing systems—similar in its way to Pynchon's anarchistic bent—was too radical to have any faith in the idealistic claims made by the organizers of the movements and the marches. All good causes in Himes's world turn out to be money-making scams; all the voices of virtuous protest are revealed as fronts for con games, money-laundering organizations, the skin trade, or the mob. Himes's novel uncovers the broken promises of an American social contract undermined by commerce, as represented in the lives of the ordinary citizens of Harlem, whose most laudable desires—for justice, equality, or empowerment—are always being manipulated for the profit of others. It is an attempt to represent the situation of ghetto residents, all looking for a better way or a way out, caught between the conspiracies of official power and the conspiracies of unofficial power, perpetually betrayed into "unorganized" and self-destructive violence. Without aligning itself with any specific political movements of the sixties, Blind Man with a Pistol represents the unarticulated and collective longings that lay behind those movements, and finds those collective longings in the concentrated and bounded space of the ghetto. The politics implied in this representation of Harlem, relentless in its cynical unmasking of the profit motive that is found to lurk behind all allegedly good causes, suggests the way that Himes both investigates the issues that are central to the noir tradition and pushes those issues past the boundaries of noir form. As in the transition from film noir to conspiracy film, Blind Man violates generic conventions of the hard-boiled novel in order to formulate a version of hard-boiled politics that is appropriate to post-sixties America.

In my earlier chapters, I discussed the ways in which noir film and fiction represent the privatized, suburban—and white—space of American consumer culture in the postwar era as a degraded and inauthentic landscape. Himes preserves this attention to consumer capitalism, but he does so by concentrating on the inner city, precisely the area that was elided from the national mainstream as America became equated with suburbs and shopping centers. Symbolically, this inner city is the polar opposite of those white-populated suburbs, but it is also, for Himes, their double. The Harlem of *Blind Man with a Pistol* is a symptomatic space, in which free-market America sees itself in a funhouse mirror. It is the flipside, or the unconscious, of consumerist America, the place where the economic machinery, the capitalist id, lurking behind the shining kitchens of suburbia and the modern elegance of the corporate boardroom is exposed to our view.

So Himes's evocation of the problem of consumer culture in America—the central political problem raised in the noir and hard-boiled texts—takes place within the symbolic space of the black urban ghetto. It is there, he suggests, that the betrayal of American ideals of equality and inclusion are most visible, there that American values are shown in what Himes sees as their true form: the value of money. Throughout his detective books, he uses Harlem not as a realistic setting, but as a crucible in which to explore the racial consequences of American hypocrisy. Like a cracked but truth-telling mirror, the ghetto with its good causes that are actually criminal scams provides for Himes a reflection of the nation: a thin layer of idealistic language that pretends to conceal the violent struggle of individuals motivated by greed, capitalism barely made decent by the worm-eaten fig leaf of democracy.[2]

I have pointed out that all beliefs and ideologies in the book are revealed to be scams; someone is always profiting, the poor are always losing their hard-earned money, and the overall atmosphere is of a money-grubbing free-for-all of individual agents. Moreover, Himes's ghetto offers a grotesque, carnival version of mainstream consumer culture, in which televisions are sold and delivered in the middle of the night; businesses begin and fail so quickly that a sign reading "Chicken Auto Insurance" hangs on one storefront; and everything, including men, women, and baboon gonads, is for sale. Himes creates surreal lists of supermarket price displays, deli signs, billboards for beer, wigs, religion, activism, and politicians, all run together to create a sense of Harlem as a rundown carnival where poverty renders the barking of commodities as a cracked chorus:

Across Lenox Avenue, on the West Side, toward Seventh Avenue, were the original slums with their rat-ridden cold water flats unchanged, the dirty glass-fronted ground floors occupied by the customary supermarkets with hand-lettered ads on their plate-glass windows reading: "Fully cooked U.S. Govt. Inspected SMOKED HAMS 55c lb. . . . Secret Deodorant ICE-BLUE 79c. . . . California Seedless GRAPES 2 lbs 49c. . . . Fluffy ALL Controlled Suds 3 lbs pkg. 77c. . . . KING CRAB CLAWS lb 79c. . . . GLAD BAGS 99c." Delicatessens advertising: *"Frozen Chitterlings and*

other delicacies." . . . Notion stores with needles and buttons and thread
on display. . . . Barbershops. . . . Smokeshops. . . . Billboards advertising:
Whiskies, beers. . . . "HARYOU." . . . *Politicians running for congress.* . . .
"BEAUTY FAIR by CLAIRE: *WIGS, MEN'S HAIR PIECES,* "*CAPILIS-*
CIO." . . . Funeral Parlors. . . . Nightclubs. . . . "*Reverend Ike; 'See and hear this*
young man of God; A Prayer For The Sick And All Other Conditions In Ev-
ery Service; COME WITH YOUR BURDENS LEAVE WITH A SONG.'" . . .
Black citizens sitting on the stoops to their cold-water flats in the broil-
ing night. . . . Sports ganged in front of bars sucking marijuana. . . . Grit
and dust and dirt and litter floating idly in the hot dense air stirred up by
the passing of feet. (50–51; the ellipses are all Himes's)

But Himes represents the ghetto as a carnival that takes no joy in the transgressive appropriation and transformation of consumer practices by the "black
citizens" who inhabit the oppressive space that is evoked here. Instead, the
orgy of demented commercialism contributes to the book's sense that Harlem
is the place where the American mainstream is revealed to be truly absurd and
truly pitiless.

Confronted with the uneven developments of capitalism suggested by this
chaotic commercial streetscape, the noir detective no longer has any capacity
to intervene. Frustrated by their failure to solve any of the book's crimes, Grave
Digger remarks to Ed that "in this mother-raping country of IBM's I don't see
what they need you and me for anyway" (139). Himes's book suggests that what
is needed is not a better or more noble detective, but a new representational
model, a discourse that can extend and renew the political critique of consumer capitalism that is made in the classic hard-boiled novels. Dismantling
the American hard-boiled detective form from within, *Blind Man with a Pistol*
sets the stage for the politics of conspiracy that the sixties have made necessary.
That politics, emerging from representations of the black inner-city ghetto in
the sixties and seventies, is another version of the politics of authenticity.

Ghetto Authenticity

Although Himes's proto-conspiracy novel produced a new mutation in noir
politics, in doing so it drew on a long-standing black cultural and artistic tradition. It seems clear, after all, that a capacious enough definition of "conspiracy fiction" would wind up encompassing nearly the whole tradition of
African American literature. The tropes of the conspiracy novel have long
been central to African American literary production, beginning with the
slave narratives' evocation of individuals trying to apprehend and escape from
a brutal commercial system in which law, society, and geography are elements
in a vast conspiracy. Consider the work of some of the major writers of fiction

in the twentieth century: Richard Wright's naturalist depiction of American society as a cunning trap of race and class in *Native Son*; the retreat to the underground of Ralph Ellison's protagonist in his shadow history of the twentieth century, *Invisible Man*; Toni Morrison's patient and precise delineation of race and gender politics in the struggles of her characters to free themselves from American racial history. The list could be extended on and on: here are texts that evince an all-too-reasonable paranoia, that reveal the traces of an oppressively pervasive alignment of social power whose existence is frequently denied by those who benefit from it, and that employ the tools of literary and popular narrative forms in the service of a far-reaching social or political criticism.[3]

If African American literature has frequently represented race as a form of conspiracy, it has also represented many forms of resistance to the structures by which racial identities and inequalities are produced. The form of resistance that emerged in novels and films of the sixties and seventies was the revolutionary counterconspiracy narrative, which eschewed the passive mapping of conspiratorial networks in favor of active resistance. Looking back to attempted slave revolts and forward to science-fictional possibilities, these counterconspiracy narratives create scenarios in which black collectives plot in secrecy and then act to take control of their own destinies, to undermine white domination, and in some cases to claim their own dominion over America or even the world. The form has its own specific lineage in African American literature, including important antecedents such as Martin Delaney's *Blake, or the Huts of America* (serialized in *The Weekly Anglo-African* 1861–1862), Sutton Griggs's 1899 *Imperio in Imperium*, and George Schuyler's *Black Empire* (serialized in the *Pittsburgh Courier* 1936–1938).[4]

Starting in the late sixties, this tradition of imagining radical counterconspiracies became one of the defining themes in African American cultural production, a development that was surely inspired in part by the founding of the radical Black Panther Party (BPP) in 1966 and its rise to national prominence in the following year. (The BPP had its origins in inner-city Oakland—it was founded in order to combat racist police brutality—and its other national chapters were formed primarily in ghetto areas of other major American cities.) Among the texts that expressed versions of this theme are John A. Williams's *Sons of Darkness, Sons of Light* (1969), Ishmael Reed's *Mumbo Jumbo* (1972), Toni Morrison's *Song of Solomon* (1977), the film *Sweet Sweetback's Baadasssss Song* (1971)—and many of the films of the blaxploitation cycle that followed *Sweetback*, though the extent to which these films imagine *collective* action is subject to debate. In these books and films, the theme of counterconspiracy becomes the occasion for revisiting America's racial history, and in particular the discourse of black authenticity. In the process, African American literature's history of engagement with the ideas of conspiracy and authenticity assumes a new form that is defined by its use of the urban ghetto as a space of political resistance.

The issue of black authenticity is a complex and unique one, informed as it is by the particular history of American slavery, the one-drop rule, miscegenation law, the politics of skin color, racial "passing," and assimilation. These and many other legal and cultural legacies of our racial history have shaped the ongoing attempts on the part of African Americans and African American literature to formulate an identity that is, to one degree or another, both "black" and "American." So this issue cannot simply be assimilated into the concept of anticonsumerist noir authenticity as I have defined it in this study. Nonetheless, I will be arguing here that in the postwar and sixties-era context the discourse of black authenticity shares an alignment with the discourse of noir authenticity that I have been tracing, defining authentic modes of black identity against modes of black middle-class identity that are perceived as participating in the dominant consumer culture.[5]

Consumption overlaps with racial authenticity in ways that predate World War II—most notably in the long tradition of selling products like skin-lightening creams and hair-straightening processes, which literally hold out the promise that consumption can make the individual less black. (This conjunction of a racial definition premised on skin and visibility with American commerce is the target of George Schuyler's satirical 1931 novel *Black No More*, in which a machine that makes black people appear white becomes fantastically profitable.) But the current structure within which commerce and black authenticity are conjoined begins to take shape in the years after World War II. As Lizabeth Cohen shows in *A Consumers' Republic*, the new "consumers' republic" in which American citizenship came to be defined by consumption also delineated the ways in which racial equality was imagined as assimilation into the marketplace, as equal citizenship within the consumers' republic.

The early phase of the civil rights movement, Cohen argues, concentrated on the fight for equal access to public accommodations, "to the stores, restaurants, hotels, housing developments, theaters, bowling alleys, and other sites of consumption where consumers were expected, and black Americans increasingly expected, to fulfill the rights and obligations of purchasers as citizens" (174). The important gains made on this front had an unintended negative consequence in that "attention to democratizing the marketplace reinforced the Consumers' Republic's orientation toward 'expanding the pie' . . . and disinterest in redistributing economic resources to achieve more fundamental socioeconomic equality" (190). The focus on opening up equal access to commercial spaces, then, led to the rise of a black consumer class—a new formation of the "black bourgeoisie."

Meanwhile, a well-documented shift in the terrain of postwar consumption, the movement of families out of city centers and into suburban areas where shopping was done by car, was an overwhelmingly white trend. (Even black veterans benefiting from the GI Bill were mostly excluded, both by racism and lack of means, from the postwar American dream of homeownership.) As cities stagnated economically, the black communities who had come—and were still coming—to Northern cities in the great migration were hit especially hard. As Kenneth Jackson has shown, the legislation put in place during the thirties to create public housing for the poor, although it was well-intentioned, was structured so that local municipalities could decide whether to build such housing, in effect restricting housing projects to large urban centers and reinforcing racial segregation and "ghettoization." By the 1960s, the black ghetto was practically synonymous with urban poverty and crime, motivating further "white flight" to the suburbs in a vicious circle.

During this period the ghetto came to signify a black authenticity defined against mainstream "white" America and especially against a black bourgeoisie figured as inauthentic, both associated with consumer culture. For example, E. Franklin Frazier's 1957 study *Black Bourgeoisie* was a sociological portrait of the postwar black middle class described in terms that suggested that this class was comparable to the American bourgeoisie that Thorstein Veblen described at the turn of the century. Frazier saw this group as emulating "white" American systems of value, their desire to assimilate leading to an obsession with status that expressed itself in conspicuous consumption: "They have accepted unconditionally the values of the white bourgeois world: its morals and its canons of respectability, its standards of beauty and consumption. In fact, they have tended to overemphasize their conformity to white ideals" (26). Frazier's analysis did for the black bourgeoisie essentially what the contemporaneous critiques of David Riesman and William Whyte did for the white bourgeoisie, diagnosing its consumerist basis as inauthentic. While the black bourgeoisie tended to offer itself as representing "the best morals and manners of the Negro" (236), other African Americans tended to regard this as hypocrisy, and to regard the class as a whole as having abandoned the larger black community, its values, and its historical situation.[6]

The discourse of black authenticity suggests, then, that individualist materialism and conspicuous consumption separate black Americans of means from the larger black community, its collective culture and meanings. This tradition has sometimes extolled the virtues of a romanticized black folk that is poor, uneducated, and generally rural. But in the sixties the romance of the hovel became a romance of the ghetto, the urban space where the "folk" are more wised-up and less passive-seeming than those in rural settings: poor but hustling, unschooled but streetwise. As Donald Bogle observes, during

the late 1960s and early 1970s . . . in rejecting the black bourgeoisie, which had seemingly often aided and abetted White America through attempts at cultural assimilation, the new militant separatist black classes sometimes came to identify blackness with the trappings of the ghetto: the tenements as well as the talk, the mannerisms, and the sophistication of the streets—all of which appeared to mark a life lived close to one's black roots. Ghetto residents seemed to have a greater ethnic identity. (*Toms, Coons, Mulattoes, Mammies, and Bucks*, 236)

This shift is especially visible in the blaxploitation films of the seventies. Self-consciously displacing the didactic middle-class "message movies" defined by the presence of Sidney Poitier, these films featured tough ghetto heroes whose quests for justice or survival connected them to their urban communities through effects of authenticity.[7]

"Blaxploitation" describes a cycle of films produced in the seventies that capitalized on Hollywood's discovery that there was an audience for films that starred primarily black actors, dramatized racism in the medium of the crime story, and mingled the comic and the horrific in narratives that were both gritty realism and outrageous fantasy. In other words, it is a genre that appears to owe a great deal to the work of Chester Himes.[8] (The two films that are usually cited as the founding blaxploitation texts both have connections to Himes; he was a friend of Melvin Van Peebles, who directed *Sweet Sweetback's Baadasssss Song* [1971]—a Himesian film if ever there was one, surreal and over-the-top—and *Cotton Comes to Harlem* [1970] was an adaptation of one of his Harlem Detective novels.) Not surprisingly, then, blaxploitation is the site where the black ghetto is represented most consistently and insistently in American cultural productions of the seventies. The inner-cityscapes of blaxploitation are both lively and dangerous, and the films present themselves as portraits of black authenticity, of a world in which a vital African American culture is inseparable from the racism, poverty, and crime that define these urban spaces. The ghetto settings in these films are sites where the discourse of black authenticity is both articulated and debated.

The effect of authenticity in these films is produced, again, through a rejection of the black bourgeoisie and its values. In a 1971 response to *Sweet Sweetback's Baadasssss Song* in *Ebony*, Lerone Bennett criticized the film for participating in this strategy, which he sees as a logic of opposition rather than of revolution:

> In the pre-black days, Negroes generally reacted to the white image by defining themselves as counter-contrast conceptions. They tried, in other words, to become opposite Negroes, the opposite, that is, of what white people said Negroes were. This symbolic strategy is being abandoned by post-Watts blacks who are defining themselves as counter-counter-contrast conceptions, as the opposite, in short, of what Negroes said Negroes were. ("The Emancipation Orgasm: Sweetback in Wonderland," 108)

For Bennett, the film never achieves the revolutionary potential that Van Peebles claimed it had because it fails to produce new and aspirational images of black life and instead falls back on an aesthetic of ghetto authenticity defined as the opposite of the black bourgeoisie. Leaving aside the fraught question of whether Bennett or Van Peebles has it right, it is clear that Bennett has identified the dominant representational mode of black resistance in the sixties era. As Ed Guerrero writes of this debate, "Clearly, beyond the mid-1960s, lower-class blacks were increasingly dissatisfied with the exhausted black bourgeois paradigm of upward mobility through assimilation and started to identify the black experience with the defiant images and culture of the 'ghetto' and its hustling street life" (*Framing Blackness*, 89). The paradigm that defines black cultural production in the post-Watts era generally, including blaxploitation and black counterconspiracy narrative, is based on ghetto authenticity as a rejection of black bourgeois representations.

The issue of authenticity and its relationship to the ghetto is also raised in the other source text of blaxploitation, *Cotton Comes to Harlem*. Many of the films begin with a credit sequence in which a theme song plays over a kind of guided tour of the film's inner-city setting (usually Harlem): the title character strutting his way through traffic in *Shaft* (1971), a couple of junkies meandering along in *Superfly* (1972). The template for these sequences is the beginning of *Cotton*, in which we follow a car as it cruises the streets of Harlem. While famous landmarks and sunlit streets slide by, Melba Moore sings a song called "Black Enough": "Ain't now, but it's gonna be / Black enough for me." The lyric was written by the film's director, Ossie Davis, and by juxtaposing it with the Harlem montage Davis suggests at the outset the extent to which his film is concerned with presenting the ghetto as the space in which to pose the question of how to be "black enough." The phrase is taken up as a motif that runs through the film, one that is sometimes appropriated by con men—this is adapted from Himes, after all—like Deke O'Malley, who asks a crowd in preacherly tones, "Am I black enough for you?" But the film takes the question seriously, and its portrait of Harlem is more fond and slapstick-comical than Himes's; it consistently finds value and vitality in the culture of the ghetto.

Cotton does not assert the authenticity of that black ghetto culture so much as it offers a meditation on the issue, one that, taking its cue from Himes's narrative setup, evokes the history that has created the conflicted desire for black authenticity in the present. The "cotton" in the title is an actual bale of cotton in which Deke O'Malley has hidden $87,000 that he has taken from Harlemites in a Back-to-Africa scam—and which every character in the film is pursuing. The combination of money and cotton is a deliberate conjuring of the legacies of slavery, especially given the way that "cotton" is rendered not only as a symbolic condensation of America's racial past but also as a sort of character that can "come" to Harlem. It is as if cotton itself has stolen the money—representing the life savings, the lifelong labor, of ghetto residents—in a revisiting of the slave past. Harlem residents react to it as such. Grave Digger, upon finding a scrap of cotton, pretends to greet it as an old friend, ironically commenting on his distance from the rural South (Ed points out that Digger was born and raised in New York City), while a woman who is asked to help move the cotton refuses to get tricked by what seems like another scam: "Don't you think I got sense enough to know there ain't no such thing as a bale of cotton in Harlem?" As these responses suggest, the film's (and the novel's) intent in bringing cotton to Harlem is to create an absurd juxtaposition, an opposition between the contemporary ghetto and the plantation past.

But the initial opposition gives way to more complicated connections between the two historical spaces, blurring the line that separates them. In her book *Black City Cinema*, Paula Massood sees in blaxploitation the emergence of a "black ghetto chronotope." In this compression of African American history rendered as a spatial representation, the images of the ghetto as a complex and recognizable space through which the films guide us are both aware of and opposed to the sociological portrait of the pathological black ghetto that sixties documents like the Moynihan Report presented. But she notes that *Cotton Comes to Harlem* represents the meeting of the ghetto formation with another chronotope familiar from cinematic history, one that she calls the "antebellum idyll," as represented in the tradition of films set in the rural South during the slave era. *Cotton* creates "interconnections between the antebellum idyll and contemporary ghetto spaces by suggesting the legacy of the rural South in the modern northern city" (90). In doing so, the film asserts the triumph of the modern ghetto over the slave past while at the same time suggesting that that past has shaped African American life in the present.

In the climactic sequence of *Cotton*, a stripper who has been yearning to make her show more socially conscious puts on a performance at the Apollo that incorporates a new prop: the ubiquitous cotton bale. Appearing on stage in slave garb, she proceeds to strip down to a bikini adorned with cotton balls while tearing at the bale in a performance of long-sought revenge and liberation. Music again provides a gloss on the action; she dances to the film's title song, a show tune with hints of funk that evokes black enslavement to cotton while warning that when cotton comes to Harlem, "we kick cotton's ass." (The performance clearly alludes to the sexual violence of slavery, but its apparent equation of liberation with striptease suggests that the show, true to the spirit of Himes, is a cynical spectacle in which the naïve desire to perform social consciousness takes the form of further exploitation.) This sequence, which also includes a white villain who lurks in the Apollo wearing a blackface minstrel disguise, suggests the extent to which *Cotton*'s consideration of the question of ghetto authenticity requires it to revisit the slave past in ways that assert the authentic value of the Northern urban blackness that will kick cotton's ass, but that have not left behind the history that links Harlem to cotton.

The film reminds us, then, that the issue of black authenticity, its contradictions and its politics, begins with the history of slavery. African American literature and other cultural productions inevitably return to the memory and the "chronotope" of the rural South with ambivalence; they return to a South that is both the reservoir of black history and the source of the economic atrocity that

FIGURE 19 *A plantation-themed striptease on a bale of cotton at Harlem's Apollo Theater.*
Cotton Comes to Harlem.

has produced a legacy of black suffering. To return is therefore both to recover that history and to confront that legacy, to attempt to locate a black American identity that is neither owned by others nor participating in the economic systems that facilitated the ownership of black subjects in the past.[9] Given this context, it is not surprising that definitions of black authenticity have tended to be skeptical of capitalist, materialist success and of the black bourgeoisie's appropriation of "white" models of economic progress and consumption.

In the sixties and seventies, the return to the South and slavery is enacted, in blaxploitation and counterconspiracy texts, through a figuring of the ghetto as the repetition and the inverse of the slave plantation, a space in which to recuperate the potential for revolutionary change that could never be realized in the context of the slaveowning South. Although the connection between these two powerfully symbolic spaces is explicit in *Cotton Comes to Harlem*, it shapes the whole blaxploitation cycle. All these films are implicitly about the Great Migration and concerned with the ways in which black urban residents, born and bred in the Northern city, have formed new kinds of communities and are plagued by new kinds of racial trouble.[10]

The connection is most vivid in blaxploitation films that are set not in the ghetto but on the plantation—notably *Mandingo* (1975) and its sequel *Drum* (1976). These are films that really put the "exploitation" back in blaxploitation— they are loaded with bizarre sex and violence, much of it interracial and all of it gratuitous and sensationalized—but they also bring the politics of the seventies ghetto to the slave plantation. As with the striptease in *Cotton*, these films combine exploitative material with a deliberate effort to revise and reverse the cinematic conventions of the antebellum narrative. *Drum*, for example, is a festival of bare breasts, blood, and bad acting that comes as a bit of a surprise after a somber credit sequence that includes African-tinged blues playing over woodcut-style images of slavery's brutality and a documentary-style voice-over introduction. As this prefatory material suggests, the film has a distinct politics, one that employs the plantation as a metaphorical space in which to imagine the possibility of black revolution in the seventies. Indeed, both films place a conflicted slave character at the center of the story—Drum in the sequel is the son of Mede from *Mandingo*, and both are played by Ken Norton—and put him into dialogue with a character who represents a more radical political position and whose martyrdom pushes the protagonist toward a potential political awakening.

In *Drum*, the title character is a house servant—the original inauthentic position—who both befriends and battles with his fellow-slave Blaise. At the film's end, Blaise leads a slave revolt in which the plantation house is burned down and many of the white characters are killed—although the rebels are then massacred by patrollers. The film ends with the image of Drum running away, his future uncertain—the image freezes and takes its place alongside the images of slavery from the credit sequence—which is at least a better fate than his father's in *Mandingo*, where Mede is boiled alive as punishment for sleeping with a white woman. Drum never identifies himself fully with the politics of black revolution, but the film nonetheless suggests a continuity in which those politics provide the link between the slave era the film portrays and the seventies context in which the film was made, a link between slave revolt and post–civil rights black militancy. *Drum* and *Mandingo*, for all their absurdities and excesses, return to the source of the American racial conspiracy in order to provide a sympathetic and tragic vision both of apocalyptic black revolution and of the conflicted character who struggles toward an authentic black identity. In doing so, they follow *Cotton Comes to Harlem* in suggesting the necessity of revisiting the space of the plantation in order to envision the kind of political action that might emerge from the space of the ghetto.

The conspiracy that begins with the economics of slavery and the confinement of slaves to the plantation finds a corollary in the seventies' cinematic portrayal of the ghetto as a claustrophobic space that bounds the lives of its inhabitants. The ghetto, like slavery, is a trap that confines people and reduces their mobility, but because it is a trap it concentrates black frustration and anger within a strictly limited geographical space. Indeed, it is the concreteness of the locale that makes the prospect of political action imaginable. Unlike conspiracy texts such as *The Parallax View*, in which consumer capitalism has ballooned to such huge proportions that it seems unassailable, these texts begin from a place where the racial and economic effects, if not the sources, of oppressive power are visible and recognized. If the ghetto appears, then, as a space where conspiratorial power operates from without on its citizens—a representation that has its own history in African American texts[11]—the black counterconspiracy narratives of the sixties and seventies approach that problem from the flipside. As in *Blind Man with a Pistol*, the ghetto here is both the opposite of the mainstream consumer culture and its double, a space outside of the marketplace and the place where the logic of the marketplace is realized as a brutal absurdity. In order to see how this conception of the ghetto enables particular visions of collective resistance, I turn now to my two examples of the counterconspiracy novel, Himes's *Plan B* and Sam Greenlee's *The Spook Who Sat by the Door*.

Uprising and Apocalypse

The Spook Who Sat by the Door, published in 1969 and adapted faithfully in a 1973 film version, tells the story of the none-too-subtly named revolutionary Dan Freeman, who becomes the first African American CIA agent—because he wants to get to know his enemy. Upon leaving the agency he returns to the Chicago ghetto where he grew up and takes employment as a social worker while pursuing his real work, organizing the local gangs into a guerrilla combat force. His inner-city background is a key credential for establishing his status as a paragon of black authenticity, and although it is the white power structure that Freeman attacks, the book makes it clear throughout that his real enemy is the assimilationist and consumerist black bourgeoisie.

When the CIA sets up a competition to find an African American worthy of joining its ranks, Freeman finds himself in "a black middle-class reunion," surrounded by men who share Ivy League backgrounds, fraternities, and social aspirations, men whom Freeman (or Greenlee) mocks for the way that they define themselves through consumption: "Drop those brand names: GE, Magnavox, Ford, GM, Chrysler, Zenith, Brooks Brothers, Florsheim. Johnny Walker, Chivas Regal, Jack Daniels. Imported beer. Du Pont carpeting, wall to wall. Wall-to-wall drags with split-level minds, remote-control color TV souls and credit-card hearts" (12, 14). This litany is like countless other critiques of consumer culture in American literature and sociology—it echoes Herbert Marcuse's claim in *One-Dimensional Man* that postwar citizens "recognize themselves in their commodities; they find their soul in their automobile, hi-fi set, split-level home, kitchen equipment" (9)—and its use here aligns the black bourgeoisie with the mainstream of American materialist individualism.

Freeman differentiates himself from this self-interested middle class through his identification with a larger black community; as one character says to him: "You hate all the Negro middle class because you think they don't do enough to help other Negroes" (53). This tension is always present in some form in black counterconspiracy texts, although it is not always the powerful antipathy that Greenlee describes. In John A. Williams's 1969 novel *Sons of Darkness, Sons of Light* the protagonist is a middle-class civil rights activist who gets fed up with his impotence and takes action in a way that ultimately touches off a black ghetto revolt and potential race war. Unlike Greenlee, who sees the black bourgeoisie as hopelessly compromised, Williams suggests that revolutionary action only becomes possible when the black bourgeoisie is radicalized and finds common cause with the black underclass: "The cops hadn't looked at status symbols, only black faces, and therefore, pounding down the streets, clubbing anything black, murdering anything black, had welded together the ghetto and the middle-class Negro" (236). The tension between the black middle class and the ghetto class provides the sixties version of an opposition that extends back to slavery and the figure of the house servant or "Uncle Tom" who fails to achieve revolutionary consciousness. As Kali Tal observes in surveying antecedents of the black counterconspiracy novel such as *Imperium in Imperio* and *Black Empire*, the genre is often centered around the relationship between two characters who represent the strain between black militancy and a moderate or pacifist humanism—as we shall see, this is true both in *Spook* and in *Plan B.*

Spook makes the militant character its protagonist and point of identification. Freeman spearheads his counterconspiracy in order to organize the ghetto collectively, with the ultimate goal of making himself irrelevant. In order to do so, he has to operate as a double agent, so he disguises himself by surrounding himself with consumer comforts, and Greenlee includes carefully chosen lists of brand names, making it clear that Freeman wants to present himself as a man defined by his purchasing choices:

> In less than a month the apartment said everything he wanted about the new Freeman. . . . He drank and served Chivas Regal, Jack Daniels black label, Beefeaters gin, Remy Martin, Carlsberg, Heineken's, La Batts and Ballantine. He had matching AR speakers in teak cabinets, Garrard changer with Shure cartridge and a Fisher solid-state amp with seventy-five watts power per channel. A Tandberg stereo tape recorder, a color television set, which could be played through the stereo system, and videotape completed the system. (81)

The lists go on like this, and we are reminded throughout the book of what car he is driving, what liquor he is drinking, what brand he is wearing. Presenting himself as a sellout who could not possibly be a revolutionary because he has too much to lose, Freeman becomes the perfect image of a class that equates taste with brand names and the good life with ownership. He imitates not the white consumer, but what he sees as the black consumer's imitation of the white: a performance of black inauthenticity.

In this project, he draws on the African American traditions of double-consciousness and "wearing the mask" and uses them to make himself the perfect undercover agent. As the double meaning of "spook" in the title suggests, to be black in America is already to cultivate the talents of an espionage agent. Freeman guards his private, revolutionary self closely and keeps it from view except when he is with his underground army. Keeping that authentic black self hidden from view, he describes his espionage work in terms that explicitly link the ghetto to the plantation, so that social workers like Freeman are the house servants and inner-city residents the field slaves; his role is to pretend to be "the house slave [hired] to keep the dangerous, dumb, nasty field slaves quiet" (186).

Freeman extends the comparison between ghetto and plantation in the history lessons that he gives to his recruits, in which the heroes are the leaders of slave revolts. He then proceeds, as in *Mandingo* and *Drum*, to undermine the historical myth of the antebellum idyll by revisiting the genre of the plantation movie: "MGM in technicolor. Big-ass house, look like the White House, big porch on the front, big white pillars. . . . Barefoot darky sittin' on the steps plunkin' a banjo" (115). Invoking the history that connects ghetto residents to their cultural past in the rural South, Freeman tells them that in order to fight well and successfully each of them must find his "nigger pride," which he compares to the precious individual items that African Americans in Northern cities have brought with them from the South: "Down inside that big trunk with the big lock, wrapped up inside tissue paper and cotton batting. . . . It's too precious to even take out every now and then to look at and feel, but they know it's there" (113). He proposes, in other words, a system of value that is opposed to the values of materialism, an alternative ethic of ownership that is based on the preciousness of connections to black traditions and history. This secret valuable, this black authenticity, must be guarded and hidden away while Freeman wears the Brooks Brothers mask and pretends to define himself in accordance with the consumerist simulacrum of values he sees in the black middle class.

If the African American is already an agent, then the ghetto and its gangs, Freeman argues, "have always been an underground" (96). Because the ghetto keeps black urban poverty separate from the rest of the city and its suburbs, it effectively renders ghetto residents as invisible. Located outside the spaces and practices of citizenship and without access to the consumption that constitutes citizenship, the ghetto's invisibility makes it potentially available for underground revolutionary activity. Like Pynchon's imagined enclaves of outsiders, it is a kind of alternative nation in which the mainstream national values are inverted and parodied. Greenlee, like a more polite version of Himes, renders the Chicago ghetto as a place that is both oppressive and vital, an alternate city defined by illegal commerce and populated by outsiders of all sorts: criminals, winos, prostitutes, junkies, and the unemployed. The ghetto is alive with the possibility of revolution, "a bomb waiting to explode," and when the revolutionaries begin their attacks on the National Guard troops that have moved in, the neighborhood becomes united as a true community in its support of the guerrillas who move "easily and silently through the ghetto which offered them affection and support, their coloration finally protective" (237). The revolution moves outward from Chicago, organizing cells in all the black ghetto communities of America's cities, uniting the many locations of this alternative black nation.

Greenlee's counterconspiracy novel provides its own version of the Two Americas model, opposing the authentically black and revolutionary inner-city to mainstream American spaces. For a contrast to the ghetto's seedy vitality, Greenlee turns to Washington, D.C. ("DC"), site of Freeman's CIA training and employment and "one of the squarest towns in the world" (33). The book uses DC not just as a representative city, but as a representation of America in city form, focusing on its pompous, ugly architecture and national monuments—remember that the book compares plantation houses to the White House—to paint a picture of DC as a microcosm of national hypocrisies, where "within walking distance of the immaculate, white, neoclassical center lie some of the worst ghetto slums in the United States" (33). The nation's capital, appropriately, contains versions of the two opposed Americas that the book describes.

In Freeman's rendering of DC as national space, it is even described, in an echo of Pynchon's vision of the sprawling disaster of California land development, as a desecration of the natural landscape: "The buildings squatted vast and ugly, a marble and granite conglomeration of the worst of neoclassical and government-modern architecture, an ugly abscess created by bulldozers and billions in the midst of the once-beautiful north Virginia woods. A cancerous abscess, he thought, sending out its tendrils of infection tens of thousands of miles" (67). If the ghetto is the space of black authenticity, DC is the spatial corollary of the nation's diseased inauthenticity, where consumer culture and government work in tandem, as with the book's descriptions of politicians selling themselves using targeted marketing techniques. The political conflict that *Spook* sets up is played out in these geographical terms, between two Americas inhabiting the nation's boundaries simultaneously: the conspiracy America, defined by consumption-as-citizenship, spreading cancerously outward from Washington, D.C., and the counterconspiracy of an authentically black America setting up points of resistance in the underground of the nation's ghettos.

While *The Spook Who Sat by the Door* envisions black counterconspiracy in terms of a clear opposition between authentic revolutionary identity and inauthentic consumerist identity as represented by the black bourgeoisie, Chester Himes employs these terms while putting them in the service of his satirical and apocalyptic vision of black revolution. *Plan B* is the tenth novel of Chester

Himes's Harlem *Série noire* cycle, and it continues to meditate on the issues raised in *Blind Man with a Pistol*. Never finished, the book was only published after Himes's death, but it is clearly the final chapter in his increasingly bleak portrayal of racial politics in the sixties and seventies. While *Blind Man* imagines the ghetto space of Harlem as the place where conspiracies of racial politics and commercial interests combine to kill off the detective form, *Plan B* describes a response to these conspiracies that begins, inevitably, on the turf of Harlem and that ends with the literal deaths of Grave Digger and Coffin Ed. Although its story unfolds in a series of convolutions and flashbacks, at the center is a Southern black man named Tomsson Black, who has spent time in the Black Panthers and other militant groups as well as studying Marxism in a tour of communist countries, and who ends up serving time in prison for raping a wealthy white woman who had invited his advances. Upon his release he receives a large check from the woman and moves to Harlem, where he founds a meat-packing company, Chitterlings, Inc., that ultimately serves to fund and front for his actual business: arming the nation's black citizens for revolution.

The book opens, arrestingly, in a seedy apartment in Harlem, where a man named T-Bone and his prostitute girlfriend Tang receive a floral delivery that is found to contain an M-14 automatic rifle and a note telling them to wait for instructions. Although T-Bone reacts with fear and skepticism, Tang is inspired by the prospect of killing white policemen. T-Bone responds:

> "Wut?. . . . Shoot a white police? Someun 'spects me tuh shoot de white police?"
>
> "Why not? You wanna uprise, don't you?"
>
> "Uprise? Whore, is you crazy? Uprise where?"
>
> "Uprise here, nigger. Is you that stupid? Here we is and here we is gonna uprise." (9)

Like Greenlee, Himes portrays the ghetto as the locale where it is possible to imagine that people are ready to "uprise," a term that already neatly combines the representation of racial equality as upward movement with the toppling of a government by its people. As in *Blind Man* and *Spook*, the representation of the ghetto in *Plan B* is central to the politics of revolution that it envisions. Himes spends one whole eventless chapter painting a picture of one area of Harlem, although the chapter begins by claiming, "No one can visualize what Eighth Avenue is like who hasn't seen it" (48). The suggestion here is that the black ghetto can only be known by those who live there, that it is comprehensible only to those who have a deep connection to and history with the ghetto. But unlike *Spook*'s use of the ghetto as a site of authenticity, *Plan B* will ultimately suggest that there is no authenticity to be found anywhere in America.

The novel pushes outside of the space of Harlem in a way that none of Himes's previous detective novels do, and initially it does so in order to revisit the Southern rural tradition that is evoked but not represented in *Cotton Comes to Harlem*. One long section early on in the book is devoted to the site where Tomsson Black's company Chitterlings, Inc. opened for business. Himes takes two chapters to describe the lives of the people associated with the Chitterlings, Inc. site, which had been a failed sugarcane plantation. The result is a wild satire of the Southern Gothic tradition—in which the South is rendered as a depraved hellhole of perpetual rape, incest, and violence—that one-ups Faulkner and then goes several degrees further. With his deadpan narrative of peckerwood idiocy and lust, dewy young maidens longing for sodomy, gang rapes, parents killing children, Himes makes the exploitative excesses of *Mandingo* and *Drum* look prudish. As in those films, the return to the antebellum South in *Plan B* creates parallels between the ghetto and the plantation; the book alternates between chapters dealing with the history behind the creation of Chitterlings, Inc. and the investigation into the gun deliveries in present-day Harlem. The two spaces are crucially linked by the history of race, but Himes finds no usable revolutionary tradition in the past, no slave revolts or black authenticity. If he is locating the politics of the present in his revisionary portrayal of the antebellum South, what he finds there is not the preciousness of black history but a chaotic carnival of atrocities, the history of race in America repeating itself endlessly.

Ultimately, the book reaches outward from Harlem and the plantation to encompass all of American life. Like *Spook*, *Plan B* is interested in the tension between the black ghetto and America as a whole, but it abandons *Spook*'s essentially realistic mode and moves instead into wildly parodic phantasmagoria. Both books draw on the politics of the sixties, and evoke in particular the 1967 appearance of the leather-clad, beret-wearing Black Panthers on the TV news—a media event that brought the image of black men with guns into the mainstream national consciousness. But whereas Greenlee envisions a logical and organized narrative proceeding from that image, in which the black men with guns go to war with the nation at large, Himes sees the blossoming of unorganized and uncontrollable violence. Greenlee establishes a clear-cut opposition between the inauthentic space of America and the space of ghetto America, while in Himes the fantastical space of his imagined Harlem—forced into the public consciousness by the appearance of deadly black men firing automatic weapons—spreads outward until all of America is engulfed in convulsions of racial absurdity.

In fact, *Plan B* is not a story of individual characters at all; Grave Digger and Coffin Ed and even Tomsson Black are pushed into the background as the narrative focus turns to the nation's black and white communities in order to exhume the American racial unconscious. Himes suggests that to write fiction about the large and complex processes of racial conspiracy and counterconspiracy requires a narrative that tracks not individuals but communities, collective entities, national policies, and economic trends. When one black gunman massacres a group of parading white policemen, the book explains that as a result "the stock market crashed. The dollar fell on the world market. The very structure of capitalism began to crumble. . . . All over the world, millions of capitalists sought means to invest their wealth in the communist east" (182). We are told what the white and black communities are feeling and what they are doing, how guilt and fear shape their actions, and what histories have contributed to the current disaster.

Like a version of Flaubert's *Salammbô* for sixties racial politics, *Plan B* describes its imagined history as an orgy of violence, acted out by collective forces, in which every gory detail is visible but anonymous. Himes even makes us privy to the grotesquely sexualized racial nightmares of randomly selected white citizens across the nation:

> One white woman dreamed that a black had gouged out one of her breasts and was thrusting his enormous black penis, which had two thick, brutal horns, into the bloody hole.
>
> A middle-aged white advertising executive dreamed that a giant nude black, with testicles hanging from his crotch like huge black bombs, was coming toward him, firing from a disembodied penis as big as a cannon barrel. He could feel each of the big solid bullets as it penetrated his body. (139)

And so on. But these fantasies are no more fantastic than the "real" narrative. They are a kind of distillation of the actual events of the book, in which the brutalities of America's racial history are brutally relived—but in which the psychoanalytic repetition does not heal but only reasserts the intractability and destructiveness of race, chronicled in the escalating madness of the book's events. Lynching is revived, and any black man appearing in public is killed on sight, so black men go underground to the sewers and conduits "made appealing by black writers" (185)—apparently a jab at Ellison's *Invisible Man*—but they are pursued by whites with guns who hunt them for sport. The collective narrative that Himes constructs, in other words, does not describe the kind of collective *action* that Greenlee writes about; in fact this kind of action is impossible in Himes's pitiless satire.

Whereas *Spook* insists on black authenticity as an alternative form of value that is opposed to the consumerist mainstream and the inauthentic black middle class, *Plan B* finds that race and consumer culture are so inextricably combined in American life that there is no authentic position for African Americans to inhabit or claim. The book's Tar-Baby-black humor is frequently expressed in scenes where the national consumer culture is mingled with ideologies of race in order to reveal all American racial identities to be parodies of themselves. At the novel's opening we meet T-Bone "laughing like an idiot at two blackfaced white minstrels on the television screen who earned a fortune by blacking their faces and acting just as foolish as T-Bone had done for free all his life" (3–4). Meanwhile this minstrel program in which whites appear black is interrupted by a commercial for a skin-lightening cream—or maybe just a cleanser—promising to take the dark taint from the buyer's skin: "*Nucreme*, a product that made dirty skin so fresh and white" (6). This is Himes's vision of race in America in a nutshell: an absurdity in which pernicious images of black people are made and sold both to white people stupid enough to believe them and to black people stupid enough to consume the images that represent them as being just as stupid as they really are. Employing this logic, *Plan B* undermines the notion of black authenticity; the images from the consumer culture that appear in this book truly reflect the book's racial vision, with white and black locked in a repulsively erotic embrace. The absurd and offensive racial representations that are daily offered for consumption are for Himes an accurate picture of America, and the book draws from the well of commercial images to create a mingling of the races that reflects the way in which they are stuck together in a gluey mess of desire and hatred, imitation and resentment.

This mingling of black and white in commerce ends in an image of apocalypse that mirrors the book's narrative trajectory. To kill a lone black gunman, the police bring out a riot tank, but it has difficulty locating him:

> The cannon seemed frustrated at not seeing a black face to shoot at, and began to shoot explosive shells at the black plaster-of-paris mannequins in a display of beach wear in a department store window.
>
> The concussion was devastating. Splintered glass filled the air like a sand storm. Faces were split open and lacerated by flying glass splinters. One woman's head was completely cut off by a piece of flying glass as large as a guillotine. Varicolored wigs flew from white heads like frightened long-haired birds taking flight. Many other men, women, and children were stripped stark naked by the force of the concussion. (181)

The pointless destruction of the mannequins—imitation black people made to facilitate the selling of products to real black people—becomes a massacre of white people that is also an unmasking, tearing away their wigs and their clothes. For Himes, there is no black authenticity to be recovered and used as a site of resistance; rather, the book's racial violence creates a frenzy in which all the imitations and disguises of race enabled by consumer culture are revealed and stripped away just long enough to make the nation's defining inauthenticity visible.

This universal inauthenticity makes *Plan B* more pessimistic about the possibility of black revolution than *The Spook Who Sat by the Door*. The black gunmen remain isolated, acting individually to create panic and chaos, and by the end Tomsson Black concludes that his plan has been a failure and that any collective and organized uprising is impossible: "Now all he could do was complete the distribution of the guns and let maniacal, unorganized, and uncontrolled blacks massacre enough whites to make a dent in the white man's hypocrisy, before the entire black race was massacred in retaliation" (200–201). Maybe African Americans will be killed off en masse, or maybe white Americans aren't quite capable of perpetrating that level of atrocity (again). Either way, Black sees violent revolution as the only viable plan. Like *Spook*'s Freeman, he rejects all forms of assimilation as hopeless, but unlike Freeman he has given up on the hope that counterconspiracy can succeed; he simply considers racial apocalypse to be preferable to the status quo.

Despite the many differences between these two books, the allegorical use to which they put their main characters links them, and suggests that these counterconspiracy texts share a common understanding of the issues they confront. The two protagonists' names contain similar allegorical resonances, ones that again suggest continuities and tensions between the ghetto and the slave past. Tomsson Black has named himself as "Black," while the suggestion that he is Uncle Tom's son serves both as a recognition and rejection of that inheritance. His self-naming is also a rejection of American icons that mirrors *Spook*'s rejection of DC-as-American icon; he was born George Washington Lincoln. Meanwhile, Freeman calls himself "Uncle Tom" in his revolutionary communiqués, so, like Black's, his name suggests that carving out the revolutionary black identity of a freeman involves simultaneously recalling the history of black servitude and taking the disguise of the assimilationist black bourgeoisie to which these characters are opposed. Just as Freeman wears the mask of the black consumer class, Black operates his Plan B while hiding behind his public persona as the assimilationist executive of a profitable commercial enterprise whose name, Chitterlings, Inc., suggests again that he makes his revolution out of a history that starts low on the hog. He smuggles blackness in under his black capitalist Uncle Tom disguise, and turns chitterlings into money and guns, the tools with which to violently dismantle the master's house.

The symbolic structure contained in these names comes to a crisis in the conclusions of the two books, in ways that reveal, again, the extent to which both books are similarly concerned with issues of authenticity and how they approach those issues differently. They both conclude with allegorical scenes in which the authentic revolutionary symbolically kills off the black bourgeoisie—the inauthentic part of himself—and is, perhaps, himself killed in the conflict. Throughout *Spook*, Freeman debates his childhood friend Dawson, who is now a policeman, and tries to figure out how to enlist him in the revolutionary cause. In the final scene, Dawson learns that Freeman is "Uncle Tom" and comes to arrest him; Freeman kills him, but in the struggle he is wounded—fatally, the book suggests. Bleeding, he sends out word to start full-scale assaults from all his ghetto cells, and the book ends at that transitional moment, Freeman perhaps dead and the revolution's future uncertain.

At the end of *Plan B*, Tomsson Black's cover is blown, too—by Grave Digger and Coffin Ed. (Although Himes never finished the book, he did draft an ending.) Himes emphasizes the importance and depth of the conflict between revolutionary action and middle-class accommodation by putting his two detectives on opposing sides. After speaking with one voice and finishing each other's sentences for nine straight novels, they now disagree, violently. When Coffin Ed threatens Black, Grave Digger shoots him dead and then is immediately killed by Black, who claims he cannot trust him. The book's final word comes from a woman who works for Black and witnesses the killings; "I hope you know what you're doing," she says, and it is hard not to share her skepticism.[12] The future that Black has described of a brutal American race war may be inevitable, in Himes's view, but it is not a triumphant vision of counterconspiracy. Instead of black collective action, sympathetic and potentially copacetic characters like Ed, Digger, and Black are pitted against one another as isolated individuals in an apocalyptic endgame.

Himes and Greenlee share an understanding of the racial issues and histories that black counterconspiracy narrative must address. In their negotiations of these issues, both books turn to the ghetto as a space where the American conspiracy of race has its most visible effects, and where the space of the antebellum slave plantation can be revisited, revisioned, and redeemed. Both created by and left behind by the mainstream consumer culture, the ghetto becomes an underground, alternative America from which it is possible to imagine a revolutionary politics originating. *The Spook Who Sat by the Door* figures the ghetto as a site where authentic black identity can be realized, and opposes this black identity to that of the black middle class, which is portrayed as inauthentically black because of its participation in the practices of consumption that serve to align it with a mainstream American identity. In *Plan B*'s more pessimistic but less didactic vision, black authenticity is desired but unattainable; instead, the ghetto reflects American commerce back to itself, a parodic imitation that reveals the original's absurdity. The ghetto is still an underground, but one that cannot support any organized political resistance; instead the introduction of revolutionary tactics into Harlem results in an engulfing chaos that makes America itself into a version of the ghetto.[13]

What links the books most profoundly is their use of the ghetto as a space within which the large forces of conspiracy can be seen and resisted, even if the resistance is unsuccessful, limited, misguided, or destructive. We have seen how *The Parallax View* and other conspiracy narratives of the sixties and seventies imagined lone characters who found themselves both powerless and emptied of agency and individuality in the face of a postnational world wholly constructed and inhabited by multinational capitalism. By turning to a specific and concrete space that large trends in capitalism and consumption, as well as race, have made into the opposite or double of the looming corporate buildings of *Parallax*, black counterconspiracy narrative reanimates the politics of resistance. Here, as it does throughout the noir tradition, consumer capitalism creates as an effect of its functioning the desire for authenticity that motivates oppositional politics. The novels by Greenlee and Himes are not, in the end, utopian depictions of communal uprising, but, like Pynchon's novels of and about the sixties, they suggest that any attempt at resistance has to take place within the framework of communities or collectivities; the response to conspiracy is counterconspiracy.

Over the course of the past three chapters I have been describing how, in the sixties era, noir evolves into conspiracy. While conspiracy narrative strips away or transforms much of the iconography and conventions of noir, it preserves the animating ideological core of noir, in which effects of authenticity are produced as an oppositional strategy that seeks to separate America as defined by consumer capitalism from a better, truer, alternative America. This struggle, as in classic noir, is staged in specific American spaces that have been produced by consumer capitalism, that contain both the aura of commerce and the possibility of an imagined opposite, an aura of authenticity. These chapters have been particularly concerned with the question of political resistance to a perceived hegemony in which capitalism and American values are conflated in an ideology that sometimes goes by the name of "the American way of life." In these texts of the noir tradition, I have been suggesting, politics and political resistance are unimaginable in the absence of a logic of authenticity. *The Parallax View* and other conspiracy texts posit that absence and in doing so find themselves unable to articulate a politics at all, while Pynchon's novels and the texts of black counterconspiracy reassert authenticity in their different ways in order to envision forms of political resistance and perhaps even action. The politics of authenticity, however, tends to appear as a politics of pure opposition, represented as a vaguely imagined "other America" or as an apocalyptic conflict in which America itself is engulfed and perhaps destroyed. In my final two chapters I turn explicitly to this problem—the apparent necessity of authenticity to noir politics—as the central problem facing the noir tradition in the era of dominant postmodernism.

PART III

Postmodernism and Authenticity

{ 6 }

Postmodern Authenticity, or, Cyberpunk

[The science of space] embodies at best a technological utopia, a sort of
computer simulation of the future, or of the possible, within the framework
of the real—the framework of the existing mode of production.

—HENRI LEFEBVRE, *THE PRODUCTION OF SPACE*

Cyberpunk is the apotheosis of the postmodern, its truest and most
consistent incarnation, bar none. It could easily have the same role
in our world that romantic poetry had at the beginning of the 19th
century. Not that I'm happy about it. Not that I like the way
it makes me feel.

—ISTVAN CSICSERY-RONAY, *"CYBERPUNK AND NEUROMANTICISM"*

In this chapter, I begin to extend my discussion of conspiracy and authenticity
to texts from the era of dominant postmodernism, beginning in the 1980s and
extending to the present of this book's writing. In the previous section, I argued
that in the sixties and seventies film noir and hard-boiled detective fiction
were dramatically transformed. Unable to sustain themselves as viable cultural
forms, the critique of consumer culture that they exemplify was taken over by
the new genre, in both film and fiction, of the conspiracy narrative. This new
genre figures consumer culture as the product of larger corporate and capitalist networks that are conceived of as so vast and complex that they can no
longer be indicted by the protagonists of the narratives, can perhaps no longer
be represented. Now I will suggest that cyberpunk—and in particular the fiction of William Gibson—takes as its project precisely the mapping, however
metaphorical, of the spaces of multinational capitalism, a project that addresses the central problem of conspiracy narrative. In doing so, I argue, these
cyberpunk texts enact their own version of noir's politics of authenticity—an
argument that provides a way of understanding why noir is such a consistent
touchstone for the texts of cyberpunk. Although postmodernism is traditionally imagined as eroding concepts such as authenticity, cyberpunk offers a version of postmodernism which posits a newly formulated authenticity that is
defined by an ethos of hybridity and bricolage.

Like the other texts of the noir tradition, the authenticity that takes shape in cyberpunk is tied to a vision of America that contains both a rejection of the nation as defined by consumer culture and a desire for an alternative nation that is envisioned as the original and lost America. Cyberpunk takes up a worldview inherited from conspiracy narrative, in which America has become so thoroughly inhabited by the functioning of global economic networks and transnational corporate entities that it no longer exists as America at all. I argue here that the emptying-out of the nation in Gibson's novels produces a form of nostalgia for the nation. His early book *Neuromancer* (1984) posited a world in which global capitalism had entirely effaced the nation as a category, producing a vision of the future that is disturbing precisely because of the nation's disappearance. In the later book *Pattern Recognition* (2003) this model is given a more explicit form as it moves from the future back to our present; in this novel the September 11 attacks force the nation back onto Gibson's map, even if it can exist only in the form of a historical wound or an absence, the nostalgic phantom of a lost limb.

Tech Noir

The genre mash-up that goes by the name of "cyberpunk" emerges decisively at the moment when postmodernism has been so broadly diffused that it can be said to define the American cultural landscape at every level—that is to say, the early 1980s. In the last section, I cited Marianne DeKoven's argument from *Utopia Limited*, proposing a model in which the postmodern was "emergent" during the sixties era, a tendency in the arts that was still in tension with a dominant avant-garde modernism. Even when early postmodernists such as Thomas Pynchon, William Burroughs, Robert Venturi, or Roland Barthes borrowed from mass culture, they did so within a model that was still rooted in traditions of the artistic avant-garde. Now I will extend DeKoven's model by proposing a periodization that locates the moment of postmodernism's full diffusion at the start of the eighties, because this is when it first becomes possible to see postmodernism expressed throughout the culture as a mass culture phenomenon as well as an artistic tendency. If postmodernism is, as Fredric Jameson argues, a "cultural dominant," then it is in the early eighties that its cultural dominance becomes visible.

Self-conscious artificiality emerged as the dominant style of the period, defining a wide range of cultural productions. In architecture, postmodernism had trickled down to shopping centers and municipal buildings, which frequently featured large artificial facades with decorative elements; the incorporation of popular style by early postmodernist architects like Robert Venturi became the new style of mass-produced building design.[1] Popular novels like Bret Easton Ellis's *Less Than Zero* and Jay McInerney's *Bright Lights, Big City* seemed to be ushering in a new wave of fictional works that attended to surfaces rather than depth; their stories and characters exist in a radically delimited and consumerist present that seems to erase all consciousness of past or history. The rise of synth-pop suggested that music, too, had become self-consciously artificial: the desired product involved synthesizers and drum machines that did not actually imitate any organically produced sound but rather drew attention to their machine-made origin.[2]

Indeed, technology, and particularly digital technology, became a crucial element in the culture's efforts to represent itself; it is not surprising that *Time's* "man of the year" for 1982 was the personal computer. The self-consciously artificial aesthetic that emerged in the eighties was an attempt to reinvent fashion, style, and design completely; to break decisively with what came before; to *be* the future that digital technology seemed to imply. In the eighties, the culture itself aspired to the condition of science fiction; the whole world seemed to want to look like *Tron* (1982), the first science fiction film to attempt to represent what goes on in a digital computer in visual and spatial terms (using the nascent CGI technology to do so). This representation, called "cyberspace" by William Gibson and then by everyone else, would become one of the central tropes of the cyberpunk genre.

In his introduction to the 1986 story collection *Mirrorshades*, Bruce Sterling offered a manifesto for cyberpunk, an attempt to define it as a coherent movement in fiction. He argued that it represented "an integration of technology and the Eighties counterculture" (x). The pastoral dreams of the sixties counterculture, Sterling suggested, had been abandoned, while the spirit of political oppositionality and subversion it contained had been taken up by a new and technologically savvy generation for whom the representative rebel antihero was now the hacker. There are many variations on this description of cyberpunk, most of which are indicative of its connections to the counterculture and to noir traditions—David Ketterer describes it as a genre concerned with "high tech and low life" (141); the editors of *Rewired: The Post-Cyberpunk Anthology* sum up its narrative concerns as "dark visions of disaffected loners contending with totalitarian corporations" (viii)—but there is broad agreement about the central features or obsessions of cyberpunk. In the *Mirrorshades* introduction, Sterling lays these out as well as anyone, arguing that the defining obsessions include: technology and in particular the implications of technology in redefining both our bodies and our sense of self, or what has come to be called the "posthuman"; hybridity and creation from found materials in the "remix culture," with an attendant interest in borders, frontiers, and "interzones"; the increase of "global integration," with particular attention to the rise of the multinational corporation; and an aesthetic that is both clinically detached and "crammed" with immersive and often disorienting floods of detail.

Although Sterling and most other commentators during the eighties tended to discuss cyberpunk as a literary movement or phenomenon, cyberpunk fiction is in fact a phenomenon in which certain postmodern tendencies are expressed across media. Its impact in film has been more powerful and long-lasting than in fiction; American films from *Blade Runner* (1982) to *Johnny Mnemonic* (1995) to *Surrogates* (2009) have explored the possibilities of the genre, and Japanese anime films such as *Akira* (1988), *Ghost in the Shell* (1995), and *Paprika* (2006) have established their own parallel tradition.[3] These anime films have often been based on manga, and American comics and graphic novels have employed similar themes; Frank Miller's 1983–1984 *Ronin* series, in particular, puts all the cyberpunk obsessions into play very early on, suggesting again that cyberpunk was a core part of the early-eighties zeitgeist.[4] Television was there, too, in the form of the still bizarre *Max Headroom* series (1987–1988) based on a British film and TV series that ran from 1985 to 1986, and these texts have all influenced the design of numerous video games, some of them based on films such as *Blade Runner* and *The Matrix*. I have suggested that New Wave synth-pop resonates with cyberpunk, and one could construct a musical lineage here as well, stretching back to Kraftwerk as well as to the avant-garde pioneers of electronic music.

In fact, any comprehensive canon also includes the tradition of texts that prefigured the appearance of cyberpunk, and this prehistory could probably be extended backward indefinitely, given a broad definition of the term.[5] But the most direct antecedents of the genre are writers from the period of emergent postmodernism, each with strong links to elements of the sixties counterculture: William Burroughs, Philip K. Dick, and Thomas Pynchon. Burroughs is important both for his style, marked by postmodern narrative experimentation and Bataille-like transgressions of sexual and societal norms, and for his association with the beat writers as forerunners of the counterculture. Dick, whose work is obsessed with altered states of reality such as those brought on by drugs and schizophrenia, brings countercultural satire and paranoia to his science-fiction stories, several of which have been adapted as cyberpunkish films: *Blade Runner*, *Total Recall* (1990 and 2012), *Minority Report* (2002), *A Scanner Darkly* (2006). An often overlooked precursor to cyberpunk is Pynchon's 1963 novel *V.*, which follows in part the doings of a group of Beat-era, proto-countercultural slackers, the Whole Sick Crew. An epic, apocalyptic festival of bodies being assembled and disassembled, of the confrontation between the animate and the inanimate, of automata that dance and plot and prophesy, *V.* posits the uncertain line between human and machine as a central concern of the twentieth century.

The line that connects cyberpunk to these countercultural and conspiracy-minded texts leads straight back, down the path I have been tracing out in this book, to noir film and fiction. If the "cyber" elements of the genre come out of its lineage in science fiction and its concern with technology, the "punk" comes from the attitude copped by Philip Marlowe and from the tough, doom-haunted legacy of noir. The two texts that initiate cyberpunk as a genre, William Gibson's 1984 novel *Neuromancer* and Ridley Scott's 1982 film *Blade Runner*, both borrow narrative models and iconography from the past in order to structure their futuristic texts: in Gibson's case the hard-boiled detective novel, and in Scott's case the classic noir. In case we somehow missed this point, the early cyberpunk film *The Terminator* (1984) includes a scene that takes place in a club prominently named Tech Noir, which could easily serve as an alternative name for the genre.

In fact, the emergence of cyberpunk coincides with the beginning of the postmodern phase of the film noir tradition, generally known as "neo-noir." Neo-noir is a catchall term, but in my introduction I argued that there is a useful distinction to be drawn between New Hollywood "antinoir" of the sixties and seventies and the postmodern "neo-noir" that begins in the eighties.[6] Many of these latter neo-noirs simply appropriate or comment on the more obvious features of noir—using a recognizable generic structure that can either reproduce the aesthetic of noir (as in, say, the 1981 *Body Heat*) or serve as an occasion for postmodern genre play (as in, say, 2005's *Kiss Kiss Bang Bang*). But cyberpunk represents a branch of neo-noir that picks up where the conspiracy texts and antinoir of the seventies left off. The conspiracy texts, while stripping away much of the generic content of noir, maintain and extend the social critique of consumer culture that noir initiates. Cyberpunk again extends this line of thought, in the form of a return; it restores much of the generic content of noir (though in the context of science fiction) while also suggesting that it is possible to at least attempt a representation of the vast interlocking systems that conspiracy implies. As a genre that draws our attention to the organization of global capital and its relationship to the aesthetic realm, cyberpunk appropriates the critique of consumer culture that classic noir makes available, and then returns it to neo-noir as the postmodern form of that critique.

My argument concerning the dialectics of authenticity, then, provides an explanation for noir's persistent intertextual presence in cyberpunk texts. Cyberpunk is the next mutation in the evolution of the noir tradition that is the subject of this book, the form that the dialectical relationship between consumer capitalism and noir authenticity takes in the era of dominant postmodernism. To see how cyberpunk approaches these issues, I begin with an analysis of three influential theoretical accounts of postmodernism, those by Fredric Jameson, Jean Baudrillard, and Donna Haraway. All three reflect the terms and concerns of cyberpunk in ways that raise the question of whether political action is possible in the context of postmodern culture. Together they suggest the extent to which an authenticity conceived of as the opposite of consumer capitalism is vital to their attempts or failures to imagine such political action.

Cybertheory

I have been arguing that the cultural diffusion of postmodernism in the early eighties is inseparable from the phenomenon of cyberpunk, an apparently subcultural movement that is in retrospect a defining feature of the postmodern.

The moment when postmodernism became visible as a cultural dominant is also the moment when the most influential theoretical accounts of postmodernism as cultural dominant were published: Jean Baudrillard's *Simulacres et simulation* was published in 1981 (with the first version of these writings appearing in English as *Simulations* in 1983); Jameson's "Postmodernism, or, the Cultural Logic of Late Capitalism" first came out in 1984; and Donna Haraway's "A Cyborg Manifesto: Science, Technology, and Socialist-Feminism in the Late Twentieth Century" followed in 1985.[7] All three of these writers approach the political issues of the present from a perspective informed by Marxism (although in Haraway's essay issues central to feminism and theories of race and sexuality are much more strongly present than in the other works), and therefore they are all concerned with what problems and opportunities the present has to offer for Left politics. Each of the three works announces postmodernism as the new and inevitable order of the day and argues that any future politics will have to proceed from within postmodernism, from within a cultural organization in which there is no longer a place untouched by both technology and consumer capitalism. In doing so, these works all end up approaching the postmodern dilemma as a dilemma of authenticity, and each deals with this central problem in ways that deploy, influence, and participate in the ethos of cyberpunk.

The year of Jameson's essay, 1984, was also the year that William Gibson's *Neuromancer* kickstarted cyberpunk fiction, and ever since then Jameson and Gibson have been, one might say, collaborators on an ongoing theorization of postmodernism. When Jameson revised his essay as the first chapter of his 1991 book *Postmodernism*, he incorporated a mention of Gibson's "representational innovations" as one crucial new way of extending conspiracy narrative's attempt "to think the impossible totality of the contemporary world system" (38). Earlier, in a 1982 essay on utopian science fiction, Jameson had practically predicted cyberpunk, analogizing the way that Raymond Chandler's plots disguised his focus on the present historicity of Los Angeles to the way that science fiction texts "fix the intolerable present of history" ("Progress versus Utopia," 152). Jameson also wrote a laudatory essay very quickly after the 2003 publication of Gibson's *Pattern Recognition*, while Gibson has referred regularly to Jameson's work in interviews. His recent novels also reflect an awareness of critical and postmodernist theory: *Pattern Recognition* includes references to Baudrillard and other theorists, while a villainous character in *Spook Country* has developed an unlikely anti-Semitic conspiracy theory involving the thinkers of the Frankfurt School, who spread cultural Marxism by "plunging their intellectual ovipositors repeatedly into the unsuspecting body of old-school American academia" (126).

The Jameson-Gibson collaboration has generally been directed toward the project Jameson calls for in the closing sections of the "Postmodernism" essay. Envisioning the totality of multinational capital's world system, he suggests, will call for an aesthetic of "cognitive mapping," a metaphorical imagining of capital that takes place in spatial terms. Here Jameson is trying to take to heart Marx's notion that it is necessary to imagine capitalism (including postmodernism, "the cultural logic of late capitalism") not only as disaster but also as opportunity, so that "the attempt to conceptualize [postmodernism] in terms of moral or moralizing judgments must finally be identified as a category mistake" (46). However, the essay is clearly in conflict with itself on this point, having spent a great deal of time describing the postmodern in terms of its lack of modernist depth, of soul, of authentic historical content that might redeem the play of commodified surfaces—as in Jameson's opposition between Van Gogh's painting of peasant work boots and Warhol's *Diamond Dust Shoes*. This conflicted quality of the essay is a result of its effort at confronting the central problem for political critics when faced with postmodernism: How to construct a political critique when there is no authentic place to begin from, no site for an Archimedean fulcrum?

> No theory of cultural politics current on the Left today has been able to do without one notion or another of a certain minimal aesthetic distance, of the possibility of the positioning of the cultural act outside the massive Being of capital, from which to assault this last. What the burden of our preceding demonstration suggests, however, is that distance in general (including "critical distance" in particular) has very precisely been abolished in the new space of postmodernism. (*Postmodernism*, 48)

Jameson imagines postmodernism as the absolute disappearance of authenticity into the late-capitalist hall of mirrors, and then tries to envision the emergence of a new approach to postmodernism that embraces its inescapable logic in order to construct the new forms of Marxist critique and action that that logic may enable. These two poles between which he oscillates, the "negative" and the "positive" conceptions of postmodernism, are formulated and elaborated in the work of Baudrillard and Haraway, respectively.

Simulations and "A Cyborg Manifesto" blur the line between theory and fiction even more dramatically than "Postmodernism." Like Jameson, both Baudrillard and Haraway suggest that postmodernism is the inescapable mode of the present, the condition our condition is in. Both also use cyberpunkish science fiction as reference points (and Baudrillard's work famously became the inspiration for the film *The Matrix*, which itself reads like a Marxist—but not, actually, Baudrillardian—primer in which the matrix's false simulations are roughly equivalent to the concept of "ideology"). Istvan Csicsery-Ronay explicitly compares their projects to that of science fiction in "The SF of Theory: Baudrillard and Haraway," arguing that "theory is merely one form of the striving to work out, in the realm of the imaginary, the contradiction in the real. In each historical order it will share the strategies of its literary counterpart, utopia or science fiction" (390). Both Baudrillard and Haraway respond to this imaginative challenge not only at the conceptual level but also at the level of style. Csicsery-Ronay calls Baudrillard's language "lyrical" and "visionary," and indeed both writers—like other poststructuralist theorists—construct a style that is more allusive than informative.[8] Each produces a quasi-literary "theoretical" writing that mingles scientific and prophetic discourses in order to address the concerns that are central to cyberpunk.

Baudrillard's vision of the present is essentially a dystopian one. When he announces in *Simulations* that we have entered the age of the hyperreal and the simulacrum, that civilization is now absolutely defined by binary codings and henceforth there can be no originals, only copies of originals that do not exist, he does so in the voice of a reluctant prophet, one who is secretly ecstatic at the ill tidings he brings. Disguised as a diagnosis, Baudrillard's work is a hyperactive lament for the disappearance of authenticity. Postmodernism here, even more than in Jameson, is the story of a "radical disenchantment" (148) brought about by the waning of creativity, originality, art, contemplation, and the real, all in decline as we make the transition to "a neo-capitalist cybernetic order that aims now at total control" (111). Authenticity now resides only in the past, and in simulated forms as a residual nostalgia. This nostalgia is made possible by phenomena such as Disneyland and Watergate; the obvious fakery at work in these examples serves as the alibi of the simulacrum, allowing us to believe that reality, truth, and value still exist elsewhere. Baudrillard leaves us no room for the possibility of political intervention; no Neo or scrappy band of freedom fighters will or can emerge to disrupt the late-capitalist matrix in which we live out our lives.

Haraway, by contrast, picks up the other end of Jameson's analysis, envisioning the postmodern as an opportunity rather than a trap. She suggests that we, those of us living through the present, are like the character Rachel in *Blade Runner*; having always believed that she is a human, she is forced to come to terms with the fact that she is a replicant, an artificial person. We, too, are artificial people in an artificial world, and there is no escaping either fact. This, Baudrillard and Haraway agree, is the condition of postmodernism, but for Haraway the postmodern is a malleable and ongoing practice, one that does not lead inevitably to paralysis—absolute loss of meaning, absolute inability to negotiate or manipulate the matrix. Rather, like a cheerier Jameson, she argues that in the late-capitalist world all political positions must be constructed in relation to postmodernism: "The entire universe of objects that can be known scientifically must be formulated as problems in communications engineering (for the managers) or theories of the text (for those who would resist). Both are cyborg semiologies" (162–63). The "cyborg" is, of course, the central figure Haraway employs in laying out the terms of her manifesto, and in articulating her political position.

The cyborg becomes a way for Haraway to formulate a position that addresses feminist reservations about postmodernism in much the same way that Jameson addresses Marxist reservations. She argues, mostly by way of implication, that feminism must now become antiessentialist, abandoning the reliance on categories like "nature" or "the goddess"—categories of essential or transcendent female being—that often informed second-wave feminist thinking. This new cyborg feminist political practice "changes what counts as women's experience in the late twentieth century" (149), imagining all identities as hybrid so as to examine the boundaries between human and machine, human and animal, but also so as to account for the challenges to a unified and essential "woman's experience" from nonwhite and working-class women. Haraway's embrace of the technological and the postmodern, her "positive postmodernism," thus suggests a much greater range of political possibilities than Baudrillard would allow. This model has been enormously influential; indeed, Haraway's essay is responsible for creating "the cyborg" as a category through which to understand postmodern culture and cultural production—a category that is appealing because it appears to solve the problem of political critique in the era of dominant postmodernism.

I would suggest, however, that the antiessentialism of the manifesto has masked the extent to which it constructs a new version of authenticity that has come to serve as the model for a postmodern resistance to global capitalist structures. Haraway's techno-utopianism is specifically countercultural, and although she playfully describes the essay as a blasphemous and "ironic political myth," its politics are blasphemous and ironic in the tradition of sixties protest strategy, with the old site of resistance—the unified and organic subject—replaced by a new site of resistance: the hybrid, technologically inflected, assembled cyborg self. As structures of consumer capitalism mutate, they produce new authenticity effects that emerge as logics of resistance in this way; the cyborg is the version of authenticity that emerges in relation to the dominant postmodernism in late-twentieth-century America. The category of the cyborg seems to construct an alternative to authenticity, but it actually constructs a new version of authenticity that is appropriate to the postmodern context, one that replicates the opposition between consumer capitalism and alternative strategies of resistance that is so central to noir and conspiracy texts. A version of Haraway's logic also informs the texts of cyberpunk; this version, inheriting the key terms of the noir tradition, locates the opposition between consumer capitalism and cyborg authenticity in the tension between commercial and national spatial organizations.

Scales of Space

Because cyberpunk imagines itself as occupying an oppositional relationship to consumer capitalism, its authors and critics are especially sensitive to the possibility of its inauthenticity. As Istvan Csicsery-Ronay puts it, "the big question for 1980s art is whether any authentic countercultural art can exist for long without being transformed into self-annihilating simulations of themselves [*sic*] for mass consumption" ("Cyberpunk and Neuromanticism," 183). This anxiety crops up throughout the critical responses to cyberpunk, with its defenders worrying about the possibility of co-optation and its detractors arguing that the whole thing was a marketing scam from the start. The editors of *Rewired: The Post-Cyberpunk Anthology* suggest that it still remains to be seen whether cyberpunk can be an oppositional "ideology" or whether it will survive merely as a "flavor" (viii). They, like many other critics, conclude that if the genre has political value, that value resides in the "attitude," suspended between skepticism and cynicism, that animates it (xii). Samuel Delany describes this countercultural attitude that cyberpunk takes toward mainstream culture: "cyberpunk is that current SF work which is not middle-class, not comfortable with history, not tragic, not supportive, not maternal, not happy-go-lucky. . . . But it's only as a negative . . . that 'cyberpunk' can signify" ("Cyberpunk Forum," 33). It exists as a principle of opposition, dedicated to a punkish undermining of the dominant culture, class, and economic arrangements.

Cyberpunk, in other words, embodies the latest version of the political contradictions and possibilities that we have seen at work in the noir tradition from the beginning of the postwar era. It has consistently been a tradition animated by strategies of negation. Hard-boiled writers, caught between modernist high art and mass consumption, tried to reject both in order to carve out a populist avant-garde. Classic film noir operated simultaneously as a rejection of consumer culture and as a commodified spectacle within which mainstream audiences could become virtual tourists on the mean streets. Conspiracy texts presented a world so thoroughly suffused by corporate interests that individuals could no longer locate the possibility of an alternative, so that resistance came to reside in (often doomed, potentially ineffectual) counterconspiratorial organizations, groups, and concepts. In trying to realize a dream of pure and oppositional authenticity, all of these texts have faced the problem of their own location within the consumer economy and have responded by attempting a radical rejection of that economy. This reactive and negative approach is the one that cyberpunk, too, takes in its critique of the capitalist world-system.

The medium of the investigation, as in earlier noir and conspiracy texts, is space. Jameson is right to suggest that cyberpunk takes as its central project the mapping of the postmodern space of global capitalism, and in doing so it borrows another icon from the noir tradition: the city. As we have seen in the conspiracy texts of the sixties, one of the central problems of late capitalism is a problem of representation. The multinational spread of corporations has created a web of connections, which is so large and intricate in its global system of seemingly endless imbrications among localities that the individual consciousness can no longer assimilate it and thus it assumes the abstract character of Baudrillard's "desert of the real." But this problem already existed in a sort of nascent form in the modern metropolis, the capitalist icon that has now been succeeded by the world-system. In his study of urban underworlds, *Metropolis on the Styx*, David Pike provides an elegant description of the metropolis in these terms:

> Once it has become impossible to grasp a city in an instant, once a single person can no longer summon up its entirety in a single image, once, to borrow Jorge Luis Borges's metaphor, the map of the city is no longer commensurate point for point with the city itself, we can say that it has become a modern city, and that new vantage points are needed from which to begin to understand it. (36)

This is precisely the problem that Jameson, building on Kevin Lynch's work on the modern city, hopes to confront; if the city required a new form of "cognitive mapping," then the postmodern world space requires yet another. And if noir and hard-boiled fiction offered one version of metropolitan mapping, then cyberpunk uses that noir vision of the city as a starting place from which to enact that mapping on a global scale.

This work is done on the territory that Neil Smith, in an essay appended to his book *Uneven Development*, calls "deep space." Smith, a Marxist geographer, is concerned with the way that capital inherently produces spatial organizations that are unevenly developed at every level from the regional to the global. He argues that late capitalism has produced a spatial arrangement that is so large and multilayered that it can only be comprehended in metaphorical terms. Like Jameson, then, Smith is interested in the possibilities of imaginative cartography; the representations of space that one finds in fiction and film can offer ways of negotiating what he calls "the conceptual abyss between metaphorical and material space" (224).[9] That abyss is an effect of late capitalism's production of space in ways that are already metaphorical—what Henri Lefebvre would call "abstract space" and what Baudrillard would call "the precession of simulacra." As Smith puts it, "The world of commodity production and exchange, the logic and strategies of accumulation, the oppressive rule of the state, the extension of transportation and communication networks—these all bring about an abstract space that is . . . disconnected from the landscapes of everyday lives, and at the same time crushes existing difference and differences" (226). As in *The Matrix*, space is produced as ideology, a simulated reality that produces oppressive conditions.

Smith goes on to argue that a political response to the problem of deep space will require an analysis of the production of *scales* of space. Capitalism, in this analysis, has produced three primary scales of space—the urban, the national, and the global—and so a strategy of "cognitive mapping" can only make sense of the contemporary world space by developing a sense of the relationships among these scales. This is the territory that cyberpunk navigates, using the noir city as a model, a metaphor through which it is possible to *re*imagine the abstracted, simulated global system, to imagine space differently than the existing order of spatial production dictates. Its texts employ the logic of scale in order to describe the already abstract space of late capitalism—a description that is also a political intervention, an attempt to map the map of postmodern global space in order to reconnect the metaphorical to the material.

In constructing its spatial representations, cyberpunk proceeds by way of a dichotomous logic appropriate to the representation of uneven development, and its initial dichotomy is borrowed from the vertical city: above versus below. By presenting the city in these terms, and using the city map as a palimpsest whose newest layer is the global map, cyberpunk makes these dichotomies a striking version, realized in metaphorical terms, of the structurally uneven developments in material space that capitalism produces. Ridley Scott's *Blade Runner* offers an especially good example of this tendency, and indeed of cyberpunk's approach to representing the city as postmodern space.[10] Its vertiginous sets draw inspiration from *Metropolis*, in which class politics are represented by the distance between the offices and playgrounds of the capitalist elite atop the city's skyscrapers and the underground city of the workers.[11] *Blade Runner* makes the street level itself a kind of underground, a seedy, crowded, multi-ethnic ghetto that is contrasted with the awe-inspiring structures that loom above it—in particular the Mayan-temple grandeur of the Tyrell Corporation, at the top of which the godlike Eldon Tyrell himself resides. There is also a secondary up-down axis in which humans with enough money have moved to off-world colonies in space: in the movie's version of "white flight" from the decaying city center to the suburbs, the new global organization of space is modeled on postwar urban dynamics.

Postwar urban space is of course the space that is most closely associated with film noir. The film's debts to noir are many and explicit, even without the hard-boiled voice-over that was used in the film's original release. But it is the images of the city and the representation of urban space in this future Los Angeles that make the connection most explicit. Los Angeles has of course been the preferred site for noir plots ever since Raymond Chandler, and the Asian presence in the street culture of *Blade Runner* links it in particular to the powerful vision of LA in the latter-day noir *Chinatown*. Polanski's film makes LA's Chinatown into a symbolic space, a place of lawless unknowability in which white characters cannot get their bearings. In *Blade Runner*, all of street-level LA is now that unknowable, noir Chinatown,[12] a seedy and anarchic mixture of ethnicities with Asian seeming to predominate, and a place where the nonwhite characters speak a creole language—"street speak"—that is not translated for viewers, a way of reminding us that we are clueless tourists here. The chaotic detail of the streets—a claustrophobic and alienating profusion of consumer culture in which advertisements suffuse the film world both visually and aurally—is matched by the ordered detail of the world above. As the camera approaches the vast and apparently smooth exterior of the Tyrell complex, the walls are revealed to contain an intricate webwork of lights, windows, movement, hivelike activity. At both the street and the corporate levels, the film immerses the viewer in a city landscape that is designed to disorient, to give the impression of an overload of detail, too much to take in, the unmappable city as a representation of a capitalism so far beyond late as to be a gothic decadence.

While *Blade Runner* looks back to film noir, William Gibson's books wear the trenchcoat of hard-boiled detective fiction. The influence is especially pronounced in *Neuromancer*, his first novel and the one most often cited as a defining text of cyberpunk. The book's final line, "He never saw Molly again," echoes the endings of two of Raymond Chandler's novels: *The Big Sleep* ("All they did was make me think of Silver-Wig, and I never saw her again") and *The Long Goodbye* ("I never saw any of them again—except the cops. No way has yet been invented to say goodbye to them"). Likewise, Gibson's famous opening sentence, "The sky above the port was the color of television, tuned to a dead channel," offers an homage that also announces the arrival of something new. The most recognizable examples of Chandler's style are his often-parodied similes: "His surprise was as thin as the gold on a weekend wedding ring" (*Long Goodbye*, 78); or "The general spoke again, slowly, using his strength as carefully as an out-of-work show-girl uses her last pair of stockings" (*Big Sleep*, 8). In sentences like these, the metaphysical conceit becomes an occasion to pull the reader out of the immediate context and into the broader atmosphere of the hard-boiled world, a seedy milieu of weekend wedding rings and out-of-work showgirls evoked like a subliminal flash. Gibson uses a similarly unexpected metaphor to signal at the outset his appropriation of Chandler's authenticity-focused worldview, now put in the service of a comparison that suggests the book's radical interpenetration of the technological and the organic.

Neuromancer contains many such borrowings, including elements of hard-boiled noir narrative, iconography, style, and ideology. The story concerns a central character named "Case" who watches as the case he is initially drawn into expands into a labyrinthine conspiracy plot involving a *femme* who is extremely *fatale* (though here she is one of the good guys), many eccentric and threatening characters, and contact with various criminal underworlds and urban dangers. The book's amoral tone and meticulous attention to detail read as echoes of Dashiell Hammett's work. The book's use of obscure (that is to say, invented) slang signals the reader's entry into an alien context, while the overloading of plot and information without explanation keeps us disoriented— both techniques are common to the hard-boiled detective genre. But, again like *Blade Runner*, what is most striking about Gibson's writing is his unusual attention to space. Gibson shares with Chandler a tendency to make space the secret center of his narratives, to create meaning and politics out of the relationship between real and metaphorical spaces.

This cognitive mapping work unfolds as the background of *Neuromancer*'s baroque plot. The "console cowboy" Case, who has made his living hacking corporations for various shady employers, has been physiologically stripped of his ability to navigate cyberspace by a client from whom he stole, and now spends his time in the darker corners of Japan's Chiba City, hoping to die. But he is called in, like some of his noir forebears, for one last heist: a mystery man is assembling a team of loners to do some work for him—including most notably the taloned and leather-clad kunoichi Molly—and he arranges an operation that restores Case's console talents. The mystery man turns out to be working for an artificial intelligence (AI) called Wintermute, which has hired the team to eliminate the safeguards that prevent it from becoming more intelligent so that it can join with its sibling AI, Neuromancer. The book links its noir aesthetic to the conspiracy plot's vastness, creating an outlaw lineage that brings both Chandler and the sixties counterculture into the technological present. Along the way the group even gets help from a sixties-style radical prankster group called the Panther Moderns who sport a punkish look that involves lots of elective surgery and heads that bristle with technology.

The book's reach is effortlessly global, moving from Japan to the Sprawl (formerly America's East Coast) to Istanbul to assorted locations off the terrestrial shore. But Gibson's most dramatic contribution to the spatial imagination is his conception and coinage of "cyberspace," the landscape within the world's linked computers and Case's "distanceless home, his country, transparent 3D chessboard extending to infinity. Inner eye opening to the stepped scarlet pyramid of the Eastern Seaboard Fission Authority burning beyond the green cubes of Mitsubishi bank of America, and high and very far away he saw the spiral arms of military systems, forever beyond his reach" (52). The extent to which this virtual geography is modeled on the complex space of the city is evident in the book's famous description of cyberspace as "lines of light ranged in the nonspace of the mind, clusters and constellations of data. Like city lights, receding" (51). Hackers like Case call themselves "cowboys," signaling a familiar linkage: the Western and the hardboiled-detective genres are both about lone men negotiating a dangerous frontier associated with femininity, whether it is the vast openness of the American West or the claustrophobic intricacy of the American city. Cyberspace, a vast and womblike space (Gibson calls it "the matrix"—the first of several elements that The Matrix borrows from him) crowded with building-like geometric representations of corporations and state institutions, combines these linked frontiers.

In appropriating these frontier spaces, however, Gibson elides what seems to be a central characteristic for both of them: Americanness. In fact, Gibson has said that in writing Neuromancer, he deliberately avoided any mention of America; instead, there is action that takes place in the long urban "Sprawl" or BAMA (Boston-Atlanta Metropolitan Axis), and discussion of particular cities. (As with Blade Runner's future version of white flight, Gibson uses the Sprawl to extrapolate the suburbanization and commercialization of the American landscape that began in the postwar era into a dystopian America now entirely made up of sprawl.) Considering Neuromancer in terms of our three scales of space, we could say that Gibson models the global scale on the urban, while eliding the national. The important entities here are distinctly postnational: corporations on the Japanese model—zaibatsus—along with criminal organizations, gangs, and also the prenational inbred clan of Tessier-Ashpool. Chandler, by contrast, made his observations at the urban scale and used the city, Los Angeles, as a microcosm of the nation, a way of representing an America that seemed to be disappearing as it became increasingly indistinguishable from the pervasive consumer culture. In his books and in many of the other texts of the noir tradition, as we have seen, the concept of an alternative and true "America" is still imagined to be available as a site of resistance—as with the Two Americas model that I described as a central feature in Pynchon's books. But in Gibson, that site of resistance, the utopian America that is always elsewhere, seems to have gone beyond reclaiming. What, then, happens to the notion of authenticity when the Chandlerian vision has reached its logical conclusion and the imaginary national space that served as its location has been entirely displaced by consumer capitalism?

Bad Machines and Good Cyborgs

I will begin to answer that question by pointing out that the fate of the nation in cyberpunk is analogous in some important ways to the fate of the human in this posthuman genre. *Blade Runner* and *Neuromancer* deserve their shared place at the center of the cyberpunk canon, in large part because both are rigorously antiessentialist and posthumanist in their outlook. In *Blade Runner*, the category of the "human" has been completely effaced or defaced by the film's end, a penciled word smudged out by a bad eraser; the replicants are as human as the humans by any meaningful measure, and the humans' uniqueness has been called into question by their own reproducibility. Is Deckard a replicant? It doesn't matter, but what does matter is that the film makes the answer completely unknowable. *Neuromancer*, meanwhile, is more elaborate, baroque even, in its debunking of essence. Every character in the book is constructed in some way: Molly, with her retractable claws and permanent mirrorshade eyes; Armitage, who assembles the team but is actually a schizophrenic basket-case whose psyche is temporarily patched together by Wintermute; the Dixie Flatline, which is a ROM reproduction of a dead man's consciousness that wants only to be erased; and on and on. And all these (sort of) human characters are essentially passive in the big picture of the novel; they are manipulated meat, doing a job, trying to survive, while the only real agents, those with motives and goals, are the two artificial intelligences.

The book is careful to offer no space of purity, to undermine anything that looks like purity, to undermine the things that look *most* like purity. The ninja Hideo, for example, is the perfect expression of the zen-calm martial-arts ideal: "His every move was part of a dance, a dance that never ended, even when his body was still, at rest, but for all the power it suggested, there was also a humility, an open simplicity" (240). He is, however, "vatgrown," a kind of replicant, a constructed thing. Similarly, cyberspace has a way of invading the space of the real, both at the level of metaphor and of the characters' experience. When Case and Molly have sex, "his orgasm flar[es] blue in a timeless space, a vastness like the matrix" (33). This sneaky infusion of constructed virtuality into what seems like fundamental bodily experience is given fuller expression near the book's resolution: Case finds himself trapped by the AI Neuromancer in a version of cyberspace that is dramatically different from the urban and geometric *Tron*-world he inhabits as a cowboy.

This reproduction appears both rural and organic, as Case finds himself living out slow days on a beach, staying in a shack with his (dead, but here alive) ex-girlfriend from Chiba City, Linda Lee. Here he has his most profound experience of nature—the waves, the gulls, the empty sea—which again is given its fullest expression in sex: "It was a place he'd known before. . . . It belonged, he knew—he remembered—as she pulled him down, to the meat, the flesh the cowboys mocked. It was a vast thing, beyond knowing, a sea of information coded in spiral and pheromone, infinite intricacy that only the body, in its strong blind way, could ever read" (232). This sounds like a reaffirmation of the body—even though it describes sex in terms of code, it does so in a lyrical register that suggests the body's code is more complex than the computer's and thus that nature trumps technology—and yet since it all takes place within a virtual model constructed by Neuromancer for Case's brain while his body lies limp at the console, the only true affirmation here is, once again, that of the technological world and the simulation.

This technological milieu, which stands outside of and simulates nature, becomes in *Neuromancer* a metaphor for the capitalist structures that stand outside of and simulate the already-obsolete nation. The figure of the machine as corporation begins to emerge at the book's climax, when Case finds himself inside of the cyberspatial core of Neuromancer and revisits his beachside idyll from the other side:

> Here things could be counted, each one. He knew the number of grains of sand in the construct of the beach (a number coded in a mathematical system that existed nowhere outside the mind that was Neuromancer). He knew the number of yellow food packets in the canisters in the bunker (four hundred and seven). He knew the number of brass teeth in the left half of the open zipper of the salt-crusted leather jacket that Linda Lee wore as she trudged along the sunset beach, swinging a stick of driftwood in her hand (two hundred and two). . . . He knew the rate of her pulse, the length of her stride in measurements that would have satisfied the most exacting standards of geophysics. (249)

Gibson returns us to the logic of conspiracy, but offers his protagonist a behind-the-scenes perspective on the sublime unknowable, which turns out again to be global capitalism. In the mind of Neuromancer, all qualities can be quantified—a mathematical logic that is also a version of the economic logic of capital, in which all value is quantified and priced within the money system.

If the AI machine stands in for corporate capital, the merging of the AIs Neuromancer and Wintermute suggests the globalization of that capital, corporate power raised to the power of everything, so that there is no longer a way to define a space outside of this new entity. Neuromancer denies Case's claim that its version of Linda Lee is just a reproduction, saying, "to live here is to live. There is no difference" (249). When the new Neuromancer-Wintermute composite appears in avatar form to Case in the book's coda, it identifies itself as "the matrix. . . . The sum total of the works, the whole show." Case wants to know how this makes things different, and it replies that "things aren't different. Things are things" (259). This is the global space of late capitalism, the thing that Gibson's cyberspatial pyrotechnics work to give us a representation of—or at least a glimpse of a representation of—while at street level it remains invisible, naturalized, reified: things are things.

Against the background created by this grand conspiratorial gesture, Gibson sets in motion a series of meditations on the nature of the corporation and corporate power in the age of multinational capital. At the center of these meditations is another dichotomy, as characteristic of cyberpunk spaces as the above/below distinction, between two figural entities that I will call the "bad machine" and the "good cyborg." This is postmodernism's version of the confrontation between consumer capitalism and authenticity, which in cyberpunk takes the form of an opposition between two ways of organizing space. The "bad machine" in *Neuromancer* is Freeside, a kind of orbiting "offshore" site for all varieties of luxury tourism, combining a sporty, Eurotrashy ClubMed atmosphere on the surface with a lively trade in gambling, drugs, and some disturbing and technologically advanced forms of prostitution below (and below that, the weird world of Straylight and the Tessier-Ashpool clan that is nominally running the corporate entity that owns Freeside; Gibson delights in the archaeological work of moving through the spatial-metaphorical layerings of such organizations). Case ultimately realizes that Freeside is a grand example of what he calls "the dance of biz," a place so wholly dedicated to the movement of capital that capital becomes invisible, a place so elaborately expensive that its simulations appear natural.

All this is, of course, what makes Freeside a tourist destination, a festival of staged authenticity. Indeed, it would not be out of place among the studies in Keller Easterling's *Enduring Innocence*, in which she examines a new kind of "spatial product" that is exemplary of postmodern capitalist space, "resorts, information technology campuses, retail chains, golf courses, ports, and other enclave formations" (1), which exist in a kind of decentered, extranational nonspace in which the commodification of experience is produced, processed, or enabled. Molly gets to the central aspect of Freeside, its biz core: "It's just a big tube and they pour things through it. . . . Tourists, hustlers, anything. And there's fine mesh money screens working every minute, make sure the money stays here when the people fall back down the well" (120). A vast machine for extracting money from people—"things," as she calls them—through varieties of manufactured touristic experience from hang-gliding to meat puppets, Freeside is a representation of consumer capitalism as a perfectly smooth and efficient machine.

Gibson's alternative to the efficient machine is the cyborg assemblage. Like the work of Pynchon and Don DeLillo, Gibson's fiction has always been fascinated by the underside of consumer culture that is represented by the production of garbage, waste, or what he sometimes, borrowing a slang word from the Japanese, calls *gomi*. Samuel Delany, picking up on Gibson's use of the word, remarks in an interview that "the bricolage of Gibson's style, now highly colloquial, now highly formal, now hard-boiled, makes him as a writer a *gomi no sensei*—a master of junk" (quoted in "On Gibson and Cyberpunk SF," 353). This stylistic bricolage is appropriate to Gibson's material, which so often pays tribute to rebuilt or reassembled gomi; his early story "Burning Chrome" gave this theme a formulation that has since become a kind of cyberpunk motto: "the street finds its own uses for things" (199). This way of putting it suggests the valuing of an aesthetic of repurposing, but also attributes the process of repurposing to collective or historical forces—"the street"—that are connoted as urban and technological.

So in opposition to Freeside, Gibson offers Zion, another space station and the home of a colony of Rastafarians who aid Case and Molly in their raid on the Freeside/Straylight complex. Putting these erstwhile Jamaicans up against the Eurotrash suggests a metaphor for capitalism's globalized uneven development—since Jamaica is the location on the one hand of a largely impoverished native population from whose numbers Rastafarianism has emerged, and on the other hand of the kind of expensively manufactured tourist enclaves that Freeside represents.[13] Although the book's championing of the space Rastas reeks of the liberal fetishization of blackness—it's counterculture catnip; pot-smoking black folks are cool, rich old Europeans suck— there is nonetheless a subtler politics at work here, too. Case is mystified by the Zionites because they are connected to the body, the "meat" that he distrusts, but theirs is a cyborg embodiment, a melding of tradition and organism with sophisticated technology—a melding that is best represented by dub, the Jamaican music that emerged in the sixties and seventies, based on a technological reworking and combining of elements from already-recorded songs: "Case gradually became aware of the music that pulsed constantly through the cluster. It was called dub, a sensuous mosaic cooked from vast libraries of digitalized pop; it was worship, Molly said, and a sense of community. . . . Zion smelled of cooked vegetables, humanity, and ganja" (102).

Cooked vegetables, cooked digital music files: there is no Levi-Straussian rawness here, but instead a deeply cooked and technologized culture in which the organic and the digital are fused in a cyborg whole that is makeshift assemblage rather than seamless simulation, as is clear in Gibson's description of the space tug *Marcus Garvey*:

> *Marcus Garvey* had been thrown together around an enormous old Russian air scrubber, a rectangular thing daubed with Rastafarian symbols, Lions of Zion and Black Star Liners, the reds and greens and yellows overlaying wordy decals in Cyrillic script. Someone had sprayed Maelcum's pilot gear a hot tropical pink, scraping most of the overspray off the screens and readouts with a razor blade. The gaskets around the airlock in the bow were festooned with semirigid globs and streamers of translucent caulk, like clumsy strands of imitation seaweed. (111)

This repurposed piece of technology, with its patched-together organization and layered surfaces that reveal history as a spatial palimpsest, is representative of the overall Zion aesthetic, and it is an aesthetic that has ethical dimensions in *Neuromancer*. The Zionites are the most genuinely likable characters in the book, and when Case is stuck in Neuromancer's beach-world construct while his body dies, it is Zion dub that pierces the simulation and acts as a lifeline that leads Case back to his body. The assemblage, as represented here by Zion, is the good cyborg that offers the possibility of resistance to the bad machine. As in Haraway's manifesto, *Neuromancer* suggests a postmodern version of the authentic, the resistance to consumer capitalism, which is based on the partiality, bricolage, and impurity that characterize "cyborg" ways of being.

We find this opposition between bad machine and good cyborg replicated in various forms in a whole range of texts that have connections to cyberpunk.[14] *The Matrix*, for example, gives us a group of freedom fighters—also using cobbled-together bits of technology, also for that matter working out of a base called "Zion"—who must contend with the ruthless efficiency of the machines who run the Matrix, and with the seamless simulations of the Matrix itself. The half-human robocop Murphy in *Robocop* (1987) must confront both the sinister corporation that made him a cyborg and the pure manifestation of that corporation, the scary ED-209—a purely machine robocop. *Terminator 2: Judgment Day* (1991) is a particularly good example. The older-model terminator (Arnold Schwarzenegger) assigned to protect young John Connor assumes the iconography of the classic American outlaw—leather jacket, sunglasses, boots, motorcycle—and over the course of the film he becomes increasingly ragged, his clothes riddled with bullet holes, his skin stripped away in places to reveal his metal skeleton and thus to give him a distinctly cyborg appearance. The new T-1000 terminator hunting down John Connor, by contrast, is a smooth and relentless machine made of liquid metal. It can take any shape, but its characteristic guise is that of a police officer—the

corporate machine operating under the shelter of an emptied-out state authority. As the cop battles the outlaw—who is accompanied by Sarah Connor,
attired and armed like a freedom fighter—we begin to see the contours of a
familiar opposition between an American identity that is inseparable from the
sleek engine of corporate capitalism and an outsider identity that is figured as
the true and authentic America.

These national concerns are not visible in any direct way in the post-
American world of *Neuromancer*. Gibson's is the most extensive mapping of
the cyborg/machine dichotomy, and his vision, again, replaces older notions of
purity with new ones of hybridity as the foundation of an authentic politics.
Hybridity is where postmodernism places its faith; bricolage is its piety. But by
eliminating the national imaginary from the opposition between consumer
culture and authenticity, Gibson's book activates an implicit nostalgia for the
effaced category of the nation. This nostalgia is created in part through noir
aesthetics, since the seedy dystopianism of Gibson's sprawl world is attribut-
able to the erasure of the nation from the cyberpunk map. That loss is a kind
of dull ache that resides unspoken at the core of the book's world; if readers
experience the book as disorienting, it is in part because a crucial aspect of our
imaginative cartography, our bearings, has been removed. Capitalism's permanent revolution seems to make the nation irrelevant, and in doing so makes
the cyberpunk mapping of the globe and the city possible; but the sinister
mood that is produced by that mapping suggests a nostalgia for the nation that
Neuromancer can never bring itself to articulate fully.

Ground Zero History

This nostalgia is given a more explicit expression in Gibson's more recent
work. These books return the scale of the nation to his fictional geography, and
in doing so enable a more direct confrontation between postmodern authenticity—now located in the form of an America that is imaginable, if not quite
present—and consumer culture. In his twenty-first-century writing, Gibson
preserves the spatial and conceptual oppositions of *Neuromancer* while using
those oppositions to reflect more directly on the present moment, creating a
kind of science fiction of the present. The book that initiates this new concern
with the present is 2003's *Pattern Recognition*. It is one of the first attempts in
fiction to cope with the terrorist attacks of September 11, 2001, and it is through
that national crisis that the novel puts America back on Gibson's map.

Cyberpunk's countercultural concern with the problem of "selling out"
takes center stage in *Pattern Recognition*, an extended meditation on the extent
to which commodification and branding have come to shape the contemporary world at every level. The nostalgia for the nation that was implied in
Neuromancer has here found a more explicit expression; the protagonist,

finding herself at a Russian meal, considers that "perhaps . . . this isn't a Russian meal. Perhaps it's a meal in [a] country without borders . . . a meal in a world where there are no mirrors to find yourself on the other side of, all experience having been reduced, by the spectral hand of marketing, to price-point variations on the same thing" (341). The character doing the considering here is a woman named Cayce, pronounced "Case" in order to signal the extent to which this book will revisit and rethink the issues raised in *Neuromancer*. She is employed by corporations as a consultant to test their logos and marketing because she has a bodily sensitivity, an allergy, to branding of all kinds. One escape Cayce finds from this sensitivity is to become part of an online community that follows "the footage," a series of brief nonsequential cinematic fragments that appear mysteriously and at intervals on the web. She is attracted to their beauty and their unlocatable quality; with its "absence of stylistic cues," the footage is blissfully free of the "semiotics of the marketplace" (23, 2). But she has been hired by a new media corporation called Blue Ant to find the maker of the footage as a way of capitalizing on its potential as a new model for marketing products to audiences inured to traditional marketing strategies.

Her investigation of the footage is a quest in which she fears that by finding the thing she desires she will destroy it, make it available for co-optation by the consumer culture. This is a microcosm of the contradictions contained within her unusual profession, which make her part of the globalizing process that elides national boundaries, "complicit . . . in whatever it is that gradually makes London and New York feel more like each other, that dissolves the membrane between mirror-worlds" (194). ("Mirror-world" is Cayce's way of describing the experience of being an American in England, where everything is just different enough to be disorienting; *Pattern Recognition* is the story of Cayce's adventures through the looking-glass.) The dissolving of national boundaries by the globalization of capital is felt as a loss of authenticity, and Cayce's physiological response to branding suggests the book's concern with the way that, in the postmodern era, commerce has inhabited human being and interaction at every level. Early on, Cayce meets a woman named Magda who works as a viral marketing tool, going to clubs, being cool and attractive, and mentioning a brand or a commodity in her casual conversations: "But it's starting to do something to me. I'll be out on my own, with friends, say, not working, and I'll meet someone . . . and they'll mention something . . . they like. A film. A designer. And something in me stops. . . . I'm devaluing something. In others. In myself. And I'm starting to distrust the most casual exchange" (85). At the core of the book is this concern, this felt loss of authenticity—and that is what Cayce is trying to find an antidote for in her investigation as she searches for the maker of the footage.

The investigation unfolds as a detective or conspiracy narrative, one that looks back to Chandler's world-weary cynicism (and his similes, again given the Gibson treatment: Blue Ant's head, Hubertus Bigend, is "a nominal Belgian who looks like Tom Cruise on a diet of virgins' blood and truffled chocolates"[15]

[6]) as well as to *The Crying of Lot 49* and its suggestion that the pattern recognition required for both detective and conspiracy narratives may always turn out to be a projection rather than a discovery. Cayce's assignment, like Case's, leads her on a global odyssey, from England to Japan and Russia, where she does ultimately discover the origin of the footage. The "maker" turns out to be Nora Volkova, the niece of a Russian gangster-businessman (and Chandler would have approved of the way Gibson uses the uncle, Andrei Volkov, to bring together in one figure the past of organized crime and the future of business and marketing). An aspiring filmmaker brain-damaged by the bomb that killed her parents, Nora's only mental life is her work on the footage, constructed on the computer. Cayce observes the process:

> She has watched a segment, or the bones of one, being built up from almost nothing. Mere scraps of found video. How once a man had stood on a platform in a station and turned, and raised his hand, the motion captured. . . . To be chosen today by the roving, darting cursor. Elements of that man's gesture becoming aspects of the boy in the dark coat, his collar up. The boy whose life, it seems, is bounded by the T-shaped city, the city Nora is mapping through the footage she generates. Her consciousness, Cayce understands, somehow bounded by or bound to the T-shaped fragment in her brain: part of the arming mechanism of the Claymore mine that killed her parents. . . . Something stamped out, once, in thousands, by an automated press in some armory in America. Perhaps the workers who'd made that part, if they'd thought at all in terms of end-use, had imagined it being used to kill Russians. But that was over now. . . .
> Only the wound, speaking wordlessly in the dark. (304–5)

The footage serves as another instance of the cyborg assemblage, one in which Gibson returns self-consciously to a scene of cognitive mapping, a purely internal space that is nonetheless urban and that is so wholly shaped by historical forces that it emerges, in a sense, without human or artistic agency; it is an expression of the specific historical brutalities of the twentieth century.

Pattern Recognition is steeped in that history, looking back in particular to the Cold War, Vietnam, and World War II through artistic assemblages and fashion homages: photographs of Zippo lighters personalized by soldiers in Vietnam, military camouflage based on digital patterns, RAF-themed cufflinks, and Cayce's own wardrobe, which features a Stasi-issue handbag and a jacket that is practically a conceptual art piece, "a fanatical museum-grade replica of a U.S. MA-1 flying jacket . . . created by Japanese obsessives driven by passions having nothing at all to do with anything remotely like fashion" (10–11).[16] All this repurposing of military history turns out to be leading us toward the wound in Cayce's own life that links her to Nora, and that is the book's other mystery: her father Win Pollard, a former Cold War security expert, disappeared in Manhattan on the morning of the September 11 attacks.

If the quest to find the source of the footage is satisfyingly complex and conspiratorial in its contours and its resolution, this second quest to find out what happened to Win Pollard is made more powerful by its lack of narrative resolution. The investigation reveals only blank fact of the sort that might describe any victim of the attacks: no one knows for sure, but it seems likely that he died in the collapsing towers. But in the process through which Cayce comes to terms with his disappearance, the book tries to come to terms with September 11 itself, described here as an "experience outside of culture" (137). In his attempt to place that experience culturally and historically, Gibson also reinstates the nation as a category within his fictional geography.

He does this by returning to the structure of spatial juxtaposition that we have seen at work in the meeting of Freeside and Zion. In *Pattern Recognition*, Cayce recalls putting up posters of Win's face in Manhattan shortly after the towers came down:

> She had, while producing her own posters, watched the faces of other people's dead, emerging from adjacent copiers at Kinko's, to be mounted in the yearbook of the city's loss. She had never, while putting hers up, seen one face pasted over another, and that fact, finally, had allowed her to cry, hunched on a bench in Union Square, candles burning at the base of a statue of George Washington.
>
> She remembered sitting there, prior to her tears, looking from the monument that was still taking shape at the base of Washington's statue to that odd sculpture across Fourteenth Street, in front of the Virgin Megastore, a huge stationary metronome, constantly issuing steam, and back again to the organic accretion of candles, flowers, photographs, and messages, as though the answer, if there was one, lay in somehow understanding the juxtaposition of the two. (186)

One object, monolithic and machine-like (the metronome suggesting unceasing, repetitive motion, the steam suggesting factories and the early machine age), resides under the sign of the branded, globalized megastore; the other, residing under the sign of America's founding (the statue of George Washington), is an assemblage devoted to a collective national mourning. The assemblage is described as "organic" but it is nonetheless, like the footage, impure and built out of found materials by an agency that is collective, unconscious, historical: the good cyborg that offers an alternative to the bad machine of global capital. Given the book's concern with how global capital eliminates "soul"—Cayce experiences not just jet-lag but "soul delay," and she posits a Baudrillardian "Tommy Hilfiger event horizon, beyond which it is impossible to be more derivative . . . more devoid of soul" (18)—it is clear that we have returned here to the political critique of consumer culture developed in earlier forms by noir and conspiracy texts. The national imaginary becomes the site of resistance that is made necessary by a felt loss of authenticity, of soul.

A second and related spatial juxtaposition also concerns the book's investigation of historical wounds, figured as a process of "digging" into the past. This takes the form of an implicit contrast between the two "digs" that are described in the novel. The first we see only in passing, as Cayce walks by a nighttime Tokyo road crew "slicing into asphalt with a water-cooled steel disk. . . . She's never actually seen soil emerge from any incision they might make in the street, here; it's as though there is nothing beneath the pavement but a clean, uniformly dense substrate of pipes and wiring" (130). This dig—which as rendered here yields no history, only the uniform innards of the urban-global machine—is contrasted with another that is closer to the center of the plot. Cayce's friend Damien is making a documentary about an annual summer dig in Russian swamps where some of the most brutal fighting of World War II took place. His email descriptions of the dig portray it as a surreal drunken carnival from which endless bones and artifacts of the war are unearthed in a search for plunder, anything that might fetch a price in the chaotic post-Soviet economy.

The literal unearthing of history and probing of its wounds that take place in this unreal and impure space assume a more specific symbolism when Cayce visits the dig in the book's coda. In a scene that revisits her crisis in Union Square, the excavation of a war-created past becomes a scene of catharsis, a site that revisits and reenacts the post-9/11 dig at Ground Zero: "she'd found herself, out of some need she hadn't understood, down in one of the trenches, furiously shoveling gray muck and bones, her face streaked with tears" (355). The unearthing of the twentieth century's wars, at the start of the twenty-first, is represented in terms of an actual unearthing. The last century has already become a subterranean pit, a wound from which any fictional attempt to imagine the space of the present or the future must begin, and the book's Ground Zero is imagined as a symbolic space in which all of America's wars going back to World War II are evoked, and mourned. The crisis of September 11 becomes again a way to return to the nation as a site of authenticity, even if the America to which the book returns is still a kind of absence and the return itself, made possible by the experience of loss, takes the form of nostalgia.

If September 11 becomes the occasion and the space in which *Pattern Recognition* imagines the possibility of an American authentic, the book is nonetheless aware that this seemingly untouchable event, set apart in its horror, can be appropriated for commercial purposes. The relationship between the megastore and the monument of national mourning may not be one of opposition, after all. At the beginning of Cayce's Tokyo sojourn, during the first hours of soul-delay, looking up "into the manically animated forest of signs, she sees the Coca-Cola logo pulsing on a huge screen, high up on a building, followed by the slogan 'NO REASON!' This vanishes, replaced by a news clip, dark-skinned men in bright robes. She blinks, imagining the towers burning there, framed amid image-flash and whirl" (125). She encounters a similar apparition in Nora's studio, where among some random tchochkes Cayce "picks up a square of clear acrylic: laser-etched in its core are the Coca-Cola logo, a crude representation of the Twin Towers, and the words 'WE REMEMBER.' She quickly puts it down" (302–3). The similarity of these two easy-to-miss moments is striking—Coke logo and twin towers, linked by a slogan—and reminds us of how consistently advertising operates by creating conjunctions such as this, spatial conjunctions, linked metonymically rather than logically or sequentially: logo-image-slogan. The national icon has now been juxtaposed with the corporate brand in a structure that is connective rather than oppositional.

The link made here, the branding of September 11, is not presented neutrally; there is a sense of recoil in the way that Cayce "quickly puts it down." *Pattern Recognition* is both hypersensitive to and disturbed by the way that all things can be appropriated by "the spectral hand of marketing"—the footage and historical trauma and Russian mafia figures too. The book suggests that there is no place of purity, outside of consumer culture, for Cayce or anyone else to occupy, but it nonetheless desires that authentic space. (In fact, the conclusion of the book is an unconvincing fantasy of authenticity restored that seems at odds with the seriousness of the issues that Gibson has put in play; Cayce loses her allergy, finds romance, and even gets her soul back.[17]) Gibson's vision of authenticity is emblematic of cyberpunk in general, constructing a variety of models in which the sleek engine of consumer capitalism is represented as a machine, while resistance to that machine takes the form of the cyborg assemblage, built from the detritus of consumer culture: implicated in the machine, but not of it. This attempt to provide an alternative to the machine of global capital consistently returns to representations of America, or of its memory. While *Neuromancer's* imagined future is dystopian and implicitly nostalgic for the nation, *Pattern Recognition* makes that nostalgia explicit and visible in the crises of the present.

In constructing these models, both books align themselves with a politics that is drawn from the noir tradition: the politics of authenticity. Although cyberpunk constructs a thoroughly postmodern, partial, impure, cyborg aesthetic, that aesthetic nonetheless becomes the basis for its assertion of a space of bricolage and hybridity that offers the possibility of authentic resistance in the era of late capitalism.[18] As with the versions of authenticity offered by noir in the forties and fifties, and conspiracy texts in the sixties and seventies, this is an essentially reactive and oppositional position, the latest chapter in the ongoing story of consumer culture's evolution and the resultant development of new forms of desire for the authentic. That point is especially important because of the tendency in so much postmodern theory and cultural production—a tendency that finds its exemplary form both in cyberpunk and in Haraway's manifesto—to embrace hybridity and bricolage uncritically, appearing to solve the political contradictions of postmodernism while in fact offering a new form of authenticity and a reaffirmation of its opposition to consumer culture.

The Space of the Clock

THE CORPORATION AS GENRE IN
THE HUDSUCKER PROXY

> The dismantling of myth in Coen films is not merely an aesthetic revolt, it is an experiment with the American dream, with the dream of capitalism, the dream of moving from one social situation to another.
>
> —GEORG SEESSLEN, *"GAMES. RULES. VIOLATIONS."*

> AMY: Who are you—what d'you do here?
> MOSES: Ah keeps the ol' circle turning—this ol' clock needs plenty o' care. Time is money, Miss Archuh, and money—it drives that ol' global economy and keeps big Daddy Earth spinnin' on 'roun. Ya see, without that capital fo'mation—
> AMY: Yeah, yeah.
>
> —*THE HUDSUCKER PROXY*

The climax of Joel and Ethan Coen's 1994 film *The Hudsucker Proxy* is also, spatially speaking, a nadir. The disgraced president of Hudsucker Industries, Norville Barnes, has plummeted forty-four floors from the top of Manhattan's fictional Hudsucker Building at the stroke of midnight on New Year's Eve, 1958. But before he hits the pavement, an unusual thing happens: time stops. Suspended in midair, Norville is approached by an angel—an echo of Clarence in *It's a Wonderful Life*, of course, but this angel is also the ghost of Waring Hudsucker, the former chief of the company, who died taking this same plunge early on in the movie. Gesturing with one of heaven's white cigars, the former corporate fatcat instructs Norville to read a letter that he has forgotten he has in his pocket, a document that will alleviate the problems that have led to his suicide attempt.

The letter, posted by Hudsucker before his death, explains how he realized that in his striving for success he lost his identity and his chance for love, worked only to achieve greater stature and profit, and thus was left empty. The letter is addressed to Hudsucker's tough, soulless second-in-command,

Sidney J. Mussburger, and Norville reads it aloud, while the angelic Hudsucker corrects his recurrent error in increasingly annoyed tones:

> "How often, Sidney, has each of us yearned for . . . a second chance—in
> business or in love? Yes, a second chance—this brings me to our com-
> pany, Sid, and its future. Our next president must have the liberty I have
> had, as owner, to experiment, and even fall"—"fail"—"without fears of
> the whims of stockholders or an impatient board. The new president
> must be free to fall"—"fail!"—"and learn; to fail"—"fall!"—"and rise
> again, by applying what he has learned. Such is business. Such is life."[1]

This brief scene contains in miniature the complex of issues that is at the film's
core. The appropriation of generic material and intertexts from the filmic past,
the theme of business success, the representation of the vertical city in the
postwar era, the disruption of conventional conceptions of time: all these will
be important to the reading of the film that I will be developing here. But most
importantly, Hudsucker's repeated corrections of Norville's mistakes draw our
attention to the film's conflation of *failing* with *falling*. In this film, failing—
whether in business or in life and love—is literalized as a forty-floor fall to the
pavement below, which is to say that it is a film whose plot unfolds in symbolic
space, in spaces that give concrete shape to intangible concepts. Employing
this strategy at several levels, the film uses cinema's history to represent the
history contained in the corporation—the postwar era's emblematic commercial organization of space—in geographical terms.

   In the course of this study, I have followed the development of the noir tradition's relationship to consumer culture as a shifting series of relationships to
commercial space. The specific and localized spaces represented in classic
noir—the supermarket and the gas station are the examples I have discussed—
are replaced, as noir film and fiction transform into the conspiracy narrative
that emerges in the sixties and seventies, by more abstract entities: first the corporation as a national institution, then the corporation as an institution that
transcends and effaces national boundaries, and finally cyberpunk's attempt to
evoke the world-space organized by global capitalism itself. In this final chapter,
I turn to *The Hudsucker Proxy*, which continues the noir-derived investigation
of capitalist space, but which does so by returning to the postwar corporation.
In doing so, it also returns to the issues surrounding organizations, organization men, and the consumer economy's eclipsing of productive labor—looking
back to the fifties from the perspective of the century's final years. Of all the
texts I discuss in this book, *Proxy* is perhaps the one whose connections to the
noir tradition are least apparent; it contains few of the iconographic or narrative
markers of film noir or of the conspiracy story. But I will be arguing here that
by reading the film in relation to its web of intertexts, we can see it as a meditation on Hollywood genre in general, and in particular on the relationship
between the screwball comedy and the film noir. That meditation enables the

Coens' film to put the issues that are central to the noir tradition—the relationship between consumer culture and authenticity—into play and to suggest yet another way of formulating those issues.

The Coens' film, like cyberpunk, represents a quintessentially postmodern approach to the relationship between consumption and authenticity that is at the core of my analysis. But unlike cyberpunk, which replaces older models of resistance to consumer culture with a form of "postmodern authenticity" based on an aesthetic of hybridity, *The Hudsucker Proxy* takes the dialectic of authenticity itself as its subject. This, as I will be suggesting in the pages that follow, allows us to see the Coen vision not as empty pastiche—which is the usual rap against it, and against much postmodern cultural production— but as a politically inflected representation of history and temporality in spatial terms.

Coen America

The films of the Coen brothers have none of the science-fictional trappings that one finds in the novels of William Gibson, but they do share with cyberpunk an interest in genre-mixing combined with a distinctly postmodern exploration of space. The Coens' films taken together offer an investigation of America conducted through the exploration of particular regional, usually rural, spaces. Often these settings are located quite specifically—in films set in Arizona, Texas, Washington, D.C., the rural South, and especially in the Minnesota locations of *Fargo*—but these real places and their traditions are always rendered unreal through the Coens' superimposition of layers of Hollywood history. As Georg Seesslen writes:

> It is not the "reality" of these places which emerges but their clichés, which are, by their nature, more real than reality. . . . These places are also one hundred percent film sets. They are not in Texas but in the film noir, not in the big city but in the world of Frank Capra. They are places, like *Miller's Crossing*, which lie at the crossroads between Fritz Lang and Howard Hawks, or somewhere between Preston Sturges and George Cukor. . . . Place becomes a stage in Coen films. ("Games. Rules. Violations," 283)

The films use Hollywood genre as a vehicle for exploring the meanings of American spaces. While employing genre conventions and references, the films simultaneously exaggerate the culture, the landscape, and above all the uses of language that are specific to a region, effectively rendering each region as a genre in itself, a set of conventions and clichés. Through combinations of repetition and variation, these conventions become sources of humor and pathos, and their structures make the larger, synecdochally connected category of America intelligible in distinctive ways.

The genre tradition that shapes the Coen films most frequently is that of film noir. Even if noir is not a genre during its classic period, it is treated as such by the neo-noir films that employ its conventions, and as a genre it has taken a central role in many of the films made by the "postmodern" generation of filmmakers. Many of the directors who define this generation—the Coens, Pedro Almodóvar, and David Lynch, in particular—employ noir as a crucial element in a larger organizational strategy that puts genres and styles from the cinematic past into dialogue with each other in order to pose both social and psychological questions about the present. So as with cyberpunk, Coen films squeeze the most lively possibilities out of genre history by creating remixes or mash-ups. Their signature recipe combines elements from the Western and the noir, a melding that frequently allows them to reveal the rural heartland of America to be as haunted and deadly as any city's mean streets—as in, say, *Blood Simple, Fargo,* or *No Country for Old Men.* Even *The Big Lebowski*—a Chandler-derived film that also features a cowboy and a tumbleweed—chooses to portray Los Angeles more as suburban sprawl than as urban icon. And the Coens' most citified noir, *Miller's Crossing,* was conceived around the unexpectedness of its eponymous locale: the place where the film's most harrowing scenes occur is a quiet spot in the woods.

American space in the Coen films frequently takes the form of commercial space, both in the noir-inflected films and in those that are not. And these representations of commercial spaces—however tenuous their connection to noir in other ways—are staged in such a way as to pose the questions about American consumer culture that are central to the noir tradition. The Coen films meditate on the opposition between consumption as the definition of America in the postwar era, on the one hand, and on the other, alternate versions of national authenticity that might challenge that definition. But even when they stage the confrontation with consumer culture specifically by employing the logic of noir, they depart from that logic. The films stand outside of that confrontation, displaying an ambivalence that recognizes the possibility of finding and representing America in its commercial spaces—one that is analogous to their finding of America in the range of consumer choices offered by the Hollywood genre film—rather than in an authentic outside. This is not, I will be arguing, an apolitical strategy of disengagement, but rather a postmodern political strategy that asserts the necessity of locating American identity in the tension between consumer economy and authentic opposition.

I made a preliminary version of this argument in the introduction, in which I suggested that the Coens' film *The Big Lebowski* draws on both the noir and conspiracy traditions, but does so in a way that is ambivalent about the logic of authenticity, which suggests that the noir detective and the supermarket may be able to coexist. A similar ambivalence can be found in many of the representations of commercial space in Coen America: the supermarket and convenience stores of *Raising Arizona,* the gas station and drug store in *No Country for Old*

Men, Hollywood itself in *Barton Fink*. That ambivalence about consumer culture is an important thematic thread in *O Brother, Where Art Thou?* (2000), whose backdrop is a regionally distinct and potentially authentic America—rural Mississippi in 1937—that is beginning to be integrated into a homogenizing national consumer culture. At the film's climax, an unexpected flood acts as a deus ex machina that rescues the protagonists, but it is not an act of God. As the film's protagonist, Ulysses Everett McGill, explains, the land is being flooded because hydroelectric power is coming and this rural area will now be put on a "grid" and made to pay. This parable of capitalism and a national mass culture coming to the South is echoed everywhere in the film. Ulysses cannot find "his" Dapper Dan brand of hair pomade at a backwater store; Ulysses and his two fellow escaped convicts are pardoned because they have recorded a song that has become a runaway hit in the new music-recording industry; banned from Woolworth's, Ulysses and Delmar wonder whether that means "the one branch, or all of 'em"—a question that invokes the network of linked and uniform commercial spaces that create another kind of national grid. In its celebration of American "roots" music, the film seems to mourn the passing of an older and more traditional folk culture, but by making the new consumer culture the vehicle both for rescuing the heroes twice and for challenging the tradition of Southern racism and the Ku Klux Klan, it also seems to figure the new America defined by commercial space as a potentially welcome development.

O Brother is certainly not a noir, but the Coens followed up their Depression-era fable with a forties film, *The Man Who Wasn't There* (2001), which revisits noir both as a genre—the film is shot in black-and-white and borrows much of its plot from the books of James M. Cain—and as a set of concerns about consumer culture in the postwar era. The plot is set in motion when the central character, Ed Crane, blackmails his wife's lover in order to raise the money he needs to invest in a new technology-driven consumer industry: dry cleaning. While working as a barber is an old-fashioned sort of job, dry cleaning is representative of the postwar romance with automating household labor. Like the TV dinner or the electric kitchen appliance, it uses technology to make housework available for purchase. Its application of chemicals to a task once done with water, and its outsourcing of a chore done in the home to an outside commercial location, make it a shining miracle of the consumer economy. The Coens bring noir and consumer culture together again, fifty years later, but in a form that makes it impossible to tell whether one is to be valued over the other, or whether any sort of authenticity is possible for the film's hollow and passive protagonist. In fact, the film ends with a self-conscious nod to the economics of noir; while he waits on death row, Ed's voiceover narration is revealed as a version of his strange and bloody tale that he is selling to a pulp magazine—he calls it a "men's magazine"—at five cents a word. The pulpy side of the film is also evident in its references to flying saucers and its campy, science-fictiony title, all of which locates the blood melodrama of noir in the realm of the commercial. Rather than identifying noir as a site of authenticity, the film emphasizes the extent to which noir is manufactured as a sensational mode of entertainment for the male consumer.

Even this cursory look at the Coen oeuvre suggests the way that it invokes and extends the issues that are at the center of this book.[2] Their films, often working with elements of noir, treating it as a genre among other genres, are alert to the representation of commercial space and the way that those representations have been employed historically in the cinema. But their way of treating those representations of commercial space suggests another mutation in the evolutionary history I have been tracing here. The commercial is no longer imagined as the diametric opposite of the authentic, and the category of the authentic itself is therefore less stable in their version of postmodern aesthetics than in the version we have seen emerging from the texts of cyberpunk. In the reading of *The Hudsucker Proxy* that follows, I will be arguing that this tendency is best expressed in their representation of the corporation as an apotheosis of American commercial space, and that it is there that the Coen approach to the dialectics of authenticity is fully realized.

The Politics of Genre

I have said that the Coens often construct their films by placing noir characters and situations in a rural setting. *The Hudsucker Proxy* reverses this formula: it is the Coens' most urban film, and yet of all their productions it appears at first glance to be the least noirish. Its dominant mode is in fact that of the screwball comedy genre, but its introduction of noir elements into that comedic framework enables the film's investigation of themes of consumerism, commercial space, and the American success story, while also making visible the continuities between the noir and screwball genres, destabilizing the apparent opposition between the two. The film opens with a scenario borrowed from the noir playbook, as we meet Norville contemplating suicide atop the Hudsucker Building: the structure in which a film begins with a (perhaps) doomed male protagonist at a moment of crisis, or even of deadness, and then circles back to tell the character's story in flashback is familiar from many noirs—*The Killers, Double Indemnity, Sunset Boulevard, The Big Clock,* and *D.O.A.,* for example. But the homey, distancing voice of the narrator—"How'd he get so high? An' why is he feelin' so low? Is he really gonna do it—is Norville really gonna jelly up the sidewalk?"—is a reassurance, and the story that follows maintains a bright, lively tone and pace, full of goofy images and exchanges that are reminiscent of screwball, even when the material seems bleak.

A brief recap of that material will allow us to see how strongly the film follows a comedic plot structure. Norville arrives in New York City late in 1958, fresh out of Muncie Business College, and goes looking for a job at Hudsucker Industries at the same moment that Waring Hudsucker, having just been told by his board that business is booming, leaps to his death from the top of the building. Norville is put to work at the bottom of the building, in the mailroom, but happens to be delivering a letter to the company's new top executive, Sid Mussburger, just when Sid is looking for an idiot to take charge of the company and depress its stock prices so that he and the board can take control. Fast-talking reporter Amy Archer goes undercover as Norville's secretary and writes a series of articles about what a doofus he is, but he redeems himself with his pet invention, the Hula Hoop. However, once the proxy president has been corrupted by his success, Mussburger finds a way to fire, disgrace, and commit him. Norville heads out onto the ledge on which the film and this chapter began, where he slips and falls and is saved in the nick of time by the angel and an unexpected assist from the film's narrator, Moses. A wiser Norville takes over the company again, and in the final scene he throws his new invention, a Frisbee, out the boardroom window, now open, that Waring Hudsucker had crashed through.

That is one way of explaining what *The Hudsucker Proxy* is about. But the question of what a Coen film is "about" can be hard to answer in the usual ways. As I suggested already, these films are, among other things, postmodern constructions that are in a certain sense "about" genre. If two of the defining features of Coen films are the linked tendencies to postmodern self-consciousness and intertextual genre-mixing, these tendencies find their fullest expression in *The Hudsucker Proxy*. Here the web of references to, and elements borrowed from, other films is so densely constructed that the conception of a film as a pastiche constructed from bits and pieces of earlier films reaches a limit of sorts, so that any interpretation of *Proxy* must necessarily account for the way that the film arranges and juxtaposes its references.

Any mapping of the intertexts present in *The Hudsucker Proxy* begins with the films of Frank Capra and Preston Sturges. As the presence of these two directors suggests, *Proxy* owes a generalized debt to the screwball comedies of the thirties and forties, and also to fast-talking newspaper films—especially *His Girl Friday* (1940), which offers the template for the character of Amy Archer, although Jennifer Jason Leigh's performance also contains elements of Katharine Hepburn's persona and filmography. *Proxy* also looks back to three iconic films about industry and urban life, *Metropolis* (1927), *À Nous la liberté* (1931), and *Modern Times* (1936), each of which constructs its critique of modernity through elaborately designed sets that evoke urban and industrial environments as the claustrophobic space of a totalitarian monopoly capitalism. These set designs are picked up much later in the baroque and dystopian ductwork of *Brazil* (1985), which is also explicitly quoted in *Proxy*. Extending this concern with the position of the individual in modern cities and workplaces to the midcentury corporate office environment, the Coens' film draws on a number of films that deal with themes of success and failure, usually in business: *Citizen Kane* (1941), *The Big Clock* (1948), *The Fountainhead* (1949),

Executive Suite (1954), *Patterns* (1956), *Sweet Smell of Success* (1957), *Will Success Spoil Rock Hunter?* (1957), *The Apartment* (1960), *One . . . Two . . . Three* (1961), *The Patsy* (1964), *How to Succeed in Business Without Really Trying* (1967), *Putney Swope* (1969), and *The Arrangement* (1969).[3] Although these films cover a spectrum that runs from broad satirical farce to earnest melo-drama, all are explorations of the way that postwar male American identity is located and contested in the drama of business success, a drama that takes place almost exclusively in corporate offices located in tall city buildings.

To accommodate this dense web of references, the film is constructed as an homage to Hollywood's past. Although the film is nominally set in Manhattan, its elaborate sets actually evoke a generalized and deliberately artificial Hollywood setting that might as well be called Metropolis or Gotham City. In fact, the radically stylized sets were constructed by creating a greatest-hits version of New York architecture in which, as production designer Dennis Gassner observes, the filmmakers "took all [their] favorite buildings in New York from where they actually stood and sort of put them into one neighborhood, a fantasy vision of New York" (*Coen Brothers*, 126). Again, American region becomes a kind of genre here and the setting is not really New York but rather Newyorkland, a version of the city so iconic and idealized that it persistently reminds us that it is a simulation, a set. This pristine quality pervades the film's design, as if every surface in the film partook of the cult of architectural new-ness present both in the Art Deco of the twenties and thirties and the postwar "international" style. Look, for example, at the perfect smoothness of Hud-sucker's leather chair at the moment he steps onto it with his perfectly shiny shoes before stepping onto the perfectly gleaming expanse of the polished boardroom table that is his launching pad into oblivion.

FIGURE 20 *Waring Hudsucker steps onto the gleaming boardroom table.*

As these stylized effects indicate, *The Hudsucker Proxy* is characterized by its postmodern distance from the material it presents. Not only the characters and their actions, but also the world of the film in its largest conception and in its smallest details, are constructed so as to put everything in quotation marks and to undermine the possibility of responding directly to the drama. This technique operates at the level of character as well as in the world-as-set. The faces of the minor characters and extras are a remarkable gallery of icons and grotesques; each unusual facial feature has been emphasized through makeup, glasses, and a casting principle of unnatural selection. The performances take this effect even further, as the actors assume absurdly exaggerated expressions and distinctive voices that emphasize the effect of the dialogue, which is itself an homage to the already-stylized patter of thirties and forties Hollywood. Consider this monologue, delivered in a rapid-fire squeal by the elevator operator, Buzz, as he takes Norville (who is carrying a top-priority "blue letter") and assorted other passengers to the upper floors of the Hudsucker Building:

> Hiya, buddy! The name is Buzz, I got the fuzz, I make the elevator do what she does! . . . Forty-four, the top-brass floor, say buddy! What takes fifty years to get to the top floor and thirty seconds to get down? Waring Hudsucker! Na-ha-ha-ha-ha! . . . Mr. Kline, up to nine. Mrs. Dell, personnel. Mr. Levin, thirty-seven. ["Thirty-six," Mr. Levin corrects, but Buzz won't abandon the rhyme.] *Walk* down. Ladies and gentlemen, step to the rear—here comes gargantuan Mr. Grier. . . . Say buddy! When is the sidewalk fully dressed? When it's "wearing" Hudsucker! Na-ha-ha-ha! Ya get it buddy, it's a pun, it's a knee-slapper, it's a play on *Jesus, Joseph and Mary, is that a Blue Letter*?!

As this manic rhyming patter suggests, *Proxy*'s style is defined by a cartoonish exaggeration that also creates emotional distance. Sound effects are amplified to create effects of comedy and mock-grandiosity, as when a corporate appointment book falls open with a long-echoing doomsday crash. When Norville and Amy kiss, the soundtrack swells to a crescendo that parodies classic Hollywood scoring, preventing rather than inviting viewer identification.

The casting and performances of the principal characters are equally precise and also precisely referential. Tall and long-limbed, gangly but handsome, Tim Robbins as Norville has a physical presence that recalls the classic Capra leading men, Gary Cooper and Jimmy Stewart. As Amy Archer, Jennifer Jason Leigh takes the part (and the hairstyle) usually reserved for Jean Arthur in Capra films, but her motormouth performance is an amalgam of Rosalind Russell in *His Girl Friday* and Katharine Hepburn in any comedy. Paul Newman is cast deliberately against type as Mussburger: he growls his lines around a well-chomped cigar, and his performance as a truculent, older-generation establishment figure recalls the characters with whom the young and rebellious

Newman character did battle in the fifties and sixties—as with, for example, his role opposite Orson Welles in *The Long, Hot Summer* (1958).

In short, everything that critics of postmodernism abhor can be found in abundance in this film: the relationship to history that is figured as a relationship to cinema history, the attention to shifting surfaces rather than modernist depth, the waning of affect brought on by the film's distancing stylization, the use of pastiche as an apparent end in itself. I will be arguing in this chapter that *The Hudsucker Proxy* is indeed a defining instance of postmodern cinema but that its postmodern structure, its organization as pastiche, is inseparable from its political logic. That is to say that the film's politics—its attitude toward the corporation and the consumer economy that it represents—is expressed, or encoded, in its use of genre and the intertextual Hollywood past.

If *The Hudsucker Proxy* is, as Georg Seesslen suggests, "a Capra story peopled by Preston Sturges characters in a Fritz Lang setting" (237; he is paraphrasing John Harkness), then it is not surprising that the film's meaning emerges out of the meeting of intertexts that it enables, and most critics have seen the comedies of the thirties and forties as central to this meaning. Both Capra and Sturges are crucial figures in the production of the "screwball comedy" from this period, although each director pursues a distinctive variant of the screwball formula. (In fact, the film usually cited as the first screwball, 1934's *It Happened One Night*, owes something to both; it was directed by Capra, and the story was based partly on the story of Sturges's 1930 elopement with Post cereal heiress Eleanor Close Hutton. Capra helped to invent screwball, but Sturges lived it.) To the extent that such a formula exists, it involves a battle-of-the-sexes romantic comedy defined by a pleasurable structure of contradiction: a romance plot that presents itself as cynical and unsentimental, a physical comedy that is defined by rapid, cutting wordplay.[4] Although the screwball comedies clearly thematize gender politics, they have also frequently been read as responses, of one kind or another, to the Depression and its class politics.[5] Powerful, and opposed, versions of that response can be found in the films of Capra and Sturges.

Frank Capra, more than any other filmmaker, directly dramatizes the national crisis of the Depression. His films, as Charles Maland points out, return persistently to the conflict between private interest and the public good, which is why they so often appear to be a cinematic corollary to the New Deal. They are also a fantasized inversion of the noir vision, in which the private interests represented by consumer capitalism have erased any possible appeal to the public good. Capra peers into the abyss—a male protagonist ends up on a ledge or a bridge or otherwise contemplates suicide—where he finds that private interest has produced a corrupt, violent, and seedy mirror-world America. Then he pulls back from that vision and reinstates an idealized small-town ethos defined by civic values as the "real" America. The male protagonist is rescued from defeat and disillusionment, usually by the intervention of a heartland community and/or the conversion of a skeptic to the side of the public good.

Preston Sturges's films also tend to involve characters brought to crisis by inequalities that emerge from American politics or economy. But if Capra's America is a place threatened by private interest that ultimately places its faith in the people as a repository of good faith, Sturges's is a wild ride up and down economic and emotional rollercoasters in which "the people" are flawed, crazy, and often kind of dumb. His characters aren't rescued by anything as organized as community or even divine intervention; most of the time they are rescued by absurd, unaccountable, and undependable luck. "What's the matter with Capra?" asks Sullivan, the wealthy director of frivolous comedies who wants to make serious films about post-Depression poverty and social themes—who aspires to be like Capra—in Sturges's *Sullivan's Travels* (1941). By the end of the movie, he implicitly answers that question: having spent time laboring on a prison chain gang, he has decided that the best thing he can do for the poor and oppressed is to make frivolous comedies (and in the process, of course, Sturges sneaks a political film into his own, frequently frivolous, comedy).[6] *Sullivan's Travels* shows Sturges's difference from Capra nicely, as well as indicating how closely the Coen sensibility is tied to that of Sturges. (*O Brother, Where Art Thou?* takes its title from the allegorical social-problem film that Sullivan hopes to make.) *The Hudsucker Proxy*'s evocation of the classic era of Hollywood is skewed in the direction of Sturges, whose manic irreverence toward the nation's institutions and unsentimental tenderness toward its inhabitants is a closer match with the Coen sensibility than Capra's responsible corniness could ever be.

So while Capra and Sturges, like two of the characters in *Proxy*, duke it out inside the Hudsucker clock in a battle for the soul of the Coens' film, we critics are left to figure out what all these issues surrounding the Depression and the New Deal are doing in a film set a generation away, in the middle of the Eisenhower administration. Ike himself calls Norville to congratulate him on the success of the Hula Hoop, but this is only one of the film's many specific historical markers. Given the constant references to the turnover from 1958 to 1959, the use of jazz, the presence of a beatnik bar, and the performance of a Dean Martin–inspired crooner, the persistent emphasis of the temporal setting is deliberately at odds with the architecture of the sets and the Hollywood intertexts, which suggest the prewar moment, the thirties.

At the film's heart, then, is a tension between the historical moment of the film's setting and the historical atmosphere of the film's references, between history and the history of cinema. Critics have noticed this tension, and have generally seen it as key to the film's politics. Walter Metz offers one version of this argument, suggesting that the film employs its thirties intertexts (in conjunction with the soundtrack, a gorgeous Carter Burwell composition that incorporates works by the Soviet composer Aram Khachaturian, notably his slave-revolt-as-Marxist-fable ballet *Spartacus*) to restore class politics to the blandly conservative culture of the Eisenhower era: "Drawing from an understanding of the 1930s

screwball comedy as a textual system in keeping with Roosevelt New Dealism ...
the film activates this generic tradition as a way of critiquing the corporate capitalism of the 1950s that threatens to engulf Norville as a Capraesque hero" (*Engaging Film Criticism*, 165).[7] Although Metz makes *Proxy* sound too much like a
straight Capra film, if not a Marxist fable in itself, he offers a useful corrective to
the reading of the movie as an empty pastiche. Paul Coughlin takes this corrective
work as his task, arguing that *Proxy* employs conventions of screwball comedy "in
order to examine its processes, expose its traditional agendas, and highlight its
inherent ideologies. The intention is not to ridicule the genre but to identify the
manner by which the screwball comedy reflects ideology, history, and meaning"
("The Past Is Now," 199). For both writers, the Coens' version of generic intertex-
tuality is a deliberate strategy with political implications.

The Coen project is in fact trans-generic, bringing together films from an
array of eras and traditions in order to make visible the obsessive American
attempt to represent to itself endless variations on the dream of social mobility,
the drama of success and failure. In doing so, the Coens construct a kind of
retrospective generic tradition of their own, or a larger structure that crosses
genres in its portrayal of success and failure as distinctive American themes. In
his book *Career Movies* Jack Boozer argues that the "business career film" is a
genre unto itself, one that is shaped by a desire to understand the way particular relationships to economy and work are intertwined with American conceptions of selfhood in the years after 1945.[8] *The Hudsucker Proxy* makes a
similar argument, but in bringing together so many different films, genres, and
traditions from the past it suggests that the business career film is only the
most straightforward version of a larger tradition that defines Hollywood film
itself. Hollywood returns perpetually to this representation of economic ambition as a form of *crisis*, so that American movies are forever staging versions of
the defining national struggle between capitalism and democracy. This is the
large opposition that we have seen at work, throughout this study, in classic
film noir and its later derivations—and noir turns out to be the final piece that
we need to fit into the Coens' generic puzzle.

To be precise, *The Hudsucker Proxy* mashes up the screwball comedy (and
the related form of the "Capra film") with the film noir, and in the process
reveals the extent to which these two forms have a perhaps unexpected set of
affinities. In his study of Depression culture, Morris Dickstein argues that
noir and screwball both take their characteristic forms from the tradition of
hard-boiled writing: "Screwball imported into comedy the kind of unsentimental crispness and cynicism that then belonged to crime stories, detective
stories, and tales of newspapermen" (*Dancing in the Dark*, 396). With the fast-
talking newspaper story as a transitional genre (one that figures as an element
in some noirs, a number of screwballs, and *The Hudsucker Proxy*), the screwball comedy put a madcap twist on hard-boiled conventions, including the
lack of conventional sentiment, the baroque plotting, the absurdist rapid-fire

poetry of the dialogue. And, of course, there is the demented gender politics. Dickstein observes that the ditzy dame and the femme fatale are versions of each other, and indeed they are: predatory women who entrap passive men who seem, mystified, to simply give themselves into the hands of an inescapable fate, whether marriage or (a life of doomed criminality ending most often in) death.

There are in fact a number of classic noirs that incorporate elements of the screwball. Dashiell Hammett is often credited as the exemplar of hard-boiled detective fiction, but his 1934 novel *The Thin Man* is already a kind of screwball comedy, one so camera-ready that it was filmed that same year. In *The Big Sleep*, Howard Hawks made significant alterations to Chandler's novel in order to create a Bogart-Bacall romance plot that is developed in comic scenes of the two prank-calling the police or getting hot and bothered talking about the races. On the flipside, Hawks's newspaper screwball *His Girl Friday*, David Thomson writes, "looks like noir coming to life" (*Have You Seen . . .?* 371). *The Big Clock*, a key intertext for *Proxy*, has the kind of plot that could go either way—a man who is compelled to conduct a manhunt for himself—and plays it for screwball laughs half the time and noir suspense the other half. Indeed, many of the best noirs are built on dialogue that would work equally well in a screwball: passages that pile comeback on comeback to create comic set-pieces of hard-boiled nonsense, like the wacky innuendos of Walter Neff and Phyllis Dietrichson in *Double Indemnity*.

Given these conjunctions, it is less surprising than it might otherwise be to notice how close noir is to the center of Capra's heartwarming comedies—in particular, *It's a Wonderful Life* from 1946. After the success of *It Happened One Night* in 1934, Capra felt the burden of his unique access to the American masses and set out to use that access to make socially significant films. The result was the series of films that made it possible to talk about a "Capra movie," defined roughly as a populist romantic-comic melodrama in which the crisis of private interests corrupting American democratic values is represented by the possibility of suicide but then becomes the occasion for a communal conversion to the side of those values: *Mr. Deeds Goes to Town* (1936), *Mr. Smith Goes to Washington* (1939), *Meet John Doe* (1941), and *It's a Wonderful Life* (1946). As I observed earlier (following Charles Maland), Capra's films always contemplate this dark abyss before flooding the world with light, but the last film in the cycle, the postwar entry, is especially bleak. George Bailey's story is such a litany of disappointments and setbacks that the only way it can be made to look appealing is by introducing an angel who shows us an alternative universe in which George doesn't even exist; and as many critics have noticed, the world without George turns out to be a film noir. As Frank Krutnik writes:

The idealized middle-American community of Bedford Falls is supplanted by the wild urban world of Pottersville. As George runs through the town, a series of tracking shots exposes the iconography of the 1940s *noir* city: a riot of neon and jazz, the main street of Pottersville is crammed with burlesque halls, dance joints, pawnbroker's stores, numerous bars.... Pottersville's urban world ... is a wasteland of non-productive excess, its public spaces dominated not by family homes but by the brash seductions of commercialized leisure. ("Something More Than Night," 85–86)

But although Capra uses the nightmare of greedy oligarchs ruling America to furnish his noir vision, and despite the apparent alignments of his work with the New Deal, this is not a leftist film; it may be vulgar, but it isn't Marxism.

Instead, as the historian Charles McGovern points out, *It's a Wonderful Life* is emblematic of postwar America's conflation of consumption with citizenship: "Bedford Falls without George Bailey is enslaved to unbridled commerce, a market in place of society, commerce without purpose or limits" (*Sold American*, 360). But George is not opposed to consumption as such; rather, he represents the Rooseveltian idea that consumption and economic abundance can be harnessed responsibly to the civic and national common good. The Bailey Mortgage and Loan is devoted to realizing the American belief that every individual or family should own a house—preferably a detached suburban one, preferably in the small-town simulacrum that is Bedford Falls—linking George's vision of consumption and civic responsibility to the midcentury rise of the suburban consumerist model. The story's final movement takes place on

FIGURE 21 It's a Wonderful Life: *George Bailey in the noir vision of Pottersville.*

Christmas, and the film endures in the popular memory because of its associations with this holiday of consumption. (Both of the "classic Christmas movies" that run on television starting each Thanksgiving are, directly or indirectly, Capra movies. *It's a Wonderful Life* is one, and the other, *Miracle on 34th Street* [1947], draws so much of its plot from Capra's *Mr. Deeds* that it should really be called *Mr. Santa Claus Goes to Town*.) Old Man Potter is not only a caricature, but a caricature of a figure whose time has passed. He is a creature of the Gilded Age, a twice-told tale of the era of robber barons and company towns. The future doesn't belong to Pottersville, with its weird and historically naïve suggestion that urban seediness will somehow be transplanted to America's small towns; it belongs to the undifferentiable tracts of commercial and suburban sprawl that will be constructed in the consumerist postwar era.

So Capra deploys noir iconography to construct a fantasy of commerce run rampant—and because it is fantasy, envisioned only so that it can be contained and ameliorated, it is a version of noir that is deprived of its potential for social critique and folded back into the system it wants to resist. While noir presents itself as the darkly authentic vision of an America lost and betrayed in the age of bland consumerism, Capra *equates* noir with consumer culture figured as rapacious commerce in order to locate the "real" America in the bland consumer-citizen ideal that noir abhors.[9]

The Hudsucker Proxy, in its skeptical interrogation of the moral structures that Capra depends upon, reintroduces the possibility of the kind of social critique that is familiar from classic noir, in which both the city and the heartland are frequently revealed as false promises, even if they promise different things. Norville Barnes, like George Bailey, has a harrowing night in the noir city and a confrontation with the abyss, but this finale is not an occasion to reaffirm the values associated with the small town and the status quo by asserting that the film's past, its story up to that point, is where goodness and truth reside. Instead, *Proxy* keeps Norville in the city, suggesting that there is no future in returning to the heartland—that there is in fact no possibility of returning to the heartland. Once you're in the city you follow the city's plot, which in its noir version leads either to disgrace and suicide or to a corrupt and soulless success. *Proxy* uses an angel and a literal deus ex machina—Moses, the godlike narrator, who resides inside the gears of the Hudsucker clock—to rescue Norville from these ugly alternatives. But along the way the film reasserts the ideological possibilities that Capra's film sought to contain; the Coens maintain a critical distance from both noir and screwball, but discover in both the possibility of a more sophisticated political response to American commerce than *It's a Wonderful Life* can offer. With this in mind, I will now turn to a consideration of the structurings of space that *Proxy*'s noir intertexts enable, as a way to begin to understand the film's representation of the spatial organization that is at its center: the corporation.

Space, Incorporated

In the preceding chapters, I have argued that the noir tradition is defined by a geography in which America in the age of consumer culture is represented concretely in the form of commercial spaces. Against these, noir posits or discovers an authentic and alternative version of America, one that exists as metaphorical representation in the spaceless space—or as the assertion of an oppositional "counterspace"—of the elsewhere. One way of conceptualizing noir's geography is offered by Kelly Oliver and Benigno Trigo in their book *Noir Anxiety*. Arguing that representations of architecture and geography in noir are manifestations of the processes of identity formation, Oliver and Trigo suggest that "the free-floating existential anxiety of film noir is an anxiety over ambiguous spaces. Its heroes are . . . wandering travelers who unsuccessfully try to escape their past. . . . Indeed, the past or time itself is often a metaphorical place or space where these characters are trapped and from which they try to run away, to no avail" (217–18). *The Hudsucker Proxy* is in fact a film that represents "time itself" in spatial terms. In doing so it reveals not the unconscious identity formation of the characters but rather something like the unconscious of the postwar corporation, in which a sleek new consumerist aesthetic is haunted by ghosts of industry and labor.

  The Hudsucker Proxy's prototype for this way of representing the corporation is the 1948 film noir *The Big Clock*. In chapter 2 I described the 1946 Kenneth Fearing novel on which the film is based, in which the term "the big clock" is a sweeping and abstract metaphor for corporate capitalism writ large. But in John Farrow's film adaptation, he and screenwriter John Latimer make the metaphor literal and spatial by putting an actual (and big) clock at the heart of the Janoth corporate headquarters. This master clock is a sophisticated-looking piece of machinery rather than a giant clock face. A cylindrical monolith with a global map bordered by clocks that tell the time in every part of the world, it is as fine an object for representing multinational capitalism—fantasized in the classic Hollywood way as a centralized monopoly capitalism—as one could ask for. It not only tells the time but also defines the order of time, controlling all the other clocks in the building and symbolizing the obsession with efficiency of the sinister corporate head, Earl Janoth. The film's straightforward social critique suggests that this servitude to time is at the core of a corporate machine that expects its employees to function like clockwork cogs. Janoth, at the center of the clockwork, exerts a kind of panoptic power; when he discovers (somehow) that a small light has been left on in a closet somewhere in the building, he demands a firing. (And when he murders his mistress in a fit of rage, the weapon he finds at hand is a sundial.)

  The film's plot revolves around the identity crisis of its protagonist, George Stroud, who is ordered to conduct a manhunt for himself; he is the "mystery man" whom Janoth hopes to frame for his mistress's murder. At the film's climax, Stroud is trapped in the Janoth building, space contracting claustrophobically around him as the dragnet he has set in motion draws closer. He takes refuge within the clock itself—a final irony, as he finds a hiding place in the belly of the beast, the nerve center that controls the whole corporate machine. Once inside, he accidentally brushes against a switch that shuts down the clock and therefore shuts down all the clocks in the building, which enrages Janoth and activates his henchman Bill, who goes to check the clock. Bill, played by Harry Morgan, is the weirdest element in the film. Unspeaking, wary, and threatening, he is inexplicable except as pure symbol, the embodiment of the corporation itself—and the inspiration for the character Aloysius in *The Hudsucker Proxy*. Clearly he cannot abide a disruption in corporate functioning like the one represented by a clock shutdown, so he goes inside the big clock, where he finds and grapples with Stroud, who eventually traps Bill in an elevator—symbol of the vertically organized corporation's power structure. The film turns out, then, not to use space as a way of understanding Stroud's identity crisis, but rather in an opposite way: it uses Stroud's internal struggle with himself as the occasion for a spatial investigation and ideological critique of the corporate organization.

Like the midcentury texts I cited in chapter 2, Farrow's film takes a critical attitude toward the corporation as a soulless machine that creates its workers as undifferentiable drones. The film suggests that this process is enabled by the corporate manipulation of time, a time organized by the clock in violation of more natural or human rhythms. The manipulation of time in the interests of commerce has a long history; as David Harvey, following Jacques le Goff, writes,

> the organization of commercial networks over space in the early mediaeval period, forced the merchant to construct "a more adequate and predictable measure of time for the orderly conduct of business." . . . Symbolized by clocks and bells that called workers to labour and merchants to market . . . merchants and masters created a new "chronological net" in which daily life was caught. (*The Condition of Postmodernity*, 227–28)

Harvey suggests that from its beginnings, capitalism has required and produced a conception of time, "symbolized by clocks and bells that called workers to labour," that organizes individuals and social structures in order to facilitate commerce. It is striking how many of *The Hudsucker Proxy*'s intertexts, in literalizing the functioning of twentieth-century capitalism, turn to images that look like updated versions of Harvey's medieval spaces. *Proxy*, *The Big Clock*, *Patterns*, and *Executive Suite* all give us urban spaces dominated at the center by tall buildings with clocks, whose bells mark the transitions of the characters' days and lives. *Modern Times* begins with a shot of an oversized clock that sets the tone for the film's depiction of Chaplin's little man caught in the gears of the industrial machine, his body subjected to repetitive labors and his life dominated by the tyranny of time. The symbolism is even more melodramatic in *Metropolis*, in which wealthy Freder takes a worker's shift and finds himself crucified on the clocklike machine he is trying to operate. Lang underlines the point by superimposing on the machine the image of the film's iconic ten-hour clock, which suggests a further development in the manipulation and production of time by commercial interests.

By employing these intertexts, *Proxy* places itself within a tradition of social critique that uses the clock as a symbol of capital's oppressive reorganization of workers' lives. Borrowing a riff from *The Big Clock*, the workers here all live on "Hudsucker Time," a point emphasized by the many shots of the Hudsucker clock, which dominates the building's profile on both the outside and inside. After the film's opening suicide, loudspeakers inform the workers throughout the building that "at thirty seconds after the hour of noon, Hudsucker Time, Waring Hudsucker, Founder, President, and Chairman of the Board of Hudsucker Industries, merged with the infinite. To mark this occasion of corporate loss, we ask that all employees observe a moment of silent contemplation" and, after a few seconds of silence, the voice concludes: "This moment has been duly noted on your time cards and will be deducted from your pay." Here the Coens appear to align themselves clearly with the populist critique of capitalist time that is present in the earlier films, echoing in particular the parodic strategies of Chaplin in *Modern Times*.

But although the Coens are clearly interested in this tradition, the film does not actually stick to the script suggested by the films it refers to. *The Hudsucker Proxy* is very much "about" time, but its techniques are mobilized throughout in order to present temporal ruptures and discontinuities, so that at every turn the film playfully violates the linear ordering; oppressive Hudsucker Time is consistently made subject to the darkly whimsical rhythms of Coen Time. Sid Mussburger keeps a Newton's cradle of clicking balls on his desk, and their constant ticking is sometimes amplified in the sound mix in order to create a sense of ominous, oppressive clock time, but when Sid realizes that Norville is the perfect patsy to put in the president's chair, he shouts, "Wait a minute!" and the balls, in a little Godardian joke, stop dead. When Hudsucker jumps and when Norville falls from the top of the building, each time the fall is stretched to absurd and agonizing lengths—a seven-second fall accomplished in thirty— rendering the death plummet as a vertiginous carnival ride. This extension of the fall reaches an illogical conclusion when Norville, and the passage of time for everyone except him, stops completely in mid-fall. But *Proxy*'s most consistent strategy of temporal organization is its extensive and parodic use of the montage sequence. By my count, the Coens use and abuse its conventions no less than five times—including a *March of Time*–style newsreel sequence à la *Citizen Kane*, but not counting several mini-montages—in order to compress a whole series of events into a passage that speeds up and slows down the flow of images at will. When time moves forward in this film, it moves not in a linear progression of scenes but in a burst of juxtaposed, and only sometimes sequential, images.

These formal tendencies are echoed in the film's thematic exploration of time, which mingles traditional Western conceptions of linear time with Eastern alternatives to such a degree that it becomes impossible to separate them effectively. Against the dominance of the clock, which shapes so much of the film, in a quiet moment Norville invokes the Hindu version of reincarnation and the notion of karma, which he describes as "a great wheel that gives us each what we deserve." This reference to an Eastern conception of time that is circular and cyclic seems to offer a kind of resistance to the dominant linear conception of time that organizes New York's rat race, but the film puts versions of circular time in the service of corporate villains, too. When Norville's Hula Hoop is a smash success and the Hudsucker board's plot appears to be thwarted, Sid Mussburger is undeterred, delivering a grimly oracular speech: "All right, so the kid caught a wave. So right now he and his dingus are on top. Well, this too shall pass. . . . Sure, sure, the wheel turns, the music plays, and our spin ain't over yet." (The film also has some ironic fun with the corporate appropriation of Eastern or transcendental thought in that scene where the loudspeaker announces that Waring Hudsucker has "merged with the infinite.") In this film, time is an ambivalent, unsettled quality, a straight path and a wheel at the same time, seemingly irrevocable and yet perpetually thwarted and disrupted, with circular time offering both rebirth and a lasting death in the crushing gears of the clock's interior and the eternal circle of its face. As the Hudsucker slogan, written in lighted letters on the clock, declares, "The Future Is Now"—a final temporal contradiction in terms.

These observations lead us to *The Hudsucker Proxy*'s defining problematic, the one hinted at in Oliver and Trigo's description of noir. This film, which appears to be organized obsessively by issues of time, is in fact organized by a principle that represents everything—especially time—in terms of space. Its project might be best understood as an instance of what geographer Edward Soja calls "simultaneity." In *Postmodern Geographies*, Soja argues that Marxist critical theory's account of capitalism has been dominated by a historicist bias that has privileged temporal understanding and obscured possible understandings of capital as "a geography of simultaneous relations and meanings that are tied together by a spatial rather than a temporal logic" (1). Writing against this tendency, Soja wants to evoke "the spatio-temporal rhythm of capitalist development, a macrospective conjunction of periodicity and spatialization. . . . The aim is to open up and explore a critical viewpoint that pointedly flows from the resonant interplay of temporal succession and spatial simultaneity" (3). The Coens' film employs a similar strategy in its use of the corporation as a spatial complex through which the history of capitalism can be represented.

The film is in fact structured by its own logic of simultaneity. I have argued that any interpretation of *The Hudsucker Proxy* has to account for its use of its many intertexts, and although the juxtaposition of the historical fifties and the cinematic-historical thirties is a key element in this accounting, it only tells part of the story. By bringing together references to and elements from films ranging from the silent era to the eighties, *Proxy* folds sixty years of cinematic history into itself, rendering that history within the simultaneous space of the film. Just as it selects and compresses New York City into Newyorkland, the film itself becomes a theme park of the Hollywood past, where the vista of genre rides can be taken in all at once.[10] Genre itself is central to *Proxy* in part because it functions in film as a spatial, architectural element; genre provides a kind of blueprint that allows a viewer, early on in the film, to perceive the structure of the film as a simultaneous whole, after which the temporal realization of, and variation upon, that structure can be comfortably enjoyed. This strategy has its formal equivalent in the Coens' characteristic manipulation of screen space through the use of wide-angle lenses—a preference that shapes the look of all their films, especially the early ones, but that is particularly noticeable in *Proxy* because of the increased scope and complexity of the sets. The wide-angle shots, by exaggerating depth relations and taking in a greater proportion of the set or scenery, provide the viewer with the sensation of seeing everything at once, apprehending a larger range of elements in the same space of any given moment. In fact, when the Coens and cinematographer Roger Deakins decided to shoot the suicide falls in wide-angle, they had to add more buildings to the set, which didn't extend far enough to accommodate the range of a 10mm lens.

This principle of construction extends to the film's specific story as well. Having shifted their focus away from the emotional attachments and plot developments that conventionally occupy the center of the viewing experience,

FIGURE 22 *The film's master shot: Hudsucker plummets into Newyorkland.*

the Coens have made a film organized largely by the motif as a principle of meaning. This choice is not unique to the Coens, of course, but since the repetition of elements in screen time ultimately creates the sensation of time's erasure or collapse, here it contributes to the overall effect of watching a film that unfolds in spatial terms. The shots of Hudsucker falling are a case in point. Their dramatic single-point perspective is reproduced in many of the shots of Hudsucker spaces that are used in the film: those of the boardroom, the mailroom, and the accounting office, for example. All are framed with strong, clean graphic lines receding to convergence, a composition that uses impossible spaces as a way to represent the corporation as an immeasurably vast entity. Meanwhile, the way that all these spaces echo the image of Hudsucker's fall make that image into a kind of master shot. The visual motif of vertiginous single-point perspective links itself to the thematic motif of falling and failing in business; falling is the image that defines all the activity that goes on at Hudsucker Industries.

But the most prominent motif in the film is, like genre, a kind of blueprint. Early on in the film, Norville explains to anyone who will listen that he has "big plans" and pulls out of his shoe the diagram that he believes will make him rich: a carefully drawn circle—"you know; for kids!" Later in the film the diagram becomes slightly more complex: a circle next to a vertical line. The joke is eventually sprung and we learn that what we have been looking at is the concept for the Hula Hoop, but by this time it has also become clear that *The Hudsucker Proxy* could fairly be described as a movie "about" circles and vertical lines. Circles recur endlessly: not just in the film's circular plot whose beginning is an end, not just in the many clocks, watches, and gears it depicts (time represented as space), but also in other symbols of corporate finance such as the tickertape spools that tell the up-and-down story of the company's profitability and the omnipresent cigars (a circle, a line) that signify success—not to mention the Hudsucker angel's halo, or his song ("She'll Be Coming Round the Mountain") or any number of other iterations. The cyclical up-and-down movement enacted by the circles also suggests the way that the circle and the vertical line, seemingly opposites, merge into a single symbolic figure in the film. Success and failure in the vertical city are registered by what floor of the building you work on, by rising and falling, and although Norville himself goes up and down like a yo-yo, Buzz points out that it can take fifty years to get to the top but only thirty seconds to get back down.[11]

The circle-and-line motif, as these examples indicate, is an expression of the film's central project: representing the corporation. The corporation is imagined here as a complex and multilayered space, simultaneously concrete and imaginary, a historically located social organization whose development also contains the development of capitalism. As with the confusion between falling and failing, the Hudsucker Building and its clock are envisioned as literalized metaphors. Its spatial organization is borrowed largely from the heavy vertical

FIGURE 23 *The blueprint: a film about circles and lines.*

symbolism of *Metropolis*, in which workers are consigned to an underground city while the bosses and upper classes occupy offices and aeries high up in the Art Deco skyscrapers above. Likewise, Norville's entry-level position at Hudsucker puts him in the infernal, dungeon-dark mailroom, where he labors alongside workers who have no apparent hope of moving up in the company.[12] Mussburger and the other board members are at the top, on the forty-fourth floor (although, true to the fable-like atmosphere of the film, "blue letters" from one executive to another are routed through the basement mailroom). The film's other images of the company present a vast and intricate machine, connected by pneumatic tubes and full of antic, absurd labors that are a parody of actual labor, such as a huge room full of men with adding machines set to the task of deciding how much a Hula Hoop should cost.

And then there is the clock, which is weirdly present to the building's inhabitants. From inside Mussburger's enormous office, part of the clock's face, the numbers and hands seen from behind, is visible—so that the clock and the building, the clock and the business of the company, are conflated visually. Working, or living, inside the clock is Moses, the film's narrator and as such a supernatural presence who watches and analyzes the film's events.[13] He turns out to have an opposite number, the sinister and unspeaking Aloysius, who carries a chisel with which to scrape the names of dead or fired executives off their doors, and who helps Mussburger to get Norville fired; he is the remorseless enforcer of the corporation's rules. (This character is borrowed wholesale from *The Big Clock*; he is a version of the silent, dangerously watchful Bill, who abhors any deviation from the proper functioning of the Janoth Corporation.[14]) When Norville's fall from the top floor suddenly stops, the cause is revealed to be Moses, who has stuck a broom in the clock's gears; when the

FIGURE 24 *The weird space of Mussburger's office, on the other side of the clock.*

Hudsucker clock stops, time stops. As does the illusion of realistic narrative: "Strictly speaking," Moses says to the camera, "I'm never supposed to do this. But have you got a better idea?" Aloysius, revealed now as another supernatural character—the time-stop doesn't include him—is incensed and bursts into the clock. Aloysius, the spirit of the machine, faces off against Moses, the ghost in the machine, while the stalled gears tremble around them. Moses wins the battle and thus enables the film's impossible happy ending, but more importantly, the sequence makes it clear that for *Proxy*, the corporation—as corporate building—is the symbolic space in which struggles over the meaning and the morality of capitalist America are played out.[15]

The character of Aloysius emerges from the history of the corporation and of its representations—specifically, from the idea that emerges in the postwar era of the corporation as a separate entity, one that transcends the interests of its human components. ("We're told businesses have souls," Gilles Deleuze remarks, "which is surely the most terrifying news in the world" [181].) The concerns that emerged during this period about the "Organization Man" were only possible in the context of a business world where the organization was perceived as paramount. And although the idea that the corporation is more important than the individuals who constitute it is attributed only to the bad-guy characters in *The Big Clock*, in other business-success films, especially fifties films such as the melodramas-for-men *Executive Suite* and *Patterns*—in which relationships among the company's executives generate the drama usually found in family relationships—we are expected to take this notion seriously.

Executive Suite, about a group of executives struggling for power after the company president's sudden death, is loaded with emotional appeals to preserve the corporate entity. The (extremely dull) climax of the film comes when

FIGURE 25 *Moses and Aloysius face off inside the clock.*

Don Walling, who unlike the other executives works in production, makes an impassioned speech about the dignity that comes from producing quality consumer goods. Both *Executive Suite* and *Patterns* offer us protagonists who are marked as different from and better than their fellow executives because they have a background in production and thus have a connection to the "real" labor of industry that underpins the functioning of the corporation. However, in both cases these protagonists articulate and act on the basis of a rhetoric that "this company is bigger and more important than any individual." Their connection to production rather than to the consumerist ethos of the Organization Man allows them to provide an alibi for corporate capitalism. In these films "the corporation" has roughly the same status that "the nation" does in a war film (or, again, that "the family" has in certain kinds of melodrama): it is the abstract entity that provides a deep and assumed motivation for all the characters' actions and passions.

The tension that is at work in these films is the same one that I described in my first two chapters, where it took the form of a crisis of masculinity. In the postwar forties and fifties, that crisis was linked to changes in the American economy; this is the moment when, to borrow Warren Susman's terms, the long-emergent "culture of abundance" decisively displaces the "producer-capitalist" culture after decades of transition. *The Hudsucker Proxy*, as we will see, approaches these issues by offering a parody of industry that depicts the corporation as an organization devoted to executive white-collar "labor," in which productive labor has essentially disappeared. This hollowing-out of the space of industry, the replacement of that space by bureaucratic and executive work, is accompanied by a kind of haunting by the symbols of industry, the ghosts of working-class consciousness and identity that operate as the "unconscious" of the corporation. This haunting is a return of what has been repressed, or contained, in the fifties business melodramas.

The transition from production to consumption economy manifested itself, in the years leading up to World War II, in the creation of the corporate city center. Production moved out of the city into surrounding areas, while the downtown locations were increasingly populated by executives, managers, bureaucrats, white-collar workers. These corporate headquarters tended in their organization to mimic the hierarchical logic of their top-down chains of command; the vertical city, more than ever, assumed its role as an objective expression of the vertical corporate structure.

So long before the Coens made their film, the architecture of the American corporate city was already a literalization, a symbolic space that expressed the newly dominant logic of the consumer society. Reinhold Martin makes this case at length in his study of postwar corporate space, *The Organizational Complex*, in which he reads the characteristic innovations of fifties architecture—the curtain wall, the module, and the grid into which those modules are inserted—as representative of a structure imagined as both standardized and flexible. Form indeed follows function here, creating an aesthetic corollary to the organization and its modular unit, the "Organization Man" as the ideal subject of consumerist America:

> While the corporate architecture of the postwar United States may appear at first to mark the apotheosis of the alienated, modernized "mass," in its historical specificity it extends a new and different vector. Not simply the vector of standardization or of the assembly line as projected in the seriality of the ubiquitous metal-and-glass curtain wall, this was the historical vector that redirected such processes and their artifacts toward a reconditioning of the modern subject. Such a tendency was already visible in the United States by the early 1930s, in a fusion of aesthetic and technological practices that presented commodities such as automobiles as an ever-evolving system of choices addressed to the perceived individuality of the new subject, who was understood fundamentally as a *consumer*. (4)

Drawing on Foucault and Deleuze, Martin argues that the consumer's individuality is constituted through patterns of choices made within standardized and interchangeable grids of possibility, and this model for the relationship between the "individual" and the society is given visual expression in the modular structure that operates at nested levels of spatial scale from the office to the building to the city. The corporation, in this model, is imagined as a "productive organism" built around the module of the worker, who is meant to identify with his or her role within the organism.

Again, *The Hudsucker Proxy*'s use of genre as a kind of spatial blueprint is a useful analogy. Genre is a system that creates apparently differentiated narratives out of grids of standardized possibilities, narratives within which viewers are encouraged to find their own individuality through modular identificatory choices. Both the Hollywood film and the corporation are in this sense information systems, networks constituted by processes of encoding and decoding. *Proxy* correlates the Hudsucker Corporation with another postindustrial "factory": the studio era of Hollywood production, from which this film's most prominent intertexts are drawn. Its self-conscious, ironic invocation of Hollywood conventions—complete with happy ending—and its grid of genre elements drawn from the cinematic past as a way of portraying the corporation as genre, suggest the extent to which both Hudsucker and Hollywood are sites for the mass-production of consumer products. You know—for kids!

The film's focus on the Hula Hoop creates an inspired microcosm for the consumerist ethos of the fifties. The Hoop's origins are so ancient as to be untraceable and bamboo hoops swung around the hips by Australian children were the inspiration for the Hula Hoop, which was put on the market by Wham-O in 1958 and became a "craze" in fifties America—just as the Coens' film describes.[16] Thus the Hula Hoop is the perfect consumer artifact, not only because it is a brightly colored, overpriced dingus distinguished by its "entertainment value" rather than its use value, but because it didn't have to be invented—it only had to be marketed. It is also, then, the perfect corollary for the consumption economy, for the corporation as a site of bureaucratic and white-collar activity in which the labor of production is menial rather than artisanal or creative.

The Hudsucker Proxy's montage depicting the Hoop's journey from Norville's conception to its realization as a product is an editing tour-de-force that cuts together the design, making, and testing of the product with the processes set in motion to name, market, and price the product. This mini-epic is structured as a parody of industry, in which absurdly vast resources and a tone of energetic seriousness are put in the service of constructing this bit of whimsical fun (in an echo, perhaps, of the construction of Hollywood product, *Proxy* very much included). A man stands ready outside the design shop like a relay runner, waiting to take the specs from a man speeding down the hallway toward him. The accountants produce a vast tome, the upshot of which is that the Hoop should cost 79 cents; an executive presented with this number frowns and adds a one: $1.79. In the time the admen take to name the product—running through The Belly-Go-Round, The Daddy-O, The Hipster, The Hoopsucker, The Hudswinger, and Uncle Midriff, among other ideas—their secretary reads through both *War and Peace* and *Anna Karenina*, the perceived seriousness of the Tolstoy she reads juxtaposed against the frivolity of her bosses' job.

The Hudsucker board, made up of undifferentiable old white men, is similarly parodied for the pointlessness of its work. There is no redeeming link to production, as in the fifties films; instead, the board operates like a hive mind organized by twin principles of inefficiency and triviality. The board members frequently speak in unison—"Long live the Hud!"—or converse in fragments, finishing or embellishing each others' sentences without ever adding anything useful. One conversation revolves around whether Waring Hudsucker fell forty-four or forty-five floors (including, or not including, the mezzanine); in another the question is raised as to how much time they have in which to depress the value of the company and three voices chime in: "Thirty days," "Four weeks," "A month at the most." Meanwhile, the repressed underneath of Hudsucker's white-collar "mind" turns out to be located right where it should be: at the top, in the center. Amy Archer, snooping in Norville's office one night, opens a door and finds herself, crazily, on a catwalk that runs through the great gears of the clock, connecting at the other side to a similar door that opens into Mussburger's office. In this symbolic spatial arrangement, the dark and dirty area of the clock's inside, signifying the memory of labor and production, is sandwiched between the two top executive offices. This space of the corporate unconscious is where Moses—the perverse imp and godlike narrator, represented as a black man in grease-stained work clothes—serves to remind us of the presence of labor that keeps the machine running.

The evocation of repressed labor and industry is also present, again as parody, in the mailroom, the underground space that resembles the workers' city in *Metropolis*. Here, as in the clock's inside, workers inhabit a factory-like landscape of machine noise and billowing steam. But these bottom-level workers, despite the oppressive atmosphere, are not really engaged in productive labor; rather, they seem mostly to run from place to place frantically, carrying unwieldy piles of letters or pushing baffling assortments of packages. It is *Metropolis* as performed by the Keystone Kops, or Kafka played as slapstick. These are not industrial "workers" in any traditional sense, but rather a sort of objective embodiment of the principle of bureaucracy: drones who carry out the pointless labors demanded by an organization that depends upon a vertical hierarchy but that seems to have no real function except to maintain the executives in their place at the top of that hierarchy.

The presence of industry has not been fully repressed or confined to "underground" spaces within the corporation, however; it also appears obliquely—in a version, perhaps, of Freudian condensation and displacement—in images displayed in the corporate headquarters itself.[17] These images, as with the architectural and cinematic homages to an earlier New York defined by images from screwball comedy, are borrowed from the anachronistic thirties. When Norville makes his first, tentative visit to the top floor, the elevator doors open to reveal a large triptych painting in high Art Deco style depicting a futuristic cityscape of huge, pristine buildings, streamlined trains, boats, bridges and zeppelins, all illuminated by the rising sun of progress. Later, when he is made president of the company, the boardroom—a space the film returns to again and again as the central topos of executive scheming and corporate power—is revealed to contain a huge bas-relief mural in a style that recalls the WPA arts projects. It shows muscular, idealized workers in hardhats and sleeveless shirts, serious in their intent, apparently involved in the construction of a building.

Taken together, these two artworks suggest a utopian vision of industry, work, and progress, a valorization of American labor whose aesthetic is straight out of the New Deal thirties and is precisely the opposite of what goes on in the corporate and bureaucratic space of the forty-fourth floor. As the camera tracks backward, the workers on the wall are revealed to be surrounded by the Hudsucker executives, laughing and smoking cigars, bringing the two sets of figures into a stark juxtaposition that is emphasized in the next shot of this montage sequence, where the same executives appear, reflected in a mirror that occupies the same space in the frame that the mural had before, replacing or displacing the workers. Again, the film's critical attitude toward the new corporate model that emerges with the consumer economy is signaled through an intertextual simultaneity that reasserts the presence of history—of labor, of the thirties—by representing that history in spatial terms.

The tricky thing about *The Hudsucker Proxy*, however, is that this portrayal of the corporation is folded into a cinematic and historical vision that cannot accurately be described as a critique of the consumer culture. The intertextual pastiche that the film employs is not empty aestheticism, as political critics of postmodernism would have it—not the "blank parody" Jameson describes— but nor is its corporate fable a Marxist morality tale. Because although the film analogizes the Hula Hoop and the Hollywood studio–era film as factory products made for mass consumption, it doesn't condemn either one. *Proxy* engineers a politically inflected parody of the corporate machine that takes children's playthings and makes them a brutally serious matter of success and failure, rising and falling, life and death; but like *Sullivan's Travels* it finds its

FIGURE 26 *Ghosts of labor: the WPA-style mural in the Hudsucker boardroom.*

own way to value the frivolous pleasures of swinging hips and funny movies. The Hula Hoop may not have the social effect that Amy, channeling Norville, suggests—"finally there'd be a thingamajig that would bring everyone together—even if it kept 'em apart, spatially"—but the film clearly enjoys the fun people have with the Hoops, and the silliness of the craze for them. The long montage showing the development of the Hoop concludes by imagining it as a failure, until one boy happens across one on the street—it sidles up to him as if the two were meant for each other—and makes such beautiful music with it that the children of New York make a run on the toy stores (and the price quickly goes from "free with any purchase" back to $1.79, then to $3.99). Here the attitude of the film undergoes its characteristic, almost imperceptible oscillation between cynical critique and wide-eyed appreciation. In that oscillation, the film reveals itself as a text that is about the dialectic of consumption and authenticity.

In the course of this book, I have been arguing that each development in the consumer culture has produced as a reaction a new set of "authenticity effects" in texts associated with the countercultural tendency in film and fiction that I have been calling the noir tradition. *The Hudsucker Proxy* is an unusual entry in this tradition because unlike the postmodern authenticity that I described as defining cyberpunk, this film takes the dialectic of authenticity itself as its subject. It revisits the postwar corporation not in order to portray it as the false image of America, in opposition to which an alternative and authentic national vision must be posited or located, but in order to portray it as a model of America seen whole. The symbolic space of the Hudsucker Building is a space of political struggle that contains the possibility of authentic citizenship as well as the possibility of a dominant consumer capitalism. In the film's ending—which of course is presented as another montage—Norville keeps his place as the president of Hudsucker Industries and redeems himself by "rul[ing] with wisdom and compassion," as Moses tells us in voice-over. In the last image, Norville unveils his latest circle-and-line "invention," a bright red Frisbee that he throws across the boardroom until it passes through the now-open window that Waring Hudsucker leapt through and flies out over the fairy-tale city.

This final evocation of space reverses the claustrophobic organization that has dominated the film, opening outward to connect the story and the corporation optimistically to the life of the city and, at a further remove, the nation. But in a film so essentially analytical in its approach to its intertexts and its construction, it would be a mistake to read this ending as a utopian overcoming of bad capitalism by good business practices, à la Capra. The film doesn't place its faith in American character or in the free market; both are shown to be capricious and corruptible, and Norville's triumph is only made possible by the intervention of the god in the (narrative) machine. If this is what it takes to succeed, or to put a wise and compassionate president in place,

then an optimistic outcome such as we have here is vanishingly improbable—
except in the world of Hollywood genre.

Proxy is a political critique of American capitalism that does not envision
an alternative that operates on any principle of authenticity, as in the other
texts in this book—the principle that those texts imagine as the unimaginable
outside of consumer culture, as the great American elsewhere. It would be
more accurate to say that the elsewhere of *The Hudsucker Proxy* is not an elsewhere at all, that it exists as an essential, internal component of consumer
capitalism itself. It exists in the form of Moses, the ghost in the machine and
the spirit of the narrative, whose presence is not utopian but inevitable, and
inseparable from his antagonist Aloysius—the relentless spirit of the corporate
machine, with its oppressive organization of time and space. This is a version
of the relationship I have been describing throughout the book, in which forms
of authenticity emerge perpetually as effects of consumer culture's pervasive
reorganization of American citizenship. And it is worth repeating that to
describe authenticity as an "effect" is not to undermine the extent to which it
represents real political desires, but rather to acknowledge that the political
resistance to consumer capitalism has no external or absolute basis; it is always
a moment in the evolving dialectic of authenticity and consumption. For the
Coens, at least in this film, what all this means is that to tell an American story
in the age of consumer culture is to describe, and if possible to enjoy, the crazy
up-and-down ride on the circles that describe the persistent tension between
capitalism and democracy.

The Coens' relationship to their characters and plots is much like that of
Moses; they are godlike tinkerers, analytically removed but sympathetic,
working impishly within the gears of genre narrative. If, as genre theorists
have often suggested, the function of Hollywood film genre is to represent
and mediate the central tensions that structure American social and cultural
life in order to provide a symbolic working-through and imagined resolution
to those tensions, then the Coens' manipulation of genre is a way of getting
inside the stories that America tells itself about itself and monkeying with the
machinery.[18] Their hackerish play with genre is a way of manipulating the
code that organizes American myth and ideology, while working at the same
time to expose that code to the viewer. The impossible resolution of *The Hudsucker Proxy* makes it clear that the resolutions of genre narrative are always
fantasies of reconciling irresolvable social tensions. One of the cultural codes
that is persistently given this treatment in their films is the assertion of a national authenticity that exists as the oppositional alternative to America as a
nation of citizen-consumers—the ideological complex that is constitutive of,
although not confined to, the noir tradition. The Coens are not unique in
their self-conscious postmodern play with authenticity,[19] but their films provide an especially complex and productive skepticism about the authentic as
an antidote to consumer culture, a skepticism that exists in dialogue with the

formulations of postmodern authenticity, which we have seen at work in the texts of cyberpunk.

Early in this chapter I suggested that it can be difficult to say what a Coen film is "about." *The Hudsucker Proxy* emerges as a meditation on the themes put into play by the noir tradition, so that we might say that the film itself is "about" the dialectic of authenticity, that it is a meditation in which the critique of consumer capitalism is accompanied by the suggestion that consumer culture and the commercial spaces that express that culture are not necessarily inauthentic. The Coens' insistence upon finding value in the devalued goes hand in hand with their skepticism about the authentic or the elsewhere as a pure principle, and both are implied in their films' obsessive theme of phonies and ersatzes. Throughout the Coen films, characters and objects are revealed to be doppelgangers or proxies, fakes or ringers, wrongly named and absurdly displaced, and this deliberate sort of literal inauthenticity shapes the way that the films use genre conventions as well. A playwright might discover, while he writes a Hollywood wrestling picture, that he is in someone else's movie that turns out to be a film noir, or maybe a horror picture, or maybe just a picture; a film noir might be narrated by a cowboy, if it is really a stoner comedy; and a screwball comedy from the thirties that actually takes place in the fifties might also be a film noir, when seen from the right angle. This pastiche of genre choices from the Hollywood factory begins to look a lot like the simultaneous array of consumer choices that are offered to the hungry eye surveying the shop window or the supermarket display. For the viewer or the shopper taking it all in, it pays to be skeptical about claims of authenticity, or about warnings of inauthenticity, because sometimes a proxy may turn out to be the real thing.

Conclusion

> *Authenticity* will be the buzzword of the twenty-first century. And
> what is authentic? Anything that is not controlled by corporations.
> Anything that is not devised and structured to make a profit.
>
> —MICHAEL CRICHTON, *TIMELINE*

The noir tradition, as I have described it in these pages, pursues a strategy of negation. It responds to the conflation of American citizenship and consumption in the postwar era by producing authenticity effects, in order to posit a version of American identity that is imagined as the opposite of the consumer republic. In the films and novels that I have discussed, the confrontation between these two versions of America takes place on the contested sites represented by particular kinds of space that are marked by commerce: the supermarket, the gas station, the office building, the inner-city ghetto, suburban real estate, the global corporation. Noir depends upon this logic of authenticity for its oppositional politics, but it is also consistently aware that its authenticity is an effect and that this effect is produced in texts that must themselves circulate within the consumer economy. Authenticity, consumer culture, national definition, outsider politics: the logic of the noir tradition is tied to issues that are important for any attempt to understand American identity. These are large issues with large histories, issues that precede the advent of noir and that continue to shape debates about American politics, culture, and national identity in the present of this book's writing. The book is necessarily only a local intervention in these debates, but I have tried to indicate here that what I have been calling the "dialectic" of authenticity and consumer culture staged by the texts in the noir tradition is a crucial, perhaps a constitutive, component of American self-understanding in the twentieth and twenty-first centuries.

There are many contemporary critics of the culture of authenticity, and their critiques take many paths, but most fall into two roughly defined groups. Either they note the desire for authenticity and assume that this must mean that the thing itself exists, because if people are fed up with fakery then surely they will rediscover or create an authentic culture for themselves (as, for instance, David Boyle argues in *Authenticity: Brands, Fakes, Spin, and the Lust for Real Life*), or they conclude that authenticity cannot and perhaps should not exist (and then, sometimes, berate the people who desire it as politically naïve morons, as Andrew Potter does in *The Authenticity Hoax*).[1] My approach has been to argue that authenticity is impossible, and also to take seriously the desire for authenticity that is performed in the texts of the noir tradition, a complex desire that contains political naïveté as well as political possibility. I have tried to make visible both the limitations and the potential of this politics of opposition, and in the process I have argued that understanding the noir tradition requires us to recognize how central the logic of authenticity is to the aesthetic construction and political vision of noir.

The self-consciousness about authenticity as an effect of commerce that noir displays is now, more than ever, present in the practice of commerce itself, and contemporary marketing theorists and strategists are at least as alert to the contradictions contained in the logic of authenticity as are cultural critics. Advertisers and marketers have long sought to portray their products as genuine or original in some way, but in the early years of the twenty-first century they are explicitly selling—or advocating the selling of—authenticity. John Zogby's chapter on authenticity in his 2008 book of polling data concludes with "a guide to marketing authenticity." In their own marketing guide, *The Soul of the New Consumer*, David Lewis and Darren Bridger argue that at the turn of the millennium we are witnessing the rise of a "new consumer" whose "soul" is inseparable from the marketplace; the key to selling things to this new kind of consumer is, of course, authenticity. Business strategists James Gilmore and Joseph Pine make this argument even more forcefully in *Authenticity: What Consumers Really Want*. Acknowledging that everything that is sold is essentially "fake," they argue that the key to a successful business is its ability to "render" products and experiences authentic. In this way, the pas-de-deux of authenticity and the commodity form continues; consumers feel themselves to have lost some truer value in acquiescing to the price-point logic of exchange value, but their desire for that lost value expresses itself in further exchanges.

These guides to the marketing of authenticity point directly back to the defining characteristics of the term that I described in the introduction. First, authenticity is conceived negatively, as the opposite of commerce and the antidote to the sense of loss or alienation or artificiality that commercial transactions produce. Second, as a negative conception, authenticity can have no proper existence; it is a desire for a transgressive outside, an unimaginable alternative to things as they are. (This is why it is so crucial to marketing, and so easily appropriated by commercial interests; when a business sells a sense of authenticity, it appeals to the desire created by consumerist alienation, which consumption promises to resolve.) To these characteristics I have added a third, one that is crucial to, but not limited to, the noir context: because consumer culture becomes conflated with American citizenship in the twentieth century, authenticity becomes a site for imagining an alternative identity that is conceived not just in individual terms, but in national terms.[2]

Within the noir tradition, the effort to imagine an authentic version of American national identity is perpetually but uneasily linked to the possibilities for the Left in American politics. Noir's critique of consumption in the name of authenticity is a version of the Left critique of capitalism as a total system, one that organizes the environment and produces the spatial arrangements that people inhabit and navigate. (In literary and cultural criticism, this approach is perhaps most closely identified with Fredric Jameson; it also informs the work of many critical geographers, a few of whom are discussed in this book.) But unlike Marxist critical theory, noir has no vision of a socialist alternative to the state of things as they are; its undermining of consumerist "mainstream" America takes place in the name of the undefinable elsewhere to which the logic of authenticity leads.

This is the crucial link between classic noir and the counterculture of the sixties era, and it is the reason why the periodizing argument of this book hinges on the turn from noir to conspiracy in the sixties and then follows the aftermath of that turn in the era of dominant postmodernism. Classic noir's critique of American consumption in the name of a better, alternative America resonates with the countercultural critique, which takes the form of a similarly powerful, similarly vague conception of conspiracy, in which the republic has been betrayed and hollowed out by consumer capitalism. In the process, the masculine self that classic noir had posited as the site of a potential reinvention of authentic American identity is also hollowed out, and only counterconspiratorial movements and forces can enact the oppositional politics that is necessary to restore America to its better, original self. In the post-sixties era, I have argued that postmodern texts in the noir tradition pursue two distinct modes of responding to the political problem they have inherited. On the one hand, cyberpunk exemplifies a postmodern version of noir authenticity, in which a "cyborg" aesthetic of bricolage becomes the new form of authenticity and thus the new form of resistance to consumer culture. On the other hand, the films of the Coen brothers exemplify a postmodern strategy that analyzes the tradition of noir authenticity without subscribing to it, creating a meditation on the dialectic of authenticity and consumption itself.

As this overview of the evolution of noir suggests, one of the most striking qualities of noir authenticity is that it claims, however vaguely, a position from which to launch an oppositional political critique of American identity in the age defined by consumer culture. The notion of national authenticity grounds that critique and makes it possible—leaving aside the question of whether we consider this kind of critique to be sufficiently sophisticated, or even worthwhile. The crisis of noir that occurs when it is transformed into the sixties conspiracy narrative comes about because in a world that is produced by multinational capitalism, political agency seems to have become impossible and the nation as a category seems to have been effaced. The texts that I have looked at from the sixties era and after have all, in one way or another, responded to that crisis of agency by restoring or revisiting some version of noir authenticity with which to construct their oppositional positions. That outsider conception of authenticity is at the heart of noir, so it is not surprising that the texts I deal with in this study that stray the farthest from a strictly oppositional authenticity—in particular Pynchon's *Vineland* and the Coens' *The Hudsucker Proxy*—are also the texts whose connections to the noir tradition are the most attenuated. They both suggest, in their different ways, that noir has to evolve out of itself in order to confront the evolving politics of capitalism in postmodern America, that the political critique of consumer culture can only continue to the extent that it finds ways to employ and accommodate elements of that consumer culture. Given our current consumer landscape, where the selling of authenticity is understood to be the job of any good marketer, it makes sense that those texts that want to find something politically useful in the noir tradition are getting out of the authenticity business, retaining noir's critical attitude toward consumer culture while abandoning its purely oppositional approach.

In the later stages of this book, then, I have tried to widen the circle, to show how the noir logic that is initiated in the forties articulates a linked cluster of issues that are central to American culture and identity, and how following the development of that logic leads us outward from noir, enabling a larger view of the ongoing dance of authenticity and consumer culture. None of the texts considered here can offer a "solution" to the problem of postwar American identity's consumerist basis; rather, the authenticity effects that they create as successive responses to that problem illuminate the historical development of the dialectic, in which new formations of consumer capitalism call forth new formulations of authenticity. Each set of texts constructs an aesthetic intervention into this problem in the politics of American culture, an effect that is appropriate to the forms of commercial space produced in its era. The journey that began in the cereal aisle and in the little roadside houses selling gas has rapidly moved outward into cyberspace's simulacra and the clockworks of the global corporation, all of which are part of the circulation of capital that has come both to define and to supersede the space of the nation. At each turn, this movement has elicited versions of the dream of a better and truer and original America—the elsewhere that noir's shadows claimed to conceal. Now, in the twenty-first century, these are the twinned halves of a legacy that Americans continue to inherit: the bright superstore and the dark unlocatable streets beyond its fluorescent oasis, the two Americas, opposed and inseparable, somehow occupying the same national space.

{ NOTES }

Introduction

1. The era of "hard-boiled" detective stories began earlier. The twenties was the decade that launched many writers' careers, the decade in which *Black Mask* magazine became the premier outlet for hard-boiled fiction. In addition to his stories in *Black Mask*, Dashiell Hammett published all of his novels in the late twenties and early thirties. James M. Cain published his best-known books in the thirties. But it is during the forties and fifties, with the film noir cycle and the novels of Raymond Chandler, that "noir" became a major cultural presence, even if it didn't have its name yet.

2. A particularly good example of this trend in noir criticism (and an excellent analysis of noir space) is Vivian Sobchack's "Lounge Time: Postwar Crises and the Chronotope of Film Noir." Sobchack argues that the absence and disintegration of the space of "home" in noir is a response to "the lived sense of insecurity, instability, and social incoherence Americans experienced during the transitional period that began after the war and Roosevelt's death in 1945, lasted through the Truman years (1945–1952), and declined as the Eisenhower years (1952–1960) drew to a prosperous close" (131). This chronology seems to me to overestimate the sense of national crisis in the immediate postwar period, and Sobchack's argument could fruitfully be extended to many texts in the noir tradition from the last few decades.

3. In his excellent 2011 book *Dark Borders: Film Noir and American Citizenship*, Jonathan Auerbach focuses on this situation of postwar alienation and its relationship to citizenship as a way of understanding film noir; he puts his explanatory emphasis on the Cold War context rather than on the consumer society.

4. Marshall Berman, a student of Trilling's, also traces the modern conception of individualist authenticity to the Romantic tradition in his 1970 book *The Politics of Authenticity*. For more on the relationship between modernism and authenticity, see Miles Orvell's *The Real Thing: Imitation and Authenticity in American Culture, 1880–1940*.

5. For more on authenticity in the existential tradition, see Jacob Golomb's *In Search of Authenticity; From Kierkegaard to Camus*.

6. Abigail Cheever's 2010 book *Real Phonies: Cultures of Authenticity in Post–World War II America* provides a useful analysis and history (circa 1945–2000) of this conception of authenticity as a problem of selfhood; "real phonies" is her term for the subjects described by Marcuse, Riesman, et al., those who have no inner self because they "find themselves" wholly in the surrounding society. See also the excellent historical work done by Grace Elizabeth Hale in *A Nation of Outsiders: How the White Middle Class Fell in Love with Rebellion in Postwar America*. As that windy subtitle suggests, Hale argues that in the postwar era, the white middle classes expressed a universal desire for, a "romance" of, rebellion. This version of the desire for authenticity took the form of identification with assorted cultural outsiders. It is much to her credit that Hale offers a political critique of authenticity while

still taking seriously the desire for authenticity; as she writes of the sixties folk revival, it "was flawed as both political analysis and social history, but it was a perfect exercise in empathy. And this, in the end, despite some revivalists' lack of a sense of the politics of their own appropriations, proved to be a route into politics" (131).

7. It might seem that the concept of authenticity could have no further use for us in the wake of poststructuralism's persuasive debunking of foundational logics of origin and presence, of all the things that are traditionally associated with authenticity. But to describe authenticity as a desire for the possibility of locating a position outside of organizing systems suggests a set of concerns that is in many ways implicitly aligned with those of poststructuralist critique. Indeed, Amanda Anderson argues that "authenticity functions throughout many poststructuralist writings as an unacknowledged informing ideal. An appeal to authenticity not only underlies the insistent poststructuralist refusal of various illusions and constraints—of metaphysics, of normativity, and of conventionality—it also fuels a whole range of appeals to valorized forms of practice and identity, however unstable or complex— however parodic, performative, or hybrid—they might imagine themselves to be" (*The Way We Argue Now*, 170). I would suggest that poststructuralist criticism evokes authenticity in this "unacknowledged" way to the extent that it desires the possibility of a disruptive or transgressive undermining of totalizing systems. Even the theorists who are most thoroughly committed to the idea that there is no outside are nonetheless often motivated by a nostalgia for the loss of that space outside of the system. See, for example, my reading of the work of Jean Baudrillard in chapter 6. One could argue, certainly, that the poststructuralist approach is dedicated precisely to articulating the way that transgression (if indeed it is possible at all) can only emerge from within the totalizing system itself; but this does not foreclose on the crucial element of authenticity as I define it here, as the desire for an outside or elsewhere. Nonetheless, I employ Anderson's argument here with some reservations; although I agree with her reading of authenticity and poststructuralism to the extent I have described here, I am not convinced by her larger ideological attack on poststructuralism.

8. This is one example of how the noir tradition is structurally similar to, though not equivalent to, Marxist critical theory; Marxism, too, is concerned with the search for a principle outside of the world-system produced by capitalism. The debate that Fredric Jameson stages between himself and Walter Benn Michaels in *Postmodernism* is instructive in this regard. Jameson, in confronting Michaels's argument that the market constitutes a "total system" within which we are always implicated and constituted, recognizes that in the context of late-twentieth-century America the terms of this problem are always conceived through the possibility or impossibility of "the critique of consumption or consumer society itself" (203). For Jameson, this raises the "very American problem" of the dichotomy between liberalism and radicalism. In these terms, we could say that authenticity as I have been using Trilling to describe it is a form of radicalism defined by absolute opposition and the search for a transgressive "outside" of the system. Jameson concludes that "critiques of consumption and commodification can only be truly radical when they specifically include reflection, not merely on the problem of the market itself but, above all, on the nature of socialism as an alternative system" (207). On those properly Marxist terms, the noir tradition fails the test, since its radicalism posits instead a (possibly conservative) national authenticity as the alternative to the American consumer society.

9. Tourism scholars Dean MacCannell, D. J. Greenwood, and Erik Cohen all take on the issue of tourism and authenticity. MacCannell's work is discussed at length in this introduction;

see also Greenwood's "Culture by the Pound" and Cohen's "Authenticity and Commoditization in Tourism." For more on the issue of authenticity in anthropological studies generally, see Regina Bendix's *In Search of Authenticity: The Formation of Folklore Studies*, Arjun Appadurai's introduction to *The Social Life of Things*, and Brian Spooner's essay in that book, "Weavers and Dealers: The Authenticity of an Oriental Carpet."

10. Boorstin's dire view of America as the place where authenticity has disappeared, replaced by images, is echoed in many works of cultural criticism that have been written since. European intellectuals, for example, love to tour the United States in order to discover its essential emptiness and simulated quality, as in for example Umberto Eco's 1973 *Travels in Hyperreality* (published in English in 1986) or Jean Baudrillard's 1986 *America*.

11. This structure creates a kind of vicious circle. The modernized subject engages in a quest for the authenticity it feels itself to have lost; this quest results in a commodification of the authentic cultural productions that it seeks out as a way of assuaging its alienation. In terms of tourism, the result is a destruction both of the tourist's authentic experience and of the meaning of the cultural productions for the members of the local culture themselves. As Erik Cohen puts it: "'Commoditization' is a process by which things (and activities) come to be evaluated primarily in terms of their exchange value. . . . The principal question in this context is, what happens to the other meanings (particularly religious, cultural, and social) of things (and activities) once they become commoditized" (380–81). Outside of the context of tourism, consider too the work of Arlie Russell Hochschild on the commodification of emotional and intimate "labors"; see *The Managed Heart: The Commercialization of Human Feeling* and *The Outsourced Self: Intimate Life in Market Times*.

12. For an extended discussion of authenticity as a problem of national identity, see Vincent Cheng's *Inauthentic: The Anxiety over Culture and Identity*.

13. This tension is the subject of Jean-Christophe Agnew's *Worlds Apart: The Market and the Theater in Anglo-American Thought, 1550–1750*, which follows the parallel histories of the market and the theater through the early modern period.

14. In Colin Campbell's *The Romantic Ethic and the Spirit of Modern Consumerism* he argues that Romanticism and consumerism emerged together in England during the Industrial Revolution as twinned expressions of hedonistic desire, a "consumption ethic" that was opposed to the Protestant "production ethic."

15. Writers who have confronted American culture since the rise of consumer culture in the postwar era have frequently offered analyses that trace American dissatisfaction, at least in part, to the affluence that seems to define us. Part of the reason why Veblen has turned out to be so influential surely has to do with the proven fact that versions of this critique can be made from just about every point on the political spectrum, so that his heirs are not limited to leftists, dour Protestants, and Scandinavian cheapskates. Although Veblen had a number of followers during the first half of the twentieth century, it was not until after 1945 that the cultural critique of affluence, in tandem with the cultural study of consumption, became a prominent discourse in America. For an extended discussion of this tradition, see Daniel Horowitz's *The Anxieties of Affluence: Critiques of American Consumer Culture, 1939–1979*.

16. The contemporary wave of scholarship on consumption gets moving around the beginning of the 1980s. In addition to the works mentioned in this introduction, see Douglas and Isherwood's *The World of Goods* (1979); *The Culture of Consumption*, edited by Fox and Lears (1983); William Leach's *Land of Desire* (1993); Roland Marchand's *Advertising the*

American Dream (1986); Jackson Lears's *Fables of Abundance* (1994); Daniel Miller's *Material Culture and Mass Consumption* (1987); *Commodifying Everything* (2003), edited by Susan Strasser; *Getting and Spending*, edited by Strasser, McGovern, and Judt (1998); and Lawrence Glickman's *Consumer Society in American History* (1999). For an early argument linking consumer culture and American identity, see David Potter, *People of Plenty: Economic Abundance and the American Character* (1958).

17. My invocation of "imagined communities" is a reference to Benedict Anderson's influential book *Imagined Communities: Reflections on the Origin and Spread of Nationalism*, which describes how nationalism is constructed and maintained through the creation and invocation of a shared identity that is claimed as both natural and distinctive.

18. There is broad agreement among scholars that the conflation of citizenship with consumption is pervasive after 1945. A number of historians also argue that the groundwork for this conflation is laid—and, some argue, the whole process is completed—roughly between 1880 and 1920.

19. In *Hollywood Genres*, Thomas Schatz observes that Chandler "was perhaps the single most significant writer—both as novelist and screenwriter—to participate in the [hardboiled detective film] genre's evolution. He provided either script or story for *Murder, My Sweet*; *Double Indemnity*; *Lady in the Lake*; *The Blue Dahlia*; *The Falcon Takes Over*; *The Big Sleep*; *Strangers on a Train*" (126). In a letter to Cleve Adams, Chandler himself suggested that his work rather than Hammett's came to be seen as the dominant image of noir because Hammett stopped publishing in the early thirties, and because *Double Indemnity* and *Murder, My Sweet* (rather than *The Maltese Falcon*) seemed to have started "the high budget mystery picture trend" (Gardiner and Walker, *Raymond Chandler Speaking*, 52).

20. I have been suggesting here that Chandler's concern with authenticity is "sentimental" while Hammett's fiction is distinctly unsentimental. In Leonard Cassuto's *Hard-Boiled Sentimentality* he argues convincingly that macho hard-boiled crime fiction is shaped by the same questions of sympathy that we generally associate with the tradition of sentimental fiction, which is associated with women and the domestic sphere. But his extensive and detailed analysis is fundamentally in agreement with the sketch I have offered here.

21. For example, by my count *The Glass Key* contains exactly zero metaphors and one simile, this: "A dark pearl in his shirt-bosom, twinkling in the fire's glow as he moved, was like a red eye winking" (142). And even that has none of the ostentation of Chandler's similes.

22. For the studies of noir that illuminate these issues, see Biesen, *Blackout*; Dimendberg, *Film Noir and the Spaces of Modernity*; Naremore, *More Than Night*; Auerbach, *Dark Borders*; and Oliver and Trigo, *Noir Anxiety*. For some useful overviews of film noir, see for example Spicer, *Film Noir*; Silver and Ursini, *Film Noir Reader*; Christopher, *Somewhere in the Night*; Server et al., *The Big Book of Noir*; and Naremore's chapter "The History of an Idea."

23. As Andrew Spicer points out, one of the most common ways of understanding film noir is as a "dark mirror" in which postwar America's cheery image is reflected back in a form that reveals anxieties and "moral anarchy" (*Film Noir*, 19). Not everyone adheres to the reading of noir as oppositional, but even a critic such as Edward Dimendberg suggests that although arguments for noir as a subversion of Hollywood or American norms "deserve to be met with skepticism, its fundamental divergence from other film types of the 1940s and 1950s seems incontrovertible" (*Film Noir and the Spaces of Modernity*, 12).

24. See Davis, *City of Quartz*; Jameson, "The Synoptic Chandler" in *Shades of Noir*. (Jameson has covered many elements of what I am calling the noir tradition in his career, having written in various places about film noir, Raymond Chandler, conspiracy film, and cyberpunk.) See also Philip Kemp's "From the Nightmare Factory: HUAC and the Politics of Noir."

25. MacCannell argues that the "still unexamined tension at the heart of *film noir* is that between senile capitalism and democracy," and that noir "witnesses" the confrontation between the two "with implacable numbness" ("Democracy's Turn," 284). In *Gumshoe America: Hard-Boiled Crime Fiction and the Rise and Fall of New Deal Liberalism*, Sean McCann locates a similar dynamic in the tradition of American detective fiction, in which he sees the drama of the New Deal's confrontation between capitalism and government playing itself out.

26. See Thomas Frank's *The Conquest of Cool* for a discussion of the marketing of countercultural style. Frank argues that the marketing of "hip" and the image of the "rebel" have defined the dominant style of consumer capitalism ever since the sixties. His generally excellent analysis is marred by a tendency to simply dismiss countercultural politics as a marketing fad. This same dismissal is at the heart of Joseph Heath and Andrew Potter's smug *Nation of Rebels*, which draws on Frank's work but is apparently impatient with the subtlety of that work. Rob Walker's *Buying In* considers the issue of countercultural marketing as a tension between consumption as a form of belonging and consumption as a way of defining individual identity.

27. Lefebvre is present in this book primarily as an inspiriting presence; for the work I'm doing here, the most relevant of his many books is *The Production of Space* (1974). In addition to the books by Soja and Sack, the works of critical geography that I discuss at greatest length in this book are David Harvey's *The Condition of Postmodernity* (1990) and Neil Smith's *Uneven Development* (1984; revised 1990 and 2008).

28. Filmmakers have been interested in the contrast between the bland consumer society and the violent excesses of the horror genre at least since George Romero filled a mall with mindlessly wandering, brain-consuming zombies in 1978 for *Dawn of the Dead*. For conjunctions of horror and consumerism that use the figure of the supermarket specifically, see the zombie film *28 Days Later* (2002) and the Stephen King adaptation *The Mist* (2007).

29. Both Naremore and Copjec (in "The Phenomenal Nonphenomenal") argue that the space of Jerry's Market is oppressive rather than cheery. Naremore sees it as part of the film's "theme of industrialized dehumanization" inherited from Weimar film and present throughout the film—in the bowling alley, the drive-in restaurant, Phyllis's house (88–89). Copjec emphasizes the emptiness of the market, arguing that it is a key example of the way that the film depletes public space and communal networks in order to show how community has given way, in the noir world, to a claustrophobic privatization. My reading here emphasizes the difference between the supermarket and the other spaces of the film rather than their continuity, but ultimately this approach does lead to a consideration of the store as private space and to the conclusion that the dark vision of noir is most fully realized in the brightly lit commercial organization of the supermarket.

30. In *Black & White & Noir: America's Pulp Modernism*, Paula Rabinowitz offers an everything-and-the-kitchen-sink reading of commodity fetishism and the role of objects in noir, among other things. Her discussion touches on the way that Phyllis Dietrichson's identity as femme fatale is an accretion of signifying objects: "Barbara Stanwyck's anklet and

heels, her cigarette and whiskey, her cat glasses and gun would indeed turn you into a femme fatale—murderous, deadly, and doomed to die in a hail of bullets" (191).

31. Lizabeth Cohen argues that this advocacy movement represents a new phase of the "consumers' republic" in that citizens come to envision political participation as an aspect of their identity as consumers.

32. In *Conspiracy Culture*, Peter Knight argues that second-wave feminist critiques of the culture frequently employed discourses of conspiracy. In Betty Friedan's 1963 *The Feminine Mystique*, in particular, Friedan's investigation of middle-class American women's dissatisfaction figures Friedan "as the lone detective chasing up the clues to the mysterious mystique" until she uncovers evidence of a conspiracy, complete with "brainwashing" (*Conspiracy Culture*, 118–19). I would add that her chapter "The Sexual Sell" even offers a Deep Throat figure, an unnamed advertising executive who gives Friedan access to reams of evidence confirming that the conspiracy against American women is in fact part of the conspiracy of consumer culture itself.

33. The question of masculinity is absolutely central to *The Big Lebowski*, in part because of the presence here of the ghost of Chandler's Marlowe and his difference from the Dude. From the use of Bob Dylan's "The Man in Me" over the opening credits, to the Dude's castration-anxiety nightmare, to the Stranger's uncertain ramblings about the Dude as "the man" and possibly a "hero," the film foregrounds masculinity as a contested category. The "big" Jeffrey Lebowski parades his romantic and heroic vision of masculinity by asking, "What makes a man. . . . Is it being prepared to do the right thing, whatever the price?" The Dude undercuts this romantic heroism (which echoes Chandler's description of the male detective-hero in "The Simple Art of Murder"), responding, between tokes, "Sure . . . that and a pair of testicles." For some intelligent discussion of masculinity in *The Big Lebowski*, see Dennis Allen's "*Logjammin'* and *Gutterballs*: Masculinities in *The Big Lebowski*"; and the BFI book *The Big Lebowski* by J. M. Tyree and Ben Walters.

34. Take for example Dudeism.com, the website of the Church of the Latter-Day Dude, which celebrates the ethos offered in *The Big Lebowski* as a preferred way of being that potentially has political implications. Dudeism is described as a "rebel shrug," and the site includes iconic images repurposed to reflect Dudeist sentiments taken from both leftist and American nationalist sources (Chinese Communist posters and Uncle Sam both tell us to "take it easy")—as in *The Big Lebowski* itself, there is a tongue-in-cheek effort here to link Left political traditions to the spirit of America.

35. For further discussion of the Dude as an exemplar of Whitman's "metaphysical loafing," see Jonathan Elmer's essay "Enduring and Abiding."

36. See David Martin-Jones's "No Literal Connection: Images of Mass Commodification, U.S. Militarism, and the Oil Industry in *The Big Lebowski*."

37. Yet another example of the film's ambivalent attitude toward consumer culture: when bowling buddy Donny dies, the Dude and Walter are alarmed at the high prices that the funeral parlor charges for urns in which to place the ashes after cremation. Walter asks the funeral director if there is a Ralphs nearby—and the next time we see them, the Dude and Walter have put the ashes in a Folgers coffee can. The sequence reads both as ironic juxtaposition of death and commerce and as a heroic cheapness, a repurposing of supermarket goods in order to avoid the funeral business's commercialization of death and mourning.

38. See Frank, *The Conquest of Cool: Business Culture, Counterculture, and the Rise of Hip Consumerism*; McCann and Szalay, "Do You Believe in Magic? Literary Thinking After the

New Left"; Heath and Potter, *Nation of Rebels: Why Counterculture Became Consumer Culture*; and Potter, *The Authenticity Hoax: How We Get Lost Finding Ourselves*.

Chapter 1

1. For an iconic image of the relationship between film noir and the gas station, consider the 1940 painting *Gas* by Edward Hopper, whose work is often considered as a kind of artistic corollary to noir.

2. Trusting "the man who wears the star" suggests a link between the gas-station attendant and the iconic sheriff of the Western genre, a figure of order and civilization in a frontier landscape. The films in the noir tradition that take place in rural settings frequently create meaning out of generic connections and tensions between noir and the Western, and the gas station can often resemble those fragile outposts of civilization that appear in various forms in the Western.

3. In her essay "Lounge Time: Postwar Crises and the Chronotope of Film Noir," Vivian Sobchack suggests that the crucial noir locations to pay attention to are "the cocktail lounge, the nightclub, the bar, the hotel room, the boardinghouse, the diner, the dance hall, the roadside café, the bus and train station, and the wayside motel" (130)—because these are the sites where noir imagines a temporary and suspended existence ("lounge time") that undermines nostalgic postwar longings for a lost and imagined American "home." One could easily add the gas station to her list, although as my argument here makes clear, my sense is that the noir gas station stages a tension between, on the one hand, something like Sobchack's (consumerist) time/space of the lounge or "idyll," and on the other, nostalgia for a productive masculine authenticity. The gas station is, after all, both a place of lounging, of temporary idylls, and a place of work.

4. Because there are so many gas station noirs to consider, I have restricted the focus of this chapter to the "classic" period of 1941–1958 (with a few prototypical earlier examples included); however, there are many neo-noirs that employ gas station scenes as well. In fact, neo-noir often eliminates the urban context in favor of a rural American space conceived of as vast, vacant, and hostile. One writer, D. K. Holm, has gone so far as to identify this tradition in noir as a generic mutation into something distinct: "film soleil." Consider for example *A History of Violence* (2005), which is a direct descendant of *The Killers* and *Out of the Past*; *Red Rock West* (1993); *U-Turn* (1997); *One False Move* (1992); and *Wild at Heart* (1990). Of particular note are the films of the Coen brothers; for example, the most memorably tense scene in *No Country for Old Men* (2007), in which Chigurh makes a baffled man call a coin flip for his life, takes place in a gas station.

5. One entertaining neo-noir example is John Dahl's 1994 *The Last Seduction*, in which femme fatale Bridget has to flee her beloved Manhattan and goes into hiding in the benighted hinterlands of upstate New York. Although she gets some pale enjoyment out of terrorizing the natives, Bridget longs to return to the city where she belongs. The film's use of classic noir's city-country dynamics to play with New York's intrastate tensions is one of its cleverest ideas.

6. The dialogue is in fact enjoyably silly throughout. One Chinese character offers a pearl of oriental wisdom that sums up pretty much everything one needs to know about the femme fatale figure in film noir: "much sorrow come from women who know not honor or truth."

7. In an essay on "rural noir," Jonathan Bell suggests that it was the development of suburban commercial areas in the forties that motivated this new version of nostalgia for the

lost heartland: "postwar sprawl . . . fueled American fascination with and romance for the truly rural" ("Shadows in the Hinterland: Rural Noir," 220).

8. It also shaped the modern credit system. The first credit cards were issued by gasoline companies in the twenties in part as a way of ensuring brand loyalty: with a Mobil card, one could fill up at any Mobil station. The credit card that could be used at many different stores followed, with the founding of Diner's Club in 1950 and American Express in 1958. Taking off in the sixties, the credit card played a major role in enabling the growth and determining the form of the postwar consumer economy.

9. Catherine Gudis argues in *Buyways: Billboards, Automobiles, and the American Landscape* that the culture of the automobile has produced two crucial and linked goals for business interests: "to package and sell motorist attention to big business, and . . . to commodify spaces for motorists to traverse and consume" (39).

10. The gas station in the forties and fifties provides an example of what Erik Cohen in his work on tourism calls "emergent authenticity," the process by which objects and places initially perceived as artificial and commercial acquire, with the passing of time, the status of "authentic" cultural artifacts.

11. The figure of the insurance-investigator-as-detective appears in several noirs, Barton Keyes in *Double Indemnity* being perhaps the most famous example. (One interesting noir-derived example of this figure is in the radio drama *Yours Truly, Johnny Dollar*. The program ran from 1949 to 1962, and its gimmick was that it was structured as an itemization of Johnny Dollar's expense account. Interestingly, one of the actors who played Johnny Dollar was Edmund O'Brien, who plays the insurance investigator Riordan in *The Killers*.) This character's role is to suggest that the insurance investigator is a more diligent and determined detective than a police investigator, because the insurance company has money at stake: capitalist business trumps government bureaucracy.

12. Mark Osteen has noticed this trend, too; in his essay on "Noir's Cars," he observes that Jeff Bailey is one of the few noir protagonists who (however briefly) actually achieves the dream of gas-station ownership.

13. The femme fatale figure and the gender issues that she raises are so central to an understanding of noir that nearly every comprehensive analysis of the films attempts to account for it in some way. Some useful studies are *Women and Film Noir*, a collection edited by E. Ann Kaplan; Karen Hollinger's "*Film Noir*, Voice-over, and the Femme Fatale"; Elizabeth Cowie's "Film Noir and Women"; and Mary Ann Doane's *Femmes Fatales: Feminism, Film Theory, Psychoanalysis*.

14. Fritz Lang's *The Woman in the Window* (1944) makes this shop-window metaphor explicit. The staid psychology professor played by Edward G. Robinson is mesmerized by a portrait of a beautiful woman that he sees in a storefront window. He then enters a dream—film noir narrative as fantasy projection—in which he meets the woman, a meeting that leads him into a world of murder, blackmail, and police investigation. Both the dangerous woman and the film noir itself are made part of the fantasy of the male window-shopper. As my reference to Laura Mulvey suggests, her groundbreaking work on the "male gaze" in "Visual Pleasure and Narrative Cinema" is a powerful tool for analyzing these persistent noir tendencies, even if it is not the tool I am using here.

15. Maybe it doesn't quite go without saying that Raymond Chandler's Marlowe is a version of Conrad's Marlow, the disillusioned modern man who narrates the story of a descent into a heart of darkness, and for whom women are always the ultimate horror.

16. The gas station/store in *The Postman Always Rings Twice* has a similar function, serving throughout the film as the visual backdrop against which Cora and Frank forge their murderous compact. Like Lorraine in *Ace in the Hole*, Cora wants more than the rural business offers, and so the gas station is both the potential vehicle for her escape (if she can make enough money) and her prison.

17. The film *Kiss Me Deadly* is vastly different from the source novel by Mickey Spillane (although it preserves the odd grammar of the title): screenwriter A. I. Bezzerides and director Robert Aldrich clearly set out to undermine Spillane's deliberate misogyny, sadism, and self-righteousness by making the film and the viewer conscious of Hammer's nastiness. The shift in setting, from New York to Los Angeles, was also crucial in that it enabled the investigation of urban space and suburban sprawl, as well as connecting the film to the tradition of Chandler's novels and thus making the film's skeptical attitude toward Hammer serve as skepticism about the hard-boiled detective figure generally.

18. See Oliver and Trigo's introduction, "Dropping the Bombshell," for an extended discussion of how *Kiss Me Deadly* brings together Cold War anxieties about nuclear annihilation with fears about women.

Chapter 2

1. The ungainly but useful term "the professional-managerial class" (or "PMC") has its origin in the essay of that name written in 1977 by Barbara and John Ehrenreich; for a discussion of the history of the term, see Jean-Christophe Agnew, "A Touch of Class." In "A Matter of Taste," Jackson Lears argues that the PMC cannot accurately be described as a "class" but is instead a Gramscian historical bloc. But whether "class" or "bloc," the model by which the PMC articulates itself as a national identity through practices of consumption that are enabled by mass culture publications is essentially the same.

2. Many studies have identified the late nineteenth century as the moment when mass production begins to dominate cultural production in America. In addition to Ohmann, see, e.g., Charles McGovern's *Sold American: Consumption and Citizenship, 1890–1945*; *Consuming Visions: Accumulation and Display of Goods in America 1880–1920*, edited by Simon Bronner; and *The Culture of Consumption: Critical Essays in American History, 1880–1980*, edited by Fox and Lears.

3. The distinction between the "writerly" (or "writable") modernist text that allows the reader to participate in the process of textual production and the "readerly" text that offers itself for easy consumption is made by Roland Barthes in *S/Z*.

4. See Horkheimer and Adorno, *Dialectic of Enlightenment*.

5. In the previous chapters I focused on concrete commercial spaces with distinct histories—the supermarket, the gas station—and with this chapter I begin to shift toward a more symbolic conception of space that will persist in the chapters that lie ahead. Nonetheless, this symbolic or social space is consistently represented in more concrete spatial corollaries in each of the texts I deal with, just as the spaces of the supermarket or gas station imply networks of circulation and exchange, both material and symbolic.

6. *The Big Clock* is not a "hard-boiled" novel, but it nonetheless raises issues that the hard-boiled authors are concerned with. I am describing it here as a "noir thriller"—it was in fact made into a film noir, which I discuss briefly both here and in chapter 7.

7. There is, despite Hagen's coldness and Janoth's lack of affect, a distinct homoeroticism in the relationship between the two men, a suggestion that the corporation exists as a

melding of male bodies as well as minds. In fact, it is Pauline's suggestion that Janoth and Hagen are lovers that causes Janoth to fly into a rage and kill her.

8. By putting Terry behind the mask of Maioranos, Chandler makes him easier to reject. There are deep strains of both misogyny and a sort of racist xenophobia in Chandler, and they are brought together in this portrait of Terry transformed into the absolute Other: an effeminate Mexican stranger.

9. McCann's chapter in *Gumshoe America: Hard-Boiled Crime Fiction and the Rise and Fall of New Deal Liberalism* is in the top rank of analyses of Chandler, along with the two essays by Fredric Jameson that I cite here, "On Raymond Chandler" and "The Synoptic Chandler," and the readings done by Erin Smith in *Hard-Boiled: Working-Class Readers and Pulp Magazines* and of Leonard Cassuto in *Hard-Boiled Sentimentality: The Secret History of American Crime Stories*. McCann also touches on some of the connections between Chandler's novel and Fearing's *The Big Clock* that I cover in depth here: the reference in both books to Henry Luce, the similarity between the "Study in Fundamentals" and the "portrait of Madison," and the overall sense that both novels are concerned with the problem of postwar mass culture.

10. The equation of crime and business is central to the politics of noir, and Fearing offers an especially nifty example in *The Big Clock*. An editor at *Crimeways* tells the story of a recent bank robbery: "The thing about this job is that the gang regularly incorporated themselves three years ago, paid income taxes, and paid themselves salaries amounting to $175,000 while they were laying their plans and making preparations for the hold-up. Their funds went through the bank they had in mind" (23). While Chandler suggests that business is a form of crime, Fearing envisions bank robbery as a form of employment that is carried out and remunerated in more or less the same way as much executive work.

11. Jameson in fact argues that Chandler reverses the tendency of certain traditions in realism to create character through spatial description, focusing on "the relative gap and distance between the character and the setting or, rather, the way in which the character type is itself predicated on that gap or tension. Unlike Balzac, for example, Chandler does not make the dwelling immediately express the truth of the character who dwells in it" ("Synoptic," 39).

12. A useful, and perhaps deliberate, contrast exists in the detective novels of Walter Mosley, which are precise in their accounting as Easy Rawlins accumulates or loses money from book to book. One of the ways that Mosley introduces race into the hard-boiled novel, as a factor that creates revisions to the genre, is to make his black PI's journey the story of a progression into and through the world of property ownership. Easy's story, too, begins in the postwar moment, and much of the drama and comedy of the first book, *Devil in a Blue Dress* (and of the film adaptation directed by Carl Franklin), concerns his attempt to maintain the sanctity of his newly acquired suburban house, which is forever being invaded. While the suburban American Dream is the focus of the white, proto-countercultural detective's contempt, it has genuine value for this historically representative black detective whose path has gone from rural Southern poverty through military service in World War II to struggling for a foothold in the segregated black middle class.

13. On the first page of *The Big Sleep*, Chandler's first novel, Marlowe enters the Sternwood mansion and finds "a broad stained-glass panel showing a knight in dark armor rescuing a lady who was tied to a tree and didn't have any clothes on but some long and very convenient hair. The knight had pushed the vizor of his helmet back to be sociable, and he

was fiddling with the knots on the ropes that tied the lady to the tree and not getting anywhere. I stood there and thought that if I lived in the house, I would sooner or later have to climb up there and help him" (3–4). The knight motif is carried though the whole book in more or less this way, suggesting that the big bad city requires a new kind of knight—one equally dedicated to doing good, but not bound to outmoded conventions of chivalry, i.e., Philip Marlowe.

14. Given the way that Chandler represents Marlowe as the embodiment of a specifically national and masculine authenticity, it is interesting that Marlowe does not seem to have served in World War II and that there is no explicit reference to his serving on the "home front," either—despite the attention that is paid to Terry Lennox's war experiences in *The Long Goodbye*. In light of the argument I have been making here it makes a certain sense, though— even apart from the fact that it is difficult to imagine the individualist, proto-countercultural Marlowe in a situation where he is part of a bureaucratic organization in which one survives by following orders. The nationalism that Marlowe represents is explicitly distanced from the "official" nationalism of the postwar period, the nationalism of the "American way of life." In his "job" as representative of the authentic and alternative America, he is absolutely set apart from other contemporary versions of national self-definition.

15. Women, as in the model that I described in the last chapter, represent the principle of commerce itself, the thing that must be rejected in order for men to claim an authentic identity. So Marlowe's attitude toward women and sex is structurally similar to his attitude toward money: both introduce inauthenticity into human relationships. When Linda Loring— another daughter of Harlan Potter, and so combining female sexuality and enormous wealth—comes to his apartment with an overnight bag but then accuses him of thinking she is "loose," Marlowe displays an anger that is similar to his reaction when accused of being cheap or money-grubbing: "'That's just another gambit,' I snarled. 'I know fifty of them and I hate them all. They're all phony and they all have a sort of leer at the edges'" (359). Sexual considerations, like economic considerations, introduce "phoniness" into the male subject's relationships with others, a phoniness that the detective has to purge from his life, at whatever cost. In this scene Marlowe is deliberately disingenuous (but not, of course, phony) about "loose women" in the same way that he is about money, claiming that he would have "made a pass" at Linda if he had thought she was a loose woman. In Marlowe's role as the street-smart knight-errant, he must pretend to covet both women and money, while actually devoting himself to battling the inauthenticity that he sees them both introducing into male affairs.

16. In *Empire of Conspiracy*, Timothy Melley traces the problem of conspiracy—the problem of the individual's loss of agency—back to the postwar cultural critics I discussed earlier, the diagnosticians of the "Organization Man": Whyte, Riesman, Vance Packard. These writers respond to the crisis of agency brought on by the consumer economy and the bureaucratic corporation's structure by positing an alternative male subject, as with Riesman's distinction between the conformist "outer-directed" man and the individualist "inner-directed" man. Melley points out that "the inner-directed . . . *also* respond to external influences—from the Joneses and, by extension, from the acquisitive logic of liberal market capitalism," so that Riesman "is forced to admit that inner-directed people were also conspicuous consumers" (54, 55). In other words, the conception of an inner-directed man who is not defined by consumer culture is an impossibility; like my description of the male detective figure, it can only exist in the alternative, oppositional, elsewhere America that we have seen defined through noir's authenticity effects.

Chapter 3

1. In describing the sixties as the moment of "emergent" postmodernism, I am following the convincing periodization that Marianne DeKoven argues for in *Utopia Limited: The Sixties and the Emergence of the Postmodern*.

2. The right-wing, nativist "paranoid style" about which Richard Hofstadter wrote was concerned with outside or "un-American" forces and ideas that might infiltrate the nation via secret societies. Both David Brion Davis and Robert S. Levine, in very different studies, have traced this "style" back to the beginning of the republic and see it as running through American culture and literature ever since.

3. Knight describes an "invisible government," operating within and as a corollary to the public government, that dates from about 1947, the year of the founding of the CIA. Anthony Chase calls it "subterranean government."

4. I am discussing the revision of the hard-boiled detective form in tandem with the revision of noir; the two forms are not equivalent, but they overlap so extensively that it is useful to discuss them together—not least because they are so strongly linked in the later developments of the neo-noir tradition.

5. Although postmodern fiction is defined in part by its appropriation of popular culture forms, it does not then become popular culture or genre fiction, any more than a *nouvelle vague* film like *Breathless* or *Shoot the Piano Player* becomes the kind of genre film to which it pays homage. Postmodern fiction—whatever its aspirations—retains the cultural capital of the literary, incorporating genre elements but remaining differentiated from genre fiction. Although I find much contemporary detective fiction to be fascinating and deserving of study, my argument here is that the ideological terms that define hard-boiled detective fiction are picked up by "literary" postmodern fiction but not, at least for the most part, by books sold as part of the detective genre. To the extent that these ideological terms live on in something that we might call genre fiction they do so in the quasi-literary science-fiction subgenre cyberpunk, which I discuss at length later in the book.

6. For an influential formalist account of this generic shift, see John Cawelti's "*Chinatown* and Generic Transformation in Recent American Films."

7. In the eighties and nineties, the conspiracy thriller took on forms that mostly stripped away the political content, unhappy endings, and pervasive paranoia of the seventies films, while reinstating competent heroic types in the protagonist role. There has been some suggestion that the post–September 11 "war on terror" and the wars in Iraq and Afghanistan have created a political climate in which a new cycle of conspiracy films that draw inspiration from the seventies films has emerged. See Jay Millikan's "Paranoid Time" and Ross Douthat's "The Return of the Paranoid Style."

8. See Allan Siegel's "After the Sixties: Changing Paradigms in the Representation of Urban Space."

9. In *The Geopolitical Aesthetic*, Fredric Jameson considers the Library of Congress scene as a quasi-religious revelation of "the impossible vision of totality—here recovered in the moment in which the possibility of conspiracy confirms the possibility of the very unity of the social order itself" (79).

10. Fredric Jameson and Anthony Chase, both of whom discuss the role of space in *The Parallax View*, also both make the connection to *North by Northwest*.

11. Peter Knight might call this a "conspiracy without conspiring," a phrase he uses to describe the conception of conspiracy that emerges in Don DeLillo's *Underworld*.

12. In *Camera Politica*, Michael Ryan and Douglas Kellner argue that this demolition of the liberal individualist subject renders *The Parallax View* incapable of articulating a useable politics. Likewise, in *Conspiracy Theories*, Mark Fenster concludes that although conspiracy theory contains a "critique of the social order and a longing for a better one . . . [it] ultimately fails as a political and cultural practice. It . . . fails to inform us how to move from the end of the uncovered plot to the beginning of a political movement" (225–26).

Chapter 4

1. Pynchon emphasizes the thematic affinity between *The Crying of Lot 49* and *Vineland* in particular by bringing back characters from *Lot 49*—the Paranoids, Mucho Maas—for cameo appearances in *Vineland*. Meanwhile Gordita Beach, the setting for *Inherent Vice*, is first mentioned in *Vineland*.

2. Mr. Jones appears in the Bob Dylan song "Ballad of a Thin Man" from *Highway 61 Revisited*, which was released in 1965, a year before *The Crying of Lot 49*. "Ballad of a Thin Man" announces the new culture of the sixties by mocking Mr. Jones (representative of square America) while subjecting him to an array of wacky goings-on, many of them with homosexual overtones that would presumably be disturbing to Mr. J. The sinister circus music in which Dylan wraps his lyrics gives the song a conspiratorial edge, as if the sixties are a haunted house from which straights of all varieties are bound to run screaming unless they take the cure the song prescribes: "you should be made to wear earphones."

3. In addition to the books by Knight and Coale, there are a number of books devoted to the postmodern conspiracy text (see for example Knight, *Conspiracy Nation*; O'Donnell, *Latent Destinies*; and Melley, *Empire of Conspiracy*) or to the postmodern detective story (early contributions include Tani's *The Doomed Detective* and Cawelti's *Adventure, Mystery, and Romance*). Thompson's *Fiction, Crime, and Empire* connects the detective tradition to what I am calling "conspiracy narrative" nicely.

4. I have been arguing in this chapter that the theme of dispossession and the division of the world into ideological binary opposites are Pynchon's central strategies for representing America. It is worth saying that these are strategies he employs in structuring *all* of his fictional subjects. As Louis Menand writes in a review of *Against the Day*, for Pynchon "modern history is a war between utopianism and totalitarianism, counterculture and hegemony, anarchism and corporatism, nature and *techne*, Eros and the death drive, slaves and masters, entropy and order" ("Do the Math," 171). Again, what I am interested in here is how consistently Pynchon brings this vast, world-organizing, big-picture thinking to bear on specifically American issues.

5. *Let Us Now Praise Famous Men* (1941), by writer James Agee and photographer Walker Evans, documents and evokes the lives of families in the rural South during the Depression.

6. As Donald Pease observes, there is a nifty irony to the fact that the term originates not with any scholar of American Studies, but with Joseph Stalin, who spoke of "the heresy of American exceptionalism" in kicking out of the Communist International a sect that had broken with the American Communist Party due to the group's belief that the United States "was 'unique' because it lacked the social and historical conditions that had led to Europe's economic collapse" ("Exceptionalism," 108).

7. In *The Crying of Lot 49*, Pynchon famously makes "waste" (or WASTE), as the devalued detritus of consumption, the secret key to American life (an idea that is picked up later in

another great postmodern conspiracy novel, Don DeLillo's *Underworld*)—giving that which is wasted or abandoned a special status, so that the excepted and unaccepted becomes exceptional.

8. Bercovitch is primarily concerned with canonical nineteenth-century American writers—although he does include a long footnote on the countercultural version of the "anti-jeremiad" that name-checks *Gravity's Rainbow*. Echoing Pease's argument about exceptionalism in which the idea of the nation and the nation itself are asserted to be the same thing, Bercovitch suggests that to critique America in the name of America is inherently to write in a way that is politically circumscribed, limited to the bourgeois, prosperity-minded worldview that he sees as the legacy of the Puritans. It would certainly be possible to place the texts of the noir tradition within the category of the anti-jeremiad. (Pynchon's approach is similar to that of *The Education of Henry Adams*, which in Bercovitch's reading "reverses all the effects of the jeremiad while retaining intact the jeremiad's figural-symbolic outlook" [195].) But although I agree that the jeremiad and the anti-jeremiad both contribute to the power of the symbol of America, I am not convinced that "in every case, the defiant act that might have posed fundamental social alternatives became instead a fundamental force against social change" (204). In Pynchon's case, as I argue here, the attempt is precisely to discover or assert political alternatives within the American tradition, to claim an American tradition that is opposed to "middle-class culture" while not prophesying the cosmic doomsday that Bercovitch associates with the anti-jeremiad.

9. The reference to key moments in American history extends to another kind of founding father, the fictional Peter Pinguid, for whom one of the book's secret societies is named. His later life is described as a tragic end by society member Peter Fallopian: "for the rest of his life he did little more than acquire wealth. . . . [s]peculating in California real estate" (51).

10. *Johnny Staccato* was a television show that ran from 1959 to 1960, in which John Cassavetes played the eponymous detective, who worked the bohe-mean streets of Greenwich Village solving cases involving beatnik poets, jazz musicians, and the like.

11. Bill Millard's essay "Pynchon's Coast: *Inherent Vice* and the Twilight of the Spatially Specific" is an excellent reading both of the book and of the spatial politics of California land development that the book engages. One of his niftiest observations is that when Doc visits Channel View Estates he parks at "what would be the corner of Kaufman and Broad" (20). Millard points out that there is no such intersection in the LA area, but that the firm of Kaufman & Broad was a major player in the construction of tract housing, one that had a large hand in producing the sprawling urban-suburban landscape of California during the sixties.

12. See *Wired* magazine's online interactive map, "The Unofficial Thomas Pynchon Guide to Los Angeles" (http://www.wired.com/special_multimedia/2009/pl_print_1708; accessed May 17, 2013).

13. In *As Seen on TV: The Visual Culture of Everyday Life in the 1950s*, Karal Ann Marling discusses this synergetic relationship of television and suburban real estate, arguing that the design of postwar suburban housing spaces and the appliances that filled those spaces (televisions among them, of course) were essentially televisual: "the picture in the picture window was like the picture on the TV set or the view into Lucy's oven [on *I Love Lucy*]. They all provided framed views of what was going on inside" (6). Dolores Hayden's *Building Suburbia: Green Fields and Urban Growth, 1820–2000* makes a similar point in its chapter on "sitcom suburbs." Hayden's book is one of several excellent studies of the history of suburbanization in the United States; see also Lizabeth Cohen's *A Consumers' Republic* and Kenneth Jackson's *Crabgrass Frontier: The Suburbanization of the United States*.

14. There is in Pynchon a version of the idea that Faulkner's fiction elaborates more fully and explicitly, wherein property ownership is a kind of original sin—an "inherent vice."

15. In their essay "Do You Believe in Magic?: Literary Thinking after the New Left," Sean McCann and Michael Szalay take Pynchon to task for his use of "magical" thinking. Their argument is that the sixties New Left and the counterculture turned to "invocations of the irrational and mysterious" (438) in challenging rational and technocratic structures as the presumed underpinning of the power structures they believed it was necessary to undermine. The second part of their argument is a wide-ranging condemnation of poststructuralist theory and postmodern fiction that connects both to the politics of the New Left; the authors assert that Toni Morrison, Don DeLillo, and Pynchon use "magic" in their work as a way of retreating from politics and from the possibility of organized social change. There is much to admire and also much to argue with in this essay. In the context of this chapter, the point I would take issue with is that the essay willfully refuses to recognize the extent to which these postmodern writers use "magic" and forms of utopian thinking productively as a way of thinking through both the problems and possibilities of the Left in America. Certainly there are moments of retreat from the political, or unsophisticated formulations of the political, in these writers' work—one might cite *Inherent Vice*'s faith in the authentic Lemuria that I have been discussing here, or the dangerous-women-ride-off-into-the-sunset ending of Morrison's *Paradise*—but as I hope my discussion of Pynchon here (and of Morrison elsewhere) shows, that work also contains a consistent, productive, and meaningful engagement with American politics and an effort to imagine new avenues for the Left to pursue.

16. Several members of the Traverse family also make an appearance in Pynchon's 2006 novel *Against the Day*, again in the context of a political struggle between competing definitions of America. Here Pynchon recalls yet another important moment in the history of the American Left, turn-of-the-century anarchism.

17. See the music video for John (Cougar) Mellencamp's 1983 song "Pink Houses."

18. I would add that *Vineland* is not just one of the few Pynchon books to contain likable and human-seeming characters, but is pretty much the *only* Pynchon book that seems to be interested in creating complex and interesting female characters. Women in Pynchon are typically either marginal figures, objects of desire, or grotesques of some sort. But the women of *Vineland*—Frenesi, Prairie, Sasha, and especially DL—are the most fully drawn characters in the book: defined by their interesting contradictions; desiring mostly each other as mothers, daughters, friends; but also acting as sexual agents, rather than serving as passive recipients of male lust.

19. The commercialization of the sixties counterculture has been the source of much head-shaking and hand-wringing for four decades; as early as 1975, on the second episode of *Saturday Night Live*, Jerry Rubin appeared as himself in a fake advertisement for counterculture-nostalgia wallpaper ("Up against the wallpaper, motherfuckers!"). See Thomas Frank's *The Conquest of Cool: Business Culture, Counterculture, and the Rise of Hip Consumerism* for an analysis of this phenomenon.

Chapter 5

1. As in any cultural paradigm shift, the chronology isn't one of straightforward cause and effect. The postmodern conspiracy novel is already emerging by the time *Blind Man with a Pistol* is published, in William Burroughs's work and Pynchon's *V.* and *The Crying of Lot 49*, for instance.

2. In *Gumshoe America*, Sean McCann connects this tendency in Himes to earlier versions of hard-boiled fiction: "Like the underworld envisioned by Dashiell Hammett and Carroll John Daly, Himes's Harlem is a fantastic image of society-as-open-market, a world deliberately stripped of almost every custom or value that cannot be reduced finally to appetitive self-interest" (283). McCann argues convincingly that this vision represents the cynical side of Himes's desire for a return to what he experienced as an edenic moment working for the WPA in the thirties. In Himes's novels McCann sees a longing to locate again some vision of communal and public good, expressed as an angry compulsion to describe the absence of that vision from American life—another expression of the betrayal of American promise that is so important to Pynchon's fiction.

3. There is a powerful tradition of conspiracy *theory* in African American culture, too. This is due in large part to the U.S. government's tradition of actually conspiring against its black citizens, as in the Tuskeegee Institute experiment in which black men were deliberately and without their consent infected with syphilis in order to study the disease, or the FBI's COINTELPRO activities directed against the Black Panthers and Martin Luther King Jr. For an overview of African American conspiracy theory, see Peter Knight's chapter "Fear of a Black Planet."

4. In her essay "'That Just Kills Me,'" Kali Tal looks at some of the key texts in what I am calling the "black counterconspiracy tradition," although she defines the tradition as one of "black militant near-future fiction," which she considers to be "a subgenre of African American science fiction" (66).

5. Authenticity also defines the racial identity of white people, in the sense that white Americans feel themselves to be inauthentic—as a result, in part, of the spread of consumer culture, with its connotations of artificiality—and one of the ways that both individual whites and the mainstream culture as a whole respond to the resultant anxiety is by appropriating elements of African American culture. (Here, too, the ghetto is important as a guarantor of black authenticity; it is almost invariably elements of black street culture that are appropriated by whites, usually as a result of their diffusion through media like film and music.) A 1999 poll asking Americans to rate celebrities and public figures as more or less authentic found that those "perceived as the most genuine in almost every category were men and women of color" (*The Way We'll Be*, 164). As E. Patrick Johnson notes in *Appropriating Blackness*, the appropriation of blackness suggests immediately that "blackness" is always a performative category with no essential content, and that its only value is in the way it circulates and acquires value in the cultural economy of authenticity. For an insightful discussion of how black elements in white popular culture have become authenticating bearers of "soul," see Harryette Mullen's "Optic White: Blackness and the Production of Whiteness"; see also Grace Elizabeth Hale's *A Nation of Outsiders*.

6. For further discussion of these issues, see Valerie Smith, "Authenticity in Narratives of the Black Middle Class."

7. The tradition that associates black authenticity with the ghetto is especially important in hip-hop culture and music. Hip-hop culture has kept the logic that I identify as beginning in the sixties and seventies alive, combining a concern with black authenticity and a distinctly conspiratorial vision of America: rappers both identify the national conspiracy against African Americans and call for, or suggest that they represent, the counterconspiracy; these two moves are nicely summed up in the titles of two early Public Enemy albums, *It Takes a Nation of Millions to Hold Us Back* (1988) and *Fear of a Black Planet* (1990).

8. Two other writers whose work has affinities with blaxploitation are Iceberg Slim and Donald Goines, both of whom published gritty-realist crime fiction set in the ghetto during the early seventies.

9. Morrison's 1977 *Song of Solomon* is a powerful example of the way that the politics of the northern urban ghetto necessitate a return to the rural South and the slave past that it contains. Its central character, Milkman, makes a literal journey from North to South in order to claim his inheritance; he thinks it is gold, but the actual inheritance is the precious family history and connections to the past that he discovers in the South—and with them, an authentic black identity that frees him from the commercial obsessions of his father, the black capitalist Macon Dead. Connected to this story is the portrait of a counterconspiracy that brings the politics of the seventies to bear on the pre–civil rights era, imagining a black revolutionary group called the "Seven Days" that seeks to enact violent racial justice through a strict numerical logic, murdering a randomly selected white person as repayment for each black victim of racist violence. For a discussion of conspiracy themes in *Song of Solomon*, see Michael Rothberg's "Dead Letter Office: Conspiracy, Trauma, and *Song of Solomon's* Posthumous Communication."

10. This attempt of African Americans with roots in the South to negotiate the northern city and the ghetto in particular is one of the great organizing themes of the Easy Rawlins detective novels written by Walter Mosley.

11. Before the sixties, fictional depictions of the ghetto, such as Ann Petry's 1946 novel *The Street*, are generally stories of survival or escape rather than active resistance.

12. This line, given to an unnamed "beautiful black woman" who is barely a character in the novel and only appears briefly at the end, is about as close as black counterconspiracy texts come to giving a female character any kind of authoritative voice. As with much of the rhetoric and leadership of real-life black militant organizations in the sixties and seventies, these books are dominated by a male perspective and are regressive in their gender politics. Black ghetto authenticity is identified as male and straight and defined against the feminizing influences of consumer culture. Indeed, black feminist analysis in the post-sixties era has provided powerful critiques of the way in which the black revolutionary subject of the sixties is constituted as male, and of the extent to which the black male claim to "manhood" involved the repression of black women and the suppression of black female identity and voices. In *The Witch's Flight: The Cinematic, the Black Femme, and the Image of Common Sense*, Kara Keeling argues, in part, that in the late sixties the Black Panther Party constructed an image of blackness as masculine in order to align themselves with "other efforts toward national liberation, including those undertaken by 'the Founding Fathers'" (84). This conception of the black nationalist subject envisioned femininity as its opposite, associated with bourgeois culture and assimilation to the white mainstream, so that to be black in the public sphere—for both men and women—was to associate oneself with masculinity. The "feminine," to put this analysis in the terms I have been using here, was figured as the definition of the inauthentic and also was symbolically linked to the consumerist black bourgeoisie against which ghetto authenticity asserts itself. As in my discussion of noir masculinity in chapters 1 and 2, the distinction that "black authenticity" insists upon is not the one between men and women but that between two kinds of male subjects—the authentic and the inauthentic—with femininity appearing as a symbolic term in this opposition, representing the principle of commerce that introduces inauthenticity into the equation.

13. The process Himes describes is imagined in an explicitly positive (and essentially nonviolent) mode in Ishmael Reed's counterconspiracy book of the period, *Mumbo Jumbo*, in which uptight white conspiracies are opposed by "Jes Grew," a virus of dancing and disorganized celebration that infects the nation. Contemporary black counterconspiracy novels—such as Colson Whitehead's *The Intuitionist* (1999) and Victor LaValle's *Big Machine* (2009)—are typically less about revolutionary violence and more about fantastic imaginings of how to represent race and community in new ways—more the children of Himes (and of Reed and Pynchon) than of Greenlee.

Chapter 6

1. A similar movement toward self-conscious artificiality occurred in eighties fashion, which was marked by a profusion of nylon and spandex splashed with bright primary colors and geometric shapes.

2. At the same time, the rise of hip-hop production introduced techniques of sampling and scratching and made rap both a creative repurposing of the cultural past and a foregrounding of the role of technology in music.

3. Another of cyberpunk's obsessions is Japan. In part this may have to do with the influence of Japanese manga and anime, and also with the extreme coolness of the iconography available in traditional Japanese martial culture (samurai, ninjas, katanas, etc.)—for example, *Neuromancer* is fascinated by shuriken, the Japanese throwing stars. But the predominance of Japanese settings and elements in cyberpunk is probably best attributed to Japan's rise to economic dominance around the start of the eighties, and the fact that Japan had come to symbolize a potent merger between technological innovation and corporate capitalism. Domo arigato, Mister Roboto.

4. *Ronin* has been weirdly ignored in critical discussions both of cyberpunk and of graphic narrative. A bridge between Miller's groundbreaking series work on Marvel's *Daredevil* title and his full-blown noir stylistics in *The Dark Knight Returns* and *Sin City*, *Ronin* is experimental, testing the limits of the comic-book form with huge multipage drawings, unusual panel arrangements and narrative structures, and expressionistic color patternings.

5. See for example the "steampunk" subgenre, which looks back to the Victorian era in books like Neal Stephenson's *The Diamond Age* (1995) and Gibson's collaboration with Bruce Sterling on *The Difference Engine* (1990). See also the Dada film *Ballet Mécanique* (Dudley and Léger, 1924). Fritz Lang's *Metropolis* (the opening montage of which echoes *Ballet Mécanique*) is practically a primer in cyberpunk conventions: the vertical city with its class poles split between the skyscrapers and the underground, the relationship between human and technology, the corporate plutocrats who create a "man-machine" android.

6. In "Kill Me Again: Movement Becomes Genre," Todd Erickson argues that although noir itself cannot be called a genre because it was not recognizable as such to the people and studios that produced it, neo-noir is a genre because it *is* consciously made to fit a stylistic and narrative template. I would suggest a variation on this claim that takes into account the postmodern uses to which noir is put in later films: although classic noir is not generally regarded as a genre, it is treated as such in its neo-noir variants.

7. The other text from this period that could be added this list is Jean-François Lyotard's *The Postmodern Condition*. Lyotard's book, like the other theoretical texts I discuss here, presents the postmodern as a cultural dominant, the present situation of "knowledge in

computerized societies," and also like them has a science-fictional orientation toward imagining a future that is unrepresentable in the terms of the present moment.

8. Both Andreas Huyssen (in *After the Great Divide*) and Marianne DeKoven have suggested persuasively that French poststructuralist theory as practiced by Derrida, Foucault, Deleuze, Irigaray, Kristeva, Baudrillard, and others takes the form of a late-modernist avant-garde writing, one that attempts to blur or erase the line between "literary" and "theoretical" language.

9. Smith is a thoroughgoing materialist, and is generally skeptical about the ability of "metaphorical" forms (such as literature or film) to have any real political effect. But here he opens up the grudging possibility—which I have opportunistically seized—that there may be some political potential in metaphorical spaces (such as those in literature and film) and metaphorical concepts (such as Jameson's "cognitive mapping"). I would argue that if late capitalism has rendered the world as a simulated "abstract space," in Lefebvre's terms, then the metaphorical cartographies of fiction and film are an important site where the political struggle over the representation of space takes place.

10. For discussion of *Blade Runner* and the postmodern city, see "From Ramble City to the Screening of the Eye: *Blade Runner*, Death and Symbolic Exchange" by Marcus A. Doel and David B. Clarke; "Ramble City: Postmodernism and *Blade Runner*" by Giuliana Bruno; and David Harvey's discussion of the film in *The Condition of Postmodernity*.

11. The exploration of city space is dramatized further through the film's motif of eyes and vision, which turns our experience as viewers of the film into a theme within the film itself. Throughout, we watch other eyes watching; we experience the visual attempt to apprehend the space that the film has created. The opening scene of the film is an entry into the city-world we are about to see, with images of the stunning, alien landscape intercut with close-up shots of an anonymous eye (Roy's?) seeing what we see. Despite his apparent centrality, Deckard himself is barely an active presence in the film; Deckard's real function in the film is to serve as a *witness*; like us, he is there to observe and preserve in memory the bright-burning drama of the replicants' lives, and to be our companion and proxy on the film's guided tour through the stylized and unassimilable spectacle of the postmodern city.

12. The Chinese American actor James Hong even has a small part in each film—although this is less impressive when we notice that Hong has been Hollywood's go-to actor for every film with a small Chinese-guy role for the last fifty years.

13. The presence of the Zion colony connects *Neuromancer* to the strain of science fiction known as "afro-futurism" for its interest in speculating about possibilities for race, racial relations, and black communities—although unlike the work of Samuel Delany or Octavia Butler, for instance, Gibson's interest in race sometimes looks like a futuristic version of the tradition Toni Morrison calls "playing in the dark," in which black characters serve as symbolic vehicles for the working-out of a text's issues rather than as characters in their own right.

14. This model draws on, but is not reducible to, the popular narrative setup (in, say, World War II films) in which a ragtag band of good guys defeat or at least sabotage an imposing and well-oiled military machine. The relationship between Zion and Freeside contains echoes, for example, of that between the Millennium Falcon and the Death Star in *Star Wars*.

15. The mention of Tom Cruise as a reference point here is another of Gibson's strategies: his characters are frequently described in terms of their resemblance to celebrities, so that a

kind of human branding or commodification operates at the level of the description. Gibson also has a fondness for extending his metaphors to absurd lengths, another inheritance from Chandler; Cayce is interested in minor celebrities "because their careers can be so compressed, so eerily quantum-brief, like particles whose existence can only be proven, after the fact, by streaks detected on specially sensitized plates at the bottom of disused salt mines" (79).

16. Many of the obscure cultural artifacts described in *Pattern Recognition*—such as the ZX81 computer or the Curta calculator—are real items. But Cayce's "Buzz Rickson's" jacket is an especially interesting case, given the book's obsession with the process of commodification. Buzz Rickson's is a Japanese company of the sort that Gibson describes, but they had never manufactured a simulation of the MA-1 bomber jacket like the one that Cayce is described as owning. After the publication of the book, they began to produce one. In an all-too-predictable twist, the jacket is now advertised online—with Gibson's blessing—as the "Buzz Rickson's 'Pattern Recognition' Black MA-1 Intermediate Flying Jacket."

17. Cayce returns briefly in *Zero History*, the third book of the trilogy that begins with *Pattern Recognition*, and her role in that book reaffirms her status as an icon of the authentic. Once again Bigend and Blue Ant are searching for the maker of a line of products that are both extremely cool and distributed outside of official marketing channels—this time instead of the footage, the item is clothing—hoping to learn from the strategies involved in the making and selling of these underground jeans and sneakers. In a nifty reversal, the maker this time around turns out to be Cayce herself, but Bigend never learns this. If Bigend represents resilient, all-embracing consumer capitalism itself, Cayce seems to represent the principle of authentic opposition.

18. The phenomenon of postmodern authenticity is exemplified in cyberpunk, but it can be found very broadly in almost any text or theoretical model that tries to find in postmodernism the potential for resistance to consumer capitalism's world-organizing structures. A recent example is Raymond Malewitz's "Regeneration through Misuse: Rugged Consumerism in Contemporary American Culture." Malewitz suggests that "rugged consumers" deliberately misuse consumer artifacts in order to strip away their status as commodities and thus enable "an original, authentic encounter with the thing" (539). As the adjective "rugged" suggests, the process as imagined (and apparently cheered on) by Malewitz employs a familiar masculinist logic; "effete commodities" are repurposed by bricoleurs who thus become masculine producers, associated with frontier primitivism, rather than feminized consumers caught in the trap of civilization.

Chapter 7

1. Norville's errors, and Hudsucker's corrections, are absent from the published screenplay of *The Hudsucker Proxy*—an unusual deviation, since the Coens are famous for translating their screenplays without alteration to the screen.

2. Another Coen film that would bear investigation in these terms is *Raising Arizona* (1987), which in addition to its several convenience stores and gas stations, contains a comic chase sequence that reaches its cartoonish climax in a supermarket.

3. The film also contains offhand references to *Miracle on 34th Street* (1947), *Singin' in the Rain* (1952), *McCabe & Mrs. Miller* (1971), *The Shining* (1980), *The Empire Strikes Back* (1980), and *The Karate Kid* (1984). Other critics have noted connections to, among others,

Shadow of a Doubt (1943), *Meshes of the Afternoon* (1943), *The Red Balloon* (1956), and *Cool Hand Luke* (1967).

4. I would propose a rough three-part categorization of the screwball genre. First there is the remarriage-courtship plot: *His Girl Friday*, *The Awful Truth*, and *My Favorite Wife*, for example. Stanley Cavell has devoted an influential book to the study of this subgenre, *Pursuits of Happiness: The Hollywood Comedy of Remarriage*. The second, the "taming of the shrew" plot, is there in the film that kicked things off, *It Happened One Night*, but after that it rarely shapes a whole film; screwball couples tend to be more Beatrice-and-Benedick than Kate-and-Petrucchio. The third plot variant, I would suggest, is Shavian; its gender dynamic resembles the weird evolutionary logic of plays like *Man and Superman* in which the woman conquers the baffled man simply by embodying the "life force": *Bringing Up Baby* and *My Man Godfrey* are excellent examples, and practically any Carole Lombard role has her playing a version of the life-force-wielding ditz.

5. See for example Richard Maltby, "*It Happened One Night*: The Recreation of the Patriarch"; Andrew Bergman, *We're in the Money: Depression America and Its Films*; Morris Dickstein, *Dancing in the Dark: A Cultural History of the Great Depression*.

6. For a useful discussion of the politics of the Capra-Sturges divide, see Kathleen Moran and Michael Rogin, "'What's the Matter with Capra?': *Sullivan's Travels* and the Popular Front."

7. For other variations on this argument, see the readings of *Hudsucker* by Erica Rowell and R. Barton Palmer in their respective books on the Coens.

8. Boozer's book discusses a number of *The Hudsucker Proxy*'s business-film intertexts at length but, surprisingly, doesn't mention *Proxy* itself at all.

9. The Coens, in their revisiting of Capra, preserve the tension between the archetypal city and the archetypal heartland setting—Norville, who is such a hick that he is named "Barnes," is from Muncie, Indiana, the city that was the basis for the classic 1929 study of prewar American mores, *Middletown*—but they gleefully trample on the moral distinctions Capra makes between the two places. Norville, like Mr. Smith, is awestruck by the city when he arrives, but Mr. Smith's awe comes from what he sees as the shining national ideals incarnated in Washington, D.C., while Norville is looking for success, and when he finds it he quickly becomes corrupt and lazy in a way that no Capra protagonist ever was.

10. In his essay "Genericity in the Nineties: Eclectic Irony and the New Sincerity," Jim Collins argues that this mode is in fact characteristic of film in the 1990s, that during that decade "genre" as a category was reconceived as Hollywood film tended toward hybrid and transgeneric forms within which the whole history of cinema became available as simultaneous array.

11. The motif of up-and-down movement cycles is expressed in other ways throughout the film, too. The psychologist Dr. Bromfenbrenner, who is called in to prove Norville's insanity, displays an up-and-down graph of Norville's psychic life (this material is borrowed from *Mr. Deeds Goes to Town*), explaining that the patient is "riding ze grand loopen-ze-loop zat goes from ze peak of delusional GAIETY to ze trrrroff of dezBAIR." More subtly, when we encounter the great gears of the Hudsucker clock for the first time, the soundtrack incorporates echoes of the famous "O Fortuna" from Carl Orff's *Carmina Burana*, with its medieval lyric invoking fortune's wheel: "Fate—monstrous / and empty / you whirling wheel / stand malevolent / well-being is vain / and always fades to nothing." The seemingly

contradictory double motif of the circle and the line is also a principle of clockworks, in which up-and-down lines stretched on pulleys drive the motion of round interlocking gears.

12. It is appropriate, then, that the first appearance that the Hudsucker name makes is in the 1985 film *Crimewave*, written by the Coens and directed by Sam Raimi, as Hudsucker State Penitentiary—implying an analogy between prison and corporation like the explicit one that René Clair makes in *À nous la liberté*. Another linked reference occurs in *Raising Arizona*; while working at his one—hated—legitimate job, Hi wears a Hudsucker Industries worksuit.

13. Moses is the film's only black character, and speaks in an imitation of Hollywood-Negro dialect from the thirties and forties. To date, the Coens have not been especially adept at creating convincing black characters—even by their standards of "character"—and seem comfortable with Moses, who is compellingly played by Bill Cobbs, only because he is safely in the realm of the "magic Negro" who watches over the fates of white characters without himself being quite real.

14. The image of the figure scraping names from an executive office's glass-fronted doors seems to have been borrowed from Sturges's *Christmas in July* (1940). Aloysius is also an incarnation of the force-of-evil character who appears in many Coen films—Leonard Smalls in *Raising Arizona*, the Sheriff in *O Brother, Where Art Thou?*, Chigurh in *No Country for Old Men*. In the Coen cosmos there is rarely a god, but there is almost always a devil.

15. It would be interesting to develop a comparison of *The Hudsucker Proxy* with Martin Scorsese's 2011 film *Hugo*. Scorsese uses 3-D effects to evoke the mazelike architecture of Hugo's home: the interior of the clock-system in a Paris train station in the early 1930s. Both films use the interior space of the clock as a means to represent the history of cinema, although for *Hugo* the dominant paradigm is not the corporation but industry, with the clockwork mechanism providing a way of looking back to the late-Victorian moment of cinema's emergence, and that industrial moment is reflected in the film's fascination with locomotives and automata and in the grand nineteenth-century design of the train station itself.

16. For some of this useful information about the Hula Hoop, I am indebted to Eddie Robson's *Coen Brothers*.

17. Condensation and displacement are key concepts in Freud's model for the interpretation of dreams: the psyche translates repressed desires or fears into the language of dreams in part by employing these tools. Condensation describes the transformation of several ideas or figures into a single representative form, and displacement moves what is central and significant to the margins, or disguises it in some way.

18. In *Hollywood Genres*, for example, Thomas Schatz argues that all film genres consider some sort of threat to the social order of American society, one that is cancelled through the formal and emotional resolution of the genre formula. In *Film/Genre* Rick Altman has pointed out that this "ritual" approach to film genre runs into difficulty when considering film noir, which on the whole does not offer this sort of fantasized solution to the social tensions it dramatizes. Indeed, this is one reason why theorists of noir have shied away from calling it a genre, or have identified it as an "anti-genre"; likewise, some Marxist critics and "ideological" theorists of genre gravitate toward noir for this very reason—because it seems to provide an antidote to the deceptions of the dominant ideology that they see as being peddled by genre narratives.

19. For example, see my article "Out of the Past, into the Supermarket: Consuming Film Noir," in which I argue that the film *Fight Club* (1999) performs a similar kind of self-consciously postmodern work on the relationship between authenticity and consumer culture.

Conclusion

1. Potter begins by suggesting that he intends to take the desire for authenticity seriously (while pursuing his argument that the market economy is in fact a positive good), but by the book's end he is denouncing that desire as "a dopey nostalgia for a nonexistent past, a one-sided suspicion of the modern world, and stagnant and reactionary politics masquerading as something personally meaningful and socially progressive" (270); he ultimately claims that the search for the authentic has led us into "sin and betrayal" (271). As this language suggests, Potter is explicit in attacking authenticity in the name of principles that he considers to represent a better authenticity. This is a frequent strategy of cultural critics—denouncing one kind of authenticity in order to champion another—and one that contributes to the vagueness of the term. See for instance Joshua Glenn's "Fake Authenticity," which opposes the fake authenticity of the Baudrillardian simulacrum to the "real" authenticity offered by existential creative individualism.

2. At the time of this book's writing, the equation of national strength with the strength of the American consumer economy is often quite explicit—in the governmental and media discourses that consider the state of the union using measures such as consumer spending and the housing economy, for instance. One moment that made this equation dramatically visible for many of us was when George W. Bush encouraged American citizens to respond to the terrorist attacks of September 11, 2001, by continuing to spend and buy—individual consumption as an act of nationalism.

{ BIBLIOGRAPHY }

Agee, James. "The Great American Roadside." *Fortune Magazine* 10 (Sept. 1934): 172–77.

———, and Walker Evans. *Let Us Now Praise Famous Men*. 1941. New York: Houghton Mifflin, 2001.

Agnew, Jean-Christophe. "A Touch of Class." *Democracy* 3, no. 2 (Spring 1983): 59–72.

———. *Worlds Apart: The Market and the Theater in Anglo-American Thought, 1550–1750*. Cambridge: Cambridge University Press, 1986.

Allen, Dennis. "*Logjammin'* and *Gutterballs*: Masculinities in *The Big Lebowski*." In *The Year's Work in Lebowski Studies*, ed. Edward Comentale and Aaron Jaffe, 386–409. Bloomington: Indiana University Press, 2009.

Altman, Rick. *Film/Genre*. London: BFI, 1999.

Anderson, Amanda. *The Way We Argue Now: A Study in the Cultures of Theory*. Princeton: Princeton University Press, 2006.

Appadurai, Arjun, ed. *The Social Life of Things: Commodities in Cultural Perspective*. Cambridge: Cambridge University Press, 1986.

Ashley, Bob, et al. *Food and Cultural Studies*. New York: Routledge, 2004.

Auerbach, Jonathan. *Dark Borders: Film Noir and American Citizenship*. Durham, NC: Duke University Press, 2011.

———. "*Noir* Citizenship: Anthony Mann's *Border Incident*." *Cinema Journal* 47, no. 4 (Summer 2008): 102–20.

Baker, Jeffrey S. "A Democratic Pynchon: Counterculture, Counterforce and Participatory Democracy." *Pynchon Notes* 32–33 (1993): 99–131.

Barthes, Roland. *S/Z*. 1970. Reprint, New York: Hill & Wang, 1974.

Baudrillard, Jean. *America*. 1986. Reprint, New York: Verso, 1998.

———. "Simulacra and Science Fiction." In Beaudrillard, *Simulacra and Simulation*, 121–28. Ann Arbor: University of Michigan Press, 1994.

———. *Simulations*. New York: Semiotext(e), 1983.

Baughman, James. *Henry R. Luce and the Rise of the American News Media*. Boston: Twayne, 1987.

Belasco, Warren. *Meals to Come: A History of the Future of Food*. Berkeley: University of California Press, 2006.

Bell, Jonathan. "Shadows in the Hinterland: Rural Noir." In *Architecture and Film*, ed. Mark Lamster, 217–30. New York: Princeton Architectural Press, 2000.

Bendix, Regina. *In Search of Authenticity: The Formation of Folklore Studies*. Madison: University of Wisconsin Press, 1997.

Bennett, Lerone. "The Emancipation Orgasm: Sweetback in Wonderland." *Ebony* 26, no. 11 (Sept. 1971): 104–18.

Bergman, Andrew. *We're in the Money: Depression America and Its Films*. New York: New York University Press, 1971.

Berkovitch, Sacvan. *The American Jeremiad*. Madison: University of Wisconsin Press, 1978.

Berman, Marshall. *The Politics of Authenticity: Radical Individualism and the Emergence of Modern Society*. New York: Atheneum, 1970.

Biesen, Sheri Chinen. *Blackout: World War II and the Origins of Film Noir*. Baltimore: Johns Hopkins University Press, 2005.

Bogle, Donald. *Toms, Coons, Mulattoes, Mammies, and Bucks: An Interpretive History of Blacks in American Films*. New expanded ed. New York: Continuum, 1989.

Bookchin, Murray. "Between the 30s and the 60s." In *The 60s without Apology*, ed. Sohnya Sayres et al., 247–50. Minneapolis: University of Minnesota Press, 1984.

Boorstin, Daniel. *The Image: A Guide to Pseudo-Events in America*. 1961. Reprint, New York: Vintage, 1992.

Boozer, Jack. *Career Movies: American Business and the Success Mystique*. Austin: University of Texas Press, 2002.

Borde, Raymond, and Etienne Chaumeton. *A Panorama of American Film Noir 1941–1953*. 1955. Reprint, San Francisco: City Lights Books, 2002.

Borges, Jorge Luis. "Death and the Compass." In *A Personal Anthology*, ed. Anthony Kerrigan, 1–14. New York: Grove Press, 1967.

Bowlby, Rachel. *Carried Away: The Invention of Modern Shopping*. New York: Columbia University Press, 2001.

Boyle, David. *Authenticity: Brands, Fakes, Spin, and the Lust for Real Life*. London: HarperCollins, 2003.

Bronner, Simon, ed. *Consuming Visions: Accumulation and Display of Goods in America 1880–1920*. New York: Norton, 1989.

Brooks, John. *The Big Wheel*. New York: Harper & Row, 1949.

Bukatman, Scott. *Blade Runner*. London: BFI, 1997.

Campbell, Colin. *The Romantic Ethic and the Spirit of Modern Consumerism*. New York: Blackwell, 1987.

Cassuto, Leonard. *Hard-Boiled Sentimentality: The Secret History of American Crime Stories*. New York: Columbia University Press, 2009.

Cavell, Stanley. *Pursuits of Happiness: The Hollywood Comedy of Remarriage*. Cambridge, MA: Harvard University Press, 1981.

Cawelti, John. *Adventure, Mystery, and Romance: Formula Stories as Art and Popular Culture*. Chicago: University of Chicago Press, 1976.

———. "*Chinatown* and Generic Transformation in Recent American Films." In *Film Genre Reader II*, ed. Barry Keith Grant, 227–45. Austin: University of Texas Press, 1986.

Chandler, Raymond. *The Big Sleep*. 1939. Reprint, New York: Vintage, 1992.

———. *Farewell, My Lovely*. 1940. Reprint, New York: Vintage, 1988.

———. *The Long Goodbye*. 1953. Reprint, New York: Vintage, 1992.

———. "The Simple Art of Murder: An Essay." In Chandler, *The Simple Art of Murder*. 1944. Reprint, New York: Vintage, 1988, 1–18.

———. *Trouble Is My Business*. 1950. Reprint, New York: Vintage, 1988.

Chartier, Jean-Pierre. "Les Américains aussi font des films 'noirs.'" *Revue du cinéma* 2 (1946): 67–70.

Chase, Anthony. *Movies on Trial: The Legal System on the Silver Screen*. New York: New Press, 2002.

Chelminski, Rudolph. "The Hard-Bitten Old Pro Who Wrote 'Cotton.'" *Life* 69, no. 9 (Aug. 28, 1970): 60–61.

Cheever, Abigail. *Real Phonies: Cultures of Authenticity in Post-World War II America*. Athens: University of Georgia Press, 2010.

Cheng, Vincent. *Inauthentic: The Anxiety over Culture and Identity*. New Brunswick, NJ: Rutgers University Press, 2004.

Christopher, Nicholas. *Somewhere in the Night: Film Noir and the American City*. New York: Henry Holt, 1997.

Clarke, David B., et al., eds. *Moving Pictures/Stopping Places: Hotels and Motels on Film*. Lanham, MD: Lexington Books, 2009.

Coale, Samuel Chase. *Paradigms of Paranoia: The Culture of Conspiracy in Contemporary American Fiction*. Tuscaloosa: University of Alabama Press, 2005.

Coen, Joel, Ethan Coen, and Sam Raimi. *The Hudsucker Proxy*. Boston: Faber & Faber, 1994.

Cohen, Erik. "Authenticity and Commoditization in Tourism." *Annals of Tourism Research* 15 (1988): 371–86.

Cohen, Lizabeth. *A Consumers' Republic: The Politics of Mass Consumption in Postwar America*. New York: Vintage, 2003.

Collins, Jim. "Genericity in the Nineties: Eclectic Irony and the New Sincerity." *Film Theory Goes to the Movies*, ed. Jim Collins, Hilary Radner, and Ava Preacher Collins, 242–64. New York: Routledge, 1993.

Comentale, Edward, and Aaron Jaffe, eds. *The Year's Work in Lebowski Studies*. Bloomington: Indiana University Press, 2009.

Conard, Mark. *The Philosophy of the Coen Brothers*. Lexington: University Press of Kentucky, 2009.

Conroy, Mark. "The American Way and Its Double in *The Crying of Lot 49*." *Pynchon Notes* 24–25 (1989): 45–70.

Copjec, Joan. "The Phenomenal Nonphenomenal: Private Space in *Film Noir*." In *Shades of Noir*, ed. Joan Copjec, 167–98. New York: Verso, 1993.

———, ed. *Shades of Noir*. New York: Verso, 1993.

Coughlin, Paul. "The Past Is Now: History and *The Hudsucker Proxy*." In *The Philosophy of the Coen Brothers*, ed. Mark Conard, 195–209. Lexington: University Press of Kentucky, 2009.

Cowart, David. "Attenuated Postmodernism: Pynchon's *Vineland*." In *The Vineland Papers: Critical Takes on Pynchon's Novel*, ed. Geoffrey Green et al., 3–13. Normal, IL: Dalkey Archive Press, 1994.

Cowie, Elizabeth. "Film Noir and Women." In *Shades of Noir*, ed. Joan Copjec, 121–66. New York: Verso, 1993.

Cross, Gary. *An All-Consuming Century: Why Commercialism Won in Modern America*. New York: Columbia University Press, 2000.

Cross, Jennifer. *The Supermarket Trap: The Consumer and the Food Industry*. Bloomington: Indiana University Press, 1970.

Csicsery-Ronay, Istvan. "Cyberpunk and Neuromanticism." In *Storming the Reality Studio: A Casebook of Cyberpunk and Postmodern Science Fiction*, ed. Larry McCaffery, 182–93. Durham, NC: Duke University Press, 2000.

———. "The SF of Theory: Baudrillard and Haraway." *Science Fiction Studies* 18, no. 3 (Nov. 1991): 387–404.

"Cyberpunk Forum/Symposium." *Mississippi Review* 16, nos. 2/3 (1988): 16–65.

Davis, Mike. *City of Quartz*. New York: Verso, 1990.

DeKoven, Marianne. *Utopia Limited: The Sixties and the Emergence of the Postmodern*. Durham, NC: Duke University Press, 2004.

Deleuze, Gilles. *Negotiations, 1972–1990*. New York: Columbia University Press, 1995.

DeLillo, Don. *White Noise*. New York: Penguin, 1985.

Dickstein, Morris. *Dancing in the Dark: A Cultural History of the Great Depression*. New York: Norton, 2009.

Didion, Joan. *The White Album*. 1979. New York: Farrar, Straus & Giroux, 1990.

Dimendberg, Edward. *Film Noir and the Spaces of Modernity*. Cambridge, MA: Harvard University Press, 2004.

Doane, Mary Ann. *Femmes Fatales: Feminism, Film Theory, Psychoanalysis*. New York: Routledge, 1991.

Douglas, Mary, and Baron Isherwood. *The World of Goods: Towards an Anthropology of Consumption*. New York: W. W. Norton, 1979.

Douthat, Ross. "The Return of the Paranoid Style." *The Atlantic* 301, no. 3 (April 2008): 52–59.

Dussere, Erik. "Out of the Past, into the Supermarket: Consuming Film Noir." *Film Quarterly* 60, no. 1 (Fall 2006): 16–27.

Easterling, Keller. *Enduring Innocence: Global Architecture and Its Political Masquerades*. Cambridge, MA: MIT Press, 2005.

Eco, Umberto. *Travels in Hyperreality*. 1973. Reprint, New York: Harcourt Brace, 1986.

Ehrenreich, Barbara and John. "The Professional-Managerial Class." In *Between Labor and Capital*, ed. Pat Walker, 5–48. Boston: South End, 1979.

Elmer, Jonathan. "Enduring and Abiding." In *The Year's Work in Lebowski Studies*, ed. Edward Comentale and Aaron Jaffe, 445–55. Bloomington: Indiana University Press, 2009.

Erickson, Todd. "Kill Me Again: Movement Becomes Genre." In *Film Noir Reader*, ed. Alain Silver and James Ursini, 307–30. New York: Limelight, 1996.

Faulkner, William. Introduction to *Sanctuary*. 1932. In *Sanctuary: The Corrected Text*, 337–39. New York: Vintage, 1987.

Fearing, Kenneth. *The Big Clock*. 1946. Reprint, New York: New York Review Books, 2006.

Fenster, Mark. *Conspiracy Theories: Secrecy and Power in American Culture*. Minneapolis: University of Minnesota Press, 1999.

Fox, Richard Wrightman, and T. J. Jackson Lears, eds. *The Culture of Consumption: Critical Essays in American History 1880–1980*. New York: Pantheon, 1983.

Frank, Nino. "Un nouveau genre 'policier': L'aventure criminelle." *L'Écran français* 61 (Aug. 28, 1946): 14–16.

Frank, Thomas. *The Conquest of Cool: Business Culture, Counterculture, and the Rise of Hip Consumerism*. Chicago: University of Chicago Press, 1997.

Frazier, E. Franklin. *Black Bourgeoisie*. New York: Free Press, 1957.

Friedan, Betty. *The Feminine Mystique*. 1963. New York: W. W. Norton, 2001.

Friedberg, Anne. *Window Shopping: Cinema and the Postmodern*. Berkeley: University of California Press, 1993.

Gardiner, Dorothy, and Kathrine Sorley Walker, eds. *Raymond Chandler Speaking*. Berkeley: University of California Press, 1997.

Gibson, William. "Burning Chrome." In *Burning Chrome*, 179–204. 1985. Reprint, New York: HarperCollins, 2003.

———. *Neuromancer*. New York: Ace, 1984.

———. *Pattern Recognition*. New York: Berkley, 2003.

————. *Spook Country*. New York: Putnam, 2007.

Gilmore, James, and B. Joseph Pine. *Authenticity: What Consumers Really Want*. Boston: Harvard Business School Press, 2007.

Glenn, Joshua. "Fake Authenticity: An Introduction." *Hermenaut* 15 (1999). http://hilobrow .com/2010/06/01/fake-authenticity. Accessed May 16, 2013.

Glickman, Lawrence, ed. *Consumer Society in American History: A Reader*. Ithaca, NY: Cornell University Press, 1997.

Golomb, Jacob. *In Search of Authenticity: From Kierkegaard to Camus*. New York: Routledge, 1995.

Green, Geoffrey, et al. *The Vineland Papers: Critical Takes on Pynchon's Novel*. Normal, IL: Dalkey Archive Press, 1994.

Greenlee, Sam. *The Spook Who Sat by the Door*. 1969. Detroit: Wayne State University Press, 1990.

Greenwood, Davydd J. "Culture by the Pound: An Anthropological Perspective on Tourism as Cultural Commoditization." In *Hosts and Guests: The Anthropology of Tourism*, ed. Valene Smith, 171–86. Philadelphia: University of Pennsylvania Press, 1989.

Gudis, Catherine. *Buyways: Billboards, Automobiles, and the American Landscape*. New York: Routledge, 2004.

Guerrero, Ed. *Framing Blackness: The African American Image in Film*. Philadelphia: Temple University Press, 1993.

Hale, Grace Elizabeth. *A Nation of Outsiders: How the White Middle Class Fell in Love with Rebellion in Postwar America*. New York: Oxford University Press, 2011.

Hammett, Dashiell. *The Glass Key*. 1931. Reprint, New York: Vintage, 1989.

Haraway, Donna. "A Cyborg Manifesto: Science, Technology, and Socialist-Feminism in the Late Twentieth Century." In *Simians, Cyborgs, and Women: The Reinvention of Nature*, 149–81. New York: Routledge, 1991.

Harkness, John. "The Sphinx without a Riddle." *Sight & Sound* (Aug. 1994): 6–9.

Harrington, Michael. *The Other America: Poverty in the United States*. New York: Macmillan, 1964.

Harvey, David. *The Condition of Postmodernity: An Enquiry into the Origins of Cultural Change*. Cambridge: Blackwell, 1990.

Haskell, Molly. *From Reverence to Rape: The Treatment of Women in the Movies*. Chicago: University of Chicago Press, 1987.

Hayden, Dolores. *Building Suburbia: Green Fields and Urban Growth, 1820–2000*. New York: Pantheon, 2003.

Heath, Joseph, and Andrew Potter. *Nation of Rebels: Why Counterculture Became Consumer Culture*. New York: HarperBusiness, 2005.

Himes, Chester. *Blind Man with a Pistol*. 1969. Reprint, New York: Vintage, 1989.

————. *My Life of Absurdity: The Autobiography of Chester Himes*. Vol. 2. New York: Thunder's Mouth Press, 1976.

————. *Plan B*. Jackson: University Press of Mississippi, 1993.

Hoberek, Andrew. *The Twilight of the Middle Class: Post–World War II American Fiction and White-Collar Work*. Princeton: Princeton University Press, 2005.

Hochschild, Arlie Russell. *The Managed Heart: The Commercialization of Human Feeling*. Berkeley: University of California Press, 1983.

————. *The Outsourced Self: Intimate Life in Market Times*. New York: Metropolitan, 2012.

Hollinger, Karen. "Film Noir, Voice-over, and the Femme Fatale." In *Film Noir Reader*, ed. Alain Silver and James Ursini, 243–60. New York: Limelight, 1996.

Holm, D. K. *Film Soleil*. North Pomfret: Trafalgar Square, 2005.

Horkheimer, Max, and Theodor Adorno. *Dialectic of Enlightenment*. 1944. Reprint, New York: Continuum, 1990.

Horowitz, Daniel. *The Anxieties of Affluence: Critiques of American Consumer Culture, 1939–1979*. Amherst: University of Massachusetts Press, 2004.

Humphery, Kim. *Shelf Life: Supermarkets and the Changing Cultures of Consumption*. Cambridge: Cambridge University Press, 1998.

Huyssen, Andreas. *After the Great Divide: Modernism, Mass Culture, Postmodernism*. Bloomington: Indiana University Press, 1986.

Jackson, Kenneth. *Crabgrass Frontier: The Suburbanization of the United States*. New York: Oxford University Press, 1985.

Jakle, John, and Keith Sculle. *The Gas Station in America*. Baltimore: Johns Hopkins University Press, 1994.

James, Henry. *The Princess Casamassima*. 1886. Reprint, New York: Penguin, 1987.

Jameson, Fredric. *The Geopolitical Aesthetic: Cinema and Space in the World System*. Bloomington: Indiana University Press, 1992.

——. "On Raymond Chandler." In *The Poetics of Murder*, ed. Glenn Most and William Stowe, 122–48. New York: Harcourt Brace Jovanovich, 1983.

——. "Periodizing the 60s." In *The 60s without Apology*, ed. Sohnya Sayres et al., 178–209. Minneapolis: University of Minnesota Press, 1984.

——. *Postmodernism, or, the Cultural Logic of Late Capitalism*. Durham, NC: Duke University Press, 1991.

——. "Progress versus Utopia; or, Can We Imagine the Future?" *Science Fiction Studies* 9, no. 2 (1982): 147–58.

——. "The Synoptic Chandler." In *Shades of Noir*, ed. Joan Copjec, 33–56. New York: Verso, 1993.

Johnson, E. Patrick. *Appropriating Blackness: Performance and the Politics of Authenticity*. Durham, NC: Duke University Press, 2003.

Jones, Thomas. "Call It Capitalism." *London Review of Books* 31, no. 17 (Sept. 10, 2009): 9–10.

Kammen, Michael. "The Problem of American Exceptionalism: A Reconsideration." *American Quarterly* 45, no. 1 (March 1993): 1–43.

Kaplan, E. Ann. *Women and Film Noir*. London: BFI, 1980.

Keeling, Kara. *The Witch's Flight: The Cinematic, the Black Femme, and the Image of Common Sense*. Durham, NC: Duke University Press, 2007.

Kelly, James Patrick, and John Kessel, eds. *Rewired: The Post-Cyberpunk Anthology*. San Francisco: Tachyon, 2007.

Kemp, Philip. "From the Nightmare Factory: HUAC and the Politics of Noir." In *The Big Book of Noir*, ed. Lee Server et al., 77–86. New York: Carroll & Graf, 1998.

Ketterer, David. *Canadian Science Fiction and Fantasy*. Bloomington: Indiana University Press, 1992.

Knight, Peter. *Conspiracy Culture: From the Kennedy Assassination to The X-Files*. New York: Routledge, 2000.

——, ed. *Conspiracy Nation: The Politics of Paranoia in Postwar America*. New York: New York University Press, 2002.

Körte, Peter, and Georg Seesslen, eds. *Joel & Ethan Coen*. New York: Limelight, 2001.

Krutnik, Frank. "Something More Than Night: Tales of the *Noir* City." In *The Cinematic City*. ed. David Clarke, 83–109. New York: Routledge, 1997.

Lasn, Kalle. *Culture Jam*. New York: Quill, 2000.

Leach, William. *Land of Desire: Merchants, Power, and the Rise of a New American Culture*. New York: Pantheon, 1993.

Lears, Jackson. "Beyond Veblen: Rethinking Consumer Culture in America." In *Consuming Visions: Accumulation and Display of Goods in America, 1880–1920*, ed. Simon Bronner, 73–98. New York: Norton, 1989.

———. *Fables of Abundance: A Cultural History of Advertising in America*. New York: HarperCollins, 1994.

———. "A Matter of Taste: Corporate Cultural Hegemony in a Mass-Consumption Society." In *Recasting America: Culture and Politics in the Age of Cold War*, ed. Lary May, 38–60. Chicago: University of Chicago Press, 1989.

Lefebvre, Henri. *The Production of Space*. 1974. Cambridge: Blackwell, 1991.

Levenstein, Harvey. *Paradox of Plenty: A Social History of Eating in America*. New York: Oxford University Press, 1993.

Lewis, David, and Darren Bridger. *The Soul of the New Consumer: Authenticity—What We Buy and Why in the New Economy*. London: Nicholas Brealey, 2000.

Liebs, Chester. *Main Street to Miracle Mile: American Roadside Architecture*. Baltimore: Johns Hopkins University Press, 1985.

Longstreth, Richard. *The Drive-In, the Supermarket, and the Transformation of Commercial Space in Los Angeles, 1914–1941*. Cambridge, MA: MIT Press, 1999.

Luce, Henry. "The American Century." *Life*, Feb. 7, 1941, 61–65.

Lyotard, Jean-François. *The Postmodern Condition: A Report on Knowledge*. Minneapolis: University of Minnesota Press, 1984.

MacCannell, Dean. "Democracy's Turn: On Homeless *Noir*." In *Shades of Noir*, ed. Joan Copjec, 279–98. New York: Verso, 1993.

———. *The Tourist: A New Theory of the Leisure Class*. 1976. Reprint, Berkeley: University of California Press, 1999.

Madsen, Deborah. *American Exceptionalism*. Jackson: University Press of Mississippi, 1998.

Maland, Charles. "Capra and the Abyss: Self-Interest versus the Common Good in Depression America." In *Frank Capra: Authorship and the Studio System*, ed. Robert Sklar and Vito Zagarrio, 95–129. Philadelphia: Temple University Press, 1998.

Malewitz, Raymond. "Regeneration through Misuse: Rugged Consumerism in American Culture." *PMLA* 127, no. 3 (May 2012): 526–41.

Maltby, Richard. "*It Happened One Night*: The Recreation of the Patriarch." In *Frank Capra: Authorship and the Studio System*, ed. Robert Sklar and Vito Zagarrio, 130–63. Philadelphia: Temple University Press, 1998.

Marchand, Roland. *Advertising the American Dream: Making Way for Modernity, 1920–1940*. Berkeley: University of California Press, 1985.

Marcus, Greil. *Invisible Republic: Bob Dylan's Basement Tapes*. New York: Henry Holt, 1997.

Marcuse, Herbert. *Eros and Civilization: A Philosophical Inquiry into Freud*. 1955. Boston: Beacon Press, 1974.

———. *One-Dimensional Man: Studies in the Ideology of Advanced Industrial Society*. 1964. Reprint, New York: Routledge, 2002.

Marling, Karal Ann. *As Seen on TV: The Visual Culture of Everyday Life in the 1950s.* Cambridge, MA: Harvard University Press, 1994.

Martin, Reinhold. *The Organizational Complex: Architecture, Media, and Corporate Space.* Cambridge, MA: MIT Press, 2003.

Martin-Jones, David. "No Literal Connection: Mass Commodification, U.S. Militarism, and the Oil Industry in The Big Lebowski." In *The Year's Work in Lebowski Studies,* ed. Edward Comentale and Aaron Jaffe, 203–27. Bloomington: Indiana University Press, 2009.

Massood, Paula. *Black City Cinema: African American Urban Experiences in Film.* Philadelphia: Temple University Press, 2003.

May, Lary. *The Big Tomorrow: Hollywood and the Politics of the American Way.* Chicago: University of Chicago Press, 2000.

McCaffery, Larry, ed. *Storming the Reality Studio: A Casebook of Cyberpunk and Postmodern Science Fiction.* Durham, NC: Duke University Press, 1991.

McCann, Sean. *Gumshoe America: Hard-Boiled Crime Fiction and the Rise and Fall of New Deal Liberalism.* Durham, NC: Duke University Press, 2000.

———, and Michael Szalay. "Do You Believe in Magic? Literary Thinking after the New Left." *Yale Journal of Criticism* 18, no. 2 (Fall 2005): 435–68.

McClure, John. "Forget Conspiracy: Pynchon, DeLillo, and the Conventional Counterconspiracy Narrative." In *Conspiracy Nation: The Politics of Paranoia in Postwar America,* ed. Peter Knight, 254–74. New York: New York University Press, 2002.

McGovern, Charles. *Sold American: Consumption and Citizenship, 1890–1945.* Chapel Hill: University of North Carolina Press, 2006.

Melley, Timothy. *Empire of Conspiracy: The Culture of Paranoia in Postwar America.* Ithaca, NY: Cornell University Press, 2000.

Menand, Louis. "Do the Math." *New Yorker* 82, no. 39 (Nov. 27, 2006): 170–72.

Mendelson, Edward. "Levity's Rainbow." *New Republic* 203 (July 9–16, 1990): 40–46.

Metz, Walter. *Engaging Film Criticism: Film History and Contemporary American Cinema.* New York: Peter Lang, 2004.

Millard, Bill. "Pynchon's Coast: *Inherent Vice* and the Twilight of the Spatially Specific." *College Hill Review* 4 (Fall 2009). http://www.collegehillreview.com/004/0040501.html. Accessed May 16, 2013.

Miller, Daniel. *Material Culture and Mass Consumption.* Oxford: Blackwell, 1987.

Millikan, Jay. "Paranoid Time: The Conspiracy Thrillers of the 1970s." *Stylus,* July 7, 2004. http://stylusmagazine.com/articles/weekly_article/the-conspiracy-thrillers-of-the-1970s-paranoid-time.htm. Accessed May 16, 2013.

Mills, C. Wright. *White Collar: The American Middle Classes.* New York: Oxford University Press, 1951.

Moran, Kathleen, and Michael Rogin. "'What's the Matter with Capra?': *Sullivan's Travels* and the Popular Front." *Representations* 71 (Summer 2000): 106–34.

Morrison, Toni. *Playing in the Dark: Whiteness and the Literary Imagination.* New York: Random House, 1992.

———. *Song of Solomon.* 1977. Reprint, New York: Vintage, 2004.

Mosley, Walter. *Devil in a Blue Dress.* New York: Norton, 1990.

Mullen, Harryette. "Optic White: Blackness and the Production of Whiteness." *Diacritics* 24, nos. 2–3 (Summer–Fall 1994): 71–89.

Mulvey, Laura. "Visual Pleasure and Narrative Cinema." In *Film Theory and Criticism*, ed. Leo Braudy and Marshall Cohen. New York: Oxford University Press, 2004, 837–48.

Naremore, James. *More Than Night: Film Noir in Its Contexts*. Berkeley: University of California Press, 1998.

O'Donnell, Patrick. *Latent Destinies: Cultural Paranoia and Contemporary U.S. Narrative*. Durham, NC: Duke University Press, 2000.

Ohmann, Richard. *Selling Culture: Magazines, Markets, and Class at the Turn of the Century*. New York: Verso, 1996.

Oliver, Kelly, and Benigno Trigo. *Noir Anxiety*. Minneapolis: University of Minnesota Press, 2003.

Orvell, Miles. *The Real Thing: Imitation and Authenticity in American Culture, 1880–1940*. Chapel Hill: University of North Carolina Press, 1989.

Osteen, Mark. "Noir's Cars: Automobility and Amoral Space in American Film Noir." *Journal of Popular Film and Television* 35, no. 4 (Winter 2008): 183–92.

Packard, Vance. *The Hidden Persuaders*. 1957. Reprint, Brooklyn: Ig, 2007.

Palmer, R. Barton. *Joel and Ethan Coen*. Urbana: University of Illinois Press, 2004.

Pease, Donald. "Exceptionalism." In *Keywords for American Cultural Studies*, ed. Bruce Burgett and Glenn Hendler, 108–11. New York: New York University Press, 2007.

———. *The New American Exceptionalism*. Minneapolis: University of Minnesota Press, 2009.

Pike, David. *Metropolis on the Styx: The Underworlds of Urban Culture, 1800–2001*. Ithaca, NY: Cornell University Press, 2007.

Polito, Robert. *Savage Art: A Biography of Jim Thompson*. New York: Knopf, 1995.

Potter, Andrew. *The Authenticity Hoax: How We Get Lost Finding Ourselves*. New York: HarperCollins, 2010.

Potter, David. *People of Plenty: Economic Abundance and the American Character*. Chicago: University of Chicago Press, 1954.

Pratt, Ray. *Projecting Paranoia: Conspiratorial Visions in American Film*. Lawrence: University Press of Kansas, 2001.

Pynchon, Thomas. *Against the Day*. New York: Penguin, 2006.

———. *The Crying of Lot 49*. New York: Harper & Row/Perennial Library, 1966.

———. *Gravity's Rainbow*. 1973. Reprint, New York: Penguin, 2006.

———. *Inherent Vice*. New York: Penguin, 2009.

———. *Mason & Dixon*. New York: Henry Holt, 1997.

———. *V.* 1961. Reprint, New York: Harper Perennial, 2005.

———. *Vineland*. New York: Little, Brown, 1990.

Rabinowitz, Paula. *Black & White & Noir: America's Pulp Modernism*. New York: Columbia University Press, 2002.

Raczkowski, Christopher. "Metonymic Hats and Metaphoric Tumbleweeds: Noir Literary Aesthetics in *Miller's Crossing* and *The Big Lebowski*." In *The Year's Work in Lebowski Studies*, ed. Edward Comentale and Aaron Jaffe, 98–123. Bloomington: Indiana University Press, 2009.

Rader, Dotson. *I Ain't Marchin' Anymore*. New York: David McKay, 1969.

Riesman, David, et al. *The Lonely Crowd: A Study of the Changing American Character*. New York: Doubleday, 1953.

Robson, Eddie. *Coen Brothers*. London: Virgin Books, 2003.

Roszak, Theodore. *The Making of a Counter Culture*. 1969. Berkeley: University of California Press, 1995.

Rothberg, Michael. "Dead Letter Office: Conspiracy, Trauma, and Song of Solomon's Posthumous Communication." *African American Review* 37, no. 4 (Winter 2003): 501–16.

Rowell, Erica. *The Brothers Grim: The Films of Joel and Ethan Coen*. Lanham, MD: Scarecrow, 2007.

Rushdie, Salman. "Still Crazy after All These Years." *New York Times Book Review* (Jan. 14, 1990): 1, 36–37.

Ryan, Michael, and Douglas Kellner. *Camera Politica: The Politics and Ideology of Contemporary Hollywood Film*. Bloomington: Indiana University Press, 1988.

Sack, Robert David. *Place, Modernity, and the Consumer's World: A Relational Framework for Geographical Analysis*. Baltimore: Johns Hopkins University Press, 1992.

Sayres, Sohnya, et al., eds. *The 60s without Apology*. Minneapolis: University of Minnesota Press, 1984.

Schatz, Thomas. *Hollywood Genres: Formulas, Film Making, and the Studio System*. New York: McGraw-Hill, 1981.

Schlosser, Eric. *Fast Food Nation: The Dark Side of the All-American Meal*. New York: HarperCollins, 2004.

Schrader, Paul. "Notes on *Film Noir*." In *Film Noir Reader*, ed. Alain Silver and James Ursini, 53–64. New York: Limelight, 1996.

Seesslen, Georg. "Games. Rules. Violations. Looking for a Trail in Coen County." In *Joel & Ethan Coen*, ed. Peter Körte and Georg Seesslen, 229–98. New York: Limelight, 2001.

Siegel, Allan. "After the Sixties: Changing Paradigms in the Representation of Urban Space." In *Screening the City*, ed. Mark Shiel and Tony Fitzmaurice, 137–59. London: Verso, 2003.

Silver, Alain, and James Ursini, eds. *Film Noir Reader*. New York: Limelight, 1996.

Simmel, Georg. *The Philosophy of Money*. 1907. Reprint, New York: Routledge, 1990.

Smith, Erin. *Hard-Boiled: Working-Class Readers and Pulp Magazines*. Philadelphia: Temple University Press, 2000.

Smith, Neil. *Uneven Development: Nature, Capital, and the Production of Space*. 1984. Reprint, Athens: University of Georgia Press, 2008.

Sobchack, Vivian. "Lounge Time: Postwar Crises and the Chronotope of Film Noir." In *Refiguring American Film Genres: History and Theory*, ed. Nick Browne, 129–70. Berkeley: University of California Press, 1998.

Soitos, Stephen. *The Blues Detective: A Study of African American Detective Fiction*. Amherst: University of Massachusetts Press, 1996.

Soja, Edward. *Postmodern Geographies: The Reassertion of Space in Critical Social Theory*. New York: Verso, 1989.

Spicer, Andrew. *Film Noir*. Essex: Pearson, 2002.

Spooner, Brian. "Weavers and Dealers: The Authenticity of an Oriental Carpet." In *The Social Life of Things: Commodities in Cultural Perspective*, ed. Arjun Appadurai, 195–235. Cambridge: Cambridge University Press, 1986.

Sterling, Bruce. *Mirrorshades: The Cyberpunk Anthology*. New York: Arbor House, 1986.

Strasser, Susan, Charles McGovern, and Matthias Judt, eds. *Getting and Spending: European and American Consumer Societies in the Twentieth Century*. Cambridge: Cambridge University Press, 1998.

Strasser, Susan, ed. *Commodifying Everything: Relationships of the Market.* New York: Routledge, 2003.

Strychacz, Thomas. *Modernism, Mass Culture, and Professionalism.* Cambridge: Cambridge University Press, 1993.

Susman, Warren. *Culture as History: The Transformation of American Society in the Twentieth Century.* New York: Pantheon, 1984.

Suvin, Darko. "On Gibson and Cyberpunk SF." In *Storming the Reality Studio: A Casebook of Cyberpunk and Postmodern Science Fiction,* ed. Larry McCaffery, 349–65. Durham, NC: Duke University Press, 2000.

Tabbi, Joseph. "Pynchon's Groundward Art." In *The Vineland Papers: Critical Takes on Pynchon's Novel,* ed. Geoffrey Green et al., 89–100. Normal, IL: Dalkey Archive Press, 1994.

Tal, Kali. "'That Just Kills Me': Black Militant Near-Future Fiction." *Social Text* 71 (Summer 2002): 66–91.

Tani, Stefano. *The Doomed Detective: The Contribution of the Detective Novel to Postmodern American and Italian Fiction.* Carbondale: Southern Illinois University Press, 1984.

Thompson, Jon. *Fiction, Crime, and Empire: Clues to Modernity and Postmodernism.* Urbana: University of Illinois Press, 1993.

Thomson, David. *Have You Seen . . .?* New York: Knopf, 2008.

Thoreen, David. "The Economy of Consumption: The Entropy of Leisure in Pynchon's *Vineland.*" *Pynchon Notes* 30–31 (1992): 53–62.

Trilling, Lionel. *Sincerity and Authenticity.* Cambridge, MA: Harvard University Press, 1972.

Tyree, J. M., and Ben Walters. *The Big Lebowski.* London: BFI, 2007.

Veblen, Thorstein. *The Theory of the Leisure Class: An Economic Study in the Evolution of Institutions.* 1899. Reprint, New York: Penguin, 1979.

Venturi, Robert, et al. *Learning from Las Vegas: The Forgotten Symbolism of Architectural Form.* Cambridge, MA: MIT Press, 1972.

Vollmann, William. *Riding toward Everywhere.* New York: Harper Perennial, 2008.

Walker, Rob. *Buying In: The Secret Dialogue between What We Buy and Who We Are.* New York: Random House, 2008.

Whyte, William. *The Organization Man.* New York: Simon & Schuster, 1956.

Williams, John A. *Sons of Darkness, Sons of Light.* Boston: Northeastern University Press, 1969.

Williams, Raymond. *Culture and Society: 1780–1950.* New York: Columbia University Press, 1958.

Wilson, Sloan. *The Man in the Gray Flannel Suit.* 1955. Reprint, New York: Four Walls Eight Windows, 2002.

Yeltsin, Boris. *Against the Grain: An Autobiography.* New York: Summit, 1990.

Zogby, John. *The Way We'll Be: The Zogby Report on the Transformation of the American Dream.* New York: Random House, 2008.

MacCannell, Dean, 10–11, 23, 252n9, 255n25
MacDonald, Dwight, 86
Madison, James, 104
Mad Men (TV series), 77
Madsen, Deborah, 139, 140
magazines, 81, 84–85. *See also specific magazines*
magical thinking, 265n15
Main Street to Miracle Mile (Liebs), 55
The Making of a Counter Culture (Roszak), 136
Maland, Charles, 224, 227
Malcolm X, 113
male gaze, 63, 258n14
Malewitz, Raymond, 270n18
The Maltese Falcon (Hammett), 17, 20
Mandingo (film), 173–174, 180
manga, 192
"The Man in Me" (Dylan), 256n33
The Man in the Gray Flannel Suit (Wilson), 86
Mann, Anthony, 62
The Man Who Wasn't There (film), 219
Marcus, Greil, 132
Marcuse, Herbert, 7–8, 81, 175
market culture, 12
marketing
    of authenticity, 248
    counterculture and, 255n26
Marling, Karal Ann, 264n13
Martin, Dean, 225
Martin, Reinhold, 239
Marvin, Lee, 128
Marx, Karl, 9
Marxism, 194–196, 226, 233, 249, 252n8
    criticism, 23
    geography, 26
    masculinity, 84–85, 112, 249
        The Big Lebowski and, 256n33
        gas station and, 51–52, 58, 64, 73, 75–76, 78–79
        nationalist, 40
        Philip Marlowe and, 17, 102, 105
Mason & Dixon (Pynchon), 141
mass culture, 8, 11, 82, 85, 146, 219
mass media, 11, 81, 96
Massood, Paula, 172
mass production, 14
materialism, 12, 69
    individualist, 169, 175
    values, 152, 177
material nationalism, 14, 44
The Matrix (film), 30, 110, 192, 195, 199, 202, 207
"A Matter of Taste" (Lears), 259n1
Max Headroom (TV series), 192
May, Lary, 25
McCann, Sean, 45, 83, 96, 97, 260n9, 265n15, 266n2
McClure, John, 126, 127
McGovern, Charles, 13, 14, 15, 228

McInerney, Jay, 190
Meals to Come (Belasco), 29
media, mass, 11, 81, 96
Meet John Doe (film), 227
Melley, Timothy, 261n16
men. *See also* masculinity
    bonding, 52, 59, 65, 67, 69, 73–76, 93
    comradeship, 20, 58
    friendships of, 64–65, 73, 94
    identity and, 58–59, 78–79, 93, 222
    male gaze, 63, 258n14
    paradigms, 105
    protagonists, 59, 78
    solidarity, 64
Menand, Louis, 263n4
Mendelson, Edward, 154
message movies, 170
metaphors, 20–21
Metropolis (film), 200, 221, 232, 236, 241, 268n5
Metropolis on the Styx (Pike), 199
Metz, Walter, 225, 226
Michaels, Walter Benn, 252n8
middle class, 81–82, 137, 146
    black, 47, 168–170, 175–177, 184
    counterculture and, 144
    PMC and, 85
    supermarket and, 28, 56
Mike Hammer (fictional character), 71–76
Millard, Bill, 146, 264n11
Miller, Frank, 192, 268n4
Miller's Crossing (film), 218
Mills, C. Wright, 82
Milne, A. A., 15
mimesis, 8, 17
Minority Report (film), 192
Miracle on 34th Street (film), 229
Mirrorshades (Sterling, B.), 191
misogyny, 19, 52, 73–74
The Mist (film), 255n28
mobility, 55–56
modernism, 7, 82, 85, 93. *See also* postmodern
    authenticity; postmodernism
    avant-garde, 190
    literary-historical, 79
    money and, 93–99
Modern Times (film), 221, 231–232
money, 9, 93–99, 104, 145
Monogram, 97
monopoly capitalism, 18
montage, 125
Morrison, Toni, 167, 265n15, 267n9, 269n13
Moscow on the Hudson (film), 29
Mosley, Walter, 260n12
Moving Pictures/Stopping Places, 51
Moynihan Report, 172
Mr. Deeds Goes to Town (film), 227, 229

Printed in the USA/Agawam, MA
May 12, 2014